AN INTRODUCTION
TO SOCIAL RESEARCH

 *Sociology Series*

John F. Cuber, *editor*
Alfred C. Clarke, *associate editor*

edited by
JOHN T. DOBY
emory university

AN INTRODUCTION
TO SOCIAL RESEARCH

2nd edition

new york
APPLETON-CENTURY-CROFTS
division of meredith publishing company

CONTRIBUTORS

JOHN P. DEAN
late of Cornell University

LOIS R. DEAN
Antioch College

JOHN T. DOBY
Emory University

ROBERT L. EICHHORN
Purdue University

ROY G. FRANCIS
University of Wisconsin at Milwaukee

JOHN C. McKINNEY
Duke University

EDWARD A. SUCHMAN
University of Pittsburgh

PREFACE to the first edition

This introductory textbook in research methods has been written to meet the methodological needs of undergraduate college students who are concentrating in the social and/or psychological sciences.

No one needs to be reminded today of the tremendous importance of the findings of science to modern man. This is evidenced by the great changes which science has made possible in our way of life and the many courses in high school and college curricula concerned with the dissemination of the findings of science. It is one of the most talked-about subjects of modern times, and perhaps one of the least understood. It is this latter aspect which we are primarily concerned with in this text; i.e., the understanding of science. What is the nature of science? What is the goal of science? How does science go about achieving its goal?

One does not answer the above questions by ascertaining what science is about. Rather one has to determine what science does and how it does it. While our curriculum has no doubt put a premium on the findings of science, it has overlooked or under-emphasized the more important function of how these findings were made. If the methods of inquiry as used by science have been so effective in producing the great ideas, and the findings of science, then it is obvious that considerable attention should be given to the important task of learning the logic and procedures for deriving "truth." This does not imply, however, that scientific logic and procedure have reached perfection, but it does intend to imply that more attention should be devoted to the study of them in order to continue to improve upon them.

Our aim is to introduce the student to the task of how to do research in the social and psychological sciences. To accomplish this end we have presented the scientific endeavor as a special type of problem-solving activity. The first part of the book is designed to present the logic and the procedural rules for scientific problem-solving, while the second half is devoted to the methods and techniques for carrying out these rules in actual research.

This book is designed as a basic introductory text for courses in the logic and methods of research and, as such, it does not pretend to be exhaustive of the field. It is planned so as to provide the core material for a one semester course. The instructor will note that there is not sufficient material here for an entire semester course without some supplementing. This arrangement is intended. Since the needs of different instructors in the area of methodology in the social sciences are varied (i.e., some undergraduate students have some formal training in logic and sufficient training in mathematics, while others do not), this opportunity to supplement should facilitate the meeting of the needs of their own situation.

J.T.D.

PREFACE *to the second edition*

Ideally, the logic, methods, and techniques of social research should be an integrated part of the substantive textbooks in sociology beginning with the introductory course. In other words, students should learn the methods and research tools appropriate to a given substantive course just as they as members of a society learn the language of their society. However, there are no such theory books or introductory texts in sociology, and until such are written it will be necessary to continue writing textbooks on the philosophy, logic, and methods of social research.

It is well known that theory, data, and methods interplay and that each conditions the meaning of the other. In general, introductory physics and chemistry texts are written so that their concepts and theories absorb and contain the methods and operational aspects of these sciences. This is possible where the conceptual structure of a field is fairly mature and systematically worked out. The fact that this is not yet true in sociology is probably most related to the preponderant existence of commonsense concepts in the field. Precision of conceptual formulation and significance of meaning are not necessarily mutually exclusive.

It is recognized that different objects, processes, and qualities exist in different degrees of availability to observation and control. Measurement is, therefore, more difficult in respect to some than others. The principal point in the foregoing is that it should be unnecessary to write such a book as this, and it is hoped that it will soon be unnecessary. It will, of course, always be appropriate to write advanced treatises on the logic, philosophy, and methods of research per se, but the existing set of working tools and ideas of research can best be learned by doing research and studying examples of substantive research.

Nevertheless, it is well known that one may learn to write and speak English perfectly by growing up with others whose English is flawless. Yet, without formal study of English grammar, our hypothetical subject may not really understand the structure of the English language and be able to make correct changes when confronted with new and difficult problems of description. The same is true in respect to the learning of methodology by the socialization process of doing research. The researcher is often confronted with a research situation where current methodology is inappropriate or inadequate and he must therefore improvise new strategies and techniques. In order to do this, formal knowledge of logic, mathematics, and the methodology of science is necessary. In other words, the logic and methodology of science evolves as does the substantive body of science. Therefore, research scientists must acquire formal skills and basic knowledge of methodology so that they may be able to improve methodology as new situations demand.

High school and college curricula have put a premium on the *findings* of science while more or less ignoring, from some points of view, the more important matter of *how* scientific knowledge is obtained. The mental perspective and the research tools of science have been extremely successful in aiding man to free himself from the shackles of invalid and inadqute ideas. Its creations and discoveries have, at times, revolutonized human thought. One is reminded of the theories of Copernicus, Newton, Darwin, and Einstein, as representing new systems of thought and knowledge which have had revolutionary effects on human thinking and behavior.

Once a system of thought is established it tends to structure subsequent thinking. Sometimes the new thinking is inappropriately extended to new facts. It is, therefore, important that students acquire critical means of analysis so that errors in reasoning and in research may be more easily discerned. The logic, methods, and techniques of research, when learned well, will go a long way toward this end.

This book is organized around three major parts: Part one, *Introduction to the Logic and Philosophy of Science;* Part two, *Methods and Techniques of Research;* and Part three, *Research Administration.* It seemed obvious that the logic and philosophy of science should be taught before specific methods and that problems of research administration derive largely from considerations and applications of research design. Therefore, methods and techniques are considered in Part two. The logic for the particular ordering of the content within Part two follows from two major considerations: *first,* that the methods and techniques to be presented first be those that are the most general and thereby provide an overall picture of the logical and temporal steps in scientific research. Such ordering eliminates needless repetition in subsequent chapters. For example, if an adequate · treatment of sampling is made in the discussion of statistical methods, then it is necessary only to refer to such when discussing survey research. *Second,* since the control of variables in social and psychological research is almost always by means of randomization, measurement, and categorical matching, it seemed desirable to present statistical methods first. In other words, most behavioral science research designs utilize some type of statistical design.

This work represents a thorough revision and expansion of the original, 1954 edition, including the addition of new chapters. While the chapters were written by individual contributors, the editor has been responsible for the overall outline and organization of the book.

Thanks are due to John Cuber, Advisory Editor, Appleton-Century-Crofts, for his critical and helpful suggestions regarding the entire manuscript.

Finally, I am indebted to the Literary Executor of the late Sir Ronald A.

Fisher, F.R.S., Cambridge, to Dr. Frank Yates, F.R.S., Rothamsted, and to Messrs. Oliver & Boyd, Ltd., Edinburgh, for permission to reprint Table No. 5 from their book *Statistical Tables for Biological, Agricultural and Medical Research* and Table No. 2 from Sir Ronald A. Fisher, *Statistical Methods for Research Workers*. Other acknowledgments are made in place.

J.T.D.

CONTENTS

PART THREE — RESEARCH ADMINISTRATION

Part one

INTRODUCTION TO THE LOGIC OF SCIENCE

I

Roy G. Francis

THE NATURE OF
SCIENTIFIC RESEARCH

The kind of scientific research with which we are here concerned is a special case of scholarship. Research which proceeds outside of this scholarly tradition will not concern us. Most of the non-scholarly research is "applied research." What we have to say is related to the so-called "pure" research. The significant thing is that the research we are dealing with is designed specifically and oriented to answering intellectual questions.

Scientific research is not the only strategy to answer such questions. There are a number of types of questions which do not concern science, but which are, nonetheless, questions worthy of intellectual concern. Certainly, not all theological questions can be dismissed as the signs of superstition and of emotionally distraught people. Moreover, questions of "beauty," "justice," and certain questions of "ought" are not answerable by the methods of science. To admit this is not to say less about science. It is a recognition that man in his intellectual capacity is not bound or limited by science. It is, then, improper to assert or insinuate that if science cannot answer the question it is not worthy of modern man.

Historically, scholarly research has been located primarily in the universities and colleges. Today, scientific work is increasingly being done in industry and government. Often, however, the work done there has not been done with a self-conscious awareness of the scholarly tradition out of which science has emerged. Moreover, since much of industrial research is regarded as private property, and some of government-sponsored research is secret, their findings are not made public. Only indirectly can their work feed into the intellectual mainstream. This is not to say that industrial and governmental research makes no contribution, but it is still true that scholarly work is located primarily in colleges and universities. Much of the governmental research which is scholarly is done by contract with professors.

Historians of science have chronicled the departure of special research disciplines from philosophy. It is not our concern to note the historical sequence of this movement. Rather, it is to note that each discipline had its origins in a common concern to know something about the world in which man lives.

It is a somewhat modern notion that scientific knowledge is particularly useful. The fundamental position has been, simply, that it would be nice to know the answer to a particular question. Scientists in the scholarly tradition are somewhat analogous to a mountain climber: the justification for climbing a mountain is that the mountain is there. The ultimate justification for scholarship is that man simply wants to know for the sake of knowing. As it will be discussed, scientists have a number of other motives; but this is the one most will have in common.

The scholarly point of view is a broad one. Though much effort is directed to making questions researchable—and this often means reducing an original question in scope—the scholar views his narrowly specified question in a broad context. To some scholars the theoretical boundaries of a specified discipline are the proper field within which the question must be put. Others prefer to see an even wider field and ultimately move to fundamental and very broad questions of the order, "What is the nature of man and his place in the universe?" This is the sort of question that makes philosophers excited by any new discovery in one of the basic sciences but it is not the sort of question that science per se seeks to answer. It is a reminder that all sciences, having come historically from philosophy, return to the fundamental quest which characterizes the scholar.

Much of what we will have to say about science will also be true of scholarly work in general. Yet we will fasten our attention on that aspect of scholarship known as science and, in particular, we will orient our thinking to sociology as a particular kind of science. For a first approximation, we will define science as that aspect of scholarly work devoted to describing the world that is, including how various aspects of that world are related.

1. SPECIFIC RELATIONS TO PHILOSOPHY

As a science, sociology is related to philosophy in at least three specific ways:

Metaphysics. Metaphysics is concerned with the basic ideas about reality. In this regard, a number of assumptions are required. The first is that we live in an essentially knowable, real world. The second is that this real world is not changed by the act of knowing, and the third is that our relation to the world and, indeed, parts of the world, may be subsequently changed by the act of knowing. The sense in which these assumptions are met is often complicated and varied according to the substantive, theoretical position of the scientist.

Unless we can agree that there is a real world somewhere *out there,* that is, not merely in the imagination of the speakers, we cannot imagine any possible test of the truth value of a statement other than logical consistency. Certainly no empirical test would be possible if the world as we know it were merely the consequence of a more or less orderly imagination. If methods are to be developed by which we can agree that a test has been made, we must first agree to some limiting condition which we will call the real world.

Unfortunately we live with statements about the world, and it is precisely these statements which are at issue. Though the world is presumably knowable, we may not know that we know it. A critical element of doubt is built into our quest. This is true of all science, but certain kinds of sociology have rather specially difficult versions of the issue.

That school of sociological theory known as "symbolic interaction" begins with the position that symbols take on meaning out of interaction between people. No symbol has intrinsic meaning, only social meaning. When both parties in the communicative transaction are responding to the symbols in similar fashion, the symbol takes on a meaning. This seems to imply that all the scientists can ever reach is consensus. When scientists agree to a point of view, according to this argument, meanings are exchanged, and the problem is solved. When one point of view is no longer seriously supported or contended for, agreement has been reached.

The exchange which took place between the scientists must, presumably, have been about something. An attempt was made to exchange meanings about a social world. Unless this is agreed to, all that follows becomes meaningless. We have to agree that in some way a social reality exists. People do exchange meanings; they do relate to each other; their relationships become organized; situations become defined. We must not confuse the necessity of actors in a situation to convince themselves and others with our scientific need to prove the correctness of our contention about those actors. That we, too, are actors will be discussed briefly below.

The second assumption about the real world that it is not modified by the act of knowing is also open to question. From the symbolic-interaction position, the theoretical assumption that "if something is believed to be true, it is true in its consequences" carries with it some doubts about knowing not modifying the world itself. A trivial instance will reveal the difficulty. Suppose that a room contains a hot stove. If we observe simply "stove," it may be hot or cold. What we do in respect to the stove depends, in part, on our judgment regarding its condition. Knowing that it is hot does not modify the heat of the stove, nor its ability to cook. It may, however, modify our behavior toward it as when we propose to heat some coffee. Now consider a social situation. The room is a scientific library in Washington, D.C. A man enters. A "man" is not a physical thing in the sense that the stove was. He has meaning in terms of our relation to him. There are various forms that the relation can take. If he occupies the position "stranger," we relate one way. If he occupies the position, "trusted friend," we relate a different way. So far, one could draw analogies to the "man-man" and "man-stove" relations. But suppose we find that he is neither of these, but "secret agent." The fact that this is known has changed things: he is no longer a *secret* agent; even if he had been a suspected agent, knowledge of his identity does change the world of social relations.

From the point of view of the actor whose activity does not include explaining the world he lives in, the entire world is relational. In one sense nouns and adjectives predispose people to action, that is behavior, in a social sense. The referent "old antique chair" does not imply the attitude of sitting. The "hot stove" doesn't either. It is only when "stove" or "chair" are viewed scientifically that their being nouns does not necessarily imply an attitude. However, the words sociology uses are primarily relational: "father," "friend," "boss," "supervisor," "peer," and the like, specify relations. Despite the arguments of the most ardent symbolic interactionist, most sociologists are willing to contend that the act of knowing does not constitute the alteration of the world. From this point of view, the dissemination of that knowledge is the process by which the world is modified. Yet who can deny that the process of being interviewed or submitting to a personality test does not alter the subject's image of himself, by making him aware of aspects of his self that he did not have before?

The foregoing argument is sufficient to force the conclusion that though the metaphysical problem is genuine, though in some ways sociological inquiry is related to it, the question of what the nature of the real world is belongs to philosophy and not science. To say this does not deny the sociologist the right to be philosophical about his science.

Epistemology. Epistemology faces the problem of determining the basis of knowledge. Classically, it asks the question, "how do we know what we know?" Scientific methodology is clearly related to that question though one may develop a perfectly consistent scientific theory without claiming "really to know" the world.

However, it is convenient, and in some ways necessary, to note a distinction regarding the basis for accepting statements. Some we simply believe, as an act of faith. All primitive definitions are of this order; all fundamental assumptions are, too. These statements we call belief. The process of accepting them we call "conviction." Science does not entirely escape from statements of this kind. It does rest on some undefined terms, on some assumptions one must accept or be unable to proceed. At times, as we observe the maneuvering of schools of thought, we are impressed with the amount of conviction underlying some assertions by scientists.

Statements purporting to be empirically acceptable to science, however, are not accepted on faith. There must be a reason for their acceptance, and these reasons must be shared with others. There must be proof, the scheme of which is only partially demonstrable. It is most likely to rest on certain fundamental assumptions, sometimes unstated. Yet if one accepts the rules of procedure, one accepts the consequences of that procedure. The rules of procedure which bind men of science to the conclusions reached by others is generally called "scientific method." The analysis of method is called methodology. But before we take up the problem specifically, there are a few more observations about the relation of science to philosophy which must be made.

Ethics. Ethics deals with concepts of "the good"; of "right or wrong." Sociology does too, but with this profound difference. To the sociologist, peoples' assertions of what constitutes "right" and "wrong," "good" or "bad" constitutes *data.* A general sociological question could include: "Under what conditions is X judged to be good?" Ethics deals with the determination of what *is* good or bad.

Ethics has as its substantive content judgments of good and bad. Sociology deals with statements *about* good and bad. Rephrasing the issue, we can define a "value" as the premise upon which (by whatever mechanism) a choice is made between or among alternatives. Sometimes it seems as if the assertion, "that is only a value judgment" ends all discussion. It is sometimes held that all values are equal. That this does not ultimately make sense can be seen in the following example.

During school vacation periods, college students are confronted with alternative ways of spending their time. They may find employment, either for casual expenses or to pay their way through college. They may simply seek a vacation. They may seek a non-paying (or low-paying) employment in a camp for deprived children. They may work on term papers or try to remove incompletes. They may go south to assist in registration of Negro voters. What choice they make depends upon their values. During the lunch period, students again make choices. They choose what to eat: cheese sandwich on white or dark bread; hamburger and french fries; milk shakes, etc. Again their choice appeals to some value. The value to choose white or dark bread may be essentially equivalent. But it becomes difficult to insist that the value on which the choice to risk one's life to aid a Negro to register is based on the equivalent of the value on which choice of bread in a sandwich is based.

It is, of course, impossible *empirically* to prove which value is superior to another, at least in this instance. But that is because the value-argument is about the way the world *ought* to be while empirical science is about the world as it *is*. Strategies for solving the empirical question do not lend themselves to the other.

One argument to assist us in clarifying what is at issue requires us to use a "means-end" analysis of a situation. In this analytical tool one observes that in a situation which has been defined, a goal is being pursued and rightly or wrongly some means are being employed to achieve that end or goal. Analytically, it is possible to perceive alternative means and/or ends in each situation, though the participants may be able to perceive only one. In that case, we would refer to the "mood" of the situation. The end upon which the means-choice rests may be called an "instrumental value" and the value upon which the end-choice is made may be termed a "transcendental value."

Given certain transcendental choices, it is sometimes possible to specify precisely which instrumental choice will maximize the likelihood of achievement. It is in the realm of transcendental values that science is silent. It can often assist, however, instrumentally. Because situations blend into each other, and the goal of one situation may be a means to achieve a higher-ordered goal (as the goal of successfully completing a course in research methods is a means to achieving a successful career in social research), some ends may rest on *relatively transcendental* values.

Since the scientist could engage in different activities than those relating to science, his scientific behavior rests on some value. It may be simply that knowledge itself is "good," that is, that the sociology major *ought* to learn how science proceeds. Whatever scientists may assert, the fact remains, science rests on a normative decision. Even the decision to be value-free or to be objective is a normative one.

2. THE ETHICAL BASIS OF ACADEMIC FREEDOM

We have just implied that many scientists publicly rest their case on the normative basis that knowledge is good, but, upon examination, that value is neither necessary nor sufficient to explain the behavior of the greater number of scientists.

The values which motivate or impel the scientist to action need not be that knowledge is good. Indeed, if he did begin with that premise, it would not be sufficient to enable him to decide which bit of knowledge he should spend his time seeking. When one observes graduate students, in the technological as well as the social sciences, one is caught up in the observation that a number of motives are involved in their being in graduate school. Some want prestige, some power, some money, some leisure and some, of course, are fleeing from the outside world. Obviously, the claim that science rests on the value that knowledge is good need not be accepted.

But science does rest on a value which, if denied, destroys the fabric of science and scholarship. That is the value which can be labelled "intellectual honesty" or "intellectual integrity." Unless the scientist is impeccably honest, the entire structure collapses. Each scientist must trust the other to report his procedures and his data honestly. If the scientist could deny this premise and report as data that information which he chose, there could be no test of a hypothesis or theory. Only if the scholar or scientist is honest can he carry out the functions of the scholar or researcher.

Freedom is prerequisite to a scientist's or scholar's honesty. He must be allowed to entertain any and all explanations of his problem. If he is denied *a priori* the right to consider a particular hypothesis, then, if his data and his research forced him in that direction, the denial of the emerging hypothesis would be a dishonest thing to do. Accordingly, the scholar demands freedom of inquiry, freedom to entertain any proposition which might enable him to explain his observations.

Academic freedom is the consequence of the demand to be honest. It is not a special case of freedom of speech. The concept of free speech is powerful precisely because it is guaranteed the liar in equal measure to the honest man. Though the scientist or scholar may be wrong, he cannot be willfully so. Academic freedom is required exactly because he must be honest. This is not to say that there are no conceivable limits on academic freedom. There are certainly debatable points which must be faced. These include the possibility of certain problems being improper to study (how can the atmosphere of the earth be so contaminated that human life is impossible?), or a method (in this example, an experiment), or the procedure by which data are to be obtained (ought a sociologist be allowed to tap phones in order to collect data?).

3. THE NEED TO STUDY METHODOLOGY

The task of science is to go beyond the data at hand. All people tend to generalize beyond their literal experience—and, usually, people err when they make generalizations. It is impossible, in such a complex society as ours, for any one to experience it all. One can interact with only a small part of the total population. Yet one usually thinks of oneself as a participant in our culture and feels free to speak of it. It can be easily demonstrated that the typical adult obtains what at best would be a biased sample. The old adage, "birds of a feather flock together," is a common-sense statement of this fact. We live in and see the world of our friends, not the whole world. Thus, the conclusions commonly reached are incorrect.

Obviously no scientist can presume to have all of the knowledge related to his field. He can possess only a very small part of the possible data; yet he must generalize. Strategies and rules help him overcome the errors of the untrained, and rules justify his generalizations.

The student of research methods is faced with a two-fold task. He must first learn to "unlearn" some commonplace ideas about science and at the same time he must learn contemporary ideas about scientific activity. The student is probably already aware of the extensive writings about science in sociology. Indeed, the extent of such writings is so great as to suggest to some that we "declare a moratorium on the use of the word 'science' " in order to avoid arguments as to whether a given piece of research is or is not scientific.[1] Such a moratorium might be well for the peace of mind of the research practitioner. However, since the student does in fact pick up ideas, erroneous as well as correct ones, about science, such a moratorium would seem to work at the expense of the beginning student.

Our culture has put a premium upon science. Advertising agencies utilizing pictures of doctors, graphs, and terminology about "scientific proof" that this or that product is superior to all competitors, stresses the importance of scientific procedure as a value in our culture. Popular literature, the comics, movies, radio and television shows, frequently involve the scientist in the key role of the story being told. The consequence is often a dramatized and erroneous account of the behavior of scientists, at least as scientists. The medical practitioner is often regarded by the lay public as the epitome of the scientist in action. Cigarette advertisements proclaiming the medical superiority of a given brand through the publication of "scientific tests" never reveal the research design which would enable one to assess more accurately the value of the test. The result is that the lay public is more likely to develop an attitude about, rather than knowledge of, scientific activity.

In addition to misleading conceptions of science gleaned from his everyday world, the student often brings with him preconceived ideas about his subject matter. When a sociological proposition about the behavior of man contradicts folk-belief, the student needs some way of deciding between the two propositions. To convince the student that the sociological one is to be preferred simply on the authority of the professor or that it is scientific may be temporarily expedient. In terms of the development of a field of inquiry such expediency has nothing in its favor. To perform the role of scientists properly, the student must learn correctly how the scientist functions.

We may draw an analogy between the student learning to be a scientist and an immigrant becoming a naturalized citizen of his adopted country. Certain similarities of belief and behavior exist between the

[1] Samuel A. Stouffer, "Sociology and Sampling," in L. L. Bernard, ed., *The Fields and Methods of Sociology*, New York, Long & Smith, 1934, pp. 486–487.

mother country and the adopted one; at the same time, the immigrant must unlearn those values of his former country which conflict with a happy adjustment to his new one. Similarly, the student must prepare himself to unlearn some notions about science and to learn the contemporary customs, traditions and mores of science. Of course, the analogy is limited: no one is "born into" a scientific culture.

There is probably one more major reason why sociologists and, indeed, social scientists in general, are acutely methodology conscious. Science is a form of human behavior. A theory which is sufficiently general to explain the behavior of the "man in the street" must also be able to explain the behavior of the scientist himself. The behavior of the scientist which his theory must explain is not only his non-scientific behavior but his behavior as a scientist as well. No other scientific theory is called upon to perform this task. A theory of nuclear fission, for example, could not be properly used to explain the behavior of the physicist. In the so-called physical sciences the relation between the scientist and his theory is not problematic in this respect.

In the social sciences, however, it is highly problematic. It would be absurd to assume intellectual processes on the part of the scientist and deny them to the object the sociologist studies. In other words, to say that the scientist thinks and that his thinking is related to his behavior, but that the man in the street either doesn't think or that his thinking is unrelated to his behavior involves a basic inconsistency.

In short, the social scientist is highly concerned with methodology for two basic reasons: he is a member of a culture which he seeks to study, and he wants to arrive at a general theory. He must develop methods which permit generality by avoiding personal and cultural biases. Further, his behavior as a scientist is a form of human behavior and is properly an area of scientific inquiry.

We commented earlier to the effect that the medical practitioner is to the layman an ideal type of scientist. Such a conception of the scientist ignores the distinction between pure and applied science. The medical doctor, in his role of administering to the sick, is applying (more or less) scientific knowledge. He may or may not be engaged in discovering new knowledge which is the activity of the pure scientist. While there is presumably a relation between pure and applied science, the two are not the same and we will restrict our consideration only to pure science, or, as we suggested earlier, science done in the context of scholarly work.

A frequently made error is to attribute to methodological statements assertions describing actual behavior. Strictly speaking, methodology is normative. Methodology simply specifies the procedures which a body of scientists have more or less agreed to as constituting a program justifying the conclusions reached. It says then, how a scientist ought to behave if his work is to be acceptable. It does not say what actually goes on. The latter belongs to the sociology of science; a particular stratum of the sociology of knowledge.

4. CHARACTERISTICS OF SCIENCE

Science includes both a goal and the means for obtaining that goal. Briefly, the goal of science is a theory. By theory we mean a "verifiable generalization of a high order which in some sense explains observed phenomena." The student is warned not to think of a theory as being "less good" than a "scientific law." Indeed, according to our usage of the term, a theory systematizes laws, hypotheses, and other generalizations of a science. Thus, science is held to include the means for obtaining a theory and we may well consider those means as an aspect of theory. Certainly, one's methodology contains theoretical implications and the student ought to be aware of that fact.

Some of the more important characteristics of science, both as substantive theory and methodology, follow:

Science Is Empirical. At some point science rests upon sense data. This characteristic of science excludes neither abstract concepts nor inferential knowledge. It merely means that science is concerned with a knowable real world.

Science Is Propositional. It deals with propositions, that is, statements which have a truth-value *about* things rather than with things. Sociology for example deals with propositions about human behavior; whatever is empirical about sociology must be reducible to propositional form.

There are several distinct levels of logical abstraction of the propositions dealt with. A statement of the order, "John Jones said he would vote Democratic" is less abstract than a statement of the order, "The lower-class, Catholic, urban factory worker tends to prefer Democratic candidates." Both propositions may be admissible to a science; the latter rests upon the correctness of propositions of the former type. Clearly, the way one argues about a proposition will depend largely upon its level of abstraction.

In some respects, the propositional character of a science is basic to an understanding of scientific activity. Kaufmann holds that the fundamental scientific act is that of deciding whether or not a given proposition ought to be incorporated into the theory of that science.[2] In general, we concur in this position, however, the specific situation faced by the scientist often involves not merely one proposition but a set of alternatives. In this case, he must have some rules which will aid him in making a decision.

[2] Felix Kaufmann, *Methodology of the Social Sciences,* New York, Oxford University Press, 1944.

It should not be imagined, however, that once a proposition has been admitted to a science it is never again questioned. In Kaufmann's terms, science has "complete control" over its propositions. This means simply, that a statement which is acceptable to science at a given time may be rejected or modified in the future. This propositional control exists at all levels of abstraction; the assumptions, definitions, and procedural rules are all subject to re-examination. This control, however, should not suggest to the student that there is no stability to the structure of scientific theory.

Indeed, the changes in science seem to follow the same general patterns of any observable type of change. It would be easy to show, for example, how the three processes discerned by Teggart in social history are present in the history of science. These processes are: (1) The persistence of certain elements. (2) The relatively slow change of certain elements. (3) The eventful changes of certain elements.[3] The analysis of these changes belongs properly in the field of history of social thought and will not be treated further here. The main purpose of indicating their existence is to aid the student in realizing the significance of propositional control in science.

Science Is Logical. Logic is defined as the discourse of argument. Analytically, logic is separable from any science; it constitutes a field of inquiry in itself. However, science is not independent of the logic supporting it. At some point in his inquiry, the scientist reaches a conclusion regarding the acceptability of some proposition (or set of propositions), and some justification for the conclusion must be made. Logic is simply the rules by which inferences are made and, therefore, is the structure of scientific argument.[4]

Science Is Operational. Logic is completely formal. The formal correctness of an argument does not depend upon the empirical content of the argument. One may logically argue that mice have a superior intelligence since, formally, logic does not guarantee the empirical existence of the classes used in the argument. How one is able to get empirical members into a logical class depends upon the operations which one is willing to perform.

As an example, consider the class of things, "neurotic personalities." Logically, we may create a definition of the class in question and proceed to engage in argument about the neurotic personality without any reference to the real world. But science deals with a knowable real world. In order to become accepted into science, the logical class, neurotic personalities, must be accompanied by an *operational procedure* by which

[3] Frederick J. Teggart, *Theory and Processes of History*, Berkeley, University of California Press, 1941.

[4] We will discuss this further in Chapters 2 and 4.

one can accurately say, "X has a neurotic personality." The operations by which class members are identified allow us to give empirical content to formal classes.

Science Is Public. In saying that science is propositional, we lay the groundwork for also asserting that science can be communicated from one scientist to another. Whatever is private to the individual researcher (his motivations, his value judgments, etc.), does not properly belong to science.

In its propositional form, science is symbolic.[5] Through consensus on the symbols utilized in a science, the objects studied by the scientist may be so well represented as to allow another scientist who does not observe the objects himself to judge the correctness of the inferences drawn. This, in turn, allows for replication of any scientific study; that is, a given piece of research can be duplicated by others and the same results may be obtained. If replication is not possible, then elements unique to the study are present and the acceptability of the study is commensurably reduced.

Science Is Problem-solving. Ordinarily, we mean by "problem" some observations which need explanation. The lack of an acceptable explanation may be due to the presence of incorrect propositions in the theory, or it may be due simply to the inadequacy of the theory.

A problem is general, and does not adhere to a unique set of observations. When unique elements are present—as, for example, when the time and space setting of the observations are intrinsically important—we speak of a "difficulty." [6] In sociology, we draw the distinction between "sociological problems" and "social problems." Generally speaking, the problem belongs to pure science and the difficulty belongs to applied science.

In the solution of a problem, the scientist formulates a *hypothesis* (or set of hypotheses). The hypothesis is a proposed solution to the problem. It is sometimes difficult to trace the source of hypotheses. Sometimes they are the result of the unique background of the scientist. When subjected to the formal test in a science, the source of a hypothesis is not particularly relevant as long as the criteria of scientific procedure are met. For the sake of semantic purity, we will say that the source of hypotheses is "inquiry" while the test of hypotheses is "research."

The correctness of the statement of the problem is paramount to subsequent scientific activity. One's conception of the problem at hand gives rise to the hypotheses to be tested, and the hypotheses, in turn, indicate which data are needed to satisfy the test. Although one may begin with only a vague feeling of the problem, eventually it must be reduced to

5 Susanne K. Langer, *Philosophy in a New Key,* Baltimore, Penguin, 1948.
6 This follows the formulation made by Professor John M. Foskett of the University of Oregon.

propositional form in order that its solution may be incorporated into science.

Science Tends to Be Abstract. Recall that we assumed a knowable real world. The propositions about the real world often are lacking in abstraction. All empirical observations, if part of science, are stated in this form. Though such propositions may depend upon rather abstract definitions and operations, such "atomic" propositions and abstract definitions are not the same thing.

As these propositions are formulated into a problem and hypotheses offered to solve the problem, the subsequent propositions become more and more abstract. At times, historically at least, scientific propositions may tend to be largely empirical; in part, science always contains at least some empirical statements. However, with the development of a theory, scientific propositions move away from the specific time-and-space statements to more general ones. Although some empirical reference is always necessary, a general scientific theory is highly abstract. As an example, the equation for the law of gravity is simply a set of abstract symbols.

Science Tends Towards a System. As scientific knowledge gets more and more abstract, as the hypotheses and laws increase both in number and generalization, scientific theory tends to incorporate uniformities among the generalizations themselves.

Since science rests so heavily on logic, there is always the danger that the system tends towards "logical closure"—that is, it is unable to accept certain empirical observations or generalizations. But science has complete control over its propositions. While certain propositions may be rejected because they contradict other known propositions, it is sometimes true that a new discovery may force a modification along the whole system of scientific theory.[7]

One of the major problems of theory, as a major component of science, is the development of a system which is able to render empirical findings consistent with each other. At the same time, the attempt to systematize empirical research gives rise to new problems and reformulation of old ones. Indeed, we must admit that some sort of dialectic relation obtains between the concepts, definitions, and permissible operations.

Science Is On-going. We may re-state the theoretical problem of systematization of scientific knowledge to indicate the vast intellectual heritage upon which any piece of scientific research rests. No one piece of research stands alone, nor does it stand and fall by itself. Of course, the source of the problem may result from this intellectual heritage. We may inherit bad ideas as well as good ones.

[7] Such a proposition would result in "eventful change," while those which are consistent but empirically new would be an example of relatively slow change, and the basic theory against which consistency is measured would be "persisting elements" referred to earlier.

5. STEPS IN SCIENTIFIC RESEARCH

For purposes of analysis, we will separate some of the more important steps in scientific research. It should be recognized, however, that the distinction between them is not as clear-cut as this presentation may insinuate. As a matter of fact, and as the student gains experience in research he will bear this out, one tends to jump back and forth from one step to another. While the temporal order of research is pretty much as given, the fact remains that "steps in scientific research" is a somewhat idealized account of how the scientist actually progresses.

Selection of Problem Area. This aspect of research is often a question of motivation and interest; many accidental things go into the selection of a problem area. The possibility of obtaining prestige, security, or even the solution of a personal problem, may determine the area in which the scientist is interested. We cannot deny the importance of such highly private considerations; but science is public. These should not become a part of science itself. Often, however, these private things later hinder the research, intruding to bias the results. This is simply true. The scientist must always be on guard against such factors and seek self-consciously to overcome them or their effects.

Acquaintance with Current Theory and Knowledge in the Area. Science is on-going, and after the scientist is aware of his problem area, he must continuously seek to know and understand the theory and problems of that area. Ordinarily, this part can be largely conducted in a library, as one would be reading the current literature on the area in question.

Definition of the Problem. This is the most crucial phase of inquiry, although it does not ordinarily come about in a clear-cut way. Indeed, as one is getting acquainted with current knowledge, he will be formulating his problem. Due to the possible motivational factors in selecting the area, or possibly to inadequacy of contemporary theory, he may poorly state his problem.

Just as there are various levels of abstraction of the propositions of science, so are there various levels of problems. Each level is solved in its own way; the solution of an empirical problem does not necessarily solve a highly abstract one. One should not imagine, then, that the formulation of a problem is an easy task. Nor are there any formal rules for telling one how to go about stating a problem. Stating a problem in such a way as to permit a solution is most difficult. It is critical to subsequent research; for only when the problem is clearly apprehended is there a possibility for the development of an adequate theory.

Development of Hypotheses. The hypothesis is, as we said earlier, a possible solution to a problem. Its source may be that of a hunch or shrewd guess by the scientist, or it may have been deduced from current theory. That is, if the theory is correct then other things ought to follow, one of which is the hypothesis in question.

Clearly, the development of hypotheses is not independent of the formulation of the problem and should be related to the phase of getting acquainted with current knowledge in an area. One important thing to remember is that good theory is abstract and tends to be general, which allows more than one hypothesis to be deduced from it. Therefore, one cannot say a priori just what hypotheses will flow from a theory: many will—and which ones are selected for test is often as much a function of the personality of the scientist as it is of the theory.

If correctly considered, the hypothesis tells what data the scientist is to gather and what to omit. Obviously, in a given piece of research, one does not look at all possible data, even at all data relevant to the field of inquiry. As a trivial example, in a study of occupational success, atmospheric information is seldom considered and the signs of the zodiac are almost ignored.

Development of the Formal Argument. Given the statement of the problem, and the hypothetical solution to the problem, how can one prove that the hypothesis (a) is true and (b) does in fact solve the problem? A decision must be made as to how the hypothesis is to be tested, what data are necessary, and what alternatives exist. Because of possible alternative findings, arguments should be formulated to face each alternative. If the argument is statistical, the tables to be used should be determined at this time.

Delineation of the Source of Data. The hypothesis tells what data are needed, and the structure of the argument tells what form they should be in. Whether one will directly observe, interview, give a paper-and-pencil test, use official documents, library materials, or whatever, must now be decided. Each source of data is liable to errors peculiar to itself and some, as secondary sources, have errors twice compounded. Many problems call for more than one source of data, particularly as the hypotheses get to be more complex. At any rate, the scientist must make certain that the data needed are available, or can become available. Clearly, if the data necessary to a test of one's hypothesis cannot be obtained, the hypothesis in question must go begging.

Creation of the Instrument. Presumably, the research is at the point where the scientist knows what data he needs and what form they are to take. The immediate task is to develop an instrument which will get him the data he wants in the form he wants. The instrument may be a questionnaire, interview, recording device, or some other means. Often, the scientist will be dealing with theoretical classes of things and faces the difficult task of properly identifying empirical members of such classes.

It is at this point that the "operationalism" of science is of critical importance, for the instrument will be part of the operations to be performed in the acquisition of data. All of the difficulties in going from abstract, theoretical definitions to concrete, empirical entities must now be squarely faced. Again, we recall that the theoretical class tends to be abstract and general; more than one identification can be made to get members of that class. The question then arises, should other identifications also be made?

To illustrate the issue: suppose we wanted an instrument dealing with "neurotic personalities" and that someone was called upon to record observed behavior. We might desire information regarding the subject's continuous washing of his hands. But neuroticism is manifest by other behaviors. Do we record them all, or only some and, if only some, how do we choose which?

Recall that there were differing levels of problems and that each had its own hypothetical solution. Each hypothesis will contain some content material, such that the level of abstractness of the hypothesis in question will go a long way in answering these questions.

Thus, the instrument should give the data called for by the hypothesis to be tested, and should be in the form which will allow us to come to a rigorous conclusion as to whether or not the hypothesis is true and, if true, if it solves the problem. We should not, however, think that operational definitions are the equivalent of theoretical definitions. The fact must be recognized that theoretical definitions must be such that an instrument can be created which will give the class empirical members; otherwise they cannot be used in research. The necessity of making operational definitions cannot be avoided. However, we must recognize the logical priority of theoretical ones and avoid the error of equating the two.

Writing a "Dummy Argument." Often there are flaws or unanticipated gaps in one's argument. Sometimes further data are needed, or unneeded data are being gathered. It is a good device, in guarding against such flaws, to write up the argument in terms of the data one expects to find. It may be held that such an action will predispose a person to certain findings and, therefore, bias the study. The fact is every scientist has some notion of what he is going to find. The suggestion is to formalize this and to see if, at this point in the research, correctable gaps exist. Much subsequent anguish and activity can be forestalled by such a simple device as this.

Pretest of the Instrument, and Possible Revision. The expenditure of the time and money necessary for full-scale research should not be engaged in unless there is definite knowledge that the instrument does give the data that is being sought. In questionnaires, for example, the wording of the questions is often misleading to certain segments of the sample. It is generally better to try the instrument out and see if it works on a small scale rather than assume that no errors exist. The creator of an instrument may be too close to it to see the changes which later develop, unless he has properly pretested it before wide-scale usage.

Formal Acquisition of Data. After the instrument has been created, and the source known to be available, the task is simply that of gathering the material—applying the instrument.

Analysis of the Data. With the method for using the data already known, a large part of analysis is somewhat routine. Often, however, some unanticipated results emerge, and the data behave differently from the hypothetical solution.[8] The scientist, if he seeks to revise his hypothesis, is essentially faced with an *ad hoc* problem. He is limited to the data at hand and this situation generally demands a reformulation of the problem, and the reformulation of hypotheses.

Formal Write-up of Conclusions Reached. This is the last step, and an important one. The write-up, generally, will be *in the form of an argument*. It will become a part of the intellectual heritage of the science in question. Subsequent researchers will read it in getting acquainted with the current theory and knowledge. The fact that it is in the form of an argument may present some difficulty to the future researchers. The temporal sequence of research is not necessarily the same as the sequence of propositions in an argument.[9]

6. SCIENTIFIC ATTITUDE

The scientist is often pictured as being detached and aloof; he is allegedly disinterested in the world about him and is completely absorbed by his experiments. We would hesitate to claim that these are necessary conditions for scientific behavior. It is true that the scientist is "passionately logical"—that is, he will accept the consequences of scientific discovery even if it makes him emotionally uncomfortable.

For our purposes, however, we will choose to emphasize the *skepticism* upon which science rests. Descartes finally concluded, "I doubt therefore I am." [10] Weber argues that the scientist is committed to the situation of being proved wrong: every known theory has undergone change and modification.[11]

Recall that science has complete control over its propositions. In the so-called induction, some intellectual leaps take place. Much research is often guided by hunches, guesses, and intuition, but, because science does not trust such sources, these are always subjected to empirical test.

8 Robert K. Merton, "The Bearing of Empirical Research upon the Development of Social Theory," *American Sociological Review, 13* (October, 1948), 505–515.

9 See Chapter 7 on Experimentation.

10 This is often written as, "I think, therefore I am."

11 H. H. Gerth and C. W. Mills, eds. & trans., "Science as a Vocation," *From Max Weber: Essays in Sociology,* New York, Oxford University Press, 1946.

Science, in its published form, is in the form of an argument. What-ever the source of the scientist's ideas, they are put in propositional form and tested. This is true even if the hypothesis is the logically necessary conclusion from the data as given. Not only does science mistrust intui-tion, but logic as well. No matter how rigorous the inference, the basic notion always is, Well, now, let's see if that's true.

This does not imply that the scientist believes nothing. He has a fundamental faith in scientific methodology—even while questioning some particular technique. He may never state it, but the scientist devel-ops a philosophy upon which his whole conception of science rests. Many of his assumptions he takes on faith; particularly if he denies any philo-sophic connection.

One issue that often brings out passionate discourse in those scientists who are otherwise detached and aloof is the question as to whether the laws discerned by science constitute a part of the real world, or whether the real world can be described by atomic empirical observations and the laws are the products of orderly human minds.

The issue is illustrated in an anecdote about three baseball umpires who were arguing about their job. Each called balls and strikes; each was bragging as to who did the best job. Said one: "I call them as I see them—and no one can do better than that." The second retorted, "That's nothing; I call them as they are." The third paused a moment, and finally added: "They ain't nothing until I call them—and then that's what they are."

Each umpire represents a different school of philosophy. The scien-tist virtually asks himself the same question, and the responses are as varied. To some, we describe uniformities of behavior as we observe them; to others science does indeed manage to describe the world as it is; to still others, scientific laws are merely the products of shrewd men.

In any case, statements of uniformities of behavior are reducible to propositional form, stand in logical relations to each other, and are sub-ject to empirical test. Regardless of the philosophy adopted, certain things are common to scientific activity: the rigorous empirical test of inferences—and hunches.

7. SUMMARY

Science is related to philosophy in at least three ways: in basic con-ceptions of reality, in basic conceptions of knowledge, and in basic ethical judgments. Without trying to impose any philosophical orientation upon the student, we notice that modifications of assumptions in these three areas lead to further modifications in science.

Science comes to us in propositional form. This leads us to consider other general characteristics of science: (1) It is concerned with a real world. (2) It is logical. (3) To get content into logical forms, science is operational. (4) Science is public in the sense of not allowing private biases. (5) Science is problem-solving. (6) It tends to be abstract, and (7) moves towards a system. No research stands by itself: Science is on-going.

The characteristics of science lead to major, analytically distinct, steps (though there is, empirically, some interaction between them). One first selects the problem area; that is largely a matter of individual motivation. Then one becomes acquainted with the current theory and knowledge in that area in order to define the problem. Formally one proposes solutions to the problem in the form of hypotheses and develops instruments to get the proper data. These will be cast in a specified form of argument and will be obtainable from a known source. After the data are gathered they are, of course, submitted to analysis. Surprising results, or modifications of hypotheses, lead to *ad hoc* problems and *ad hoc* hypotheses.

Science is geared to change. Accepted beliefs of today may be rejected tomorrow—and re-accepted the next. This gives rise to, and reinforces, the skeptical attitude. Science does not trust intuition, though it utilizes hunches, shrewd guesses, etc. It does not trust logical inference—everything is put to test.

Value-judgments, as matters of private convictions, are not a part of science, though they may be proper subjects for scientific analysis. There is, however, a fundamental value-orientation of science and that is summarized in the concept intellectual honesty. Intellectual honesty is the *sine qua non* of science. The contradiction of it destroys the basis of science. It follows that whatever social forces impinge upon intellectual honesty, impinge also upon the scientific mind.

SELECTED REFERENCES

Francis, Roy G., *Rhetoric of Science,* Minneapolis, University of Minnesota Press, 1961.

Kaufman, Felix, *Methodology of the Social Sciences,* New York, Oxford University Press, 1944.

MacIver, Robert M., *Social Causation,* Boston, Ginn, 1942.

Ramsperger, Albert G., *Philosophies of Science,* New York, Appleton-Century-Crofts, 1942.

Russell, Bertrand, *Human Knowledge: Its Scope and Limits,* New York, Simon and Schuster, 1948.

Searles, Herbert L., *Logic and Scientific Methods,* New York, Ronald, 1948.

2

Roy G. Francis

SOME ELEMENTARY LOGIC

1. INTRODUCTION

Before one can argue in such a way as to force his conclusions from his premises, he must have a structured pattern of movement. In its most elementary form, the argument deals with classes of things. In this case, each member of the class is treated as being identical (as far as class membership is concerned) with every other class member. These classes are organized into sentences. Eventually, one proceeds to ask the question, Does knowledge of the truth-value of one sentence imply knowledge of the truth-value of some other? Logic involves an examination of the way in which sentences can claim to be related. Argument flows from correct utilization of the character of these various relationships.

It really doesn't matter if the sentence is as simple as the kind we will deal with in this chapter or not. Indeed, a mathematical formula can be considered as a logical argument. Various sentences would give numerical values for the terms in the formula and one would give the formula itself; working the arithmetic would be a simple algorithm for deducing the conclusion. However, we will not deal with the logic of arithmetic here, but with simple, categorical logic.

A reflection on the first paragraph will reveal that we need some rules to ascertain "class membership," not in the operational sense of getting real-world, kickable members, but in the abstract sense. These rules will be true at least by definition. We will need to know something about the kind of simple sentences we will make—what they assert, and the scope or breadth of the domain about which they are true. Finally, we will need to know how simple sentences can relate to one another. Given this, the structure of simple argument will be readily apparent.

2. RULES OF THOUGHT

The use of a quasi-psychological language is a bit unfortunate; but this is what some specifications have been called for so long as to be so entrenched we dare not invent new names. However, do not think that these specify how one thinks. Rather, consider that these must be true, "must hold," if an argument is going to be sustained. Of course, if the material we deal with cannot be contained under these rules, our kind of logic won't work. But we are not required to specify rules for all logics; we are content to deal only with that which is consistent with these rules.

The Rule of Identity. In any discourse or argument, the meaning must remain the same throughout the argument. To define a term one way and then argue later as though it meant something different denies correct use of logic. Thus, if adolescent is defined to mean any young person between the ages of 15 and 23 and then later used to mean immaturity, an ambiguity is introduced and the argument has no weight. Symbolically, we may denote the class as S. This rule simply says $S = S$. If the object does not belong in class S, it belongs in class $-S$ (read: not $-S$).

The Rule of Contradiction. Remember that our classes are going to be put into sentences. In a simple sentence, we will have one class in the subject (denote it S) and one in the predicate (denote that class P). The rule of contradiction denies that an S can be both P and the contradiction of P (*i.e.*, $-P$). Thus, if the predicate term about adolescents is "adjusted," then we cannot argue that a particular adolescent is both "adjusted" and "not-adjusted" with respect to the same referent. If our theory says there is a class of things that are "both adjusted and not adjusted," then this rule says that an adolescent cannot belong to this class (note how cumbersome the language rapidly becomes) and to the class, "adjusted." Symbolically, we could state it as: $S \mathbin{/} (P \cdot -P)$. In this case, the slash (/) signifies a denial and the period in the parenthetic term signifies "and."

The Rule of the Excluded Middle. This asserts that the things dealt with in our subject class S must be either P or $-P$. Notice that we are dealing with "dichotomies." A dichotomy is a dimension admitting only two classes. In the real world, there may be many classes—consider height or weight. If we can identify a person's height as six feet three and two-sevenths inches, he must be either that tall or not. The latter includes both those taller and those shorter. Symbolically, with V signifying "or," we could have: $S = (P \mathbin{V} -P)$.

3. FORMS OF SENTENCES

That there are four possible forms of a classical two-term proposition should be readily deduced if we consider that the sentence will (a) either talk about all of the members of the subject class or only about some of them; and will (b) either affirm something or deny it. If the sentence is about all of the S's, it will be a "universal" one; otherwise it will be a "particular" one. If it is positive in its assertion, it will be "affirmative"; if it denies something, it is "negative." Thus, we have the following:

Universal Affirmative: All S Is P. Traditionally, this has been pictured in diagrams. A circle denoting *S* is put inside a circle denoting *P*, thus:

Of course, *S* and *P* could be identical; the statement would be true, but it would be misleading to indicate that *P* is larger or more inclusive. Hence, one cannot tell from the sentence how the circle diagrams are to look. A more convenient form is to put the information contained in the sentence in a "two-by-two" table. Notice that the claim, "All *S* is *P*," says that there are no cases where *S* is also —*P*; symbolically, the class $S . -P = 0$.

In a two-by-two table, this would appear in this form:

	S	—S
P		
—P	0	

The Universal Negative: No S Is P. It would appear this way:

	S	—S
P	0	
—P		

Notice that in neither of these two cases is there a commitment to the existence of any *S*. They merely assert that should any exist, they cannot be joined as indicated in the tables.

The Particular Affirmative: Some S Is P.

	S	—S
P	X	
—P		

In specific, note that one is not claiming that only some of the *S* is *P* or, in another way, simply that some *S* is not *P*. For the latter, one uses the specific assertion.

The Particular Negative: Some S Is Not P.

	S	—S
P		
—P	X	

These four exhaust the scope and mood of two-term propositions. From these we build up the formal structure of categorical argument.

The student should note that the form of logical analysis presented here, the two-by-two table, is identical in structure to certain statistical arguments to be discussed later. For a fuller treatment see the *Rhetoric of Science* by the author of this chapter.

4. RELATIONS BETWEEN PROPOSITIONS

Given two sentences, Q and R, does the knowledge of the truth-value of Q require any conclusion regarding the truth-value of R? The answer depends on how the truth values of Q and R are related to each other. It would seem clear that the possibilities are the following:

    a. They can both be true
    b. Q can be true and R false
    c. Q can be false and R true
    d. They can both be false

To specify how these connect, we must develop a notational system. If the truth of Q is randomly associated with the truth of R (if they are independent of each other), then knowledge of the one implies nothing of the other. We would denote this with an empty 2×2 table, viz.,

	Q	$-Q$
R		
$-R$		

It turns out that we can specify logical relations when we are able to deny one or two of the four possibilities. This condition lends itself to the power of logic in denying inference and results in the inability of science ever to prove, without doubt, anything.

Consider a statement of the following formal kind: "If Q, then R." This holds that it is impossible for Q to be true and R to be false—a denial of *b* above. In our notation,

	Q	$-Q$
R		
$-R$	0	

This is the hypothetical; sometimes it is called the relation of "implication."

"Subimplication," in which "Q is implied by R," would be denoted as follows:

	Q	$-Q$
R		0
$-R$		

This is a denial of c above. The difference between these two is significant especially when our theory requires one proposition to precede the other. If either can be considered as antecedent or consequent with equal theoretical thrust, then implication and subimplication are mere notational differences. However, if one's theory can identify one or the other as antecedent, then these relations take on a new significance.

If Q specifies a condition held to be antecedent to R, then subimplication is the same as "necessary conditions." An inspection of the table reveals that this is so, for the possibility of R being true when Q does not obtain, is denied. Moreover, when Q is theoretically held to be antecedent to R, the hypothetical turns out to specify "sufficient conditions." Again, an inspection of the table shows that other conditions than Q can result in the truth of R; but given the truth of Q, it follows that R cannot be false.

The "necessary and sufficient conditions" turns out to be an "if and only if" relation:

	Q	$-Q$
R		0
$-R$	0	

An enormous amount of fuzzy thinking is generated when a person believes this latter describes the relation when, in fact, a weaker condition (either of the two earlier examples) is correct.

Other logical relations specify degrees of contrariety. These involve the denial of a and d in our schema. When both are denied, we have the relation of contradiction:

	Q	$-Q$
R	0	
$-R$		0

This relation denies that the two statements can either be true together or false together. This leaves only the possibility that the truth of either is associated with the falsity of the other. It is a strong alternative: either Q or R is true; not both.

Weaker relations exist, too. Thus, if we simply deny that both can be false but admit that both could be true, we would have:

	Q	$-Q$
R		
$-R$		0

and if we deny that both could be false, but admit that both could be true we have:

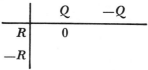

In theoretical discussions we are often asked to choose between competing theories. Frequently some research associated with one of the contending ideas may be presented. We are asked not only to judge the argument for which some data are presented, but to make judgments of the others as well. Unless we know, or have good reason to believe, the kind of contrariety existing between the ideas in contention, we cannot proceed to make the second judgment. In particular, theoretical arguments based on the assumption of contradiction are themselves false if the relationship is one of the weaker forms.

5. ARGUMENT BASED ON THE PRECEDING RELATIONS: THE SYLLOGISM

Formally, the syllogism is a two-premised argument. The major premise contains an asserted relationship; the second premise an existential commitment; and the third sentence contains a conclusion. The logical question is: Does the conclusion flow from the premises? The conclusion may be empirically true and still the argument can be false. We will consider only the hypothetical and the contrary syllogisms.

The hypothetical Syllogism:

$$\text{Major premise: If Q, then R}$$
$$\text{Minor premise: R}$$
$$\text{Conclusion \quad : Q}$$

Is this a valid conclusion? Consider the two-by-two representation of the hypothetical:

	Q	$-Q$
R		
$-R$	0	

Given the truth of R we have no way, upon entering the table, of knowing whether to put the case under Q or $-Q$. Hence, we are not *forced* to conclude Q; it may or may not be true. This illustrates the sin of "affirming the consequent" for, had the relation been subimplication, a 0 would have been entered under $-Q$ and we would have been forced to conclude Q.

Suppose, however, that we had proceeded as follows:

$$\text{Major premise: If } Q \text{, then } R$$
$$\text{Minor premise: } -R$$
$$\text{Conclusion \quad : } -Q$$

Now, is the argument forced? Looking again at the tabular representation we find:

	Q	$-Q$
R		
$-R$	0	

In this case, given $-R$, upon entering the table we find we cannot enter the column headed Q, since that can have no cases. We are forced to accept $-Q$, and the conclusion is logically forced.

Should we have had the strong relation of "if and only if," we could have proceeded in either case. Our table would be:

	Q	$-Q$
R		0
$-R$	0	

The minor premise of R would force the conclusion, Q; and the minor premise $-R$ would force the conclusion, $-Q$.

The major premise is a theoretical argument (based, or established, in part by previous research and in part by logical consistency). The minor premise is often the whole purpose of research. Clearly, however, the design of the research—whether it can or cannot answer a particular question—is contingent upon an appraisal of the major premise.

We are often asked to choose between contending hypotheses. In this case, our theoretical analysis must establish the character of contrariety. The alternative syllogism has, as its major premise, an assertion of "either Q or R" and, as we said, this may be a strong or a weak choice.

Consider the following:

> Major premise: Q contradicts R
> Minor premise: Q
> Conclusion   : R is false

Is this a forced conclusion? Consider the diagram:

	Q	$-Q$
R	0	
$-R$		0

If Q is affirmed, then one is forced to conclude that R is false. Had R been asserted in the minor premise, one would have to conclude that Q is false. Had R been denied by the research operation, one would be forced to accept Q; and, similarly, for the denial of Q in the minor premise.

The weaker, or "contrariety," relations also obtain. While contradiction requires a denial of a and d in our set of possible alternatives, contrariety simply involves a denial of only one or the other. Thus, if we were to assert "Q or R," allowing both to be true, our table would be of the following:

	Q	$-Q$
R		
$-R$		0

This stands in contrast to either contradiction or the other weak contrary relation:

	Q	$-Q$
R	0	
$-R$		

One must notice specifically the implications for the alternative syllogism in the different cases.

Consider the following argument:

> Major premise: Either Q or R
> Minor premise: R
> Conclusion   : $-Q$

Is the conclusion valid? Clearly, the answer depends upon which of the three cases holds. If contradiction obtains, the conclusion is proper; if the second case (which denies d) obtains, the conclusion is false. If the third case correctly described the relation, the conclusion would be forced.

Evidently, the character of the alternative relation is of critical importance. Think back to the issue of "necessary and sufficient conditions." There, you will recall, "sufficient conditions" was of the logical form of the hypothetical. Frequently, we are asked to choose one from a set of hypotheticals. If these hypotheses were contradictory the problem of design would be simple: attempt to affirm or deny a particular alternative. However, in sociology, *it is possible to conceive of many hypotheses being true under differing conditions.* If this is the case, then these alternatives could be "contradictory" only under highly specified conditions. In general, they would be simply contrary.

From this it follows that we must begin to ask questions regarding the conditions under which one hypotheses holds and not another. That is to say, we ought to be less concerned with attempting to put down contending arguments and more with examining the conditions under which our—or any—hypothesis holds.

6. A FINAL COMMENT

Because we deal with imperfect measurements, we ought not expect to find zeroes in the cells required by our formal logic. Instead, we ought to expect to find small frequencies. If this is so, then we must learn how to combine probability reasoning with categorical logic. This is one of the issues facing statistical inference, a point to be covered later.

SELECTED REFERENCES

Francis, Roy G., *The Rhetoric of Science*, Minneapolis, The University of Minnesota Press, 1961.
Angell, Richard B., *Reasoning and Logic*, New York, Appleton-Century-Crofts, 1964.

3
John T. Doby

CONCEPTS AND THEORIES

1. INTRODUCTION

Francis Bacon wrote that "knowledge itself is power." One can judge the relative degree of maturity of the various scientific disciplines by noting the degree of control or power which each affords man over aspects of nature. If one were currently to rank the divisions of science according to their problem-solving power it is quite likely that most authorities would agree that the physical sciences would rank first, followed by the biological sciences and then the social sciences.

We can more clearly appreciate the role of concepts and theories in science if we look at the basic developments in the scientific disciplines and note the relation between new conceptualizations and subsequent increases in problem-solving power. Because of the cumulative nature of scientific progress a discipline is always more successful in its recent history than in the past. For example, the physical sciences have become very successful since World War I. They have progressed from the description of natural processes, through the explanation of these, into the control of them. Physics has advanced from a description of wave phenomena, to an explanation via atomic theory, to a controlled release of atomic energy. Biology has progressed from conceptual models which at first merely described the qualitative behavior of nature, à la Darwin, to more recent models which explain genetic transmission. Sociology, psychology, economics, and anthropology are still primarily functioning at the level of qualitative description of empirical relations, intuition, and trial and error research.[1] Even so, these disciplines have radically transformed man's views and thinking about human nature. Many conditions and characteristics of man which were once thought to be immutable are now being controlled. For example, the power of education

[1] Some important reference sources for keeping up with recent scientific research are: "Current Contents," "Science Citation Index," and "Science Information Exchange," available in any good library.

and social organization to release and aid in the development of human potentialities and the power of economic theory to enable governments to control inflation and deflation are resources which were once believed impossible. Many other examples could be given in the field of social and psychological problems, such as mental health, mental retardation, poverty, and community development.

Up until the twentieth century, the principal advances, particularly practical advances, in the physical sciences were the result of intuition, empiricism, and trial and error. The nineteenth century scientist observed phenomena, described it and interpreted it, but was able to make very few accurate quantitative predictions.

The steam engine was not developed as a result of advances in thermodynamics; rather the converse was true, and thermodynamics developed as a branch of physics partly in order that the steam engine might be more fully understood. By contrast, the atomic reactor was conceived and predicted and developed as a direct result of the theory of relativity; and the maser and laser were conceived and developed by the direct application of quantum mechanics.[2]

It should be clear from the foregoing that concepts and theories provide the scientist with a perspective or view of aspects of reality which is not available by direct observation. In other words, concepts and theories provide constructed pictures of reality which, when tested by appropriate scientific procedures, give meaning and control over aspects of reality.

Without adequate concepts and theories the scientist is, in his efforts to explain and understand reality, very much like John Saxe's six blind men of Indostan in their efforts to describe the elephant. That is, their view of the elephant seemed to depend entirely upon the part of the animal which they accidentally touched. For example, those who touched his trunk thought he was like a tree; those who touched the tail thought the elephant looked like a rope; and so on.

In a common-sense manner of speaking, concepts and theories are not peculiar to science. They are as essential to everyday communication as they, in their more refined form, are basic to scientific thinking and research. It is man's ability to represent experience and objects of experience by means of language that most clearly distinguishes him from other members of the animal kingdom. Everyday experiences and interaction do not require the precision, reliability, and validity of concepts and theories that science does. Man, in respect to his everyday interaction, often lives by myth and yet manages successfully. This is also true in regard to his scientific endeavors, but the consequences of myth to the

2 Bryce Crawford, "New Trends in Graduate Study in the Physical Sciences," in Everett Walters, *Graduate Education Today*, Washington, D.C., American Council on Education, 1965, p. 218.

scientific world are more pronounced, more consciously tested, and more quickly discovered and eliminated. In fact, one of the major tenets of scientific procedure is to doubt one's premises and to arrange to test one's doubts as a means of establishing their validity. Something like this also takes place in everyday experience, particularly social behavior. However, the results of this kind of testing do not accrue in any formal way to the body of science. The reason for this is quite clear, namely, that *the conceptualizing of problems is on a level of abstraction which is outside the realm of direct or indirect sensory contact of the layman.* In other words, the formulation of the problems of daily living are at one level of experience and the scientists' formulation of scientific problems are at another. Let us illustrate this difference by referring to the elementary concept of mass in physics. The ordinary person usually implies nothing more than the idea of bulk in his use of this term. However, the student of introductory physics knows that the physicist specifies a different meaning. To the physicist the concept of mass involves weight, force, acceleration, inertia, and gravity. Moreover, he is interested in the specific relationships among these factors. For example, force is equal to the product of the mass of a body and its acceleration, or $F = MA$; mass is then equal to the ratio F/A.

Scientists and philosophers of science are in basic agreement that the principal objective of all the sciences is *explanation* of empirical uniformities, that is, describing and explaining the empirical regularities of the real world or aspects of the real world. If we ignore for the moment the role of methodology and mathematics in scientific explanation, then we can say that the task of explanation lies with *concepts* and *theories*.

2. CONCEPTS

It is the scientist's task to make theoretical sense out of his observations. Let us make it clear at the outset that by "observations" we are referring to controlled or measured observations of aspects of the real world. If science is to tell us anything about the world of reality, it must somewhere contain empirical elements in its observations. In this regard we assume that *information* about the world comes to us by experience alone and it is by experience alone that propositions about the world are tested. Moreover, since our experience is always limited, the limits of possible experience cannot be drawn. In other words, our conceptions of experience are limited by experience; that is, we view experience from within our experience.

Fundamental to all experience is perception and, just as perception is conditioned by experience, so is conception. This in turn conditions subsequent perception. There is, to be sure, the argument of some philosophers who contend that experience is uniquely and ineluctably private and that only the objective, external world is problematic and therefore subject to science. In the opinion of this writer, Professor Kaplan properly disposes of this belief when he says:

. . . the solipsism to which such an epistemology is inevitably impelled is, for methodology at any rate, a reduction to an absurdity. Science itself is a social enterprise, in which data are shared, ideas exchanged, and experiments replicated. It is precisely the cumulation of empirical evidence which shapes a welter of diverse opinions into scientific knowledge common to many minds.[3]

If it is through the interpretation of experience that the scientist explains his empirical observations, then this is often quite difficult since it means essentially the *choosing of the right concepts* to guide the process of observation and to interpret the results. But we have earlier implied that we cannot be certain of the meaning assigned experience even though knowledge is dependent upon experience. In other words, as knowledge is dependent upon experience, so also is meaning. This form of empiricism, called by Kaplan "semantic empiricism," does not deny truths which transcend experience and therefore depend on faith; rather, it denies the possibility of assigning scientific meaning to statements involving ideas which transcend experience. To illustrate what we mean by the distinction between knowledge and meaning let us note that we have some knowledge of the workings of the DNA molecule in hereditary transmission but we do not, as of now, know what this *means* in regard to human learning, perception, and, in short, to behavior. Again, we may have knowledge of what someone is doing, but it may require additional experience with him to determine the meaning of what he is doing.[4] For our purpose here it is sufficient to say that Charles Pierce's formulation of meaning is closest to what we are trying to convey. To borrow from and rephrase Pierce, *a statement is meaningful if it enters into the making of a decision and its meaning is the difference it makes to the decision made.*[5] If we formulate a statement implying cultural determination of behavior then this affects our decision regarding research strategy as well as our beliefs about what is or is not effective therapy procedures for controlling behavior. In other words, to believe a statement is in effect to make a choice among alternative sets or courses of action. The word action should be construed in the broad sense

---

[3] From *The Conduct of Inquiry: Methodology for Behavioral Science,* by Abraham Kaplan, copyright © 1964 by Chandler Publishing Company, San Francisco, pp. 35–36. Reprinted by permission.

[4] For a more detailed discussion of this see *Ibid.,* pp. 36–45.

[5] See Charles S. Pierce, *Collected Papers, Pragmatism and Pragmaticism,* vol. 5, eds. Charles Hartshore and Paul Weiss, Cambridge, Harvard University Press, 1960. And Charles S. Pierce, *Collected Papers, Science and Philosophy,* vol. 7, ed. Arthur W. Burks, Cambridge, Harvard University Press, 1958.

to include theoretical and methodological action as well as practical or applied.

General Functions. The individual in adjusting to his environment uses his sensory capacity to become aware of and to interpret aspects of the world about him. His specialized sense organs, including the higher processes of the brain, permit him to sift the welter of stimuli about him and to respond specifically to some of its aspects. This selection of a few impressions which have relevance, from a mass of impressions and the organizing of these into a primary image or view, we call "perception." Perceiving, then, is a way of ordering the environment by playing up certain features and playing down others.

Any sharp distinction between perception and conception is arbitrary. However, we will use perception to refer to the results of past learning which interact with brain structure and functioning to determine one's interpretation of stimuli. People encounter new situations containing strange elements for which current perception does not provide adequate meaning. In addition, there are also elements in reality that are relevant to its understanding, but not directly perceivable. Given the foregoing situations of new or strange elements and/or hidden elements, and the necessity for responding, one has to act on the basis of *conception* by making certain assumptions. Therefore, one of the psychological functions of conception is to remove the blocks to perception. A dramatic illustration of the blocking of perception and the need for conception to enable the person to overcome the perceptual obstacles is given in the following quotation from *The Evolution of Physics* by Einstein and Infeld. To be more precise one would say that the following is an example of the *postulational character of science.*

In our endeavor to understand reality we are somewhat like a man trying to understand the mechanism of a closed watch. He sees the face and the moving hands, even hears its ticking, but he has no way of opening the case. If he is ingenious he may form some pictures of a mechanism which could be responsible for all the things he observes, but he may never be quite sure his picture is the only one which could explain his observations. He will never be able to compare his picture with the real mechanism and he cannot even imagine the possibility or the meaning of such a comparison. But he certainly believes that, as his knowledge increases, his picture of reality will become simpler and simpler and will explain a wider and wider range of his sensuous impressions.[6]

Thus it should be clear that under such circumstances absolute knowledge is probably never attainable, but if man is sufficiently clever he can circumvent the obstacles to perception through ingenious conception and achieve an increasingly accurate approximation to reality. In such a case conception serves the same purpose as perception; that is, it

[6] Albert Einstein and Leopold Infeld, *The Evolution of Physics*, New York, Simon and Schuster, 1938, p. 33. Reprinted by permission of the Estate of Albert Einstein.

permits adjustment or provides a new orientation. In this regard there is a mutual or reciprocal relationship between perception and conception: perception aids conception and the new-found concepts feed back into perception giving old percepts new meaning. Thus a concept is not only an aid to perception, but it is also a *way of conceiving*.

It is in this latter aspect of the concept that we are most interested. The history of science is rich with examples where scientists when confronted with problematic phenomena have, in their efforts to explain them, suggested the *existence of something not directly perceived*. Some examples of such concepts are bacteria, molecules, genes, electricity, motives, and attitudes. This function of a concept, as a way of conceiving the nature of phenomena, is effectively expressed by Professor Herbert Blumer.

> Perhaps it might be better to say that, on the basis of given tangible perceptual experiences which were puzzling, certain individuals fashioned constructs which would give these experiences an understandable character. As far as I can see, scientific concepts come into existence in this way. They refer to something whose existence we presume, but whose character we do not fully understand. They originate as conceptions occasioned by a series of perceptual experiences of a puzzling character which need to be bridged by a wider perspective. I hasten to add that the concept does not merely suppose the existence of something which bridges perceptual experiences, but it implies that this thing has a nature or certain character.[7]

The concept is formulated in response to experience and it also represents the content of experience. For example, the child, as its knowledge of language increases, learns to use words which stand for some common property of a variety of objects, persons, or situations. Thus the young child may be able to name correctly such animals as the horse, dog, cat, and mouse, but it is not until sometime later that he is able to group these under the single unifying concept of animal. In other words, the abstraction of experience from the world of particulars, and the holding on to this, is possible only through conceptualization and this necessitates concepts.

This process of developing concepts by learning to group objects or experience in terms of common properties is called "abstraction." It is clear that one of the important functions of concept formation is to enable the observer to focus on relevant factors and ignore the irrelevant. By identifying the isolated particulars of experience one is able to group them in terms of their common content and characteristics. Once a set of concepts has been developed and given labels or identifying symbols, then three developments of paramount importance for science are made

[7] Herbert Blumer, "Science Without Concepts," an unpublished mimeographed copy of an address delivered before the Ninth Annual Institute of Social Research, University of Chicago, August 20–23, 1930, p. 3.

possible by the process of abstraction in forming concepts. *First,* the common content conceived from the mass of particulars may now become the object of separate investigation and study; *secondly,* the content may become the experience of others since it is identifiable by a language or symbols which are common to others and this makes possible collective action and cumulative results; and *thirdly,* it makes possible the unity and systematic nature of science by linking together the particular elements and ideas in a pattern. Science gets its systematic nature through the coherence of its concepts.

One or two examples should make clear the linkage function of concepts in science. The concepts of chromosome and gene in biology have formed a pattern which has guided research in that field. The concepts of culture, institution, status, and role have guided research in sociology. The development of concepts in science provides the web of ideas which connect the various individual research efforts and enables the organization and reorganization of experience through time.

In summary, the main points which we have made so far in connection with the *psychological* and *social* functioning of concepts in science are: (1) the scientific concept provides a way of viewing or picturing that which cannot be directly observed and thus circumvents obstacles to perception, (2) the content of the scientific concept consists of abstracted materials which may be socially shared with others and therefore become the subject of additional study, (3) the concept because of its verbal or symbolic nature may be shared with others which allows for the cumulation and extension of science, and (4) the logical interrelations of scientific concepts make possible the systematic structure of science.

The foregoing functions of concepts are more or less common to the functioning of common-sense or ordinary language concepts. Let us now look more specifically at what concepts *do* in scientific research and thinking.

Functions of Concepts in Science. Recall that the principal purpose of science is to explain empirical phenomena by establishing predictable cause-effect relationships. In order to do this the scientist is guided in his formulation of the problem and his observations of the data. What does the guiding and what are the "seeing eyes?" The reader should be warned that we are not referring to the process of creativity that goes on in the mind of the scientist. Instead we are referring to one of the essential elements that he uses in the creative process. This element is the *scientific concept.* It is common knowledge that Pasteur in his study of the causes of disease was guided by his phrase "seek the microbe." In other words, he had a concept of microscopic organisms as disease bearing organisms, and he used this concept to guide and order his research. Following this, as most everyone knows, the mysteries of fermentation, anthrax, septicemia, and rabies yielded to the new approach made possible by his concept of microscopic organisms. We may now conclude that the *first* function of the concept is to *guide research by providing a perspective and point of departure*. In other words, Pasteur's concept of the microbe provided him with a way of looking at his problem and this resulted in bringing new facts into existence. That is to say, concepts provide a way of looking at things and also a way of making relationships observable which were formerly not observable. In Pasteur's case the particular invisible relationship brought into conscious existence is the relationship between bacteria and disease.[8]

We can only speak of the functions of scientific concepts in terms of the intentions of scientists and their meanings are scientifically valid only if what they intend becomes actual; that is, if problems are solved and new problems discovered as research continues. In other words, a scientific concept is a set of specifications as to how to proceed in an inquiry. The meanings assigned the concept and the specifications provided vary with the context within which the concept is applied; therefore, the *guiding* function of a concept varies with its context. For example, the concept molecule means one thing in physics and another in chemistry and the concept of culture means something quite different among art patrons from what it means to an anthropologist.

The specification of a point of departure or perspective is not sufficient to enable the point of view to become instrumental in inquiry. It is not enough to say, "seek the microbe" or "look at culture." In addition the concept specifications must include an account of not only what is to be observed and where, but also *how* it is to be observed; that is, the concept must include properties which will enable the fulfilling of the purpose of the researcher. This will enable us to state the *second* function of scientific concepts, namely, *to specify the operations necessary to observing the categories or variables which will tell us more about our subject matter*. For example, the concept of intelligence specifies mental age divided by chronological age and this multiplied by 100 as specifying an IQ score. Ideally it is desirable to specify a variable as an equation then it can be treated according to the rules of mathematics. For example, in physics W designates weight and V stands for volume, then D or density is written as $D = \frac{W}{V}$ and can be treated according to the rules of algebra. Thus $W = DV$ and $V = W/D$. It must be noted that it is still the defining equation for density and does not define weight or volume. The algebraic rearrangement is merely a convenient means for calculating W or V. It presupposes that W and V have already been defined.

It is of interest to note how a conceptual point of view determines the data to be selected for research. Blumer notes that perhaps "the mill-

---

[8] We are not concerned here with the historical fact of who first conceived the idea, for example, Fracastoro, Leeuwenhock or some other, instead we are concerned with an *example*.

ing and halting condition of our own science does not come directly from the inadequacy of our techniques, as almost everyone contends, but from the inadequacy of our point of view." [9] From the point of view of this text, we would argue that the techniques follow from the types of conceptualization. Blumer cites a good illustration of our point of view.

Through conception objects may be perceived in new relations, which is paramount to saying that the perceptual world becomes reorganized. It is well to bear in mind that in the process new problems may arise, new techniques may appear, and new interpretations may suggest themselves. An entire new field may open up; scientific energy may be released in new productive ways. As I see it, this has been the experience of science on the adaptation of a new orientation or, what is equivalent, on the adaptation of a new conceptual framework. A conspicuous case which may be given in illustration is the origin of modern physics. The work of Galileo is usually chosen, with good reason, as marking the change from the metaphysical preoccupation of the medieval logicians to the scientific endeavors of modern scientists. This work is significant not only for the introduction of experimental technique but also for the development of new concepts which became the basis for the new attack of modern physics. These concepts are familiar. Mass, motion, inertia, force, came to take the place of the concepts of medieval logicians: essence, quality, substance, potentiality. They provided a new perspective; they opened up a new field of endeavor. They raised new problems and suggested new techniques; they sensitized perception to new relations and guided it along new directions; they made experimentation possible, and ultimately they yielded new forms of control. A similar picture, I suppose, is being presented in contemporary physics in the new orientation and conceptual framework surrounding the work in relativity and quantum relations.[10]

We may summarize the above two functions as follows: concepts specify the roads or avenues to follow in research and the means or methods of travel upon these roads. That is, concepts provide a point of view thereby releasing activity and, in addition, direct such activity with varying degrees of effectiveness. The success of the activity is, of course, dependent upon the validity of the concepts.

A third function of concepts arises out of the consequences in practice of the foregoing two. Once concepts have delineated research paths or roads and have provided the instrumental foundations for pursuing the paths, then, by the use of rules of logic new road networks or junctures may be deduced. In other words, one may, by deduction, generalize to new concepts and new problems. Thus the *third* function of the concept is its *deductive consequences.*

The deductive nature of science applies not only to new or future conditions, or "prediction," but also to past behavior, or "post-diction." For example, the researcher in geology may use the concepts of physics

9 Blumer, *op. cit.*, p. 9.
10 Blumer, *Ibid.*, p. 9.

to make deductions about geological deposits; the sociologist may apply sociological theories to ancient or past civilizations which may be confirmed by historical research. The historians of mathematics have made it clear that the major concepts of the number system and mathematics in general arose out of man's efforts to solve physical problems. However, in each case these developments were elaborated and extended into complex new systems by logical growth and in many instances have far outraced experience.

We have stressed the instrumental and freeing or enriching function of concepts in guiding research. But we must be aware that as soon as we formulate or accept one form of conceptualization, this automatically sends us down one road rather than another and that this blinds us to other and perhaps better road possibilities. We are caught in a paradox. We need proper concepts in order to get started, but we also need some way to formulate better concepts. In other words, while concepts are freeing they are also binding.

The reconstructed logic of science is much simpler than the actual activities and procedures which a scientist engages in while solving a problem. As Kaplan has so well pointed out:

> The appropriate conceptualization of the problem already prefigures its solution. Ask someone to arrange six matches into four equilateral triangles; he will find it impossible, until he realizes that they need not all be in the same plane, whereupon the tetrahedron becomes obvious. But he must first be able to free his conception of geometric figures from the restriction to the plane. Such freedom is as hard to come by—and to live with—as any other.[11]

We must be prepared to formulate a precise and complete conceptualization, but we must be equally prepared to abandon it in favor of another one if it does not work.

3. THE CONCEPTUAL PROCESS: CONCEPTS AND THEORIES

It should be clear from the discussion in section two that concept formation and theory formation are two different aspects of the same general process of scientific explanation. In so far as science is concerned they go hand in hand and are interdependent.

The process of conceptualization usually begins with some *actual* puzzling observation or from some *hypothetical,* but new situation, deduced from existing theory. The problem then is to conceptualize the new situation so as to permit an appropriate effort to solve or explain it. As knowledge of a particular subject area grows, our conception of the subject matter of the area changes. As our concepts improve, we learn more. Our knowledge never becomes complete, but it does continuously become a better approximation to reality. As our concepts improve we

11 Kaplan, *op. cit.,* p. 53.

are able to deduce better theories and as we acquire better theories we are able to formulate better concepts. Whether or not ultimate success will occur is problematic, but the scientist, nevertheless, operates on the assumption that it will. A good illustration of what we mean is provided by Dr. Einstein's hypothetical example of a connection between general relativity and geometry.

Let us begin with the description of a world in which only two-dimensional and not, as in ours, three-dimensional creatures live. The movies have accustomed us to two-dimensional creatures acting on a two-dimensional screen. Now let us imagine that these shadow figures, that is, the actors on the screen really do exist, that they have the power of thought, that they can create their own science, that for them a two-dimensional screen stands for geometrical space. These creatures are unable to imagine, in a concrete way, a three-dimensional space just as we are unable to imagine a world of four dimensions. They can deflect a straight line; they know what a circle is, but they are unable to construct a sphere, because this would mean forsaking their two-dimensional screen. We are in a similar position. We are able to deflect our curve lines and surfaces, but we can scarcely picture a deflected and curved four-dimensional space.

By living, thinking, and experimenting, our shadow figures could eventually master the knowledge of the two-dimensional Euclidean geometry. Thus, they could prove, for example, that the sum of the angles in a triangle is 180 degrees. They could construct two circles with a common center, one very small, the other large. They would find that the ratio of the circumferences of two such circles is equal to the ratio of their radii, a result again characteristic of Euclidean geometry. If the screen were infinitely great, these shadow beings would find that once having started a journey straight ahead, they would never return to their point of departure.

Let us now imagine these two-dimensional creatures living in changed conditions. Let us imagine that someone from the outside, the "third dimension," transfers them from the screen to the surface of a sphere with a very great radius. If these shadows are very small in relation to the whole surface, if they have no means of distant communication and cannot move very far, then they will not be aware of any change. The sum or angles in small triangles still amounts to 180 degrees. Two small circles with a common center still show that the ratio of their radii and circumferences are equal. A journey along a straight line never leads them back to the starting point. But let these shadow beings, in the course of time, develop their theoretical and technical knowledge. Let them find means of communications which will enable them to cover large distances swiftly. They will then find that starting on a journey straight ahead, they ultimately return to their point of departure. "Straight ahead" means along the great circle of the sphere. They will also find that the ratio of two circles with a common center is not equal to the ratio of the radii, if one of the radii is small and the other great.

If our two-dimensional creatures are conservative, if they have learned the Euclidean geometry for generations past when they could not travel far and when this geometry fitted the facts observed, they will certainly make every possible effort to hold onto it, despite the evidence of their measurements. They could try to make physics bear the burden of these discrepancies. They could seek some physical reasons, say temperature differences, deforming the lines and causing deviation from Euclidean geometry. But sooner or later, they must find out that there is a much more logical and convincing way of describing these occurrences. They will eventually understand that their world is a finite one, with different geometrical principles from those they learned. They will understand that in spite of their inability to imagine it, their world is the two-dimensional surface of a sphere. They will soon learn new principles of geometry, which though differing from the Euclidean can, nevertheless, be formulated in an equally consistent and logical way for their two-dimensional world. For the new generation brought up with a knowledge of the geometry of the sphere, the old Euclidean geometry will seem more complicated and artificial since it does not fit the facts observed.[12]

While the situation of two-dimensional creatures on a two-dimensional surface was hypothetically conceived in relation to these same creatures on a three-dimensional surface there is nothing hypothetical or constructed about the referents. The referents are real and observable even though indirectly. The sociologist may directly observe a man's choice of a candidate on an opinion poll by watching him mark one place instead of another, but he does not observe the dynamics which determined the choice, these are not visible and must be inferred. It is at this point where *theories* are necessary to connect the physical referents to the explanatory variables, which are nonetheless physical, but only indirectly observable. The theories allow us to make inferences between the concepts whose referents are directly observable, such as a verbal statement, and the concepts which are indirectly observable, such as the motives, attitudes, or values which are the presumed connection between what is directly observed and what the indirect term signifies. We may directly observe hair and eye color, but we *infer* a connection between these and genes. If the inference is confirmed then these indirect observables are as much a part of the real world as are the ones directly observable by the ordinary senses. Since science is primarily concerned with the establishment of relationships between a set of problematic data and a set of explanatory data the connections between these are always inferred and, therefore, indirect. The more advanced a science becomes the more indirect inference is necessary since the number of logical and empirical steps between the problematic and explanatory increases. We will now examine some of the problems involved in relating concepts by theories.

4. SOME PROBLEMS IN CONCEPT FORMATION

First, scientific knowledge requires that all statements of science be capable of being tested by reference to evidence which is public, that is it

[12] Einstein and Infeld, *op. cit.*, pp. 236–238. Reproduced by permission of the Estate of Albert Einstein.

can be secured and checked by independent observers.[13] To this end, data which are to be used as scientific evidence should be obtained under the guidance of concepts whose use by scientists is marked by uniformity and correspondence.

We have implied that concepts refer to things; that is, objects, organisms, persons, and properties or characteristics of things. Animals, plants, factories, streets, men, sex, and thought are concepts since these are terms which refer to things or their properties, that is, nouns and adjectives. Concepts also refer to events or actions of things. These are predicates or verbs. A third class of concepts refers to the relationships among things, events, and their properties. In this third type of concept the evidence is more complicated than in the other two because it is indirect. People can directly observe dogs and they can observe them fighting or playing, but the relationship between the animal and the properties which evoke the fighting or playing are less accessible to direct observation. This creates problems of definition, observation, and measurement.

A still more abstract class of names which is sometimes called a concept, but for our purposes is more appropriately labeled a *"construct"* refers to *hypothetical boundaries* of concepts. The content of a construct is freely created by the scientist and represents the logical extreme of a known thing, event, or relationship. The use of constructs allows the scientist to construct theoretical limits which constitute boundaries between which empirical things, events, or relationships can vary. Knowing the hypothetical boundaries the scientist can formulate equations under specified conditions to predict behavior within these boundaries. For example, in mathematics one may construct straight lines, circles, and cones and by the use of equations which describe them we can calculate the dimensions of actual circles, lines, and cones and thereby determine variation from the model. The notion of a vacuum, a frictionless engine, and perpetual motion are examples of constructs in physics. We can logically construct a "frictionless" society, a perfectly integrated personality, and a completely rational man, but instances of these are not to be found. If this is so, then of what value are constructs? The answer is that they are necessary to science. All concepts are simplifications of reality. Man "in general" is never the same as any particular man. Since the essence of a concept is an abstraction of selected elements from reality it invariably loses in concreteness and individuality. As Professor Einstein noted in the analogy of the watch referred to previously, man in his observation of things and events is always limited and therefore finds it necessary to invent, that is, construct what conceivably could account for what he observes. These constructions are hypotheses.

Scientists aim toward ever simpler systems of explanation of their

[13] This statement, of course, does not refer to primitive terms and the axioms which relate these to concepts—one has to start somewhere with an assumption.

observations. Thus the logical relations among concepts are constantly undergoing revision and reformulation. As a field of science becomes more complex this becomes quite difficult since the empirical referents are often only indirectly observable. Therefore, it is important for conceptual clarity that the relations between the concepts and their referents be clearly specified. Indeed, as Hempel says:

> . . . the entire history of scientific endeavor appears to show that in our world comprehensive, simple, and dependable principles for the explanation and prediction of observable phenomena cannot be obtained by merely summarizing and inductively generalizing observational findings. A hypothetico–deductive–observational procedure is called for and indeed is followed in the more advanced branches of science: guided by his knowledge of observational data, the scientist has to invent a set of concepts—theoretical constructs, which lack immediate experiential significance, a system of hypotheses couched in terms of them, and an interpretation for the resulting theoretical network; and all this in a manner which will establish explanatory and predictive connections between the data of direct observation.[14]

Here Hempel is not using constructs in the sense that we have, namely, as boundary notions, instead he is using the term as an indirect observable. The idea is similar, but not the same. Weber's ideal type is close to what is here meant by construct. Likewise is McKinney's notion of the constructed type. These will be discussed later in the chapters on construction typology.

As Kaplan says:

> . . . no observation is purely empirical—that is, free of any ideational element— as no theory (in science, at any rate) is purely ideational. . . . All inferences implicate theories, in the broadest sense of the term. . . . the human being is himself an instrument of observation and requires, like other instruments, a theory for its proper use. . . . It is by way of the norm as well as by way of the idiosyncratic that theory enters into observation. When we see that someone is pleased or angry, we are relying on a whole framework of ideas about cultural patterns in the expression of emotion, just as we understand what is said not just on the basis of what we hear but also in terms of a whole grammar somehow brought to the hearing. Such theories are tacit, loose, and above all, perfectly familiar, like the geometrical optics with which we make out what we see at a distance. Its very familiarity may hide it from use, but it is at work for all that. I once heard a distinguished experimental physicist seriously deny that theory plays any part in his observations of nuclear reactions on photographic plates in cloud chambers and the like! Does the chess master "see" what is happening in the game or does he "understand" it? Both "see" and "understand" are manners of speaking.[15]

---

14 Carl G. Hempel, "Fundamentals of Concept Formation in Empirical Science," in the *International Encyclopedia of Unified Science,* vol. 2, no. 7, pp. 36–37, Chicago, The University of Chicago Press, 1952.

15 Kaplan, *op. cit.,* pp. 58–59.

Theories and concepts are two interrelated aspects of the general process of scientific explanation. A theory consists of a set of statements which connect a set of concepts in a logically unified way and provide an interpretation of an empirical law or laws. In a broader sense theories are constructions which serve to integrate or organize the entire set of empirical laws in a field into a single deductive system. To be sure this effort is not always successful but, nonetheless, it is the aim irrespective of the state of development of a field. A theory is practical; that is, it works to the extent that it allows for fruitful deductions which are later confirmed by appropriate scientific tests. Early research on malaria suggested that "bad air" was causally related to the disease. Consequently observations were made and data collected relating the incidence of malaria to exposure to bad air. The concept of malaria had to evolve from some theory, however, implicit, as to the cause of the malady. The term "malaria" was simply a symbolic representation of the theory. Since the theory was invalid the concept led the investigators to blind alleys. The interrelation of theory and fact are unquestionable. However, when it comes to creativity and the advancement of science it is the invention of significant new theories that mark the new landscapes. Conant says: "The history of science demonstrates beyond a doubt that the really revolutionary and significant advances come not from empiricism but from new theories." [16]

The degree of refinement and flexibility of concepts and theories improves as the data in a field grow and improve. Some concepts are very crude and others highly refined. Let us next examine concepts in terms of the various symbolic forms by which they are defined.

5. THE SYMBOLIC REPRESENTATION OF CONCEPTS

Usually the following discussion would be found under the heading of measurement and types of scales. However, from the point of view and purpose of this chapter, it is more appropriate to label the section "symbolic forms or levels of concepts."

A fruitful concept ties in with its body of theory in such a way as to suggest new problems and new principles, rather than stalling thinking by operating like a bottomless, closed system. Analytically and provisionally, a closed system represents an assumed final state of a science not its development and on-going state.

We have emphasized several times before that concepts refer to sense data somewhere along the logical chain. Therefore, observation is a necessary part of concept formation, but it is not sufficient. The observer must have accurate data in order to build new concepts.

[16] James B. Conant, *Modern Science and Modern Man*, New York, Columbia University Press, 1952, p. 30.

Types of Variables. We contend, as we have implied elsewhere, that the primary purpose of science is to explain by establishing a connection between a problematic variable and one or more explanatory variables. These are sometimes referred to as dependent and independent variables, respectively. To illustrate, we will define as problematic data the different learning scores of a sample of subjects on the same material and who have had the same training on these materials. The explanatory data are the data derived from the hypotheses which tentatively account for the differential performance. Suppose, in this case, this is the subject's attitude toward the motives to be learned. Suppose further that this variable (attitude) completely accounts for the variance in the dependent variable (learning). Then attitude completely explains the problem, at least in an empirical or functional sense. We recognize two types of these variables; namely variables that are *continuous* and variables that are *discrete*. A continuous variable is one which can be represented by any value or fractional value between any two points on a scale. Consider the height of individuals; our unit of measure is the inch. However, we could use $\frac{1}{2}$, $\frac{1}{4}$, $\frac{1}{8}$, or $\frac{1}{16}$ of an inch as our unit of measurement. We could continue to take even smaller units, assuming our measuring instruments permit. The point is no matter how small we make our unit of measurement it can always, in theory at least, be made smaller. A discrete value can only fall at separated points on a scale, for example, at 0, 1, 2, 3, 4, 5 and so on. If we are speaking of the number of people in a room, then, the answer is a whole number.

To the scientist the formation of concepts involves some form of measurement treatment of variables.

Levels of Concept Formation or Types of Scales. We earlier defined a concept as representing a class and/or properties of things. Suppose we are observing the sex of human beings; there are only two values of this variable—male and female. Such natural classifications, when they occur, are of great value to science, particularly when exclusiveness and exhaustiveness in classification are satisfied not simply as a matter of definition or logical consequence of the determining criteria, but as a matter of empirical fact. This implies an underlying empirical law and thus gives some measure of systematic coherence to the classificatory concepts involved; for example, the division of human beings into males and females, the marriage institution into monogamy, polygamy, and polyandry. These are not logically or empirically exhaustive, but to the extent which such are factually so, they possess systematic importance. The basis for such classification is in regard to *classes* of objects rather than individual objects. That is, the above type of classification takes the form: characteristic A belongs to the things of class B. This implies that characteristic A invariably is associated with class B either on logical grounds or as a matter of fact. It does not say that objects can be individually described, and then divided into groups forming a natural classification. To summarize, we may say that a classificatory concept represents a characteristic which any object in the category under consideration must either have or not have. Such a scale is unordered, that is the characteristic in question is not arranged in ascending or descending order of amount and is called a "nominal scale."

The properties or attributes of concepts which form a nominal scale may be analyzed experimentally or observationally to determine other characteristics with which they are associated. Classificatory or categorical concepts are generally used for description of observational findings, and for the formulation of initial empirical generalizations. When the necessity for a more precise and flexible set of concepts occurs, classificatory or nominal concepts are replaced by other types which make it possible to deal with amount or degree of characteristics; that is, to treat the variable as a continuous variable. Instead of the categorical nature of classificatory concepts, these represent terms or ranks of "more or less" and metrical terms of a quantitative nature which assigns to each item in the category a certain real number or numbers. The "more or less" concept is an "ordinal scale" and the metric is an "interval" or "ratio" scale.

An ordinal scale assigns an upper and lower boundary to a homogeneous set. In such a case the number of observations are arranged so that we can say that one observation represents more or less of a given variable than another. Thus, comparative ordering consists of determining for any two objects in a given category whether they are the same in respect to some characteristic and, if not, which of them has more or less of the characteristic. For example, in respect to mineral objects a comparative concept of hardness could be arrived at for any two minerals within a category by determining whether they are of equal hardness and, if not, which of them is less hard. Mohs scale of hardness in geology is such a scale. To derive a truly comparative concept it must be possible to arrange the object or attributes of a given category in serial order (an object precedes another if it is smaller than it), whereas objects of equal characteristics coincide, *i.e.,* share the same place. We may line up a group of individuals along a wall and by comparing them one to another arrange them in order from the tallest to the shortest. We may assign the rank of one to the tallest, two to the next, and so on until the last or shortest. Our observations would then represent an ordinal scale.

Although the ranks will enable us to say whether one person is taller or shorter than another, they will not tell us the degree of difference. This will require another type of scale, that is, a scale which will allow us to ascertain not only rank order, but magnitude of difference between ranks as well. The simplest is called an "interval scale." The interval scale provides equal intervals from an arbitrary point of origin. The problem is to find both a unit of measurement and a point of origin. An example is the centigrade scale. Zero and one hundred are arbitrarily assigned as the freezing point and the boiling point respectively and the temperature range between these is divided into a hundred equal intervals known as "degrees Centigrade." Arithmetical operations cannot be performed on the assigned values *themselves*. A temperature of 40° C cannot be said to be twice as high as one of 20° C, although it is twice as far from 0° C to 40° C as it is from 0° C to 20° C. This is because the point of origin is arbitrary. In other words, we can perform operations of addition or subtraction on interval concepts and still maintain the essential properties of the scale. The reason for this is that the origin or zero value is arbitrary. Adding or subtracting a specified number for each value on an interval scale only shifts the point of origin. It does not change the essential properties of the scale.

As the foregoing shows it is not appropriate to take ratios of any two values on an interval scale. If we do, we change the nature of the scale. Ratios can be taken with respect to the *differences* between the values of an interval scale.

The only scale on which ratios can be formed between values of a variable is one in which we have an interval scale with an *absolute zero*. Such a scale is called a "ratio scale." Weight, as measured in ounces or pounds, or length, as measured in inches, are ratio scales for the origin on these is an absolute zero corresponding to no weight or length at all. Here it is appropriate to state that a person who weighs two hundred pounds is twice as heavy as one who weighs one hundred pounds. In ratio scales only the unit of measurement is arbitrary; the zero point is fixed. We cannot therefore add or subtract a given number to each value of the variable and still maintain the properties or nature of the original ratio scale. All the members can be multiplied by a constant without affecting anything, since this only changes the unit.

All attempts to measure an intangible quality must, of course, be indirect in nature. However, there must be provided, at least, a distant empirical referent or interpretation for the quantity so that we may know what to expect from Y when the scale indicates a certain value of X. Review the discussion in section 2 above on the function of concepts and constructs to find the traditional answer to this problem.

Kaplan reminds us,

It is to be remembered that, if measurement in general is the mapping of objects into an abstract space, the range of possibilities is basically limited only by our imagination and ingenuity in constructing such spaces. The act of measuring does not consist merely in applying a yardstick of some sort, *but also in devising the stick to be applied.*[17]

This latter phrase refers to the need to formulate concepts and constructs to indicate the nature and units of the "yardstick." Therefore, let

17 Kaplan, *op. cit.*, p. 197. Italics added.

me suggest that the order of events in the development of a science is to identify fundamental variables through the development of theories and concepts and the logic of the data deriving from these will suggest or imply the mathematical problem of measurement.

6. SUMMARY

Concepts provide the foundation for the development of scientific theory by serving as a guide for controlled observation of the empirical world. Concepts function in research by: (1) providing an empirical point of departure or point of view; (2) providing a set of specifications which will allow for the measurement of intangible qualities; and (3) permitting the deduction of new problems and facts. Concepts, data, and theory interplay, *i.e.*, concepts and theory guide research in search of new facts, new facts give rise to new concepts and theories, and new concepts and theories provide old concepts and old facts with new meaning. This interplay characterizes the development of science.

Finally, we formulated the notion of levels of concept formation in terms of degree of abstractness and flexibility for mathematical treatment. In this connection, we noted four levels of scales; nominal, ordinal, interval, and ratio.

SELECTED REFERENCES

Adler, Franz, "Operational Definitions in Sociology," *American Journal of Sociology*, 1947, vol. 52, no. 5, pp. 438–444.

Bergmann, Gustav, and Kenneth Spence, "Operationism and Theory Construction," in Melvin H. Marx, *Psychological Theory*, New York, Macmillan, 1951, pp. 54–66.

Cicourel, Aaron V., *Method and Measurement in Sociology*, New York, Free Press, 1964.

Hempel, Carl G., "Fundamentals of Concept Formation in Empirical Science," in the *International Encyclopedia of Unified Science*, vol. 2, no. 7, Chicago, The University of Chicago Press, 1952.

Kemeny, John G., *A Philosopher Looks at Science*, Princeton, Van Nostrand, 1959. See especially chapters 1, 3, 7, and 9.

Madden, Edward H., *The Structure of Scientific Thought*, Boston, Houghton Mifflin Co., 1960.

Marx, Melvin H., "The Dimension of Operational Clarity," in H. H. Marx, ed., *Theories of Contemporary Psychology*, New York, Macmillan Co., 1964, pp. 187–201.

Paps, Arthur, *An Introduction to the Philosophy of Science*, New York, Macmillan, 1959.

Woodger, J. H., "The Technique of Theory Construction," *International Encyclopedia of Unified Science*, vol. 2, no. 5, Chicago, The University of Chicago Press, 1939.

Zetterberg, Hans L., *On Theory and Verification in Sociology*, rev. ed., Totowa, N.J., Bedminster Press, 1963.

4
John T. Doby

EXPLANATION AND PREDICTION

1. INTRODUCTION

A. Commonsense Explanation

One of the major aspects of research is the necessity for ordering and interpreting the data, or facts, observed. In a general sense this is the problem of making the facts have a clear meaning. This is a task not only of science, but also of everyday human interaction, but with an important difference. Let me, in this introduction, try to make this difference clear.

Our everyday efforts to explain are relatively simple. They consist of conveying our motives, intentions, goals, and actions to others so that others can hopefully understand or perceive them as we do. Meaning in this sense consists of the simple and straight-forward task of using a set of words which carry the meaning one wishes to express and also convey the same understanding to others. When one has made himself intelligible to others, he has in the sense of everyday or common-sense explanation, "explained." His explanation may not be equally satisfactory to all who hear it simply because different people have different levels of general understanding. What is intelligible to one may not be to another and some may already comprehend and not even need an explanation. Explanation in this context is essentially a matter of creating shared meanings. Thus explanation in everyday interaction consists of describing one's behavior with words that permit another to understand and accept what he understands. On the other hand, one may explain and another may not accept the explanation; that is, he understands, but cannot accept the reasons given as satisfactory. In this context common-sense explanation of behavior should be distinguished from justification of behavior.

Examples of everyday explanations are: he does not work because he is lazy or he is a criminal because he loves a life of crime. Such statements only describe the problem in other words and do not explain anything;

they do not relate or connect one process or event with another process or event. To understand in this sense is essentially a form of psychological empathy and not scientific. The trouble is not in the things to be explained but in the confusing of what constitutes explanation; particularly the equating of truth with subjective and personal meaning. Common-sense is often remarkable in the insights it yields. Much information has been acquired in the course of ordinary experience and this information is, within limits, quite accurate. An illustration of this is man's adaptation and survival. However, all this common-sense knowledge is seldom if ever accompanied by any explanation of why the facts are as alleged. Man learned how to make ships float without knowing the principles underlying buoyancy; he learned how to fertilize crops without understanding what was really involved. In other words, much significant technology has arisen for the application of common-sense to experience. The foregoing should be sufficient to dispense with the idea which occasionally shows up in the social sciences that one has explained when he describes the same thing all over again, but in different words or terms. This in no way is to be confused with scientific explanation.

B. The Concept of Scientific Explanation

The problem of scientific explanation is similar to that which confronts a man trying to solve a cross-word puzzle. He has available certain clues in the form of given letters, and it is the task of the observer to fill in the missing letters so that a system of interconnections emerge. When all the relations are ordered so that each makes sense within the whole according to the rules, then the puzzle has been explained. The elements of the puzzle are explained by showing the place that each connects in the overall pattern. The pattern of relations is not constituted out of our perceptions, but out of a network of "demonstrable relations." We will discuss later, under the heading of prediction, just what we mean by demonstrable relations.

It is not easy to explain what is meant by "explanation." In the first place, it must be realized that any statements which attempt to explain the process of scientific explanation are *reconstructions* of scientific practice or logic and are therefore idealized and abstracted statements. Actual practice always entails some logical patchwork in addition to the general rules. In the second place, it is difficult to describe or specify scientific explanation because the methodology and logic of explanation also undergo growth and change, and new methodologies and new systems of logic often evolve.

Earlier we stated that scientific explanation consisted of establishing the interconnections among a set of variables. But how does one objectively establish a set of interconnections? The process is one of applying deductive reasoning under the guidance of theory and the pragmatic testing of conclusions by data. What is required is to show a logical necessity between the explanatory premises and the facts to be explained, and some correspondence of this to related sensory or empirical findings. This, of course, is far too simple a statement for two reasons. First, assuming that the premises do provide for deductions which logically include the fact or problem to be explained and thereby presumably explain it, how do we *know* the premises are really true? And what controls the dynamics assumed in the premises? In regard to the first question, can we show that our explanations are inherently necessary to account for the facts observed? The answer is admittedly a weak one. But, it is not possible to provide such explanations or would any scientist or philosopher of science argue that it can be shown that given explanations can be demonstrated to be inherently necessary and final. In regard to the second question, or what explains the premises, this question is based on a false assumption, namely, that one has to reduce an inquiry to first causes before explanation is complete. On the contrary, finality of explanations is a characteristic of common-sense explanations and pseudo explanations, not scientific ones. We simply stop and assume our inquiry is finished with what is unproblematic in a *given* context. If an explanation raises new questions in a different context and hence suggests more to be explained, this is good. One of the tests of a good explanation is whether it *adds* new ideas and new problems. Science is on-going and it is unnecessary to assume an ascertainable or knowable beginning or ending.

The logical and methodological model required to answer a given scientific question or problem depends upon what the problem *is* and *how* it is posed. In other words, it depends to some extent upon what is asked and how "what is asked" is asked. Moreover the same problem can be posed in many different ways and, therefore, what is necessary to explain the problem will change. To illustrate: Durkheim asked, why do Catholics have a lower suicide rate than Protestants? His answer was that they lived under more cohesive institutional arrangements than Protestants and that the more strongly knit social bonds of Catholics provided greater security during periods of personal stress. As posed, this question implies a statistical model which correlates suicide rates with living under different degrees of social cohesion. But, since Durkheim was dealing with data from the latter part of nineteenth century Western Europe, we are not sure that his findings would apply to other countries or even to Western Europe today. Had our question referred to particular persons rather than a class, the proposed explanation for the first question would not be sufficient. There are two principal reasons for this. First, Durkheim's argument was not concerned with individual cases, but with aggregates. And secondly, the explanatory premises in his argument are not fully or precisely stated. For example, it is not clear *how* or *why* reduced social cohesion is supposed to affect suicide. In other words, if we find a Protestant suicide case having a network of highly impersonal social relations and associates all unconcerned about his personal well-being we cannot be sure that the next person in such a circumstance will commit suicide when faced with severe personal stress. This raises an old but fundamental question in the logic of inference, namely, why are some inferences justified as reasonable and others rejected as unreasonable though both go beyond available empirical evidence? One traditional answer to the foregoing question is that one of the inferences is in accord with or conforms to known empirical regularities. In other words, it is in accordance with general theories which have worked in the past.

But let us carry the argument further. There are cases where the theory has always worked in the past, but one would still be uneasy about asserting that it will always apply to similar cases in the future. On the other hand, there are cases where it has always worked in the past and yet one would have no hesitancy about asserting its continued truth for the future. For example, one would not feel comfortable about asserting that after one case of suicide under conditions of anomie suicide will surely occur in the next such case. However, one would have no hesitancy in asserting that other pieces of copper will conduct electricity after observing that a given piece of copper conducts it.[1] Why do we accept the one and reject the other? Goodman answers by saying that the hypothesis involved in the statement on the piece of copper is based on a *law-like* or universal principle whereas the other is a statement of contingency or perhaps even an accidental generality. This does not really answer the question because it does not allow us to be able to clearly identify a law-like statement. In other words, the meaning of a law-like statement is not completely clear. It does, however, seem clear that when projections are made on the basis of explanatory premises which are statements of universal law, such projections or inferences appear unquestionable or fully justified. This suggests that explanations within a *given context* may range from complete, to partial, to contradictory, or to no explanation at all. Nagel gives an example of an explanation based on a universal law as follows:

Why does ice float on water? The explicandum (the fact to be explained) in this example is not a historical fact, whether individual or statistical, but a universal law which asserts an invariable association of certain physical traits. It is familiarly explained by exhibiting it as a logical consequence of other laws—the law that the density of ice is less than that of the water, the Archimedean law that a fluid buoys up a body immersed in it with a force equal to the weight of the fluid displaced by the body, and further laws concerning the conditions under which bodies subjected to forces are in equilibrium.[2]

[1] Nelson Goodman, *Fact, Fiction and Forecast*, Cambridge, Harvard University Press, 1955, p. 73.
[2] Ernest Nagel, *The Structure of Science—Problems in the Logic of Scientific Explanation*, New York, Harcourt, Brace & World, 1961, p. 17.

The foregoing type of explanation is traditionally called the deductive model, a formal type of argument in which the fact to be explained is a logically necessary consequence of the explanatory premises. In other words, the explanation is based on laws that are capable of enabling the event in question to have been predicted. One is tempted to conclude that this is perhaps the ideal structure of scientific explanation, but it is certainly not the only model. It may be that the others are logical approximations to the deductive model. This is a problem for the logicians to settle. Nevertheless, *there is explanation without prediction and there is prediction without explanation.* It will help our general understanding of explanation if we consider examples of each of these.

2. EXPLANATION WITHOUT PREDICTION

It is true that on occasion a successful explanation, particularly a casual explanation, also allows us to predict the event in question and thus afford a complete test of the explanation. A good example is the prediction of atomic energy from Einstein's relativity theory. Such prediction in the physical sciences is quite recent and probably reflects the growing body of casual theory in the physical sciences as contrasted with earlier hypotheses based on correlations. This suggests that it is perhaps premature to draw too sharp a distinction between explanation and prediction. In other words, as new fields of science such as biology, psychology, sociology, and economics develop more complete explanations for given contexts, they may be expected to find more explanations which also allow for prediction.

In the meantime, however, much valid information exists in these fields which currently allows for explanations, but not predictions. For example, sociology can explain much delinquency in modern society on the basis of knowing that children in slum neighborhoods or socially disorganized communities experience severe strain on behavior due to a large gap between their socially structured goals and socially accessible, legitimate opportunities. This simply says that perceived lack of opportunity and failure in school are frequently the causes of delinquency. That is, these factors are, under certain conditions, sufficient to produce delinquency. There are also some unknown causes of delinquency, but the majority of the cases of delinquency are preceded by the conditions described. The intention here is to show reasonable explanations of delinquency can be given even though we are unable to predict that any particular individual will become delinquent.

Although the point is the same it may be helpful to take an example from another field. As of now the medical sciences do not know the cause or causes of cancer. However, they do know some of the conditions which when present are *frequently* followed by cancer. For example, a high level of radiation exposure can cause skin cancer and excessive cigarette smoking, lung cancer. If a farmer comes into a clinic with a growth on his face or ears and the physician diagnoses it as skin cancer, and if the physician can discover no other evidence for other known causes, he is in a good position to assert that the cause was excessive exposure to the sun.[3]

Hempel and Oppenheim warn that if we cannot derive the fact or event to be explained from known general laws and theories which connect it with antecedent conditions, we are likely to deceive ourselves if we retrospectively explain by reference to those antecedent conditions.[4] This suggestion is plausible and should be observed.

Explanation based on statistical laws may be quite good, but may not allow for significant prediction. However, as the body of knowledge grows by means of statistical theory the likelihood of more general theories being derived is increased. And as a body of theory grows so does explanation improve, but partial explanation is still explanation. One of the clearest examples of explanation without prediction is polio. The causes of the three kinds of polio are known and vaccines now exist. However, prior to the vaccines, the causes were known, but we could not predict the occurrence of individual cases or even where a community outbreak would be expected to occur.

3. PREDICTION WITHOUT EXPLANATION

The percent of votes which President Charles de Gaulle received in his 1965 run-off election was predicted exactly. However, the explanation of his victory was far less precise. Ancient astronomers were able to make quality predictions, but their explanations or theories were poor indeed. Such predictions are usually made on the basis of well-established, empirical generalizations. In other words, it is possible to make predictions on the basis of indicators rather than causes.

4. EXPLANATION AND PREDICTION

In a strictly deductive, experimental model the time order of events in the experiment and the logical requirements of prediction are virtually the same. Yet there are certain formal differences between explanation and prediction. Scriven argues that "to predict, we need a correlation between present events and future ones—to explain, between present ones and past ones." [5] This seems to oversimplify the matter. It is true that in order to explain the fact to be explained must be deducible from the explanatory premises. But this logical requirement must also be bol-

[3] This example was suggested by a similar illustration by Michael Scriven, "Explanation and Prediction in Evolutionary Theory," *Science*, vol. 130, no. 3374 (August 28, 1959), p. 480.

[4] C. G. Hempel and P. Oppenheim, "The Logic of Explanation," in H. Feigl and M. Brodbeck, eds., *Readings in the Philosophy of Science*, New York, Appleton-Century-Crofts, 1953, p. 323.

[5] Scriven, *op. cit.*, p. 479.

stered by the reasonableness of the premises in regard to other known but related facts. Hanson cites the case of "Blackett's, recognition, in 1933, that the arguments of Dirac and the quite distinct arguments of Anderson terminated in a prediction of the same particle, the positron." [6] This along with the on-going nature of science suggests the tentativeness of all scientific explanations.

When theory and law (fact) are sufficiently powerful, explanation and prediction go together. The neutrino, radio waves, and the elements which filled empty places in the periodic table were predicted from theory before they were discovered. Therefore, the men who made these discoveries knew what to look for from the start. Kuhn points out that such foreknowledge does not make the task of discovery less difficult, but it does allow one to know when the goal has been reached. Theory which is powerful enough to allow prediction enables one to identify and name his findings, whereas discoveries that are not predicted by theory are generally difficult to label or identify—for example, the discovery of x-rays and oxygen. These could not be predicted from accepted theory at the time and it was sometime after their physical discovery before they were actually identified for what they are.[7]

Prediction involves a reference to the time of happening of the event predicted. In a logical sense it is possible to predict the past. Howard Becker labeled such as "retrospective-prediction." Such prediction would apply to aspects of geology, archaeology, historical sociology, and paleontology. Explanations always entail a fact or an empirical regularity and even though the explanation is wrong it sometimes is still useful, whereas nothing corresponds to a false prediction.

Much work goes on in clinical medicine, interpretative sociology, and economics where shrewd, successful forecasts are made which could not be formulated from the available explanations. These are not guesses, but are reasoned forecasts derived from the partial knowledge of sensitive observers. This kind of prediction without explanation has characterized all sciences in their early development and continues to characterize advanced sciences in areas where strong, theoretical generalizations are lacking. It is useful to encourage activity with the hope of improving predictive techniques in areas where adequate explanations are lacking.

5. BASIC REQUIREMENTS FOR EXPLANATION

A. The Deductive Model

Hempel and Oppenheim list two sets of conditions as the requirements for adequacy in scientific explanation.[8] These are requirements for

---

[6] Norwood R. Hanson, "Scientists and Logicians: A Confrontation," *Science*, vol. 138, no. 3547 (December 21, 1962), p. 1313.

[7] Thomas S. Kuhn, "Historical Structure of Scientific Discovery," *Science*, vol. 136 (June 1, 1962), p. 761.

[8] Hempel and Oppenheim, *op. cit.*, pp. 321–322.

logical adequacy and for *empirical* adequacy. There are three requirements for logical adequacy: (1) The fact to be explained, that is, the
problem must be a logical consequence of the explanatory law and
premises. Unless the problem or fact is logically deducible from the explanation, it has not really been explained. (2) The explanatory statements must contain at least two independent premises one of which is a
universal law. Unless there are at least two independent premises the
explanation would be a pseudo-explanation—the substitution of other
words or labels for a fact already stated. (3) The third requirement is
obvious, the requirement that the explanatory premises contain empirical
content capable of being checked by experiment or observation.

Hempel and Oppenheim list only one requirement for empirical
adequacy. This is that the statements which make up the two or more
premises of the explanation be true. They admit that this requirement
can seldom, if ever, be met. Therefore, a weaker rule or requirement is
usually given, namely, that the premises be highly confirmed on the
basis of the best available evidence. The reason for this is that sometimes
subsequent, empirical findings reveal that what was earlier thought to be
true is not, in fact, true. The earlier explanation was not a correct
explanation.

Suppose, as is frequently the case, that among the explanatory statements are premises which are part of a more comprehensive, theoretical
system. Is it appropriate to characterize them as either true or false? Even
though this appears to be a moot question among some scientists, and
some would deny that the labels true or false are appropriate in this
event, we feel that some such requirement is necessary to give stability
and continuity to science. Otherwise, premises could be invented at
will.[9]

There are other models or types of scientific explanation. These
have some elements in common with the deductive model, but they also
have important differences. I suspect that the differences are more related
to the logic of the problem formulated and to differences in the state
of development of existing theory available for different subject areas,
than to intrinsic differences among fields. The same condition obtains
in respect to the kinds of explanatory laws used as explanatory premises
in different sciences.

B. Types of Scientific Laws

The type of scientific law most frequently thought of, but least
frequent in occurrence, is the *causal* law. There is no completely satisfactory definition of a causal law. Nagel identifies four conditions which
supposedly satisfy the requirements for a causal law. For our purposes

[9] For a detailed discussion of the nature and requirements of scientific laws see
Nagel, *op. cit.*, pp. 29–78.

it will be sufficient to list only two of these. First, the relation is an invariable one—when the alleged cause occurs, the alleged effect always follows. Operationally this means that the cause constitutes both a necessary and a sufficient condition for the occurrence of the fact or effect. In practice, however, the event picked out for the cause is normally one which culminates or completes a set of sufficient conditions for the occurrence of the effect. The one chosen for the cause is regarded for theoretical purposes as being the most significant. For example, we assume that a cold virus is the cause of the common cold, but we assume in addition the presence of other conditions, such as lowered resistance of the host or lack of immunity against colds. Secondly the casual relation has a temporal sequence or character—the cause is said to precede the effect.

Nagel identifies four other types of laws that are used as explanatory premises, but are not of the causal variety. The first of these he identifies as *laws which describe the properties of natural substances,* for example, laws which describe the color spectrum, the density of objects, melting point, or other determinable properties. In human behavior the intensity of attitudes, the cohesiveness of groups, the properties of intelligence would, when properly defined, be other examples. A second type of law asserts an invariable, sequential order of dependence among events or properties. Most developmental laws of organisms or sociological laws of the development of societies are of such a type, although in the strict sense such have not been formulated in sociology. Nagel illustrates this by the law, "The formation of lungs in the human embryo never precedes the formation of the circulatory system." Developmental laws usually state only a necessary condition for the relationship and not a sufficient one; therefore, they are not causal unless the sufficient conditions are identified and described. Both the laws of determinable properties and the developmental laws are more on the order of empirical laws than causal laws. They could, with additional information, be reformulated as causal laws.

The third type of law, statistical law, is common to all the sciences, but most frequently found in the biological and social sciences. It asserts an invariable, probabilistic relation between events or properties. One such law is that if an unbiased coin is tossed a large number of times the distribution of heads to tails will be equal. Statistical laws do not assert an *invariable concomitance,* but instead they assert that in a sufficient number of trials one event is accompanied by another with an *invariable relative frequency.* Such laws are themselves not causal although the facts they describe may be given causal interpretations by the introduction of valid, theoretical laws.

A fourth type of law is one which expresses a functional dependence (in the mathematical sense of function) between two or more measured variables of properties or processes. Such a law usually describes a concomitant variation in magnitudes between two or more properties. Nagel cites the example of the Boyle-Charles' law for ideal gases, that is, $pV = aT$, where p is the pressure of the gas, V its volume, T its absolute temperature, and a a constant that depends on the mass and the nature of the gas under consideration. This law only asserts that a change in T is concurrent with changes in p or V. It is not, therefore, a causal law, although, it does allow for explanation as well as prediction.

A second type of functional law is one which describes how a change in a magnitude per unit of time is related to other magnitudes. Galileo's law of falling bodies is such an example. Given an adequate conceptualization of the variables involved, it is believed that this type of law has great potential for describing socio-cultural and behavioral changes per unit of time.

Nagel does not claim that the foregoing four types of non-causal laws are exhaustive of all the laws in use in scientific explanation. However, his classification seems to be a useful and basic one. It clearly shows the value of empirical laws in scientific explanation.[10]

6. EXPLANATION IN THE SOCIAL SCIENCES

Let me first dispose of the idea held by some that explanation in the social sciences is somehow different from the other sciences. I thoroughly agree with Nagel, Braithwaite, Hempel, and Oppenheim, and Kaplan that the basic model of scientific explanation is the same in all the sciences. It seems clear that the sciences with the more elaborate bodies of data and more precise conceptualizations have evolved the simpler and more rigorous scientific explanations. Since the sciences have unequal time spans of development and, therefore, unequal evolved bodies of knowledge, it follows that one would not expect them to employ the same explanatory models irrespective of differences in types of data and problems of measurement. To be sure the methods of observation and techniques are different in all the sciences, but the basic rules of logic and methodological procedure are the same.

From the point of view of scientific explanation it is very important to distinguish (as Znaniecki and later, the late Howard Becker have so clearly done) between action as defined by the actor being observed and from the point of view of the scientist or observer. The scientist's interpretations follow logically from his constructed explanatory system and not from the private, subjective, and phenomenological interpretations of the actor. The process of confirmation or denial is in respect to the logical and empirical requirements of the observer's explanatory system and not the actor's.

It has been argued by some that since man lives in three time di-

10 Nagel, *Ibid.*, p. 74.

mensions (past, present, and future) that much of his behavior is determined by the future and, therefore, the deductive model is inadequate
and some form of a teleological model is needed. To be sure, man has
goals and he applies these to the future. But it is nonsense to assume that
the future acts causally on the present. This kind of reasoning is a clear
example of misplaced concreteness. The emphasis should be placed on
the *desires* of the actor for a certain kind of future, and not the future
itself, as being causally responsible for the behavior. When conceived in
this way a teleological explanation becomes a perfectly sound, functional
type of proposition.

There are very difficult problems involved in research on human
behavior, but these have not been identified by those who contend that
human behavior is beyond the pale of natural science. The more tough-
minded thinkers are hard at work describing and analyzing, not com-
plaining that "it can't be done." Such prophets of failure have sat on
the sidelines of the development of every science from the beginning of
that science to the present and most likely others of the same kind will be
on the sidelines of the new sciences in the future.

Let us identify some of the legitimate major difficulties of research
on human behavior. First, if we assume that cultural systems such as
social institutions and organizations are adaptive systems which determine much human behavior, the rapid, even accelerating rate of
change within these systems produces serious problems in describing them
and relating social variables to behavior. Moreover, as man learns more
about his own behavioral systems he applies this knowledge and again
changes the system. This suggests that scientific prediction could play
a very important part in man's social knowledge and its applications. It
also implies that the predictions as well as explanations would be more
successful on a short-term basis. If more fundamental conceptualizations of social and psychological variables are developed, this may not
become too great a difficulty. At present, most of the data of the social
sciences consists of correlations which are time-bound for the same reasons that predictions are and, therefore, also short-term.

From the standpoint of developmental laws both of a societal and an
organismic or individual nature it seems that better ideas and more
factual information are needed on two kinds of potentialities—genetic
and cultural. The concept of potentiality was more of a stumbling block
in the physical sciences than an asset, but I do not believe this to be the
case in the behavioral or life sciences. One of the major aims of these
sciences is to better understand man's adaptive capacity and, hence,
potentiality for change. Therefore, it is necessary to have a better knowledge of genetic functioning and the interaction of cultural and other
environmental resources with behavioral development. It may prove to
be easier and more desirable to program and alter culture patterns than

to program the genetic processes. The question of how human behavioral systems evolve and change is a problem of paramount importance to man. This appears to be a problem area where the application of evolutionary theory by means of functional laws (in the mathematical sense) holds great promise or, at least, seems an appropriate model.

7. SUMMARY

The fruitfulness of a good hypothesis lies in its powers of explanation and prediction. The nature of scientific explanations is open or on-going; science does not assume a knowable beginning or ending. As the requirements for scientific explanation made clear, all explanations are conditional and approximate. They apply to the stated conditions covered in the premises and old explanations are improved upon by subsequent and more precise ones. This process is theoretically infinite.

Science was conceived as a problem-solving activity and theory, in logical conjunction with empirical fact, as the problem-solving tools.

The deductive model was viewed as representing the basic scientific model, but other models are also used in scientific explanation. Nagel identified three widely used models; statistical or probabilistic models, functional or teleological models, and genetic or developmental models.

It was recognized that genuine causal explanations, although few in occurrence, also allow for prediction. However, there is explanation without prediction and there is prediction without explanation. Explanation with prediction allows for an immediate recognition of the object or process discovered, but prediction without explanation usually is associated with controversy over just what has been discovered.

Finally, a discussion of explanation and prediction in the social sciences concluded that the basic process was the same as in other sciences, but that the data and techniques called for explanatory models appropriate to the logic of the problem and the data.

SELECTED REFERENCES

Braithwaite, R. B., *Scientific Explanation,* Cambridge, England, Cambridge University Press, 1955.

Chapin, F. Stuart, *Experimental Designs in Sociological Research,* rev. ed., New York, Harper & Row, 1955.

Feigl, H., and May Brodbeck, *Readings in the Philosophy of Science,* New York, Appleton-Century-Crofts, 1953.

Fisher, R. A., *The Design of Experiments,* 4th ed., Edinburg, Oliver & Boyd, 1947.

Greenwood, Ernest, *Experimental Sociology,* New York, Kings Crown, 1945.

Kaplan, Abraham, *The Conduct of Inquiry—Methodology for Behavioral Science,* San Francisco, Chandler Publishing Co., 1964.

Marx, Melvin H., *Theories in Contemporary Psychology*, New York, Macmillan, 1964.
Mill, John Stuart, *A System of Logic*, New York, Longmans, 1930.
Nagel, Ernest, *The Structure of Science—Problems in the Logic of Scientific Explanation*, New York, Harcourt, Brace & World, 1961.
Popper, Karl R., *The Logic of Scientific Discovery*, New York, Basic Books, Inc., 1959.

Part two

METHODS OF RESEARCH

5
Roy G. Francis

STATISTICAL METHODS

I. INTRODUCTION

1. Statistics in Research: The Problem

The fundamental problem of empirical research is the explanation of observed variation. The variation might be in terms of quantity, as in variation of weight gained resulting from different diets; the variation might be in terms of proportions, of probabilities, as in the proportion of marriages ending in divorce. The basic element of variation as central to a research problem should never be forgotten. The need for statistics in scientific inference arises largely from it.

Had the traditional logic of classes been adequate to account for empirical variation, it is not likely that statistics would have arisen, or, if it had arisen, would play the role in contemporary research that it does. For that matter, a straight-forward mathematical statement of functional relations is not sufficient for empirical research since some variation around the mathematical line ordinarily exists and must be accounted for.

Another way of saying this is to say that had all conceptual classifications resulted in completely homogeneous empirical members, there would have been little need for statistics. Let us explain what we mean by an example. If the empirical operations used in arriving at the classification of neurotic personalities had been such that every member of each type of neurotic personality was precisely the same as all others, so that one could say all neurotics of type one experienced traumatic experiences as children, the "qualitative logic" would have been sufficient for making subsequent inferences. Due either to an intrinsic variation in the real world, or to inadequate conceptualization, or to inadequate operational definitions, such statements are impossible to make. We generally are reduced to making "particular propositions," i.e., some neurotics of type one experienced traumatic experiences as children. As

65

we shall see, we are limited in the type of inferences possible when our premises are of this sort.

This state of affairs has led to two directions, both related to statistical inference. On the one hand, we have the development of a probability logic to enable us to come to decisions about particular propositions. On the other hand, we have an emphasis upon quantification of the basic variables. The emphasis on quantification—and the problems on quantifying social data are by no means solved—attempts two things. First, by being precise the influence of biases on the part of the scientist are explicated and attacked. Second, clearer statements of the amount and kind of variations observed are made possible. That it is necessary to have original, precise data is easily appreciated. No statistical juggling can improve on bad or poorly defined data.

Another type of variation which flows from statistical inference is that of "sampling." Recall that science trusts neither intuition nor inference. All propositions are subjected to verification. The question becomes, "Will all tests of the same hypothesis give precisely the same results?" If the answer is negative (and, in fact, it is negative) we again observe a case of variation. Do the results of a series of tests differ by chance, or are the differences real? This is a basic question which is partially solved through statistical inference.

Again, is it possible to study every instance of some problematic event or behavior? Suppose one wanted to explain neurotic behavior. Could one reasonably be expected to study every neurotic? The answer is obviously not. Not only is the scientist limited in terms of the money and facilities available to him, but also time. Even if he studied all neurotics up to some specific date there would be subsequent cases still to occur. Only a partial study can be made; that is, the scientist must study a sample of some population. He wants to make inferences about the population. Will each sample give precisely the same result? Even if one knew he was studying a single population, he would observe "sampling variation"—that is, differences due entirely to the fact that a sample was studied. To distinguish between results flowing from sampling variation and from having actually studied two or more populations is a fundamental task of statistical inference.

This type of variation is critical to modern empirical science. Unless there is such uniformity (as, presumably, in certain chemical mixtures) that variation from test to test is negligible, observed variation needs to be explained. Statistical theory is simply a system of thinking, made possible by the admission of certain assumptions and postulates, which allows for rigorous inference in the case of variation. We generally study only a sample of the objects in which we are interested; sampling theory, a fundamental part of statistical theory, provides a guide in drawing the necessary inferences.

2. *The Logic of the Statistical Argument*

One of the most potent devices of traditional logic is the two-premised argument, the syllogism. In particular, we should understand the structure of the alternative syllogism. If we have two propositions, A and B, such that they cannot be false together (but admitting that they might be true together), then one can use the following form of argument:

> Major premise: Either statement A or statement B is true.
> Minor premise: Statement A is false.
> Conclusion   : Statement B is true.

If, in the minor premise, we affirmed one of the propositions, we could not conclude the falsity of the other since both could be true.

Consider also the hypothetical syllogism. Suppose we have two statements, P and Q, such that the relation of implication exists between the two. Then one could use the following form of argument:

> Major premise: if P is true, then Q is true.
> Minor premise: Q is false.
> Conclusion   : P is false.

Remember that in the hypothetical syllogism the truth of Q implies nothing about the truth of P, i.e., the affirmation of the consequent does not imply the truth of the antecedent unless they are related strongly: if, and only if, P, then Q.

These two syllogisms are basic to statistical inference. Suppose we have two measures of divorce, x_1 and for rural marriages and x_2 for urban marriages. Suppose, further, that these measures are not numerically identical. The question is how can we explain our observed variation? Is it due simply to variation from sample to sample? Or is it due to "real" differences between rural and urban marriages? The *form* the argument takes is this. Alternatives are set up.

Either (1) there is only a sampling difference between the two measures, or (2) the amount of divorce is greater for one area than the other. Clearly, they cannot be false together though one might argue that they could be true together. We are not concerned with that possibility, except to argue that we can decide between the two only through the falsification of one of the alternatives. Verification of either does not force the denial of the other.

Now, we will assume that the two measures differ only to the extent of sample variation. This assumption is our premise P in the hypothetical syllogism. If this is true then (as we shall later learn) there is a statistic S which is smaller than the number, 2. This is our conclusion, Q, in the hypothetical syllogism. If empirically this number S is greater than 2, we have a *contradiction* and Q is false, hence P is false. But P was simply proposition A in the alternative, so that if P is false, A is false also. And we know from syllogistic argument that if A is false, the alternative B must be true.

The student should notice the difference between the form of the argument and the content of the argument. The statements A and B may or may not stand in an alternative relationship when one deals with empirical classes. The possibility of their being true or false together is a theoretical issue and must be examined prior to any test of their relationship. If this inference is not explored prior to the use of the subsequent statistical argument, the possibility of their being alternatives is an *ad hoc* problem. Of course, this situation is quite common; we often use a statistical technique without being quite sure of our theoretical assumptions. After we have made our "statistical analysis" we then often look for the theoretical assumptions which must be made to warrant the techniques being used. While we do not deny that through such activity much has been learned, we wish to repeat that the *ad hoc* problem may develop, but never tests, the hypothesis in question.

The structure of the hypothetical syllogism (which is called the "null hypothesis" in statistical literature) flows from statistical theory. The main effort in this chapter will be to indicate the correctness of this type of reasoning.

3. Relation to Other Logical Forms

It is all but obvious that statistical inference is predicated on what we have called "qualitative logic." Recall that we could write any formula as a system of premises and conclusions. This fact, coupled with the syllogistic structure of the statistical argument, should convince the student what we have tacitly assumed; namely, that it is incorrect to pose the problem of qualitative or quantitative logic.

While beyond the scope of this text, it would be possible to indicate the postulates of categorical logic, those of quantitative logic, and those of probability logic. We could see that one does not deny earlier postulates, but, rather, builds on them. Instead of saying, What logic do I prefer? one should ask himself, What is my problem? What is my substantive hypothesis to solve that problem? What data does my hypothesis call for? *What logical postulates are met by the data needed to solve my problem?* For instance, if my data satisfy the assumptions of a mathematical equation describing a functional relation, then I must "fit a curve" to the data. If the assumptions of statistical inference are met, then I must reason statistically. If only the postulates of categorical logic are satisfied, then I will use categorical logic. Let the problem define the logic to be used, not the converse.

Certain logical operations (e.g., curve-fitting, analysis of variance, chi-square, mathematical model construction) may be the current fad. But to select first the operation, and then the data to fit it reverses the development of theory. It must be repeated that an argument is a solution of some problem. Arbitrary use of logical operations must involve arbitrary assumptions and arbitrary definitions of problems. If science is indeed problem-*solving,* then it seems necessary to spend time defining the problem in such a way that it can be solved. Only after one knows the problem ought he determine the structure of the argument he is to use.

Statistical formulas do not exhaust the ways scientists justify their conclusions. For certain types of problems and for certain types of data, statistical formulas are apparently necessary for rigorous inference. But the burden of proof as to the applicability of the formula rests with the user. Simply because one knows some technique does not mean he must use it; the use of an equation is a decision about a proposition which must be defended before we can admit its proper place in science. The student must always put scientific problems ahead of the techniques of science.

A BRIEF SUMMARY OF DESCRIPTIVE STATISTICS

1. Collection and Classification of Data

Statistical methods are used in analyzing and in drawing inferences from a number of repetitive events which do not all have the same outcome. The event may be, for example, marriage and the outcome may be divorce or its absence. An event may be placing a rat in a maze, and the outcome may be 3 weeks, 24 days, or whatever. In each situation two features are forced on us; first, we can observe a large number of events of similar content and second, there is a certain amount of variation in respect to the outcomes associated with the events in question. If there were no such variation—that is, if each event had the same outcome— there would be no statistical problem.

Statistical analysis begins with the definition and observation of events, and the subsequent classification of them in terms of possible outcomes. Of course, the outcomes must also be defined and operations must be performed which will allow us to classify the event properly. From our earlier discussion of scientific method, we should recall that the logical steps in inquiry involve the definition of the problem, the statement of an hypothesis to solve that problem and the creation of an instrument to obtain the necessary data. "Creating an instrument" is simply a shorthand statement of defining the operations by which the various classes of events and outcomes will have empirical members.

Of particular concern is an understanding of classification in terms

of the possible outcomes. The events to be studied are ordinarily categorically defined and are shared by all objects in the inquiry. The
problematic variation is in the outcomes which may be observed. The
general principle is to define the outcomes in such a way that each object
is a member of one and only one possible outcome class. Another way
of saying this is to assert that the classification scheme must be mutually
exclusive and exhaustive. Further, only one basis of classification at
a time may be used. For example, if the event was, "occupation," one
would use such classes as "lawyer," "minister," "blacksmith," and would
not use "rural" since the latter refers to residence.

There are, in general, three types of possible classification systems:

Categorical. The categorical set of classes involve only the issue of
whether or not the object is a member of the class. If there are two categories we speak of a dichotomy; for example, "male" and "female."
There may be more than two classes, as in the distribution of classes of
budget expenditures.

Ordinal. If the classes are so defined that one of the outcomes is
larger or smaller than another, but the amount of the difference is unstated or unknown, we speak of ordinal classes. We may, then, classify
people as "old," "middle aged," or "young." The student will immediately perceive the possibilities for ambiguous definitions unless the
classes are defined in terms of units of time.

Cardinal (quantitative). If the membership in a class depends upon
the size or the amount of the object, the classes are quantitatively defined.
Age in years is a good example, as is income. There are two basic types
of cardinal data; the "discrete" and the "continuous." An example of
discrete data is size of family since only integers are used to define
membership. Age and income are both continuous since a decimal (or
fraction) can be used to separate classes.

If the data to be used properly belong in a cardinal system, by dis-
carding certain information (e.g., precision as to amount of difference)
we can deduce ordinal relations. From cardinal data, ordinal data can be
derived without additional knowledge. But if we know only that people
are "old" and "young," we cannot get a cardinal system of age and, obviously, age-categories are impossible. While much statistical analysis is
concerned with cardinal data, such data do not exhaust the use of statistics. Indeed, the power of statistics lies in the fact that arguments about
categorical data can be rigorously made, even in the face of particular
propositions.

2. *Tabular and Graphic Representation of Data*

Let us suppose that we are studying how long it takes a group of
students to complete a true-false test. It may be that, for our purposes, we
operationally define time taken to complete a test as a measure of the

difficulty of the test. Obviously, there are other ways to define the difficulty of a test, and there are theoretical deficiencies in the definition given. Such issues are not primarily statistical and must be decided before statistical analysis proceeds. Let us agree, in order to illustrate statistical techniques, that we are justified in using this definition.

We first note that the *range* of time taken by the 138 students to complete the test is from 21 minutes to 54 minutes, i.e., the smallest and largest values. The issue is: what size of *interval* should we use in defining the classes of "time taken." We may leave the data in raw form and ungrouped. This is the same as having classes of one member each. With 138 objects to be analyzed, 138 classes seem too many to carry around and, clearly, if we had 1380 objects, we would need some system of reducing the number of classes.

The important thing in defining the size of the class interval is to recognize that in defining classes we will be losing a certain amount of precision. This is so since we will treat each member of a class as though its true value equaled the mid-point of the class in question. As one would guess, the mid-point is a value half-way between the lower and upper class limits. If the data are discrete, the mid-point is obtained by adding the lower and upper limits and dividing by two. If the data are continuous, the mid-point is obtained by adding the lower limit of the interested class to the lower limit of the class just above and dividing by two. This is a device aimed at avoiding unpleasant and nonsensical decimal values for the mid-point. The number of classes, and their size, can be answered only in terms of how to reduce the difficulty in computation without distorting the data. We can give only a rule of thumb to resolve the issue.

The general rules follow from these considerations. We first note the range and decide on the size of the interval; this decision fixes the number of classes as well as the mid-points of each class. In general, one avoids "open-end" classes as much as possible, e.g., 5 years and more renders the determination of a mid-point somewhat difficult. We will go through an example to make concrete the issues involved.

The range of minutes to complete the exam was from 21 to 54 minutes, or 33 minutes. If an interval of 5 would not distort the data, we would have 7 classes. The smallest number was 21; if we chose, we could simply add 5 to that number and get, immediately, the lower bound for each succeeding class. Again, for convenience, we can decide to have the first class begin at 20 minutes, even though no one used precisely that time; rounded numbers always seem easier to work with.

Having defined the classes, the next step is to classify the students into their proper classes. All those who used between 20 and 24.9 minutes belong in the first class, those who used between 25 and 29.9 belong in the next one, etc. When all have been properly classified, we can draw up a table which is one way of presenting the data.

The table's title will be, in general, a simple declaration of the event.

TABLE 5.1. TIME TAKEN TO COMPLETE A TRUE-FALSE TEST

Class interval	Mid-points	Frequency
20 to 24.9	22.5	3
25 to 29.9	27.5	17
30 to 34.9	32.5	27
35 to 39.9	37.5	39
40 to 44.9	42.5	31
45 to 44.9	47.5	16
50 to 54.9	52.5	5
	Total	138

Source: Hypothetical.

To the left is the "stub," in which the possible outcomes are defined, and to the right is a column showing the frequency of members of each class.

A certain amount of information is gained from the table itself. We get some picture of how the time used was distributed among the students of the class and, after some experience in dealing with this kind of data, one can guess pretty closely to what the average time is. To most people, however, the numerical differences of various classes are not appreciated, unless the differences are great. Some sort of graphic presentation seems useful.

The most common graph for such data as these is the "histogram." Along the horizontal line (or X-axis), we put the class intervals; and along the vertical line (or Y-axis), we put the frequency for each corresponding class. For each class interval we extend a bar (equal in width to the class interval) up to the number designating the frequency of that class. The bar extends from the lower class limit to the upper class limit of each class. If we have a constant size interval for the classes the interval can be regarded as a unit which is numerically equal to one. Then the area of each bar is equal to the frequency, i.e., the height times one. Since the total number is the sum of the frequencies, the area under the histogram equals the number of frequencies and can be obtained by summing the area of each bar.

We may put the relative frequency on the Y-axis, instead of the frequency. This is, simply, the frequency divided by the total number. In this case, the area of each bar represents the relative frequency of the particular class interval, and the total area of the histogram equals one.

While one gets a better picture of the distribution from the histogram, the significant point for us is the relation between the area and relative frequency. Originally, we can compute the area from knowledge of the frequency, but subsequently, a knowledge of the area allows us to

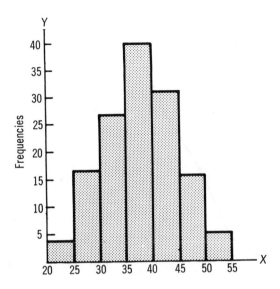

Figure 5.1. Histogram. Note use of class limits on X-axis.
Source: Table 5.1.

infer the frequency for each class. This relation between area and relative frequency is the fundamental notion of statistical inference.

Another useful graph, and rather widely used, is the "frequency polygon." Like the histogram, it is based on the frequency tabulation in Table 5.1. Unlike the histogram, the frequency polygon is constructed from the mid-points of each class. The mid-point and the relative frequency for each class determine a point (X, Y). These are then connected by straight lines, as in Figure 5.2. However, to insure that the total area under the curve equals 1, the distance between each class mid-point is again regarded as a unit.[1] Further, the line is extended from the smallest mid-point used to the mid-point of the class to the left of the smallest one with members. The line is similarly extended to the mid-point of the class next above the largest one with members. In our case, the class 15-19.9 has no members and is to the left of our smallest class. Hence, we would draw in line from the point (22.5,3) to the point (17.5,0).

Again, a knowledge of the area under the curve of the frequency polygon allows us to infer the relative frequency of the segment of the X-axis being considered.

[1] This is using relative frequencies; in the case of using absolute frequencies, the total area equals the number of objects being considered, i.e., N.

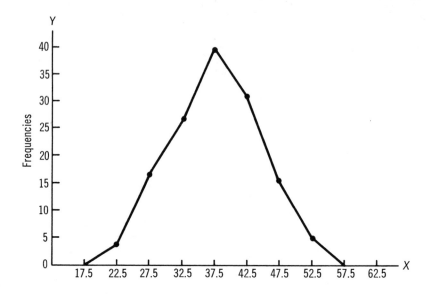

Figure 5.2. Frequency polygon. Note use of mid-points and extension of graph one class above and one class below the range of the empirical data. The area of this graph equals that of Figure 5.1.
Source: Table 5.1.

3. The Basic Statistical Idea: The Frequency Distribution

The concept of the frequency distribution simply formalizes what we have stated in terms of the classification and tabulation of data. This involves the assumption that some causal system functions in such a way that there is associated with each possible outcome some relative frequency of its occurrence. The relative frequencies of possible outcomes are connected in some sort of system. This system is the frequency distribution.

Although heuristically we may think of the frequency distribution as "looking like" our tabulated data, the two are not the same. For one thing, the data which we gather do not completely exhaust the theoretical distribution; we deal only with a sample. How one can argue from a sample to the "parent population," as the theoretical distribution is sometimes called, will be treated later. Indeed, this is the crux of the statistical argument.

The frequency distribution can generally be described in terms of a mathematical equation. The equation allows us to plot a curve on a graph, in much the same way as we did the histogram and frequency polygon. In fact the same relationship obtains: from a knowledge of the area under the curve (associated with a specified segment of the X-axis), we can deduce the relative frequency of the occurrence of the outcome. The student should realize that different segments of the X-axis define different possible outcomes and that the length of these segments defines the size of the class intervals.

Mathematically, the curve which describes a frequency distribution is a function of one or more constants. In reference to the population described by the frequency distribution, these mathematical constants are called "parameters." The sample equivalent of a parameter is called a "statistic." Some curves, as we suggested, can be described by only one or two parameters; others require more. It happens that the curve most frequently used in statistics, the "normal curve," uses only two such parameters. The important point is that from a knowledge of these two parameters one can completely describe the normal curve. From our knowledge of a normal curve, we can immediately deduce the relative frequency of the various possible outcomes. Evidently, we will need to know more about these measures if we are to proceed with statistical inference.

4. Describing the Distribution

Measuring Central Tendency. When one has a set of data, such as that in Table 5.1 or, generally speaking, cardinal data, a measure that describes in some way the information given is desirable. Among the measures in use we will use mostly the arithmetic "mean," the most common concept of average.[2] This is found by summing the size of each object and dividing by the total number of objects measured. If any particular outcome occurs more than once it is added as often as it occurs.

Symbolically, the mean is given by the formula,

$$M = \frac{\Sigma X}{N}. \tag{1}$$

The Greek letter Σ (sigma) symbolizes the *operation* of summing the values designated by X. The symbol X does not mean, as might be supposed,

---

2 Other fairly well known measures of central tendency are the mode and the median. The mode, generally speaking, refers to the outcome which has the largest relative frequency. In the data used above, the class 35 to 39.9 is the *modal* class. Sometimes a distribution may have two classes with the same or nearly the same number of members. This is spoken of as a "bi-modal distribution" and often suggests the use of two bases of classification instead of one.

The median is a measure of position such that there are as many objects larger than the median as there are smaller. In the case of a uniform distribution (the same frequency for each class) this cuts the X-axis in half. In the normal distribution, the mean, median, and the mode all define the same outcome. Unlike the mean, the mode and the median are independent of extreme values in the distribution. However, the mean is subject to algebraic manipulation and the others are not; for that reason, among others, it is preferred in the development of a theory of statistical inference.

to multiply sigma by X, but to sum all of the X values. N refers to the total number of frequencies. To get the mean the sum of the X values are divided by N.

Equation (1) generally refers to ungrouped data. If any X value occurs more than once, it is convenient to write (1) as,

$$M = \frac{\Sigma f X}{N}. \tag{2}$$

The symbol f denotes the frequency of each grouping of X-values. The X-values are multiplied by the corresponding frequencies and then summed. After being summed the quantities are divided by N, the total number of frequencies.

If the data are classified as those in Table 5.1, we do not have the "true" X-value for each object. We have classified them into intervals size five. For purposes of calculation we treat them as if they all had the size designated by the mid-point. We will denote the mid-point as $\hat{X}$. In such a case, we write (2) as,

$$M = \frac{\Sigma f \hat{X}}{N}. \tag{3}$$

We will illustrate the use of formula (3). Note, first, what information must be known before it can be used. We must have the mid-points and the frequencies of each class and also the product of the frequencies and the mid-points of each class. We then must sum the information gained by this multiplication process. The next step is to set up a table which will give us this information. This is done by creating a column for the different kinds of information needed as in Table 5.2 below.

Summing column two, we find that $N = 138$. Summing column three, we find that $\Sigma f \hat{X} = 5215.0$. We simply insert this information into

TABLE 5.2. TIME TAKEN TO COMPLETE A TRUE-FALSE TEST

Mid-points $\hat{X}$ (1)	Frequencies f (2)	$f\hat{X}$ (3)
22.5	3	67.5
27.5	17	467.5
32.5	27	877.5
37.5	39	1462.5
42.5	31	1317.5
47.5	16	760.0
52.5	5	262.5
Total	138	5215.0

Source: Table 5.1.

equation (3) and perform the indicated division. The mean is thus found to be $M = \dfrac{5215}{138} = 37.79$, rounding off to two decimals.

Although the numbers used in this example were relatively simple for the calculation of the mean, an inspection of column three shows some rather large numbers. With larger numbers, or with a more complicated set of mid-points, it is easy to see that calculation of the mean by (3) could become cumbersome. A formula that lends itself to simpler calculation processes (for the more difficult the operation the greater the likelihood of error) seems to be useful.

If the size of the intervals is constant, a simpler formula may be obtained by *transforming* the $\hat{X}$ values to integers. We make this transformation by subtracting the mid-point of any convenient class; normally the class with the greatest frequency from the mid-points of all the classes used. We then divide this difference by the size of the interval. Denoting the transformed information by the letter d, the symbolic representation is given by,

$$d = \frac{\hat{X} - A}{i}. \tag{4}$$

In Table 5.3 below, we have designated a column d. Notice that certain d-values have negative algebraic signs. Thus, to get the d-value for the smallest class, letting i denote the interval, 5 in this case, and choosing $A = 37.5$ for convenience,

$$d = \frac{22.5 - 37.5}{5} = \frac{-15}{5} = -3.$$

The algebraic signs must be retained and used in computation.

Since we have subtracted a constant value we must add it back in our subsequent calculation of the mean. Further, we divided by another constant, i, so we must multiply our results by the same constant. The mean can then be found by the equation.

$$M = A + i\left(\frac{\Sigma fd}{N}\right). \tag{5}$$

In Table 5.3 we anticipated this result. Notice again what information (5) calls for: we need to know the d-values for each class, the frequencies for each class, and the product of the frequencies and the d-values for each class. Our table is constructed so as to give us this information. We find that

$$
\begin{aligned}
A &= 37.5 \\
i &= 5.0 \\
\Sigma fd &= 8.0 \\
N &= 138.0.
\end{aligned}
$$

TABLE 5.3. TIME TAKEN TO COMPLETE A TRUE-FALSE TEST

$\hat{X}$	d	f	fd
22.5	−3	3	− 9
27.5	−2	17	−34
32.5	−1	27	−27
37.5	0	39	0
42.5	1	31	31
47.5	2	16	32
52.5	3	5	15
		Total 138	+ 8

Source: From Table 5.1.

Inserting these values into (5) gives us,

$$M = 37.5 + 5 \left(\frac{8}{138} \right) = 37.79,$$

which agrees with equation (3).

Measuring Dispersion. In addition to a measure of the average value, the use of the normal curve necessitates a knowledge of the amount of variation in the distribution. The variation is measured in terms of deviation from the mean. It is called the "standard deviation." The importance of the standard deviation lies in the fact that the area of the normal curve above the X-axis in the segment comprising one standard deviation unit on each side of the mean consists of about 67% of the total area under the curve. The characteristic of being able to compute the area under different segments of the normal curve—and hence the corresponding relative frequency—from a knowledge of the standard deviation is the foundation of statistical inference. The square of the standard deviation is called the "variance."

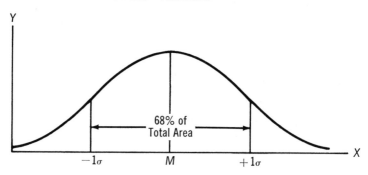

Figure 5.3. Normal curve.

The operational definition of the standard deviation is given in the following steps: (1) subtract the mean from each X—(or $\hat{X}$) value, (2) square the differences, (3) multiply the squared differences by the corresponding frequency (in ungrouped data the frequency equals one for each class), (4) sum these products, (5) divide by the total number of objects; this gives the variance. To get the standard deviation, step (6) is to extract the square root. These steps operationally define the standard deviation though the conceptual definition includes its relation to the area under the curve.

Obviously, these steps can become quite troublesome. Therefore, some computational formulas would be useful. We will give them in the form of variance. The student should always remember to extract the square root to obtain the standard deviation.

Denoting variance by σ^2 (the lower case Greek letter sigma), for ungrouped data

$$\sigma^2 = \frac{\Sigma X^2}{N} - M^2 \tag{6}$$

and for grouped data,

$$\frac{\Sigma f X^2}{N} - M^2. \tag{7}$$

When the data are arranged in classes variance is found by,

$$\frac{\Sigma f \hat{X}^2}{N} - M^2 \tag{8}$$

and, again, $\hat{X}$ denotes the mid-point values of each class.

The student should again notice what information is called for by each equation. Illustrating the process of arithmetic computation by (8), we find we need the following information: the mid-point values for each

TABLE 5.4. TIME TAKEN TO COMPLETE TRUE-FALSE TEST

$\hat{X}$	f	$f\hat{X}$	$f\hat{X}^2$
22.5	3	67.5	1518.75
27.5	17	467.5	12856.25
32.5	27	877.5	28518.75
37.5	39	1462.5	54843.75
42.5	31	1317.5	55993.75
47.5	16	760.0	36100.00
52.5	5	262.5	13781.25
Total	138	5215.0	203612.50

Source: From Table 5.1

class; the squares of these numbers; the frequencies of each class; the sum of the frequencies; the product of the class frequencies and the squares of the mid-point values; the sum of these products; and the square of the mean. We will then arrange Table 5.4 so as to give us this information. By direct computation, we find the following values:

$$\Sigma f\hat{X}^2 = 203612.50$$
$$N = 138$$
$$M = 37.79$$
$$M^2 = 1428.0841$$

Inserting these values in equation (8),

$$\sigma^2 = \frac{203612.5}{138} - 1428.0841 = 47.37$$

Clearly, the computation of variance by (8) can become a cumbersome process. The numbers dealt with are large, even with these simple data. The issue of rounding off decimal places is present at each step. An easier computational formula would be useful. Analogous to equation (5) for the mean, variance can be found by,

$$\sigma^2 = i^2 \left[\frac{\Sigma fd^2}{N} - \left(\frac{\Sigma fd}{N} \right)^2 \right]. \tag{9}$$

where the symbols are the same as for (5). Notice that in (9) the computation does not involve the arbitrary starting point of A.

TABLE 5.5. TIME TAKEN TO COMPLETE A TRUE-FALSE TEST

X	d	f	fd	fd²
22.5	-3	3	- 9	27
27.5	-2	17	-34	68
32.5	-1	27	-27	27
37.5	0	39	0	0
42.5	1	31	31	31
47.5	2	16	32	64
52.5	3	5	15	45
	Total	138	+ 8	262

Source: From Table 5.1

Table 5.5, above, gives the information needed in (9). The information required by (9) is found to be,

$$\sigma^2 = 25 \left[\frac{262}{138} - \left(\frac{8}{138} \right)^2 \right]$$
$$\sigma^2 = 47.38.$$

The difference between this value and that given by (8) is due to the rounding-off of decimal places in (8). If one used $M = 5215/138$ instead of $M = 37.79$, the two results would have been identical.

Since variance equals 47.38, the standard deviation is the square root of that number. It is found to be equal to 6.88. The area under a normal curve corresponding to the segment of the X-axis ranging from 30.91 to 44.67, or the mean plus and minus 6.88, is approximately 67% of the total area under the curve. A glance at Figure 2, the frequency polygon, indicates that there is a fairly close fit. The distribution in Table 5.1 is approximately normal..

5. Basic Ideas of Probability

To understand the mathematical conception of probability the student must be prepared to give up some common sense ideas. For one thing it makes no mathematical sense to discuss the probability of a unique event. The idea of recurrence of an event is fundamental to a precise conception of probability. In fact, we will define probability by formalizing the idea of relative frequency of an outcome. Thus, some notion of an arithmetic ratio will be present in the definition of probability. Such terms as "improbable" will at best be translated into numerically small ratios. But at what point a relative frequency is sufficiently small to allow one to talk of the improbability of an outcome is quite arbitrary.

Definition. If an event can occur N times and an alternative outcome (denoted by o_i) can occur f times, the probability that o_i occurs is $p_i = f/N$. Since the outcomes are mutually exclusive and exhaustive, $\Sigma f = N$ and $\Sigma p = 1$.

In the case of a dichotomy we ordinarily speak of "successes" and "failures." By success we simply mean one of the two alternative outcomes; generally, the outcome of substantive theoretical interest. In this case, the probability of success is denoted by p, and the probability of a failure is denoted by q. The value of p is found by obtaining the ratio of the number of ways a success can occur to the number of ways a success can occur plus the number of ways a failure can occur. The value of q is similarly obtained.

If one is given a probability system it is often desirable to be able to deduce the probabilities of another system comprised of various combinations of the outcomes involved in the first system. Thus, if one knows the probability that a student will complete an examination in a certain amount of time and also knows the probability a student will receive a certain grade on that examination, we may want to deduce the probability that he will finish the exam at a given time and receive the grade in question.

Certain rules for such inference have been derived, based on the assumption of statistical independence of the two probability systems. The inference which is drawn may then be tested empirically. Later we will learn how to be able to decide whether or not the two systems were in fact independent of each other. Evidently such knowledge will give us a powerful device to aid in making decisions about the acceptability of certain propositions.

Rule of Addition. When dealing with two mutually exclusive outcomes, *A* and *B*, if outcome *A* has the probability of p_1 of occurring and outcome *B* has the probability of p_2 of occurring, the probability that either *A* or *B* will occur is the sum of probabilities $p_1 + p_2$. This can be generalized to any number of mutually exclusive outcomes.

Rule of Multiplication. If outcome *A* has the probability p_1 of occurring and outcome *B* has the probability of p_2 of occurring, with or after *A* in one possible way, the probability that both *A* and *B* will so occur is the product of the probabilities, $p_1 p_2$. This, too, can be generalized.

Suppose we want to obtain the probability of getting 3 heads (successes) out of a toss of 5 coins. Labeling the coins *A*, *B*, *C*, *D*, and *E*, we associate with each coin an outcome of interest. For example, the outcomes for *A*, *B*, and *C*, are successes each having a probability *p*. The outcomes for *D* and *E* are failures each having a probability *q*. Since we are interested in these outcomes occurring together, we use the Rule of Multiplication. The probability for this one set of probabilities is found by,

$$P = pppqq.$$

Since the *p*'s are of the same value, and the *q*'s are of the same value, we may write this as,

$$P = p^3 q^2.$$

To generalize our symbols we will say we tossed *n* coins, of which *r* were to be heads. Obviously, there would be $n - r$ tails. With these symbols, we would write,

$$P = p^r q^{n-r}. \tag{10}$$

If we assume that we have "true" coins, we can associate $1/2$ with the probability *p*; this implies that *q* is also equal to $1/2$. Then, the numerical value of obtaining 3 heads in a toss of 5 coins *in one way* is found by,

$$P = (1/2)^3 (1/2)^2 = .03125.$$

In deducing such combinations of probabilities the possible ways of arranging the outcomes in question is of some importance. This is so, since the combinations of outcomes *A* and *B*, etc., can occur in more ways than one. Each way it may occur has the same probability. Rather than laboriously counting each combination, some algebraic equation would simplify the work involved.

Rule of Combination. If an event can occur n times, a successful outcome can occur r times and a failing outcome can occur $n - r$ times, the number of ways in which successes and $n - r$ failures can occur without regard to order is found by the formula,[3]

$$_nC_r = \frac{n!}{r!\,(n-r)!}. \tag{11}$$

Suppose one were tossing a set of 5 coins. It might be of interest to know the number of ways 3 heads could be obtained. One way of finding out would be to identify each coin by some unbiasing mark and enumerate all possible ways of getting exactly 3 heads disregarding the order in which the different coins fell. This may be a simple task with only 5 coins, but with larger numbers the physical counting would take considerable time. By inserting the proper values in (11), however, one could obtain the same result easily. In this example, $n = 5$, $r = 3$, and $n - r = 2$. By (11), we obtain,

$$_5C_3 = \frac{5!}{3!\,2!} = \frac{5 \cdot 4 \cdot 3 \cdot 2 \cdot 1}{3 \cdot 2 \cdot 1 \cdot 2 \cdot 1} = \frac{120}{12} = 10.$$

Each of these different arrangements has the same probability of occurrence.

To obtain the probability of obtaining 3 heads in a toss of 5 coins, one must determine the probability for each of the ways in which it might occur and, in accordance with the rules of addition, to sum them. Each probability of obtaining 3 heads in a toss of 5 coins is the same. We can either add the 10 identical values, or can multiply the probability by 10. The latter is easier, and we obtain, in symbols,

$$P = {}_nC_r p^r q^{n-r}. \tag{12}$$

Taking into account the 10 possible ways of getting 3 heads and 2 tails in a toss of 5 coins we find, from (12),

$$P = {}_5C_3 p^3 q^2 = 10\,(.03125) = .3125.$$

That is, if the tossing of 5 coins were continued long enough, slightly over 31% of the time we would get 3 heads and 2 tails.

THE BINOMIAL DISTRIBUTION AND THE NORMAL CURVE

In high school algebra we learned that we can expand the expression $(p + q)^n$. To refresh our memory, we shall expand this expression letting $n = 5$.

---

[3] The symbol $n!$ is read "n factorial." This means to take the number n and multiply it successively by integers reduced by 1. Thus, if n equals 4, $n!$ is found by multiplying $4 \cdot 3 \cdot 2 \cdot 1$. By definition, $0!$ equals 1. Of course, $r!$ is likewise obtained.

$$(p + q)^5 = p^5 + 5p^4q + 10p^3q^2 + 10p^2q^3 + 5pq^4 + q^5 \qquad (13)$$

One of the terms in this expansion seems to be familiar: $10p^3q^2$. It is the expression for getting the probability of obtaining 3 heads in a toss of 5 coins. The general term for the binomial expansion is the formula for getting the probability of obtaining r successes in n trials.

Formula (13) can be written as,

$$(p + q)^n = \Sigma_n C_r p^r q^{n-r}. \qquad (14)$$

Since $p + q$ must equal 1, the term on the right of formula (14) also equals 1. This equation is important for deducing probabilities from the knowledge of p and q.

Out of n trials, r can range from 0 to n. That is, we can ask, what is the probability of getting no successes in a toss of 5 coins, as well as, what is the probability of getting 5 successes in a toss of 5 coins. There is a unique probability associated with each value of r. These are given in Table 5.6 below.

TABLE 5.6. PROBABILITY FOR GETTING r SUCCESSES OUT OF n TRIALS

r	nCr	p^r	q^{n-r}	Numerical value
0			$(1/2)^5$	.03125
1	5	$(1/2)$	$(1/2)^4$	.15625
2	10	$(1/2)^2$	$(1/2)^3$	.31250
3	10	$(1/2)^3$	$(1/2)^2$	.31250
4	5	$(1/2)^4$	$(1/2)$	.15625
5		$(1/2)^5$		.03125

$n = 5$

An important modification of the summation operator is needed. From the knowledge given in Table 5.6, we may want to make some additional combinations. We might, for example, want to know the probability of obtaining either no successes or 1 success; this may be put, "the probability of no more than 1 success." From the rule of addition, we simply sum the probabilities when $r = 0$ and when $r = 1$.

To show this operation in terms of Σ we will put $r = 0$ below the summation sign to indicate the first term to be summed and the number 1 above the sign to indicate the last number to be summed; that is,

$$\sum_{r=0}^{1} {}_n C_r p^r q^{n-r}.$$

Similarly, to find out the probability for obtaining 3 or more heads (at least 3 heads), we would put $r = 3$ below the summation sign and n above it.

The probabilities in Table 5.6 can be represented graphically as in Figure 5.4 below. We will show them as a histogram. Recall that the relative frequency—the probability—of any r-value is shown as a bar extending up from the X-axis with a width equal to the class interval. The r-values are integers: what are the class limits for the histogram? The r-values are taken as the mid-points of their respective classes. To obtain the lower class limit we subtract .5 from the r-value and to get the upper class limit add .5 to it.

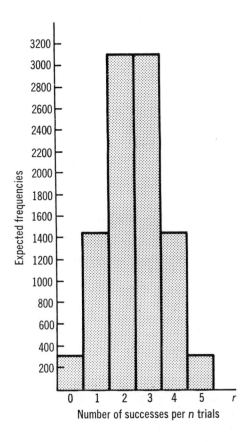

Figure 5.4. Histogram of binomial for n = 5. N = 10,000.

We clearly have unit widths for the class intervals. The probabilities, shown on the Y-axis, can be thought of as the heights of the bars. Again, the area in the histogram corresponds to the probability associated with a segment of the X-axis. The total area equals 1.

Just as we could compute the mean and standard deviation from the data in Table 5.1, we can compute the two values for the binomial. To illustrate this, we must change the probabilities to frequencies since, by our definition, $p = f/N, Np = f$, where N is the number of times n coins are tossed. For convenience, let $N = 10,000$. Now we can set up Table 5.7 allowing us to use Formulas (5) and (9) for the mean and standard deviation. Inserting the proper values in our equations, we find that the mean is 2.5 heads out of a toss of 5 coins. The standard deviation (the square root of variance) is found to be approximately 1.12.

TABLE 5.7. EXPECTED FREQUENCIES OF OBTAINING r SUCCESSES
OUT OF N TRIALS

r	d	f	fd	fd^2
0	-2	312.5	-625.0	1,250.0
1	-1	1,562.5	-1,562.5	1,562.5
2	0	3,125.0	0	0.0
3	1	3,125.0	3,125.0	3,125.0
4	2	1,562.0	3,125.0	6,250.0
5	3	312.5	937.5	2,812.5
	Total	10,000.0	5,000.0	15,000.0

Instead of using these equations some simpler ones are available for the binomial distribution. As long as n is small the binomial expansion

$$M = np = \text{mean of the binomial} \qquad (15)$$

$$\sigma = \sqrt{npq} = \text{standard deviation of the binomial} \qquad (16)$$

is not too difficult to use to compute probabilities. When n is large, however, the separate calculation becomes burdensome. However, when n gets large, the step differences of the Y-axis of a histogram get smaller and smaller. For instance, if n equals 500 a frequency polygon of the binomial expansion would be virtually a continuous curve. Indeed, a theorem of mathematical probability proves that as n gets larger the binomial approaches the normal curve. That is to say, computation of probabilities from the normal curve involves a progressively smaller error as n gets larger, providing np is greater than 5.

As we indicated earlier, it will be useful to learn how to calculate probabilities from the normal curve. Recall that the area under a segment of the curve equals the probability of the outcome identified with the corresponding segment of the X-axis. Recall, also, the property of the standard deviation; transformation of the X-axis into standard deviation units allows an inference of the area covered by the segment involved.

Probabilities are calculated in terms of standard deviation units from

TABLE 5.8. AREAS UNDER NORMAL CURVE

$\dfrac{x}{\sigma}$	Area	$\dfrac{x}{\sigma}$	Area
.25	.09871	1.75	.45994
.50	.19146	2.00	.47725
.75	.27337	2.25	.48778
1.00	.34134	2.50	.49379
1.25	.39435	2.75	.49702
1.50	.43319	3.00	.49865

Source: Reprinted with permission from Q. McNemar, *Psychological Statistics*, New York, Wiley, 1949.

the mean. Fortunately, areas corresponding to standard deviation units have been mathematically computed. One needs only to know how to transform the X-axis into the proper units. The transformation is quite simple. We first compute the *mean deviate* value by subtracting the point of interest on the X-axis from the mean. Then we divide this number by the standard deviation. The resulting quotient is the number of standard deviation units the original X-value is from the mean. Associated with the number is the corresponding area under the curve. This area equals the probability that an object will fall between the mean and the X-value chosen. Symbolically, this operation is given as,

$$Z = \frac{x}{\sigma} = \frac{X - M}{\sigma}. \tag{17}$$

Table 5.8 gives the corresponding area of the normal curve for selected values of (17). It can best be used by drawing a picture of the normal curve and identifying the area we want to know. Suppose we

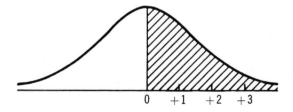

Figure 5.5. $\dfrac{x}{\sigma}$ areas under the normal curve.

want to know the probability of obtaining 12 or more heads out of a toss of 15 pennies. The area desired is shown in the shaded area of Figure 5.6.

Notice that the lower limit is 11.5, our X-value. To use (17) we need the mean and σ. $M = np = (15)\,(\frac{1}{2}) = 7.5$.

$$\sigma = \sqrt{npq} = \sqrt{(15)\,(\tfrac{1}{2})\,(\tfrac{1}{2})} = 1.94 \text{ (approximately)}.$$

Inserting these into (17) we obtain,

$$\frac{11.5 - 7.5}{1.94} = \frac{4}{1.94} = 2.06.$$

The X-value of 11.5 falls 2.06 standard deviation units from the mean. Using Table 5.8, we find that the corresponding area under the curve equals .4803 of the total area. However, the portion of the curve we wanted extends from 11.5 to infinity. Clearly, the space from the mean to

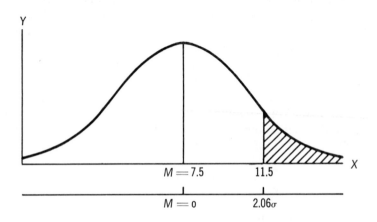

Figure 5.6. Normal curve showing area needed to solve the problem. Second base line indicates a transformation of the first base line to $\frac{x}{\sigma}$ units.

infinity comprises only one-half of the total area under the curve. Therefore, to obtain the desired area we subtract .4803 from .5000. Doing this we obtain the number .0197; this is the probability that we will get 12 or more heads from a toss of 15 coins. The binomial gives .0176 for the same problem. The difference amounts to only .0021 of the total area. Even when n equals only 15, the normal curve seems to be a fairly good approximation.

INFERENTIAL STATISTICS

1. Sampling Theory: Standard Errors and Confidence Limits

A scientist seldom, if ever, deals with a population; he usually deals with a sample. If he does possess all the data comprising the population the problem may lack sufficient generality to be of scientific interest. But, usually, for one reason or another he simply does not possess all of the data.

When one has only a sample to deal with some way of estimating the population value is needed. Samples can vary due to sampling alone, as we saw in the case of tossing coins. The question is, then, how can we measure sampling variation?

First, consider the population distribution of the sample values—all possible samples. Instead of the frequency distribution of X-values, consider a distribution of sample means. The mean of all possible sample means is the population mean itself. If we could transform the sample-mean axis into standard deviations of the mean, we could estimate the probability of obtaining specified sample values from a known population.

The standard deviation, when referring to a population value, is called a "standard error" and is denoted by the Greek letter epsilon, ϵ. Mathematically, it functions exactly as does the standard deviation we have already used. If we measure on the X-axis two standard error units from the parameter, we will cover 95% of the area of a normal curve. This band covers 95% of all possible sample values.

Now ask the question, How often am I willing to be wrong? We have tacitly assumed that we would be willing to be wrong 5 times in 100. This means that those sample values that fall beyond the band covered by 2 standard error units from the population mean are rejected as estimates of the parameter. The rejection would be in error 5 times in 100.

But we don't know the parameter value. We know only the statistic. We will use the statistics to estimate the parameters and use an analogous argument about the confidence of our estimate. Using what are called,

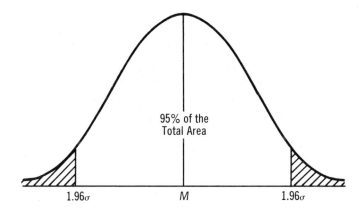

95% of the
Total Area

1.96σ M   1.96σ

Figure 5.7. Normal curve showing traditional 95% confidence limits.

"95% confidence limits," we argue this way: if we measure a band around our sample mean two estimated standard errors on each side of the mean, the chances are 95 in 100 that we have included the parameter value in our estimate. The smaller the range of tolerable error, the more confidence we have in our estimate.

The sample mean is taken as an estimate of the population mean. We need to know how to estimate the standard error. We know the standard deviation of the sample distribution. It turns out that the standard error of the mean (i.e., the distribution of means) if found by,

$$\epsilon m = \frac{\sigma}{\sqrt{N}} \tag{18}$$

where σ is the sample standard deviation and N is the size of the sample. For proportions, the standard error is estimated by,

$$\epsilon p = \sqrt{\frac{pq}{n}}. \tag{19}$$

It is clear that the larger the sample, the smaller the standard error, if all other assumptions have been met.

Size alone is not the criterion. Two assumptions have been made in the argument which must be made explicit. First, we assumed a normal distribution. In the case of means we can find some comfort in the fact that means tend to be normally distributed even if the original distribution was not. This is true particularly in large samples. Second, we assumed "random sampling." Random sampling means that each object in the study had an equal chance of being drawn.

The end result is that the way in which a sample is taken is of fundamental importance to the inferences which are possible. To insure confidence in our knowledge we wish to minimize the amount of sampling error. Failure to abide by the assumptions of statistical theory admits the possibility of uncontrolled error.

2. Sampling Theory: Testing Hypotheses

Instead of considering whether a statistic estimates a given parameter, consider the case of two statistics which are numerically different. This poses a problem of variation and two major explanations can be offered. The numerical difference may be due to sampling variation, or the differences may be real. In the Introduction to this chapter we found that the argument essentially involves an alternative syllogism; the student should review that discussion.

We will justify the test of the null hypothesis which asserts that sampling variation is a sufficient explanation for the observed difference. Assuming that this is true, this implies that all *pairs* of samples are drawn from the population and that a distribution of the differences between these pairs exists. Further, if the parent population was normally distributed, the population of differences is also normal. Since the samples are from the same population the mean difference will be zero. If we knew the sampling error of the differences we could transform the X-axis and measure in standard error units the distance a given sample difference is from the mean. This would allow us to assert the probability of getting a difference as large or larger than the one observed. If the probability is small enough, the arbitrary choice of 5 times out of 100, we would be justified in rejecting the hypothesis that the mean difference is zero. The transformation is called the "critical ratio." Symbolically, it is given by,

$$\text{C.R.} = \frac{S_1 - S_2}{\epsilon_d}. \tag{20}$$

This relationship is illustrated in Figure 5.8. Notice how the relation between area and probability has persisted since we first learned how to draw a histogram. We encountered the idea in the discussion of the binomial and the normal curve approximation to the binomial. We saw it again in the relation between sample values and population values and find it again in the *difference* between two sample values.

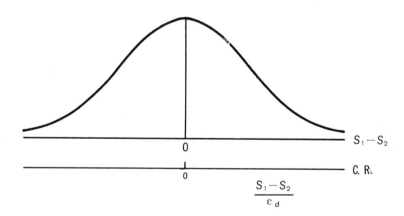

Figure 5.8. Illustration of a normal distribution of critical ratios. Compare with Figure 5.6. Note how second base line now transforms the difference between pairs of statistics into critical ratio values.

Apparently, we need to know an equation for the *standard error of differences*. This is given as,

$$\epsilon_d{}^2 = \epsilon_1{}^2 + \epsilon_2{}^2 - 2\, r_{12}\, \epsilon_1\, \epsilon_2 \tag{21}$$

where subscript 1 refers to one sample and subscript 2 refers to the other. Notice that a term involving a new symbol r is present. This symbol refers to a measure of correlation (see section 10 below). If the samples are drawn independently of each other, then $r = 0$, and (21) reduces to,

$$\epsilon^2_d = \epsilon_1^2 + \epsilon_2^2. \tag{22}$$

The standard error terms to use in either (21) or (22) depend upon the type of statistic used. If one is discussing means then the standard error of a mean is used. If the statistics refer to proportions, or relative frequencies, then the standard error of proportions is used.

We will give two illustrations of a test of the null hypothesis. The first will illustrate standard errors of proportions and the second will illustrate a special case of the difference between correlated means. For this latter example we will give a formula for its standard error.

Suppose we drew a random sample of 400 urban marriages and, after 10 years of marriage, observed that .32 of these resulted in divorce. Independently, a random sample of 350 rural marriages was drawn and after an interval of 10 years, .23 ended in divorce. Is the difference of proportions of divorce due to sampling error, or is there a real difference?

Assume that the difference comes from a population of differences with a mean equaling zero. With 95% confidence limits this implies that the critical ratio will be smaller than 1.96 since 1.96 standard error units around the mean corresponds to 95% of the area of the normal curve. Then insert the proper numbers in (22) and determine the empirical value of the critical ratio.

We find that $S_1 = .32$; p_1 also equals .32 which implies that $q_1 = .68$; $n_1 = .400$. $S_2 = .23$, the same value being p_2. This implies that $q_2 = .77$; $n_2 = 350$. Inserting these in (20) we get,

$$\text{C.R.} = \frac{.32 - .23}{\sqrt{\dfrac{(.32)\,(.68)}{400} + \dfrac{(.23)\,(.77)}{350}}}$$

$$= \frac{.09}{\sqrt{.00055}}$$

$$= 3.91.$$

But this contradicts the inference that C.R. is less than 1.96, making the assumption that the statistics came from a common population, false. This implies that the divorce rate is higher in urban areas than in rural ones.

Suppose, for another example, we wish to find out the influence of a lecture in modifying attitudes towards defacing public property. A random sample of 10 delinquents is drawn and an attitude test is given them regarding defacing public property. They are then given a lecture on the subject and again their attitudes are measured. Since they comprise the same group a certain amount of correlation is obviously present and the critical ratio formulas already given cannot be used.

A formula for the standard error of matched differences is available which does not involve the calculation of the amount of correlation, but which nevertheless corrects for whatever correlation there may be. In Table 5.9, we are given the hypothetical "before" and "after" scores on the attitudinal test. Note that one column is labeled d, which denotes the numerical difference for the two scores for each person. Another column is headed d^2 which is the square of these differences.

TABLE 5.9. ATTITUDE SCORES, BEFORE AND AFTER LECTURE
ON DEFACING PUBLIC PROPERTY

Individual	Score before	Score after	Difference d	d^2
A	8	10	-2	4
B	9	8	1	1
C	8	10	-2	4
D	6	5	1	1
E	7	7	0	0
F	5	6	-1	1
G	9	8	1	1
H	6	4	2	4
I	8	9	-1	1
J	4	6	-2	4
Total	70	73	-3	21

Source: Hypothetical.

Directly analogous to (6) we get the sample standard deviation of the difference,

$$\sigma_d = \sqrt{\frac{\Sigma d^2 - \frac{(\Sigma d)^2}{N}}{N}}. \tag{23}$$

And the standard error of difference is found to be,

$$\epsilon_d = \frac{\sigma_d}{\sqrt{N}}. \tag{24}$$

Notice that Table 5.9 is set up to give us the necessary information.

In this case, the null hypothesis asserts that the mean differences within the 95% confidence limits equals zero. The formula for the critical ratio is,

$$\text{C.R.} = \frac{(M_1 - M_2) - 0}{\frac{\sigma_d}{\sqrt{N}}}. \tag{25}$$

From Table 5.9, we get the numbers necessary to compute the critical ratio. Recall that the null hypothesis implies that the C.R. <1.96 on the assumption that the "true value" of $\bar{d} = 0$. Simple calculation shows that in this case $\bar{d} = -.3$, $\sigma_d^2 = 2.01$. Since $N = 10$, the critical ratio is given by,

$$\text{C.R.} = \frac{7 - 7.3}{\sqrt{\dfrac{2.01}{10}}}$$

$$-.71$$

This is certainly less than 1.96; we have not contradicted the implication of the null hypothesis. Although we have not unequivocally proved that sampling variation explains the difference between observed $\bar{d}$-value $(-.3)$ and the assumed one $(\bar{d} = 0)$, we have no better explanation. Hence, we say that chance *can* explain the difference.

3. A Chi-square (χ^2) Test of the Null Hypothesis

Quite often in social science research the assumption of a normal distribution is not met. Further, the outcomes of the events being studied are often categorically or ordinally defined. This implies that frequencies of occurrences, rather than quantitative variation, must be explained.

To illustrate the issue, suppose one were studying the effect of educational policy on management policy in modern industry.[4] Are the higher levels of management selected from higher levels of education, or can the grade-school graduate work his way up to executive positions? To answer this question one must be able to assert the relationship which exists between education and management levels.

In Table 5.10 we have "cross-tabulated" 220 employees of a hypothetical plant in regard to employment category and amount of education. There are three columns for educational level and three rows for employment category. Is there a relationship between the two systems of outcomes, or are they independent?

If membership in the employment categories is independent of membership in educational levels the laws of probability are sufficient to explain the observed frequencies. On the other hand, if we can contradict the laws of probability we also contradict the assumption of statistical independence. This, in turn, implies at least some relationship between the two systems.

From the Rule of Multiplication we know that if the probability that *A* occurs (the outcome "laborer"), is independent of the probability that

---

[4] Robert C. Stone, "Mobility Factors as They Affect Worker's Attitudes," *American Sociology Review*, vol. 17, no. 1 (February, 1952), pp. 58–63.

TABLE 5.10. RELATION BETWEEN EMPLOYMENT CATEGORY AND AMOUNT OF EDUCATION

Employment category	Amount of Education			Row Totals
	Grade School	High School	College	
Laborer	65	50	10	125
Foreman and Supervisor	10	30	5	45
Executive	5	20	25	50
Column totals	80	100	40	220

Source: Hypothetical.

B occurs (the outcome "grade school education"), then the probability that the joint outcome ("grade-school education and laborer"), is the product of these two probabilities. By selecting the proper column and row we can then determine the expected probability for any "cell." A cell is that part of the table where a row and column overlap. Thus, the first row and the second column gives rise to the cell "high school and laborer."

The probability of any row outcome is found by dividing the row total (called the marginal total of the row) by the total number (the sum of the row totals). The probability of any column outcome is similarly found. Note that the sum of the column equals the sum of the new totals. We can symbolize any row total by n_i and a column total by n_j. Denoting the total by N, the expected probability for any cell is found by (n_i/N) (n_j/N). This in turn can be transformed into expected frequencies denoted by f_e, simply by multiplying the probability by N:

$$f_e = n_i n_j / N = (n_i/N)(n_j/N)(N). \tag{26}$$

Repeated use of (26) will give us the expected frequencies for each cell in the table. If the laws of probability are sufficient to explain the observed frequencies (f_o), the differences between the f_o and the f_e values ought to fluctuate around zero. Observe that sampling variation will account for some differences from zero. How great should the variation be before we reject the laws of probability?

A statistic has been devised to answer this question. It has a chi-square (χ^2) distribution and is, therefore, called "the chi-square test." It is found by,

$$\chi^2 = \sum \frac{(f_o - f_e)^2}{f_e}. \tag{27}$$

Notice that if f_o equals f_e in every case; χ^2 equals zero. Table 5.10 has been so constructed as to give us the required observed frequency information.

Table 5.11 is constructed so as to yield the necessary information for obtaining chi square. The sum of the last column gives us chi square. Its calculation is simple. We record the observed frequencies, and then compute the corresponding expected frequencies. Then the difference is obtained. Since the sum of f_o equals the sum of f_e, the sum of the differences equals zero. Hence, the differences are squared and these squares are divided by the corresponding expected frequencies. The sum of these last values gives us chi square. In this case it is found to be 62.27.

TABLE 5.11. EMPLOYMENT AND EDUCATION:
ARRANGED FOR COMPUTATION OF χ^2

Observed frequencies f_o	Expected frequencies f_e	$f_o - f_e$	$(f_o - f_e)^2$	$\dfrac{(f_o - f_e)^2}{f_e}$
65	45.45	19.55	382.20	8.41
10	16.36	- 6.36	40.45	2.47
5	18.19	-13.19	173.71	9.56
50	56.82	- 6.82	46.51	0.82
30	20.45	9.55	91.20	4.46
20	22.73	- 2.73	7.45	0.33
10	22.73	-12.72	162.05	7.13
5	8.19	- 3.19	10.18	1.24
25	9.09	15.91	253.13	27.85
		00.00		$\chi^2 = 62.27$

Source: From Table 5.10.

To decide whether or not 62.27 sufficiently differs from zero, one must know the probability of obtaining a chi square as large, or larger, through the laws of probability. Just like in testing the null hypothesis with the critical ratio, the null hypothesis is rejected if the probability of obtaining a chi square is "sufficiently small"—recall the arbitrary 5 times in 100.

The probability of obtaining any size of chi square depends upon what are called the "degrees of freedom" involved in its calculation. In the chi square we have discussed this refers to the table originally used. The degree of freedom may be thought of in this way. We used the marginal totals in the computation of the expected probabilities. We can then regard the marginal totals as being fixed. How many cell values are independent of the marginal total? For instance, given the first cell in the first row do we know what the other cell values must be? Since the difference between the marginal total of the row and the first cell goes into two remaining cells we do not. But, if we know the values of two cells in a three cell row, the frequencies in the third cell is also known since the three must equal the marginal total. The same argument applies to the columns. The question becomes, how many cells in the table are, in this sense, free. The answer is simply, the product of the free cells in the row and the free cells in the column. Denoting the number of free cells in the rows by r, and the number of free cells in the columns by c, the degrees of freedom are computed by the equation,

$$d.f. = (r - 1)(c - 1). \tag{28}$$

In Table 5.12, we give the probabilities for obtaining given chi-square values to 10 different degrees of freedom. The first column gives the degrees of freedom and the second and third designate the probabilities for obtaining the chi squares as large or larger than the ones entered in the cells of the table. Thus, the third column gives the .05 probability of obtaining chi-square values associated with various degrees of freedom. For one degree of freedom, the probability for getting a chi square as large or larger than 3.841 is .05.

TABLE 5.12. SELECTED VALUES FOR χ^2: .05 and .01
LEVELS OF SIGNIFICANCE

d.f.	.05	.01
1	3.841	6.635
2	5.991	9.210
3	7.815	11.277
4	9.488	13.277
5	11.070	15.086
6	12.592	16.812
7	14.067	18.475
8	15.507	20.090
9	16.919	21.666
10	18.307	23.209

Source: Table 5.12 is abridged from Table 2 of Fisher: *Statistical Methods for Research Workers* published by Oliver & Boyd, Ltd., Edinburgh, by permission of the author and publishers.

In our example, we had 3 rows and 3 columns. Using formula (28), this gives 4 degrees of freedom. We find 4 in the first column of Table 5.12 and, reading under the column labeled ".05," the entry is 9.488. We can now formally state our null hypothesis: with 4 degrees of freedom at the .05 level of confidence if the true chi square is zero, the empirical chi square is less than 9.49. Our empirical value is greater than the one designated in the conclusion; therefore the premise that the true chi square is zero is false. This implies that some relation exists between educational level and employment level.

This hypothesis, while verified, is "elliptical"; that is, a certain amount of the content is unstated. Precisely what the relationship is was not stated. Suppose, for example, that our hypothesis asserted that a specific pattern existed; that grade school graduates tended to be foremen and supervisors and that college graduates tended to be executives. In such a case if it turned out that high school graduates tended to be executives and college graduates tended to be supervisors we could reject the null hypothesis and still be unable to accept the alternative. This means that for a rigorous test, the content of the alternative must be stated before the test. This, in turn, means that the alternatives must have real theoretical importance prior to a test. Unless this is done the *content* of the verified hypothesis is *ad hoc* and still must be subject to empirical verification.

STATISTICS

1. Prediction and Correlation

The idea of linear relations can be developed from two somewhat different strategies. The first one is that of hypothesis testing and the second one is that of prediction. The arithmetic operations are quite the same. The difference is mainly in interpretation and what scientific activity one wants to perform. To those who feel that the goal of science is to predict, the development through prediction probably makes the most sense. However, to those of us who feel that the goal of science is the development of a theory, of which prediction is one kind of empirical test, the argument through hypothesis building is preferred. Above all the student ought not think that the two are so different as to require a choice. Both have their proper place in statistical thinking. No well-trained person can afford to ignore either; the operation which one chooses to emphasize depends ultimately on his view of science. Biases are exposed in favor of theory building. An orientation to prediction can lead to a narrow operationalism, whereas theory building at least forces the researcher into a broader perspective of his problem.

The concept of correlation, or of functional relation, has a strong appeal in scientific argument. If it can be shown that one quantitative variable varied with another quantitative variable, a functional relation is said to exist between them. The simplest function is that of a straight line, i.e., $Y = a + bX$, where a and b are constants.

The Line of Best Fit. The categorical logic we discussed in an earlier chapter does not exhaust the kind of relations of interest to sociology as a science. In this aspect of statistical assertion we are concerned with quantitative statements and how they are related.

In particular we are concerned with the situation in which both the problematic data statement and the explanatory statement involve quantities. Our problem at this point is not how to obtain measurements which give us quantities. Strictly speaking, measurement is more of a theoretical problem than a statistical one. Our concern here is with developing testable hypotheses given the fact that our data are indeed mensurable.

If we have a variable such that the *mean* makes sense, our problem resides in how to explain the variation that is attached. Note that the mean makes sense only if there is variation which is not too skewed. Highly skewed data are not well represented by the mean. If there were no variation and the mean was literally a constant, there would be no problem; no matter what other variable one wanted to associate with the problematic datum, the answer would be the same. For example, if Y has a constant value, $Y = 6$, and taking another variable Z with values 1, 2, and 3, we would have to assert the following: if $Z = 1$, then $Y = 6$; if $Z = 2$, then $Y = 6$; and if $Z = 3$, then $Y = 6$. Such argumentation would make nonsense—there would be no problem.

If, however, Y is indeed a variable, then we can seek some other variable such that the variation in one is at least associated with variation in the other. If their associated relationship could be described by a mathematical function, knowing the value of one X we could deduce (or predict) the value of the other. Thus, if $Y = 2 + 3X$, then if $X = 1$, $Y = 5$; if $X = 2$, then $Y = 8$; and so on.

X	0	1	2	3	4
Y	2	5	8	11	14

In scientific research the hypothesis might be simply that a straight-line function exists, but the values of the constants must be computed from the data. Thus, the data for pairs of X's and Y's might be that of above, and some way for inferring the values of a and b must be known. The determination of these constant terms is the problem of "fitting a straight line" to a set of data.

The problem is solved in the following equations:

$$b = \frac{N\Sigma XY - \Sigma X \Sigma Y}{N\Sigma X^2 - (\Sigma X)^2} \tag{29}$$

and

$$a = M_y - bM_x. \tag{30}$$

The subscripts denote which variable is being considered. From (29) we can see how to set up a computational table for the determination of the constant terms. We need (1) the sum of the X values; (2) the sum of the Y values; (3) the sum of the cross-products, i.e., the sum of the values found by multiplying each X by its corresponding Y; and (4) the square of the X's, and the sum of those squares. Later, we will need the square of the Y's and the sum of those squares.

Let's see whether or not (29) and (30) will give us the constant terms

TABLE 5.13. ILLUSTRATION OF TABLE FOR COMPUTATION
OF CONSTANTS IN LINEAR EQUATION $Y = a + bX$

X^2	X	Y	XY
0	0	2	0
1	1	5	5
4	2	8	16
9	3	11	33
16	4	14	56
30	10	40	110

Source: From Table 5.12.

of the equation $Y = a + b(X)$. Table 5.13 is set up to give the required
information.

From Table 5.13, we find:

$$N = 5$$
$$\Sigma X = 10$$
$$\Sigma Y = 40$$
$$\Sigma XY = 110$$
$$\Sigma X^2 = 30.$$

Inserting these in (29), we obtain

$$b = \frac{5\,(110) - (10)\,(40)}{5\,(30) - (10)^2} = 3.$$

The mean of the Y values is easily found to be 8 and the mean of the X's
is found to be 2. Inserting these, with the value of b found above, into
(30), we find,

$$a = 8 - (3)\,(2) = 2.$$

These values are the same ones used in the earlier example. While we
have not proved anything in particular the student should have confidence that the equations work.

The Range of Predictive Error. If a functional relation between two
variables exists, and persists through historical time, the question can
be used for predictive purposes. That is, if the equation $Y = 2 + 3X$
was and is "true," for future values of X corresponding values of Y could
be predicted. The accuracy of the prediction could be used to test the
correctness of the constant terms as well as the line itself.

The issue can be seen graphically. On the X-axis the X-values are
given; on the Y-axis the Y-values are given. The corresponding points for
the pairs of values (X, Y) are then plotted and these points connected by
a straight line. Notice, particularly, that a one-one correspondence exists
between the X- and Y-values in the illustration. In such a case there is
presumably no predictive error.

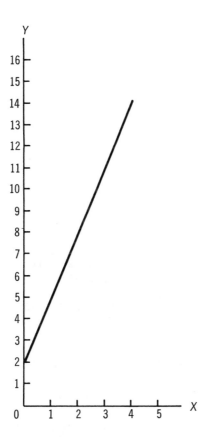

Figure 5.9. Graph of a linear function, $Y = 2 + 3X$.

This situation seldom, if ever, exists in social science research. Generally, there is no unique correspondence between X- and Y-values; for any given X-value several Y-values may be associated. A more realistic example would be the relationship between age at first marriage for husbands and wives. The data would look like this:

Before we calculate the line of best fit we could plot the paired values of X's and Y's. Letting the husbands' ages be the X-values and the wives' ages be the Y-values, we would make a "scatter diagram" (Figure 5.10). Note that for any X-value, more than one Y-value is given. Apparently, no straight line can connect all the points.

However, there seems to be a "linear trend." The equations (29) and (30) will give the *best possible straight line* in the sense that the deviations from the empirical points to the line will be as small as possible. We will later compute the values for a and b; now, we should reflect on the fact that, whatever the line will be, there will be deviations from it. This

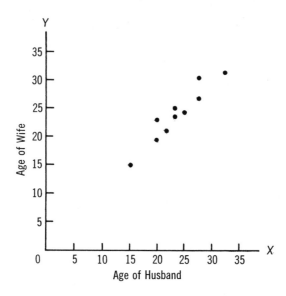

Figure 5.10. Scatter diagram for data in Table 5.13. The trend seems quite linear.

means that the equation for the line will predict only the most likely values of Y for given values of X.

Just as we sought a measure of variation around the mean when we estimated the parameter, we want a measure of variation around the line. The smaller the variation around the line, the smaller the predictive error. With the proper measure of variation we could estimate the bands around the line within which 95% of the values would fall. This measure is called "scatter," and is found by the equation,

$$S_y = \sqrt{\frac{\Sigma Y^2 - a\Sigma Y - b\Sigma XY.}{N}} \qquad (31)$$

When (31) has been calculated a predictive equation stating the amount of expected variation would be, for 95% confidence,

$$Y = a + bX \pm 2S.$$

The calculations below use the data in Table 5.14 to illustrate fitting a line and estimating scatter. Note that the table is constructed to give us all the necessary information. Since scatter involves a knowledge of the constants a and b, we will compute them first.

TABLE 5.14. AGE AT FIRST MARRIAGE FOR TEN COUPLES

Husband X	Wife Y
18	15
21	20
22	23
23	22
25	24
25	25
27	25
30	31
30	28
35	32

Source: Hypothetical.

$$b = \frac{(10)\,(6492) - (256)\,(245)}{(10)\,(6782) - (256)^2} = .9632$$

$$a = 24.5 - (.9632)\,(25.6) = -0.158$$

$$S^2{}_y = \frac{6233 - (-0.158)\,(245) - (.9632)\,(6492)}{10}$$

$$= \frac{6233 + 38.7 - 6253}{10}$$

$$= 1.87; S_y = \sqrt{1.87} = 1.37$$

$$\sigma_y{}^2 = \frac{6233}{10} - \frac{(245)^2}{100} = 23.05$$

$$Y = -0.158 + (.9632) \pm 2\,(1.37)$$

It should not be imagined that a and b are always positive. They both may be negative, or one negative and one positive. When Y decreases as X increases, b, the slope of the line, will be negative.

The Amount of Correlation. We may restate the problem of correlation from prediction to explanation. In the latter case, the basic observation is twofold: first, the arithmetic mean of the Y-values has to make sense; not only must an average be taken, but the distribution must be at least approximately normal. If all of the values are bunched toward either extreme (in which case we speak of the distribution being skewed), the median or the mode may be a better average. The second aspect of the problematic observation is the variation which is present. If all of the Y-values had the same value, there would be no problem. As one would guess, the amount of variation in Y can be measured by variance.

It is this variation we seek to explain. The fundamental hypothesis of linear correlation is that the amount of variation in Y is reduced by the introduction of X. If the X-value completely determined the Y-value, we would have a perfect fit. If, as in the example from sociological research, the line is not perfect but some scatter is present, X is not the sole determinant of the Y-values.

The variation of the Y-values around the line is measured by scatter. Clearly, scatter measures the variation of Y not associated with X. The ratio of scatter to the variance of Y is the percent of the variance of Y not associated with X. The percent of variance which is associated with X must be the difference between the percent which is not associated and 100%.

TABLE 5.15. AGE AT FIRST MARRIAGE: ARRANGED TO COMPUTE
LINEAR REGRESSION AND CORRELATION

Husband X	Wife Y	X^2	Y^2	XY
18	15	324	225	270
21	20	441	400	420
22	23	484	529	506
23	22	529	484	506
25	24	625	576	600
25	25	625	625	625
27	25	729	625	675
30	31	900	961	930
30	28	900	784	840
35	32	1225	1024	1120
Total 256	245	6782	6233	6492

Source: From Table 5.14.

Denoting the amount of correlation by r^2, the percent of the variance of Y which is associated with X is defined by,

$$r^2 = 1 - \frac{S_y{}^2}{\sigma_y{}^2} . \qquad (32)$$

To obtain r^2 we simply insert the values for scatter and variance of Y in (32) and obtain,

$$r^2 = 1 - \frac{1.87}{23.05} = .919.$$

However, r^2 can be obtained from a computational formula which does not involve the actual computation of either scatter or variance of Y. Using the same symbols as before,

$$r^2 = \frac{(N\Sigma XY - \Sigma X\Sigma Y)^2}{[N\Sigma X^2 - (\Sigma X)^2] \quad [N\Sigma Y^2 - (\Sigma Y)^2]} . \tag{33}$$

From Table 5.15 we obtain the needed numbers and compute r^2 to be, as before,

$$r^2 = \frac{[(10)\,(6492) - (256)\,(245)]^2}{[(10)\,(6782) - (256)^2] \quad [(10)\,(6233) - (245)^2]}$$

$$= \frac{(2200)^2}{(2284)\,(2305)}$$

$$= .919.$$

2. Correlation and Measurement

The sociologist is often in the situation in which his conceptual scheme is far ahead of his measurements. Indeed, he may feel that his scaling procedures simply give him a "first approximation" to the best assignment of numbers. He may feel that his scaling, though highly loaded with his major dimension, is also loaded with a lot of other things and he can't measure the extent to which random error is mixed in.

What, then, is the problem in respect to interpreting correlation? Recall the formula for correlation:

$$r = \frac{N\Sigma XY - \Sigma X\Sigma Y}{\sqrt{N\Sigma X^2 - (\Sigma X)^2}\ \sqrt{N\Sigma Y^2 - (\Sigma Y)^2}}.$$

Part of the difficulty lies in the fact that there are dimensions, X and Y. If both measures were equally inflated with error the interpretation would be simpler. If, however, both were identically involved with error (such that if the score was made larger for both X and Y in similar increments, or made lower similarly), the correlation would be inflated.

Assuming that the error is not, in itself, correlated between the two measures but is random in both, the consequence is simply that, if anything, the correlation is likely to be dampened. Any random error would result in an over estimation of variance making the denominator inflated and implying a deflation of the ratio. A random error would affect the sum of the cross products similarly so that the ratio would be a bit lessened.

However, if one of the measures was more affected than the other by random error, the interpretation would be more difficult. It would not be immediately clear just what the consequence would be. Of course, it would be much like the case of randomness in both.

For this reason, one often finds it more convenient to shift his data to z-scores. The z-score, you will recall, consisted of a mean deviate divided by its standard error. Note what happens to the slope of the line:

In mean deviate form, where $y = Y - \overline{Y}$ and $x = X - \overline{X}$

$$r^2 = \frac{(\Sigma xy)^2}{\Sigma x^2 \Sigma y^2} \,.$$

Note that $\frac{\Sigma x^2}{\Sigma x^2} = 1$, and any number multiplied by 1 is itself.

$$r^2 = \frac{(\Sigma xy)^2 \Sigma x^2}{(\Sigma y^2)\,(\Sigma x^2)^2} \,.$$

In mean deviate form this is,

$$b = \frac{\Sigma xy}{\Sigma x^2}$$

and thus,

$$b^2 = \frac{(\Sigma xy)^2}{(\Sigma x^2)^2}$$

$$r^2 = b^2 \frac{\Sigma x^2}{\Sigma y^2}$$

Since

$$\Sigma x^2 = N\sigma^2$$

$$r^2 = b^2 \frac{N\sigma_x^2}{N\sigma_y^2}$$

Extracting the square root we have,

$$r = \frac{b\sigma_x}{\sigma_y}$$

and solving for b,

$$b = \frac{r\sigma_y}{\sigma_x} \,.$$

In the linear equation, expressed as mean deviates,

$$y = bx$$

so that,

$$y = \left(\frac{r\sigma_y}{\sigma_x}\right) x.$$

Dividing both sides by σ_y results in,

$$\frac{y}{\sigma_y} = \frac{rx}{\sigma_x}$$

which, you will recognize, is a "z-score notation,"

$$z_y = rz_x.$$

In this case, the slope of the line equals the correlation, and is often denoted β (read, beta);

$$z_y = \beta z_x.$$

In this notation the predictive argument is cleaner and one is enabled to see more clearly the preceding argument on the inflation of variance with error. The implication seems to be quite clear—we ought not worry too much about measurement error. This is especially true in the case of using correlation simply to test a hypothesis regarding the existence of some relation between two measures.

3. Analysis of Variance

The Basic Problem. From our discussion of correlation, the student will recognize the general character of the problem. If we have a dependent variable which is quantitative in character, the variation present can be described in terms of variance. The problem is to explain, in some sense, the variance. Further, in linear correlation the basic hypothesis was that the amount of variance could be effectively reduced by correlating the dependent variable with another variable, X.

Recall that a quantitative variable can be *reduced* to categories. Also, note that a hypothetical independent variable may, conceptually, be categorical in nature. For example, if we wanted to explain variation in delinquency rates we may conceive of "types of childhood training" as an independent variable. Certainly, such a variable is categorical in nature. We may also wish to avoid the implications of linearity. We may feel that the relation between the dependent and independent variable may be curved rather than a simple straight line.

Analysis of variance is a technique which essentially takes into account the above possibilities. The independent variable is "categorized." Let us recall the general formula for the sum of squares used in variance. For later convenience we will introduce some new symbols. The general symbol for each number appearing as the independent variable will be X_{ij}. The subscript j refers to the column of the independent variable in which the X's are cross-tabulated. The subscript i will refer to which one of the X's in the j column reference is being made. The mean of all X_{ij}'s will be denoted as $\overline{X}$, to distinguish it from the mean of a column which will be denoted $\overline{X}_j$.

Using these symbols, the sum of squares for variance is written,

$$\Sigma(X_{ij} - X)^2. \tag{34}$$

It is an algebraic rule that we can add zero to any quantity we want, and the quantity remains the same. If we add and subtract the same quantity, we are really adding zero to the old quantity. If we add and subtract X_j to (34), we obtain,

$$\Sigma(X_{ij} - \overline{X}_j + \overline{X}_j - \overline{X})^2. \tag{35}$$

By simple algebraic manipulation this becomes,

$$\Sigma(X_{ij} - \overline{X}_j)^2 + \Sigma(\overline{X}_j - \overline{X})^2. \tag{36}$$

The importance of (36) lies in the fact that we can see that the total variance is made up of two sources of variance. One is the variation of the column values around the column mean. This is the term $\Sigma(X_{ij} - \overline{X}_j)^2$ in (36). The other source is the variation of the column means around the grand mean. This is the remaining term, $\Sigma(\overline{X}_j - \overline{X})^2$, in (36).

Both of these terms can be used to estimate variance. These are only "sums of squares." When divided by the degrees of freedom, sums of squares can be used to estimate variance since they are of the form of equation (6). The question becomes, do they estimate the same thing? If they both estimate the same thing, the introduction of the independent variable has not reduced the observable variance. In other words, the independent variable does not explain any of the variation in the dependent variable. On the other hand, if they are estimating different variances, we have effectively reduced the variance in the dependent variable and the independent variable is real.

Instead of testing for significance of differences as one might suppose, we take a ratio of the between column estimate to the within column estimate of variance. This ratio is called the "F-ratio." For given degrees of freedom, if there is no difference between the two estimates, the laws of probability will explain some variation. Hence, after selecting the level of confidence, one argues in the general null hypothesis manner, viz., for the given degrees of freedom at the .05 level of confidence, if chance explains the difference, the F-ratio will be less than some number.

TABLE 5.16. SELECTED VALUES FOR F-RATIOS
AT .05 LEVEL OF SIGNIFICANCE

d.f. for Denominator	d.f. for Numerator					
	1	2	3	4	5	12
1	161.00	200.00	216.00	225.00	230.00	244.00
2	18.51	19.00	19.16	19.25	19.30	19.41
3	10.13	9.55	9.28	9.12	9.01	8.74
4	7.71	6.94	6.59	6.39	6.26	5.91
5	6.61	5.79	5.41	5.19	5.05	4.68
10	4.96	4.10	3.71	3.48	3.33	2.91
15	4.54	3.68	3.29	3.06	2.90	2.48
20	4.35	3.49	3.10	2.87	2.71	2.28
24	4.26	3.40	3.01	2.78	2.62	2.18
25	4.24	3.38	2.99	2.76	2.60	2.16
30	4.17	3.32	2.92	2.69	2.53	2.09
40	4.08	3.23	2.84	2.61	2.45	2.00
60	4.00	3.15	2.76	2.52	2.37	1.92
∞	3.84	2.99	2.60	2.37	2.21	1.75

Source: Table 5.16 is taken from Table 5 of Fisher and Yates: *Statistical Tables for Biological, Agricultural and Medical Research*, published by Oliver & Boyd Ltd., Edinburgh, and by permission of the authors and publishers.

It happens that both the numerator and denominator of the F-ratios have a chi-square distribution. The chi-square distribution is a function of the degree of freedom. For that reason, the F-table must take into account the degrees of freedom of the numerator and the denominator. Certain selected values are presented in Table 5.16. The entire table is for the .05 level of confidence; if the F-ratio is equal to or greater than the number found, the null hypothesis is rejected. The first row of the table labeling the different columns designates the degrees of freedom in the numerator. The first column labeling the rows designates the degrees of freedom in the denominator. Thus, if the numerator has 12 degrees of freedom, and the denominator has 30, the F-ratio at the 5% level is found to be 2.09.

The analysis of variance technique is not without its restrictions. These restrictions exist in the assumptions made in the derivation of the F-ratio. Although we did not make the derivation here, the assumptions must be known. The distribution of the X_{ij} values for each column is presumed to be a sample drawn from a population denoted to the jth category (column). The j samples are assumed to be random, independent of each other, normally distributed, and having the same variance. This latter assumption is called the "homoscedasticity"; since the within-column variances are averaged for all the columns, wide variation in column variances could not be tolerated.

One-way Classification. We will here give the computational set-up for analysis of variance with one independent variable. The symbols are the same as in the preceding section. Numerical examples will be given in Chapters 6 and 7. The dependent variable, symbolized by X_{ij}, is sorted out into m columns (i.e., $j = 1, 2, \ldots, m$). There are n values in each column. Thus $N = nm$. Observe, in particular, the row denoting column totals (X_j).

TABLE 5.17. DUMMY TABLE FOR ANALYSIS OF VARIANCE

Treatments			
1	2	$\ldots$	m
X_{11}	X_{12}	$\ldots$	X_{1m}
X_{21}	X_{22}	$\ldots$	X_{2m}
.	.	.	.
.	.	.	.
.	.	.	.
X_{n1}	X_{n2}	$\ldots$	X_{nm}
$X_{.1}$	$X_{.2}$	$\ldots$	X_m

For convenience in making computations an Analysis of Variance Table is constructed. This table indicates the source of variance and its equational equivalent. The degrees of freedom and the mean square obtained by dividing the sum of squares by the degree of freedom is shown. Finally, a column indicating the F-ratio to be taken is indicated. This, in turn, indicates how to set up a computational table by showing precisely what data are needed.

TABLE 5.18. ANALYSIS OF VARIANCE

Source	Sum of Squares	d.f.	Mean Square	F
Total	$\Sigma X_i{}^2{}_j - \dfrac{(\Sigma X_{ij})^2}{N}$	$N - 1$		
Between	$\Sigma X.{}^2{}_j - \dfrac{(\Sigma X_{ij})^2}{n}$	$M - 1$	$\dfrac{\dfrac{\Sigma X.{}^2{}_j}{n} - \dfrac{(\Sigma X_{ij})^2}{N}}{M - 1}$	$\dfrac{\dfrac{\Sigma X.{}^2{}_j}{n} - \dfrac{(\Sigma X_{ij})^2}{N}}{M - 1}$
Within	$\Sigma X_i{}^2{}_j - \dfrac{\Sigma X.{}^2{}_j}{n}$	$N - M$	$\dfrac{\Sigma X_i{}^2{}_j - \dfrac{\Sigma X.{}^2{}_j}{n}}{N - M}$	$\dfrac{\Sigma X_i{}^2{}_j - \dfrac{\Sigma X.{}^2{}_j}{n}}{N - M}$

From the analysis of variance table, we observe that we need (1) the square of each item summed $(\Sigma X_{ij})^2$; (2) the sum of each item squared $(\Sigma X_{ij}{}^2)$; (3) the square of each column total summed for the m columns $(\Sigma X^2._j)$; (4) the number of items in each column (n); and (5) the total number in the table (N).

The computational table would then be,

TABLE 5.19. COMPUTATIONAL TABLE FOR ANALYSIS OF VARIANCE

		Treatments				
	1		2	...	M	
	X_{11}	$X_{11}{}^2$	X_{12}	$X_{12}{}^2$	... X_{1m}	$X_{1m}{}^2$
	X_{21}	$X_{21}{}^2$	X_{22}	$X_{22}{}^2$	X_{2m}	$X_{2m}{}^2$
	.	.	.	.	.	.
	.	.	.	.	.	.
	.	.	.	.	.	.
Column totals	$X._1$	$(X^2)._1$	$X._2$	$(X^2)._2$	$X._m$	$(X)^2._m$
Square of $X._1$	$(X._1)^2$		$(X._2)^2$		$(X._m)^2$	

4. Summary

One of the major tasks of science is to reach a decision regarding a proposition. We have learned that under special conditions statistics allow us to make decisions about a particular kind of proposition. The fundamental task of statistical inference is to enable one to decide whether an observed variation is explicable by the laws of probability, or if it must be explained by some other influencing factor.

The steps in this learning process are, despite new word symbols, quite direct. The first task is to make a frequency distribution and to graph it. The graph has the characteristic of having correspondence. We then modify "frequency" into "relative frequency," showing that the area and the frequency associated with that area to be in one-to-one ratio, and relative frequency becomes "probability." Thus a graph of probabilities would enable us to estimate probabilities.

After formally defining probability and various rules for combining probabilities, we observed that the binomial $p + q$ could be expanded into a series which could be graphed. Hence we could use the graph to estimate probabilities. Then we noted the similarity between the graph of the binomial and the normal curve. Under the general assumptions of normality and random sampling, the normal curve could be used to measure probabilities.

Thus the probable occurrence of any statistics having a normal distribution could be estimated. Some major statistics having such a distribution are means, differences between means, proportions, and differences between proportions. Knowledge of the probable occurrence of a statistic provides a basis for judging whether or not the event is too rare to be attributable to chance. This involves a prior agreement as to the range of error, or confidence limits, one wants to employ.

Two other major types of distribution, with essentially the same argument, are the chi-square and F distributions. The former allows one to draw inferences about a statistic called "chi square" and the latter allows inferences about the ratio of two estimations of variance. The latter estimation is fundamental to analysis of variance.

Another significant statistical argument is that of correlation. Again, the problem is that of variation. As in analysis of variance, linear regression can start with variance as a measure of variance. Utilizing the argument of concomitant variation, the general hypothesis is that the dependent variable is a linear function of another variable. Equations for obtaining the best constants from a set of empirical data are given. Variation around the resulting line allows for two things: first, to give a range of predictive error and second, to measure the percent of the original variance which is not associated with the introduction of the independent variable.

As a closing comment, the student should be reminded that no statistical technique can improve upon poor data. Further, each statistical equation implies a solution to some problem. Prior to using any statistic, one must make certain that the problem solved by the equation is relevant to the research problem at hand.

SELECTED REFERENCES

Clark, Charles E., *An Introduction to Statistics,* New York, Wiley, 1953.

Hagwood, Margaret J., and Daniel O. Price, *Statistics for Sociologists,* rev. ed., New York, Holt, Rinehart and Winston, 1952.

Jackson, Robert W. B., and Palmer O. Johnson, *Introduction to Statistical Methods,* Englewood Cliffs, N.J., Prentice-Hall, 1953.

Lev, Joseph, and Helen M. Walker, *Statistical Inference,* New York, Holt, Rinehart and Winston, 1953.

McCormick, Thomas C., *Elementary Social Statistics,* New York, McGraw-Hill, 1941.

6
John T. Doby

PRINCIPLES OF EXPERIMENTATION

1. INTRODUCTION

We indicated in Chapters 2 and 4 that the process of scientific explanation involved the *construction* of concepts and theories which would allow for a logical deduction of the empirical facts to be explained and would at the same time be consistent with other established, related facts and theories. This means that concept specification and theory construction must meet the requirements of logical and empirical adequacy.[1]

The purpose of experimentation or any other major scientific method is to facilitate the advancement of scientific knowledge. This, of course, does not mean that any particular experiment is necessarily good or even well designed, or that only experimental data contributes to the advancement of science. The Michelson-Morley experiment in the late 1870's was one of the greatest experiments of all time, and its results were negative. Nevertheless, these results led Albert Einstein to formulate Relativity Theory in 1905. Experimentation and measurement are each guided by theory. Hence, an accurate measurement as well as an adequate experiment depend upon precisely formulated concepts and theories. Whether or not an experiment is conducted on human behavior depends less on the characteristics of human behavior than on the imaginativeness of the researcher and the adequacies of his theoretical formulations which enable him to conceive appropriate empirical matter to experiment upon.

It is clear that a principal reason why one sees so few experiments in the social sciences is that these abound with theories that are not really theories. For example, role theory, social change theory, social organization theory, and reference group theory among others, are cases of crude

This chapter is an adaptation of Chapter 12 of the author's *Introduction to Social Psychology*, New York, Appleton-Century-Crofts, 1966.

[1] See C. G. Hempel and P. Oppenheim, "The Logic of Explanation" in H. Feigl and M. Brodbeck, eds., *Readings in the Philosophy of Science*, New York, Appleton-Century-Crofts, 1953, p. 323.

generalizations based on imprecisely formulated clusters of concepts. If the concepts and theories are not clearly and precisely formulated, it is difficult if not impossible to effectively experiment. In other words, experimentation or any other kind of good research presupposes something to be observed, counted, or measured and, unless we know what that something is, no indexing or measuring can have any significance.

The chapter which follows is concerned with some applications of experimentation in the social sciences. Therefore, this chapter will concern itself with some elementary principles.

It is assumed that the student has already learned a good deal about this subject in introductory psychology and in introductory courses in the natural and physical sciences; the principles of experimentation should not be entirely new to him. Then why is the subject treated here by way of a single chapter if the student has already been exposed to many of the ideas? First, the training in principles of experimentation which the student receives in all the other courses which represent empirical science are principally aimed at orienting the student for *those* disciplines, but somehow the student fails to understand that the logic of science and the general principles of experimentation are common to *all* empirical science and what is different are the *techniques* of application of these principles. In other words, transfer of training does not successfully occur.

Secondly, a given field of science tends to *emphasize* particular aspects of the general principles of experimentation and, therefore, some specific attention must be given to the principles and techniques which will help the student better understand the empirical procedures and findings of the field under study at the moment.

In summary, then, this chapter is not intended as the student's first introduction to the subject, but instead it aims (1) to remind the student that what he has already learned in this area is relevant but must now be refocused to the context of social behavior, and (2) to provide selected techniques which will be helpful in understanding the empirical procedures and findings of social psychology and sociology.

The experimental method more nearly approximates the ideal application of the logic of science than any other method in scientific use. Loosely speaking, it can be said that the experimental method is the concrete embodiment of the ideal logical structure of science. The adequacy or degree of approximation of a given experimental design to the ideal logical model of experimental inference depends upon many things. Among these are the state of development of the theory and the adequacy of the instruments of observation within the field. These instruments may range all the way from paper-and-pencil tests to elaborately contrived hardware. It might also be added that the most important ingredient is the imagination and cleverness of the scientist himself. Furthermore, the methods and procedures for experimentation are themselves constantly undergoing evolution and improvement. For example, the classical form of the ideal experiment was to hold constant all the independent variables except the one which the investigator was interested in testing. He would systematically vary it and observe the effect on the dependent variable or outcome factor. Usually, the method of holding constant was by means of direct manipulation, such as controlling the temperature of a gas or the amount of certain chemicals included in a solution.

It does not take much imagination to detect the shortcomings of this early idealized form of experimentation. Suppose that a factor under study functions jointly with another factor. The investigator would probably conclude that it was not significant. If his procedures only allowed for varying one factor at a time, then it is unlikely that he could have discovered joint effects since to do so would assume that he could simultaneously vary at least two factors. Thus, one of the major shortcomings of the traditional experimental model was that it could not deal successfully with multiple factors.[2]

Another difficulty was the implicit assumption that control of the variables depended upon some form of direct manipulation. For example, this sort of reasoning suggests that one would have to manipulate the moon itself, in order to observe its effects upon the earth. Why not simply assume that it is not necessary for the investigator to control the moon in order to scientifically study its effects on the earth. Why not, as a beginning, simply observe the properties of the moon and the earth, say the tides, which vary together. This is commonly called *concomitant variation*. It is the degree to which two factors or a set of factors vary together in a way predicted by an hypothesis. Such occurrences are the basic raw materials of any science. In Chapter 4 we labeled such occurrences as empirical regularities or uniformities. These regularities are the realities of nature with which the scientist is concerned. For example, temperature X varies with altitude Y and human attitudes A vary with amount of education B. In other words, the fundamental basis for experimental inference is that one must first have established a concomitant relationship between two or more variables.

In order to establish concomitant variation it is not necessary to attempt direct manipulation as in the oversimplified classical notion. All that is necessary is for the relationship to be so defined as to enable the investigator to at least *count* the instances of occurrence or, preferably, to measure the units of observation.

2. SETS AND FUNCTIONS

The units under observation are determined by the variables under investigation. One variable may be deviant behavior and the researcher may be trying to connect this variable with some environmental property,

---

[2] It should be pointed out that one of the principal reasons for this was that the mathematics necessary for multiple factor analysis were not available in that era.

let us say, social stress. The units under observation would be the specifications of deviant behavior and the specifications for stress. With two
factors under observation the units will be in pairs or sets of two. A collection of objects or items is designated in the language of mathematics as
a "set." A set is usually represented by the capital letter S. There exist
infinite sets, the number of whose elements is unbounded. Our concern,
however, will be with *finite* sets, namely those having exactly n elements
for some nonnegative integer n. For example, consider the sets of four
aces in a deck of cards (diamonds, hearts, spades, clubs), or the set of two
letters in the alphabet (a, b). These sets have *four* elements and *two* elements, respectively. Some finite sets are very small and some are very
large. The set of all housewives in America is quite large and the set of all
living presidents of the United States is very small. In statistical theory as
well as general mathematics we find considerable use for a subset called
the "empty" or "null" set. By way of illustration let us consider all subsets
of the five-element set of five true-false examination questions. There is
one empty subset (no question answered correctly). It is generally designated by ϕ. This set should not be confused with the set {0} which contains
one object, namely, the integer 0. There are five subsets consisting of one
element (one question answered correctly). There are ten subsets consisting of two elements, that is, two questions answered correctly, and so
on. The total number of possible elements or ways would be 2^5 or 32.
Let S be the total set of 32 ways. The empty set would be the subset of
five questions all of which were answered wrong, that is, the subset where
none is answered correctly. There is obviously only one such subset. The
students who remember the binomial theorem will recognize that these
numbers are the coefficients of the powers of x from 0 to 5 in the expansion of $(1 + x)^5$.

A set B is a subset of a set A if every element of B is an element of A.
This is symbolized as, $B \subset A$. This may be read as, B is contained in A.
If $A = (a, b, c)$ and $B = (b, c)$ then $B \subset A$. But, every set is a subset of
itself, $A \subset A$, since each of its elements is contained in the set. In scientific research we are more likely to be concerned with a subset that does
not contain all of the elements of the other set. Such a set is called a
"proper" set and is defined as follows: a set B is a proper subset of a set A
if every element of B is an element of A, but not every element of A is an
element of B. Thus, in the true-false test example above, the set of no
correct answers, the empty set, ϕ, is a subset of A.

Sets may be combined in several ways. Let $X = (X_1, X_2, \ldots, X_{10})$
and $Y = (Y_1, Y_2, \ldots, Y_{10})$. These two sets may be arranged in a square
table such as Table 6.1.

The pair of elements (X_i, Y_j), formed as indicated in Table 6.1 is an
"ordered pair." It is ordered in the sense that the first member of the
pair is always an element of X and the second is always an element of Y.
Such a subset or ordered pair is a "relation." The relation will be called

TABLE 6.1. SCHEMATIC REPRESENTATION OF A TWO-WAY
CLASSIFICATION TABLE ILLUSTRATING A SET OF ORDERED PAIRS

x Set (Rows)	Y Set (Columns)							Row Means
	1	2	3	...	j	...	k	
1	X_{11}	X_{12}	X_{13}	...	X_{1j}	...	X_{1k}	$\overline{X}_{1.}$
2	X_{21}	X_{21}	X_{23}	...	X_{2j}	...	X_{2k}	$\overline{X}_{2.}$
3	X_{31}	X_{31}	X_{33}	...	X_{3j}	...	X_{3k}	$\overline{X}_{3.}$
.	.	.	.	.	.	.	.	.
.	.	.	.	...	.	...	.	.
.	.	.	.	.	.	.	.	.
i	X_{i1}	X_{i2}	X_{i3}	...	X_{ij}	...	X_{ik}	$\overline{X}_{i.}$
.	.	.	.	.	.	.	.	.
.	.	.	.	...	.	...	.	.
.	.	.	.	.	.	.	.	.
R	X_{R1}	X_{R2}	X_{R3}	...	X_{Rj}	...	X_{Rk}	$\overline{X}_{R.}$
Column Means	$\overline{X}_{.1}$	$\overline{X}_{.2}$	$\overline{X}_{.3}$	...	$\overline{X}_{.j}$	...	$\overline{X}_{.k}$	$\overline{X}$

a function if it is "single-valued," that is, if to each first coordinate there corresponds one, and only one, second coordinate. The set X is the "domain" of the function and the range of the function is contained in Y. The range of elements or values contained in Y may or may not consist of the whole set Y. Let us assume that Y refers to a population of people and X refers to intelligence quotient; for a given set of X values there is a given number of people with these IQ values, but this number may not be all the people with these IQ values.

Referring again to Table 6.1, R is the number of rows and k is the number of columns. Let us assume that the X variable refers to persons or individuals and that the Y variable refers to experimental conditions; then the score for the ith subject in the jth condition is X_{ij}. The mean score for the ith subject is represented by $\overline{X}_{i.}$, and the mean score for the ith experimental condition is represented by $X_{.j}$. The mean of all observations is represented by $\overline{X}$.

We accept the notation (X_i, Y_j) as representing an ordered pair in which X_i is called the "first coordinate" and Y_j is called the "second coordinate." The set of all first coordinates (in the ordered pairs) is called the "domain" of the function. The set of all second coordinates is called the "range" of the function. As indicated before, this assumes that for each first coordinate there is one and only one second coordinate. A look at Table 6.1 will show that this is the case in that table. This does not mean that any given pair must have only one frequency. For example, if the pair (X_{12}) represents an IQ of 100 and an age of 10, then there may be a large number of children in a given population who have an IQ of 100 and are age 10, but each child has one, and only one, IQ.

Recall that in Section 1 of this chapter we introduced the notion of concomitant variation. From the point of view of research, our interest in concomitant variation is in determining if the variation in Y is *dependent* on a variation in X.

3. BASES FOR ESTABLISHING THE EXISTENCE OF RELATIONSHIPS

How does a researcher determine if the variation in one variable is dependent upon one or more independent variables? As the preceding statement implies, we are using the term "dependent variable" to refer to the effect or outcome to be explained, and the independent variables as the factors for explaining the effect or dependent variable.

To answer the question that was just posed, let us begin by noting that there is no means of direct observation by which one can demonstrate that Y depends on X. Rather, we are *always* in a position of *inferring* a relation between a set of problematic data and a set of explanatory data. The degree of confidence in the inference may approach certainty; in fact, the scientist may be certain that X produces Y. Let us say that he has, by *controlled* observation, demonstrated this over and over again. Suppose we know that a certain virus, A, produces a certain kind of cold, B. But does it produce it every time it is present in a person? No, not necessarily; in other words, it produces it only under certain conditions and bodily states of the person. The existence of a relationship is dependent upon the *conditions* which contribute to, or intervene, in connection with the relationship. Thus, for these reasons alone, if we observe enough cases there will always be some discrepancy between actual outcomes and theoretically expected outcomes. There is always some error to be expected in prediction because the conditions of functioning are never *exactly* the same and there is, therefore, always some error. This is true irrespective of the field of science in question. One really can only say that the degree of confidence in a scientific inference can only *approach* certainty.

It might be added that there are other reasons by which such a conclusion is justified. One of these additional reasons is that irrespective of how refined a measuring instrument is, there are always further refinements that can be made. Another reason is that there is always some variation which results from sampling fluctuations. Therefore, one may always expect errors due to crudeness of measurement. But given whatever confidence we have in our inferences, what evidence is necessary to justify such inferences? In other words, if one wishes to test the hypothesis that the behavior of variable Y depends on the behavior of variable X, what does he have to establish in order to conclude that it does?

4. CONCOMITANT VARIATION

Perhaps the first and most obvious bit of necessary evidence is whether a change in X is accompanied by a change in Y. Assuming that it has been shown that a change in variable X is accompanied by a change in variable Y, at least four important questions may be asked about the covariance. (1) Does the variation in Y *depend* on the variation in X? (2) Is the variation in Y independent of the variation in X in the sense that both X and Y depend on some other variable or variables? (3) Are the variations in Y and X "joint functions," that is, do they interact? (4) Maybe Y and X are not related at all and the covariation observed in the sample is a chance event? How do we decide which of these four is correct? The answer to this question is a matter of experimental design and control. We shall now discuss a few ways which will enable us to answer these questions. Let us first take up the question of whether there is, in the first place, a covariation and if so, how much?

Simple Linear Correlation and Simple Regression. Suppose that we have a set of n pairs of values; we know each value of Y that is associated with each value of X and both measures are on the same individual or object. Therefore, we know that Y_1 and X_1 go together, Y_2 and X_2 go together, and so forth.

Suppose we have the following 10 hypothetical observations,

X	Y
0	1
1	3
2	5
3	7
4	9
5	11
6	13
7	15
8	17
9	19
10	21

It is noted that X and Y increase together and that the points with (X_i, Y_j) as coordinates, form a straight line.

From any two points on the line, we can find the rate of change of Y for a change in X. This is generally called the "slope" of the line in analytic geometry and the "difference quotient" in calculus.

It should be clear that if Y is related to X, a change in X should be accompanied by a change in Y. The slope or difference quotient is a measure of such change. This is given by,

$$\text{Slope} = \frac{Y_2 - Y_1}{X_2 - X_1}.$$

In the case of the hypothetical data indicated by the coordinates in Figure 6.1 below, the slope is,

$$\frac{15 - 11}{7 - 5} = \frac{4}{2} = 2.$$

This means that for a given unit change in X, Y changes two times this amount.

The equation is $Y = bX$ and the student should recognize this as the straight-line equation when the line passes through the zero point of origin of both the X and Y axes; b is a constant and is called the "regression coefficient" or slope as defined above. From now on we shall refer to it as the regression coefficient.

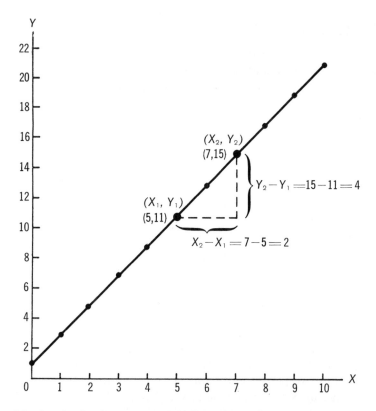

Figure 6.1. Graph of a linear or straight-line relationship.

When the point of origin or line of intercept of the Y axis is not at zero, the effect will be to introduce an additive constant into the formula $Y = bX$. This constant is denoted by a and is called the Y "intercept." In such a case we have two constants and the relation is described by the equation, $Y = a + bX$. Such is the case in the hypothetical data shown above. The student will note that when $X = 0$, $Y = 1$. Therefore, the formula which describes the relation between X and Y above is, $Y = 1 + 2X$.

The above data are "positively" related as Figure 6.1 indicates; that is to say, as X increases Y increases and the regression coefficient, b, is positive. Sometimes the regression coefficient is "negative" which means that as X increases Y decreases. The same general reasoning may be extended to include additional or multiple variables. This, of course, presupposes that the linear assumption still holds. If the relationship is curvilinear, then other techniques are called for.[3]

Notice in Figure 6.1 above that the curve completely describes the relationship in that all the points fall on the line. This is not often the case. Generally there is error or scatter around the line and the problem then is to determine the line of "best fit"; that is to say that the constants a and b must be calculated in such a manner that the error variance will be at a minimum. A suitable method for doing this is the method of *least-squares*.[4] This will not be illustrated here. However, a method for calculating a and b whether there is or is not error around the line will be given for "ungrouped" data; data which have only one value in an interval. This is the case with the data given above, except that there were not any errors in these data; that is, the curve represents a perfect fit of the data.

Suppose we have the following ten pairs of scores,

X	Y
6	11
4	8
3	2
7	15
8	17
2	7
5	4
4	7
3	4
5	9

[3] For the student who is interested in multiple variable relations he might begin with Philip H. DuBois, *Multivariate Correlational Analysis* New York, Harper & Row, 1957, and Mordecai Ezekiel, *Methods of Correlation Analysis,* 2nd ed. New York, Wiley, 1949.

[4] Ezekiel, *Ibid.,* p. 64.

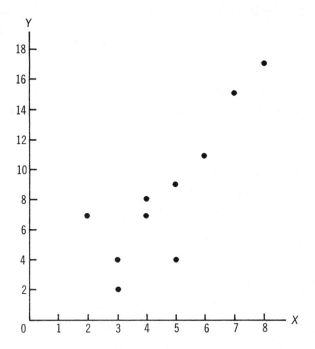

Figure 6.2. Estimating regression from imperfect data.

In plotting these data the degree of scatter or departure from a straight line will be apparent (Figure 6.2).

Obtaining a line of best fit for the above data involves a process of curve fitting which will minimize the quantity

$$\Sigma(Y - \tilde{Y})^2$$

where Y denotes the observed values of the dependent variable and $\tilde{Y}$ denotes the estimated values of the dependent variable as given by the regression equation,

$$\tilde{Y} = a + bX.$$

The constants a and b may be calculated directly from the raw scores of the X and Y variables.

For b we have,

$$b_{yx} = \frac{\Sigma XY - \dfrac{(\Sigma X)\,(\Sigma Y)}{N}}{\Sigma X^2 - \dfrac{(\Sigma X)^2}{N}}$$

where N is the total number of observations, which in the above example is 10.

For *a* we have,

$$a = \frac{\Sigma Y - b\Sigma X}{N}.$$

Obviously, if we divide Y and X by N we get the mean of Y and the mean of X, which yields the equivalent formula, $a = \overline{Y} - b\overline{X}$.[5]

It is clear that when the value of b has been obtained, a can then be derived, so we will calculate b first. To do so we will need the following table:

TABLE 6.2. CALCULATING TABLE FOR REGRESSION CONSTANTS
a AND *b* FOR UNGROUPED DATA

X	Y	X^2	Y^2	XY
6	11	36	121	66
4	8	16	64	32
3	2	9	4	6
7	15	49	225	105
8	17	64	289	136
2	7	4	49	14
5	4	25	16	20
4	7	16	49	28
3	4	9	16	12
5	9	25	81	45
Total 47	84	253	914	464

$$b = \frac{464 - \dfrac{(47)\,(84)}{10}}{253 - \dfrac{(47)^2}{10}} = \frac{69.2}{32.1} = 2.15,$$

and

$$a = \frac{84 - 2.15(47)}{10} = -1.71.$$

Recall the main idea of the regression coefficient as being the amount of change which occurs in a dependent variable, Y, per unit change in an independent variable, X. Let us take a further look at the intuitive meaning of the terms in the b formula in relation to the basic definition of b. Let $x = X - \overline{X}$ and $y = Y - \overline{Y}$, that is, letting x and y be *deviates from*

[5] A more detailed presentation of these is found in most introductory statistics textbooks. See, for example, Morris Zelditch, *A Basic Course in Sociological Statistics*, New York, Holt, Rinehart and Winston, 1959, pp. 96–98. Also review Chapter 5 of the present textbook.

their respective means, where the mean is defined as $\dfrac{\Sigma X}{N}$, then the point of intercept of the X on the Y axis is no longer at X equals zero, but shifts to the point of intersect of the means of the X and Y axes. On the basis of these definitions of x and y we can set up the following algebraic equalities of b_{YX} where the subscript $_{YX}$ means the regression or dependence of Y on X.

$$b_{YX} = \frac{\Sigma XY - \dfrac{(\Sigma X)(\Sigma Y)}{N}}{\Sigma X^2 - \dfrac{(\Sigma X)^2}{N}} = \frac{\Sigma XY - N(\overline{X})(\overline{Y})}{\Sigma X^2 - N(\overline{X})^2} = \frac{N\Sigma XY - \Sigma X\Sigma Y}{N\Sigma X^2 - (\Sigma X)^2}$$

$$= \frac{\Sigma xy}{\Sigma x^2}.$$ This latter is the main deviate form of b.

It is helpful to think of Σxy as the amount of covariance or varying together of X and Y. The term Σx^2 is the sum of the squared deviations from the mean which represents the variation of the independent variable alone, and $\dfrac{\Sigma xy}{\Sigma x^2}$ is the ratio of the varying together of X and Y to the variation of X alone. Hence, b is the measure of the amount of variation in Y which corresponds to a unit change in X.

Perhaps it should be recalled that the fact that two variables tend to increase or decrease together does not imply that one necessarily has any direct or indirect effect on the other. Both may be influenced by other variables so as to produce a strong mathematical relationship. The presence of a strong mathematical relationship is necessary to establish a functional dependence between two variables, but it is not sufficient. In other words, more information about the nature of the covariation is necessary before such a decision can be made. Of particular importance is information concerning the time order of the events; does the independent variable always precede the dependent variable in time, and when it does is it followed by the dependent variable or outcome? Also, when it is absent is the effect also absent? These questions imply a one to one relationship which is almost never the case. If more than one independent factor is involved or if interfering factors are uncontrolled, then, obviously, the one independent factor could not account for all the variation. In the case that multiple factors are involved, then a multiple correlation and regression analysis would be called for.[6] Another method for establishing concomitant variation is called the "Analysis of Variance" and was developed by the late professor, Sir Ronald A. Fisher.

[6] The student who is interested and who has the necessary mathematical background is invited to read the section on "Multiple Linear Regression" in Paul G. Hoel, *Introduction to Mathematical Statistics*, 3rd ed., 1962, New York, Wiley, 1962. Also, Mordecai Ezekiel, *Methods of Correlation Analysis*, 2nd ed., New York, Wiley, 1949.

5. ANALYSIS OF VARIANCE

Introduction. In most cases there are several variables in addition to the ones which the investigator has controlled which need to be controlled if the research design is to yield fruitful and valid results. In some cases these interfering variables can be controlled by laboratory means, but others can be controlled, and are often only possible to control, through the use of statistical designs. We wish to briefly introduce two principles which are fundamental to statistical designs which have as their aim the improving of the process of drawing inferences from experimental results. These principles are called "randomization" and "replication." Let us now consider their meaning. A good example of the use of these is provided by Hoel:

Consider an agricultural experiment in which two different seed varieties are to be tested on a piece of land. If the piece of land were divided into two equal pieces and one variety planted on each, the difference in yields could not be used as a valid estimate of the differential effect of the two seed varieties, because of the possible difference in the soil fertility of the two pieces.

Experiments can often be made valid by applying the principles of *randomization* and *replication*. Thus, in the present illustration, if the piece of land were divided into a number of small plots of equal size, and if one variety of seed were planted on half of these plots and the other variety on the remaining half, with the selection of the plots for each variety determined by a random process, then the varying fertility of the land would affect the two varieties approximately equally and therefore the difference in varietal yields would represent a valid estimate of the differential effects of the two seed varieties.

Randomization by itself is not necessarily sufficient to yield a valid experiment. For example, if one merely tossed a coin to determine which half of the original piece of land should be planted with one of the seed varieties, the selection would be random but it would not permit the two seed varieties to be equally affected by any varying soil fertility. If the two seed varieties were equally productive but the two halves of land were markedly different in fertility, then regardless of which seed variety was selected for each half, the conclusion would invariably be that the seed varieties differed in productivity. In order to insure validity, it would be necessary that the piece of land be divided into a sufficiently large number of similar plots so that the probability of having one of the seed varieties largely located on the more fertile plots will be very small. This repetition of an experiment or experimental unit is called replication. Thus, to insure validity in an experiment, randomization should be accompanied by sufficient replication.[7]

Randomization and replication are useful in enabling a clear interpretation of experimental results. It is also an essential part of most statistical models. We shall now consider one basic model for which randomization is a fundamental assumption.

The model which was discussed in the section of this chapter en-

[7] Hoel, *op. cit.*, pp. 246–247.

titled Simple Linear Correlation and Simple Regression has been called a "linearity model." The hypothesis underlying that model implies that the relationship between the two variables takes the form of a straight line. If this is not actually the case, the linear correlation coefficient will underestimate the degree of relationship. In other words, it will measure only the amount of straight-line relationship between X and Y.

The basic problem in the linear correlation model is to determine the amount of relationship about a geometric line.[8] In the analysis of variance model the fundamental purpose is to separate the total amount of variance into individual parts, each part assignable to a known source, factor, or condition. This allows one to assess the relative magnitude of variation resulting from different sources and to determine whether a particular part of the variation is greater than chance expectation. There are many forms of the analysis of variance and the particular form used depends upon the particular research problem and its related experimental design.[9]

The Concept of Variance. Perhaps the simplest and quickest way to indicate the meaning of the concept of variance is by way of an example. Suppose we have a set of test questions and that we administer the test to a sample of subjects with the following distribution of right answers.

The table below is a frequency distribution with a class interval of 1. The symbol f_i denotes the frequency of occurrence of the particular value X_i. Multiplying each value of X_i by its frequency and adding together the products, $f_i X_i$, we obtain the sum of 37. The arithmetic mean $\overline{X}$, is 37 divided by 14, or 2.64.

In general, where $X_1, X_2, X_3, \ldots, X_i$ occur with frequencies $f_1, f_2, f_3, \ldots, f_i$, and k is the number of different values of X (in Table 6.3 this is 6), then the weighted arithmetic mean, $\overline{X}$, equals

$$\frac{f_1 X_1 = f_2 X_2 + F_3 X_3 + \ldots f_i X_i}{N} = \frac{\sum\limits_{i=1}^{k} f_i X_i}{N}$$

where

$$N = \sum_{i=1}^{k} f_i$$

---

[8] The correlation model can, for some purposes, be more clearly presented in the form of a variance ratio. See T. C. McCormick, *Elementary Social Statistics*, New York, McGraw-Hill, 1941, pp. 182–183, and Philip H. DuBois, *op. cit.*

[9] For a clear and fundamental introduction to some of these designs see George A. Ferguson, *Statistical Analysis in Psychology and Education*, New York, McGraw-Hill, 1959, chaps. 15 and 16. For a more advanced and more complete set of techniques see B. J. Winer, *Statistical Principles in Experimental Design*, New York, McGraw-Hill, 1962.

TABLE 6.3. CALCULATING VARIANCE FOR FREQUENCY DISTRIBUTION
OF TEST SCORES

(1) Test Score X_i	(2) Frequency of Right Answers f_i	(3) $f_i(X_i)$*	(4) Deviation from the Mean $X_i - X = x_i$	(5) Frequency Times the Deviation $f(X_i - \overline{X}) = f_i x_i$	(6) Frequency Times the Deviations Squared $f(X_i - \overline{X})^2 = f_i x_i^2$
0	1	0	-2.64	-2.64	6.97
1	2	2	-1.64	-3.28	5.38
2	3	6	-0.64	-1.92	1.22
3	4	12	+0.36	+1.44	.52
4	3	12	+1.36	+4.08	5.55
5	1	5	+2.36	+2.36	5.57
	14	37			25.21

*Frequency multiplied by X.

and the summation is over k terms, i.e., the number of different values of X. Also

$$\sum_{i=1}^{N} = \sum_{i=1}^{k} f_i X_i.$$

Our immediate interest is in the concept of variance, but in order to understand it we need to understand the mean. The notion of variation or deviation assumes knowledge of a point or characteristic around which the variation occurs. In respect to the concept of variance the point around which the variation is measured is the mean. In other words, variance is a particular measure of departure from the mean or central tendency.

Let us symbolize variance by the symbol s^2

$$s^2 = \frac{\Sigma f(X - \overline{X})^2}{N}.$$

We see that variance is the mean of the squared deviations from the mean. Another way of saying this is to note that it is the sum of the squared deviations from the mean divided by N or the total number of observations. The square root of the variance is known as the *standard deviation*.

Let us now calculate the variance in Table 6.3 above.

$$s^2 = \frac{\Sigma f(X - \overline{X})^2}{N} = \frac{\Sigma f x^2}{N}, \text{ where } N = \sum_{i=1}^{k} f_i$$

$$s^2 = \frac{25.21}{14} = 1.80.$$

Keeping in mind the foregoing concepts of the mean and variance, let us now turn to a consideration of the analysis of variance.

The term "analysis of variance" is somewhat ambiguous since its application is primarily concerned with procedures for testing hypotheses about the *means* of populations. This technique is used to test the significance of the differences between the means of three or more different samples. It can be applied to two means, but other, more conventional techniques are generally used when only two means are involved.[10]

Analysis of Variance: One-Way Classification—The Basic Problem. The problem is to explain the variation among a set of means from k different sample populations. The method is to divide the sum of squares $\Sigma(X - \bar{X})^2$ into two additive components. These are then used to test whether the k samples have been drawn from the same or different populations.

We may wish to test the different effects of k treatments on some dependent variable. These may be different ways of instructing, different ways of memorizing, different types of childhood training, or different dosages of a drug. A different treatment is applied to each of the k samples and each sample contains n members. The members are assigned to the treatments by means of some randomizing process. The means of the k samples are calculated. The null hypothesis asserts that the samples are drawn from populations having the same mean.[11] In other words, the hypothesis of equal means is stated, which is a way of saying that the differences among treatments are not statistically significant. If the variation cannot be attributed to sampling error, we reject the null hypothesis and accept the alternative hypothesis that the treatments applied were significant in their effects.

Consider a psychological experiment to compare success of learning at 3 different levels of difficulty of materials to be learned. Suppose that we randomly assign 10 subjects to each of the three levels; we then have a grand total of 30 experimental subjects. Thus $k = 3$ treatments and $n = 10$ subjects per treatment. Assume that the subject matter differs only by level of difficulty and that the subjects were assigned randomly to each experimental level. The mean number of right answers is computed for each sample of 10 subjects for each level of difficulty. Differences in rate of learning are reflected in the variation among the 3 means. If this variation is of such magnitude that it could arise in random sampling in less than 5 percent of the cases, then we normally reject the null hypothesis and accept the alternative hypothesis, that the amount of learning varies with the level of difficulty.

---

10 See, for example, Critical Radio Test in Chapter 5.
11 The student who is interested in the whys of the null hypotheses is invited to try his hand with Karl R. Popper, *The Logic of Scientific Discovery*, New York, Basic Books, Inc., 1959.

The basic table for a one-way classification problem using analysis of variance may be represented as follows (Table 6.4).

TABLE 6.4. ILLUSTRATION OF GENERAL NOTATION OF A ONE-WAY CLASSIFICATION TABLE FOR ANALYSIS OF VARIANCE

	Category				
	Group A	Group B	Group C	Group k	
(1)	X_{11} X_{21} X_{31} . . . $X_{10\ 1}$	X_{12} X_{22} X_{32} . . . $X_{10\ 2}$	X_{13} X_{23} X_{33} . . . $X_{10\ 3}$	X_{1k} X_{2k} X_{3k} . . . $X_{10\ k}$	
(2)	Total T_A . . .	T_B . . .	T_C . . .	T_k	T = Table Total
	Mean $\overline{X}_{.1}$	$\overline{X}_{.2}$	$\overline{X}_{.3}$	$\overline{X}_{.k}$	$\overline{T}$ = Table Mean

$T_A = X_{11} + X_{21} + X_{31} \ldots X_{10\ 1}$ and the same for groups B, C, and so on.

T (Table Total) $= T_A + T_B + T_C + T_k$.

$$\overline{X}_{.1} = \frac{T_A}{10}; \overline{X}_{.2} = \frac{T_B}{10}, \text{ and so on.}$$

$$\overline{T} = \frac{T}{40}.$$

Element X_{32} in category B designates an observation on the third person in treatment class B. In general, this is designated as X_{ij} or an observation on element i or subject i in treatment class j. Notations for the totals required in the computation of the sums of squares appear in part (2) of the above table. For example, T_A designates the sum of all observations in treatment class A, and $\overline{X}_{.j}$ designates the mean of a particular treatment class.

What basic computing formulas are needed? Let us attempt to logically deduce the kinds of formulas needed. Recall that the basic idea underlying the analysis of variance is that the *total* sum of squares may be partitioned into independent and additive parts, each part resulting from an identifiable source of variation. The null hypothesis specifies the nature of the relationship among these components.

Let us begin by calculating the total sum of squares.

Analysis of Variance: One-Way Classification—The Required Sums of Squares. We have denoted the sum of all the observations in a particular group by T_j:

$$T_j = \sum_{i=1}^{n_j} X_{ij}.$$

The sum of *all* the observations in all the k groups is denoted by T:

$$T = \sum_{j=1}^{k} \sum_{i=1}^{n_j} X_{ij}.$$

This may be read as the sums of the j categories.

The computation formulas are now readily obtainable. The formula for the *total* sum of squares is,

$$\sum_{j=1}^{k} \sum_{i=1}^{n_j} (X_{ij} - \bar{X})^2 = \sum_{j=1}^{k} \sum_{i=1}^{n_j} X_{ij}^2 - \frac{T^2}{N}; \quad N = \sum_{j=1}^{k} n_j.$$

We simply find the sum of squares for all the observations and subtract T^2 / N.

Recall that in a table involving a single variable or one-way classification our interest is in assessing the treatment effects and their differentials, if any, as these are reflected in the column means. Hence the principal interest is in *between-treatment variation*. Since the different columns or categories represent different treatments, it is presumed that the column means will show significant differences if the different treatments do in fact produce different effects. Thus, another sum of squares of principal interest is the *between-group* sum of squares. The formula is,

$$\sum_{j=1}^{k} n_j(\bar{X}_j - \bar{X})^2 = \sum_{j=1}^{k} \left(\frac{T_j^2}{n_j} \right) - \frac{T^2}{N}.$$

Obviously, if there is not significant variation of the column means around the total or grand mean, then the different treatments did not produce statistically significant differences. In such a case all the variation except random column variation would be found to be *within* the columns. This leads us to the final sum of squares for consideration in a one-way classification table and it is generally labeled the "within-groups" sum of squares.

$$\sum_{j=1}^{k} \sum_{i=1}^{n_j} (X_{ij} - \bar{X}_j)^2 = \sum_{j=1}^{k} \sum_{i=1}^{n_j} X_{ij}^2 - \sum_{j=1}^{k} \left(\frac{T_j^2}{n_j} \right)$$

The fraction,

$$\sum_{j=1}^{k} \left(\frac{T_j^2}{n_j} \right)$$

is the sum of squares of the column totals divided by the corresponding number of cases.

The above formulas are also applicable to treatment groups of unequal or equal sizes.

A numerical example should help clarify the foregoing formulas. Suppose an experimenter is interested in evaluating the effectiveness of three methods of teaching a given course. A group of 30 subjects is available to him. This group is assumed by the investigator to be a random sample from the population of interest. Three subgroups of ten subjects each are formed at random; the subgroups are each taught by a different one of the three methods of teaching. Upon completion of the course, each of the subgroups is given the same test covering the material in the course. The symbol n designates the number of subjects in a subgroup and k the number of treatments, in this case the number of teaching methods employed.

The hypothetical scores are given in Table 6.5 below.

Referring now to the formulas for calculating sums of squares and substituting the appropriate numerical results from the table below will

TABLE 6.5. COMPUTATION PROCEDURES FOR THE ANALYSIS OF VARIANCE: ONE-WAY CLASSIFICATION

		Teaching Method		
	1	*2*	*3*	
	6	4	8	
	8	4	10	
	5	3	12	
	9	8	14	
	7	7	13	
	4	5	10	
	6	2	11	
	7	3	9	
	5	6	15	
	8	5	7	
T_j	65	47	109	$\sum_{1}^{3} T_j = T = 221$
n_j	10	10	10	$\sum_{1}^{3} n_j = N = 30$
$X_{.j}$	6.5	4.7	10.9	$\dfrac{T^2}{N} = 1628.03$
$\sum_{i=1}^{n_j} \overline{X}_{ij}^{2}$	443	253	1249	$\sum_{j=1}^{k} \sum_{i=1}^{n_j} X_{ij}^{2} = 1945$
$\dfrac{T_j^{2}}{n_j}$	422.5	220.90	1188.10	$\sum_{j=1}^{k} \dfrac{T_j^{2}}{n_j} = 1831.50$

give us the required sums of squares. First, the total sum of squares is:

$$1945 - 1628.03 = 316.97.$$

The between-group of squares is $1831.50 - 1628.03 = 203.47$. The within-group sum of squares is $1945 - 1831.50 = 113.50$.

Notice that the between-group and within-group sums of squares for a one-variable table must necessarily, when added together, equal the total sum of squares or a computational error exists.

The computational results of the analysis of variance are usually displayed in summary form as indicated in Table 6.6 below.

TABLE 6.6. SUMMARY OF ANALYSIS OF VARIANCE
FOR THE DATA OF TABLE 6.5

Source of Variation	Sum of Squares	Degrees of Freedom	Mean Square or Variance Estimate	F – Value
Between-Groups	203.47	$k - 1 = 2$	101.74	
Within-Group	113.50	$N - k = 27$	4.20	24.22
Total	316.97	$N - 1 = 29$		

The within-group variation is the pooled variation within each of the subgroups. When divided by the appropriate degrees of freedom (which will be defined below), it may also be thought of as the experimental error or mean square error.

The hypotheses about the equality of the population means can be tested by the F-ratio (after Professor R. A. Fisher, who originated the test). For a one-variable table the F-ratio is the ratio of the between-group variance to the within-group variance or the experimental error. Hence, in this case:

$$F = \frac{\text{Between-group variance}}{\text{Within-group variance}}.$$

We now need to refer to a table of theoretical F values in order to evaluate the above obtained F. See Table 5.16 in Chapter 5 for such a table. The table is first entered at the degrees of freedom associated with the numerator, and next for the denominator; in this case, at 2 and 27 degrees of freedom respectively. The critical F value at the 5 percent level for 2 and 27 degrees of freedom is 3.35. The observed F value for the above data is 24.22. Since it is larger than the critical value of 3.35, we tentatively reject the hypothesis that the column means are equal and accept the hypothesis that they are unequal. This means that the different methods of teaching presumably made a real difference in mean results per method. We emphasize the tentativeness of the conclusions, since they are based on a chance probability of .05. The critical value chosen was at the .05 chance level. This means that with a greater mean square of 2 degrees of freedom and a lesser mean square of 27 degrees of freedom, an F value as large as 3.35 can occur by chance not more than 5 times in 100 cases. Since the observed F value in the foregoing illustration is much larger than 3.35, it would be expected to have a chance value considerably smaller than 5 percent. Obviously, the smaller the probability of chance, the greater the probability of a real or systematic effect.

If we wanted to increase our confidence in the results, we could choose a more stringent critical value, say, the 1 percent level. In this case, with the same degrees of freedom the critical F value is 5.49 and the probability of such an F value occurring by chance is only one in a 100 times. Of course, as we decrease the probability of accepting a relationship as significant when in fact it is *not,* we also increase the probability of rejecting it as false when in fact it is real. In other words, there are two kinds of errors which one should beware of in testing statistical hypotheses. These are sometimes called type I and type II errors. The *rejection* of a true hypothesis is a type I error and the *acceptance* of a false hypothesis is a type II error. Suppose one sets the null hypothesis as the hypothesis to be tested, and the test results in the decision to reject the null hypothesis when in fact it is true; this is a type I error. On the other hand, if one accepts the null hypothesis as true when in fact it is false, this is a type II error. Of course, in regard to any given hypothesis one can make only one of these errors. The only way to guard against both of these kinds of possible errors is to increase the degrees of freedom by increasing the number of observations or sample size.

We have used the term "degrees of freedom" without defining it and we will now attempt to show its meaning. In the first place, the term "degrees of freedom" refers to the number of *independent* observations on a given source of variation—independent in the sense that a subsequent observed result is not dependent upon the previous one. Suppose we have the following column of observed values and its resulting total:

$$
\begin{array}{c}
1 \\
2 \\
3 \\
4 \\
5 \\
\hline
15
\end{array}
$$

The concept of degrees of freedom may be illustrated as follows: Given a fixed sum, how many of the numbers may be assigned arbitrarily? That is, how many are free to vary? In the case of the above column of values with the sum of 15, exactly 4 can be assigned arbitrarily; the fifth number has to be such that the total is 15.

In other words, the degrees of freedom is the number of independent observations minus the number of constants or fixed values used in estimating the variance. The number of degrees of freedom for each subgroup or column in the teaching methods experiment is, $n - 1$ or $10 - 1 = 9$. The number of degrees of freedom for the within-group variation or all the subgroups pooled is, $k(n - 1)$ or $N - k$ which is $3(9) = 27$ or $30 - 3 = 27$.

The problem in the foregoing one-way classification illustration was to determine whether the three treatments were equally effective in respect to the mean result. This assumed that the subjects who were randomly assigned to the subgroups did not differ in respect to previous background in the course subject matter. In other words, if the subgroups differed significantly in respect to past training in the subject matter, then this would obscure or depress any actual effects of the teaching methods. To prevent this interference with the experimental results, the factor of previous training would need to be taken into account. This would involve a two-factor or two-variable analysis of variance design.

Analysis of Variance: Two Variables of Classification. The variations in the observations in the analysis of variance experiment in the section of this chapter entitled *Analysis of Variance: One-Way Classification* were, as we saw, caused by different methods of teaching. But the variations may also have been due to a difference in the background training of the subjects.

The development of the analysis of variance procedure for a two-way classification with single observations per cell may be illustrated in the following table (Table 6.7).

In this table the double subscripts identify the row and the column. The first subscript identifies the *row;* the second identifies the *column.* Thus X_{12} is the score in the first row and the second column. In general,

TABLE 6.7. ILLUSTRATION OF TWO-VARIABLE CLASSIFICATION
WITH SINGLE OBSERVATION PER CELL

		First Variable			
		A	B	C	Row Mean
Second	a	X_{11}	X_{12}	X_{13}	$\overline{X}_{1.}$
Variable	b	X_{21}	X_{22}	X_{23}	$\overline{X}_{2.}$
	c	X_{31}	X_{32}	X_{33}	$\overline{X}_{3.}$
	Column Mean	$\overline{X}_{.1}$	$\overline{X}_{.2}$	$\overline{X}_{.3}$	$\overline{X}_{...}$

X_{rc} denotes the measurement in the rth row and the cth column. The dot notation in the row and column totals is used to designate means. The symbol $\overline{X}_1.$ refers to the mean of the first row, $\overline{X}_2.$ to the mean of the second row and so on. Similarly, $\overline{X}._1$ refers to the mean of the first column, and $\overline{X}._2$ to the mean of the second column. The grand mean, the mean of all N observations is $\overline{X}$ without any dot designations although some designate the mean of all observations by $\overline{X}$ . . .

In the previous case of a single variable classification an estimate of the variance was obtained for the column means. Here we shall also obtain an estimate for the row means because we are interested in seeing if both factors affect the variance. The computation is illustrated for the following hypothetical data for three treatments A, B, C and three background levels or types a, b, c.

TABLE 6.8. ILLUSTRATION OF TWO-VARIABLE CLASSIFICATION
WITH SINGLE OBSERVATION PER CELL, USING HYPOTHETICAL DATA

	A	B	C	T_r
a	5	8	11	24
b	7	10	13	30
c	10	14	18	42
T_c	22	32	42	96

The procedure for obtaining the desired sums of squares is the same as before. The sum of squares used in estimating the population variance from column means is computed as before and is,

$$\frac{(22)^2}{3} + \frac{(32)^2}{3} + \frac{(42)^2}{3} - \frac{(96)^2}{9} = 1090.66 - 1024.00 = 66.66.$$

Similarly, the sum of squares for estimating the population variance from the row means is,

$$\frac{(24)^2}{3} + \frac{(30)^2}{3} + \frac{(42)^2}{3} - \frac{(96)^2}{9} = 56.00.$$

The total sum of squares is,

$$5^2 + 7^2 + 10^2 + 8^2 + 10^2 + \ldots 18^2 - \frac{(96)^2}{9} = 1148 - 1024 = 124.$$

The student should note that the denominator in each term used in computing the foregoing sums of squares is the number of items which have been added in the total which appears in the numerator.

The sum of squares which corresponds to the experimental error in a two-way analysis of variance is sometimes called the "remainder" or "residual sum of squares" and is equal to the total sum of squares minus the sum of the column and row sum of squares, in this case, 124 — 122.66 or 1.34.[12]

The above results may be viewed more clearly if we summarize them in a table (Table 6.9).

TABLE 6.9. SUMMARY TABLE FOR TWO-WAY ANALYSIS OF VARIANCE, SINGLE OBSERVATION PER CELL

Source of Variation	Sum of Squares	Degrees of Freedom, d.f.	Mean Square or Variance Estimate	$F-$ Value
Column means	66.66	2	33.33	98.03
Row means	56.00	2	28.00	82.35
Residual	1.34	4	.34	
Total	124.00	8		

The total degrees of freedom is $N — 1$ or $9 — 1 = 8$. The degrees of freedom for the residual sum of squares is obtained by subtracting the sum of the degrees of freedom for the columns and rows from the total degrees of freedom. In this case, that would be $8 — 4$ or 4.

The F-test for the hypothesis that the row means are equal can be made by comparing the variance estimate for rows with the residual variance estimate.

The F-ratio is, $F = \dfrac{28.00}{.34} = 82.35$. The critical F-value at the 5 percent level with 2 and 4 degrees of freedom is 6.94. Since our obtained value is 82.35, we conclude that the three groups differ in subject-matter background. The test for column means is,

$$F = \frac{33.33}{.34} = 98.03.$$

Hence, we conclude that the column means also differ. The theoretical F-value which will not be exceeded by 95 percent of the samples is 6.94 for 2 degrees of freedom associated with the numerator of the F-ratio and for 4 degrees of freedom associated with its denominator.

In order to appreciate the increased sensitivity obtained by eliminating the variation due to differences in background training when testing the hypothesis that the treatment or column means are equal, consider how the hypothesis would have been tested if the row classifications were not available. This would be the situation, for example, if the three treat-

[12] This applies to two-way analysis of variance with one observation per cell. The case would be different with repeated observations per cell or with repeated observations per cell with unequal n's.

ments had been assigned to the nine cells at random. This, of course, would be a one-variable or one-way analysis of variance. Table 6.10 below summarizes the results when the row classifications are not available.

TABLE 6.10. SUMMARY OF ANALYSIS OF VARIANCE OF DATA
IN TABLE 6.8 WITHOUT ROW CLASSIFICATION INFORMATION

Source of Variation	Sum of Squares	d.f.	Mean Square or Variance Estimate	F-Ratio
Column means	66.66	2	33.33	$F = \dfrac{33.33}{9.56} = 3.49$
Within groups	57.34	6	9.56	$F_{.95}(2,6) = 5.14*$
Total	124.00	8		

*To be read as, The theoretical F-value which will not be exceeded by 95 percent of the samples is 5.14 for 2 degrees of freedom in the numerator of the F-ratio and for 6 degrees of freedom in the denominator.

It is interesting to note that when the row classification was not available, the F-value for the column means or treatment effects is *not* significant. Thus, failure to control for background effects in the above case totally obscured the real effects of the treatment variable. The important principle in experimental design which this result points to is that, in addition to the randomization process in assigning subjects to treatments, it is also necessary to *control* as many interfering variables as one can. From this point of view the one-way analysis of variance is much like the simple correlation coefficient in that it may not be sensitive enough to discover the relationships which are actually present.[13]

A comparison of the F-ratio for column means when the second variable was controlled with the F-ratio for the same when the second variable was *not* controlled, is very striking. The F-ratio for the column means with the second variable taken into account was 98.03 and it fell to 3.49 when the second variable was *not* taken into account. We thus see the increased sensitivity of the test as additional related variables are controlled.

A thorough treatment of the bases for establishing relationships would require a detailed analysis of all the major types of experimental design as well as an analysis of the logic and methods of inference. This, itself, would require the space of a very large textbook. Our analysis of simple linear correlation and one- and two-way analysis of variance represented statistical techniques for establishing relationships, but by *themselves* they are not sufficient to determine the precise nature of the

[13] It is beyond the scope of this text to consider the more complex designs but the student should begin now to read a text like Allen L. Edwards, *Experimental Design in Psychological Research*, rev. ed., New York, Holt, Rinehart and Winston, 1960.

relationships. That is to say that further evidence and conditions must be established before one can show that *X produces Y* rather than simply *varies* with *Y*. Some of these conditions and methods of inference will be discussed in the next section.

6. METHODS OF INFERENCE AND INTERPRETATIONS OF RESEARCH RESULTS

Suppose that a researcher has established by either an appropriate correlation analysis or an appropriate analysis of variance that two factors are related. What does such a concomitant relationship mean? To answer this question one needs to know *how* the variables are related. Are they positively related or negatively related? A relationship may be described as positive when an increase in *X* is accompanied by an increase in *Y* or a decrease in *X* is accompanied by a decrease in *Y*. A negative relationship means that an increase in *X* is accompanied by a decrease in *Y*, or a decrease in *X* is accompanied by an increase in *Y*. Another question is, Are they *jointly* related; that is, do they interact? Recall the discussion of the regression coefficient in Section 4. It was conceived as the ratio of the covariation of the two variables to the variance of the independent variable or $b_{yx} = \frac{\Sigma xy}{\Sigma x^2}$. This, of course, is a measure of the amount of change in *Y* per unit of change in *X*. It can also be reversed. In this case, we would consider *X* as the dependent variable and *Y* as the independent variable, and we have $b_{xy} = \frac{\Sigma xy}{\Sigma y^2}$, when $\Sigma xy = \Sigma XY - \frac{\Sigma X \Sigma Y}{N}$ and $\Sigma y^2 = \Sigma Y^2 - \frac{(\Sigma Y)^2}{N}$ when *X* and *Y* refer to raw scores.

If b_{yx} and b_{xy} are each significant, this means that *Y* and *X* are affecting *each other;* in other words, they are intercorrelated. The same question could be asked and answered by using an analysis of variance technique. For example, is the effect of the columns and rows in combination different from the sum of their separate effects? If the effect in combination is significantly greater than the sum of the separate effects, then there is interaction present.

The task of determining *how* a set of factors is related in terms of a sequence of cause-and-effect relationships is sometimes very complex. All we can hope to do in this regard at the introductory level is to present some of the more common research designs used to clarify research results.

Basic Types of Experimental Designs

The classical statement of experimental methods is by John Stuart Mill (1806–1873) who was able to systematize the logic of research of his day within the framework of five methods.[14] As much as I am tempted, I

[14] John Stuart Mill, *A System of Logic*, 8th ed., New York, Harper & Row, 1900, pp. 278–291.

shall not present Mill's methods and canons in his own words; however, it is strongly recommended that the student read them in the reference cited. We will list his methods and discuss them in relation to our general question of how to explain an observed relationship. Mill derived five methods which he used to describe all the types of logical procedures required in ordering data. These are: *Method of Difference; Method of Agreement; Joint Method of Difference and Agreement; Method of Concomitant Variation; Method of Residue.*

This text stresses the idea that a research problem exists when a researcher observes an empirical regularity which existing knowledge will not adequately explain. This empirical distribution we have designated operationally as a "dependent variable." Assuming that the investigator has determined by theoretical and/or empirical means which variables are to be defined as the independent variables, which are the intervening variables, and which the dependent variable, then the beginning phase of the process of explanation is to relate by some correlation or variance analysis technique an independent variable to the dependent variable. If the dependent variable varies in any manner whenever the independent variable varies in some particular way, then the researcher concludes that the two are at least statistically related and probably functionally related. This is the basic idea of concomitant variation.

Since we have conceived of the research process as beginning with a problem of variation, we shall now discuss more fully concomitant variation designs.

Method of Concomitant Variation. The fundamental idea of concomitant variation should already be clear to the student from the discussion of correlation analysis earlier in this chapter and in Chapter 5. Nevertheless, it will not be out of order to restate some of the ideas. The usual concomitant variation design involves the following:

1. A range of measures, scores, or frequencies of an independent variable are systematically obtained.
2. Corresponding measures, scores, or frequencies are obtained on a dependent variable.
3. If the dependent variable varies systematically in relation to the independent variable, then the researcher concludes that the two variables are related.

An illustration of this method is as follows: an experimenter was interested in discovering what relationship existed between high school grade average and college grade average. To do this he might select a random sample of college seniors and calculate the average grade of each for the four years in college. He would also, of course, have to obtain the corresponding high school grade averages for each student. These scores would then be arranged in terms of a set of ordered pairs and the amount of correlation calculated.

Suppose he discovered that there was a positive relationship which indicated that the students with the highest high school averages also obtained the highest college average. This indicates one kind of concomitant relationship. Let us symbolize it by $+ +$.

A relationship may be of the sort that the dependent variable decreases as the independent variable decreases; this would also be a positive relationship and we will symbolize it by $- -$. This may be illustrated by noting that as the strength of an attitude decreases, the interest of the person in the object of the attitude also decreases.

A third type of concomitant relation is where the independent variable increases and the dependent variable decreases. A study at Indiana University showed that as per capita income, X increased, it was accompanied by a decrease in the suicide rate, Y.[15] This type of relationship we shall symbolize as $+ -$.

A fourth type is when the independent variable decreases and the dependent variable increases. This is symbolized as $- +$. This is simply the reverse of the third type. An illustration of the fourth type would be: as the amount of information on vital issues, X decreases, rumor production, Y increases.

Take the frequent statement that crime and divorce rates vary concomitantly with urban areas. This statement is often contrasted with such rates in rural areas. The inadequacy of such a statement is evident if we find crime and divorce in *both* areas since under such conditions area could hardly be considered the cause. This is like saying that age is correlated with knowledge. Age is a time index. The fundamental question is what happens during time that is actually related to an increase in knowledge. The same is true about the statement which contrasted rural and urban areas. What *processes* and *conditions* are present in the urban areas that are not present in the rural areas which also vary concomitantly with crime? This requires an extension of our method to include additional methods.

In conclusion, it can be said that the Method of Concomitant Variation is not a method of proof of cause-and-effect relationships, but it can suggest such when the degree of concomitant variation is high. It is certainly true that nothing can be the cause of an effect if the effect does *not* vary when the alleged cause varies. The method of correlation analysis and the method of analysis of variance treated earlier are the two main methods for dealing with data collected under the Method of Concomitant Variation.

We indicated above that the Method of Concomitant Variation needs to be supplemented by other methods. We shall deal next with the Method of Difference as supplementary to the Method of Concomitant Variation.

[15] Unpublished Master's thesis reported in John H. Mueller and Karl F. Schuessler, *Statistical Reasoning in Sociology*, Boston, Houghton Mifflin, 1961, pp. 282–283.

Method of Difference. In some of the examples which dealt with concomitant variation we noted the difficulty of the independent factor varying not only with the effect, but also with its opposite. Obviously, this makes for difficulty in interpretation. For example, suppose the independent variable is the order of birth of children and the hypothesized dependent factor is high anxiety of the firstborn. Suppose that by actual observation or check it turned out that half of the firstborn are classifiable as being anxious and half are not. In such a case it is unlikely that birth order is related to the production of anxiety, although it still might be a contributing factor, but this would have to be ascertained through additional information. The Method of Difference is useful in enabling us to gain a more precise picture of the relationships involved and to disentangle such confusing results.

Perhaps this is a good place to point out that generally a researcher does *not* use just one of these methods at a time, and if it does not work, then he tries some other. More often in any good research design many different methods are *combined* into one major research design. This is always the case in any research beyond a simple exploratory description of the problem. We are here treating the various methods separately only for purposes of exposition.

The modern application of the Method of Difference is best illustrated by the use of an experimental group and a control group. The researcher proceeds as follows:

1. Two groups of subjects are selected by matching, by randomization, or by both and are presumed to be equal in all relevant respects except for measurable chance differences.
2. One group is designated the control group and the other the experimental group. The experimental group is properly exposed to the independent variable or variables, and the same is withheld from the control group.
3. If a change occurs in the dependent variable in the experimental group, but such a change does not occur in the control group, then the researcher attributes the change to the independent variable he manipulated in the experimental group.

The social psychologist may make use of this method; he selects a population of subjects and divides them into two or more subgroups which are equal in regard to relevant variables. The equalizing of the groups in regard to relevant factors is achieved by random selection and factor matching or measurement matching. Suppose we wanted to match the groups by sex; then we would simply have an equal number of males and females per group. If it were relevant to match for education and IQ, then they would be matched by number of years of education and IQ score. The principal idea is to compose the groups so that they are as nearly equal as possible on all factors known to influence the dependent variable. By "equal as possible" we mean that the groups are the same except for random sampling differences. The experimenter would then introduce the treatment variable to one or more of the groups and withhold it from the other group or groups.

The literature of psychology and social psychology is replete with such experiments.[16] A classical example in social psychology is Sherif's experiment on the formation of group norms. Among the questions which interested Sherif was one about group effects on individual response to an objective but unstable stimulus. In his study of group effects on judgment he employed the well-known autokinetic effect phenomenon to obtain the objective unstable stimulus situation. In complete darkness or in a closed, unlighted room when there are no lights visible, a single small light seems to move, and it may appear to move erratically in all directions. This is an example of the autokinetic phenomenon. If the point of light is presented repeatedly to an individual, it will seem to appear at different places in the room. The position of the point of light is at all times constant.

Sherif asked the subjects to judge the distance which the light appeared to move. Since the light actually did not move but was perceived to move, then the estimated distance was a function of subjective factors. The experimental problem dealt with the question of whether one's judgment of the perceived movement was affected when rendered with the knowledge of others' judgment of the perceived movement. To answer this question it was necessary to study the perceived movement in two situations. First, the subjects responded to the experienced movement when alone, except for the experimenter, and then a second time when the individual was in the group situation. The control group, of course, responded both times under the alone condition.

The experimental group was divided into two subgroups. One was exposed to the group situation after being experimented upon when alone. The other was first introduced to the group situation and was afterwards exposed to the alone situation. This was done to determine whether the effects produced under the group situation would persist in the alone situation.

Other controls were utilized in the study but the above should suffice to illustrate the Method of Difference. This method is not a method of discovery, since in its application it is necessary that the researcher have knowledge beforehand of the factor or factors that he varies. That is, Sherif, for example, believed that the social situation would produce significantly different responses than the alone situation. To test this assumption he had two groups that differed in respect to the social situation

[16] See Gardner Murphy *et al., Experimental Social Psychology,* New York, Harper & Row, 1937 and Eleanor Maccoby *et al., Readings in Social Psychology,* New York, Holt, Rinehart and Winston, 1958; also, the *Journal of Social Psychology* and the *Journal of Abnormal and Social Psychology.*

and observed their responses in regard to the same dependent variable or outcome.

It is, of course, difficult to adhere strictly to the requirements of the Method of Difference. For example, it is very difficult to find or to create conditions which are exactly alike except for the factor or factors in which one is testing. Mill recognized this and provided this rule of application: "But to determine whether this invariable antecedent is a cause, or this invariable consequent an effect, we must be able, in addition, to produce the one by the means of the other: or, at least, to obtain . . . an instance in which the effect 'a' has come into existence, with no other change in the pre-existing circumstances than the addition of 'A.' " [17] In the above example, a change in judgment was capable of being produced by the introduction of the responses of other subjects, while other pre-existent circumstances were kept as stable as possible.

The principal value of the Method of Difference is that it can help a researcher decide whether a given variable could *not* be the cause of a given effect. The principal rule is that *no variable can be the cause of a phenomenon if it is absent when the phenomenon occurs.* It should now be clear that the advantage of this method is that it permits the use of a control group.

Its principal weakness centers around the fact that it is not a method of proof in the sense that it can show that *A* causes *B*. It can show that *A* is one of the factors or conditions which will produce *B*, but suppose that there are multiple factors which will produce *B*. In such a case, the application of the Method of Difference gives only a partial answer and does not conclusively establish proof.

At this point it should be noted that experimental methods or any other research methods can only establish whether a relationship exists between some antecedent factor or condition and some subsequent outcome or effect. It cannot determine what event or outcome is important for investigation or what antecedent factors or conditions are *relevant* to examine in connection with the effect. Knowledge about the relevant conditions and alleged causal factors has to come from previous research experience and from the theorizing of the researcher.

Returning now to the Method of Difference, suppose that a researcher has found in one instance that when he introduces antecedent factor *A*, effect *B* occurs and when factor *A* is not present, *B* does not occur. He now recommends his treatment to his friend and his friend tries it, but he does not get the effect, *B*. Assuming that the researcher in the first instance was correct, then we are forced to conclude that other factors may also affect *B*. This necessitates a closer examination of the alleged relationship between antecedent *A* and effect *B*. A modern interpretation and application of Mill's *Method of Agreement* will help clarify the results.

17 Mill, *op. cit.,* p. 282.

Method of Agreement. In the immediately preceding section we saw that the Method of Difference was principally a means for determining the contribution of a given factor to a particular effect. But if the one factor only partially explains, then we need to look for other factors. Suppose that we hypothesize that some other factor is also related. Let us see how the Method of Agreement would enable us to test this.

The basic ideas of the Method of Agreement are:

1. The researcher observes two or more instances of an effect or outcome.
2. Each time the effect occurs he notes the factors present which seem to be related to the outcome or effect.
3. He makes repeated observations using different combinations of the independent factors until he ascertains the one or ones which are always present when the effect or dependent variable occurs.
4. He infers that the factor or factors that are always present when the effect occurs are related to the effect.

Suppose a sociologist or a psychologist were studying the factors related to occupational success. He could examine the college and professional school records of a sample of practitioners in a number of occupations. In addition, he might follow up the leads provided by a study of the records with interviews of the sample subjects. Suppose he found that in each case of a successful practitioner, he had known early in life what he wanted to become. The application of the Method of Agreement would suggest a relationship between early occupational commitment and occupational success. Likewise, the investigator might find a number of other factors held in common by successful occupants of occupations, such as high intellectual ability and strong motivation. Each of these may actually be related.

If the investigator finds that there are multiple factors involved, then the research problem becomes one of determining the individual effects of each variable, the joint effects of variables, if any, and finally the combined or total effects of all the variables under investigation.[18] However, the basic logic still remains, that of the two-variable analysis discussed in connection with the Method of Concomitant Variation, Method of Difference, and the Method of Agreement.

We will not discuss the Method of Residue, but will conclude the presentation of methods with a discussion of the Joint Method of Agreement and Difference.[19] It should be clear to the reader that the Methods of Agreement and Difference are complementary.

---

[18] Such an undertaking is sometimes called "multiple factor analysis." Students are introduced to such techniques in intermediate and advanced statistics and courses in advanced experimental designs.

[19] For a discussion of the Method of Residue the student may refer to Mill, *op. cit.,* ch. 8, or Herbert L. Searles, *Logic and Scientific Methods,* New York, Ronald, 1948, pp. 203–205.

Joint Method of Agreement and Difference. This type of research design utilizes the following procedure:

1. The experimenter determines whether two or more instances of the occurrence of an effect have only one factor in common.
2. He then tests to determine if, in two or more instances where the common factor is absent, the effect does not occur.
3. The conclusion is that since the two situations only differed with respect to the presence and absence of one factor, then that factor is related to the effect.

We will borrow an example from Searles to illustrate concretely the Joint Method. The problem concerns the determination of the cause of a case of ptomaine poisoning. Searles says:

Suppose that we have a party of six people who eat at a cafeteria and that afterwards three develop ptomaine poisoning. An inquiry is made into the details of their menus, and it is found that every item of their meals differed with the exception of chicken. All of those stricken with the poisoning had eaten this one thing, and only this, in common. According to the Method of Agreement, the chicken would be regarded as the cause of the poisoning. But if we wished to make a check in order to be doubly sure, we would supplement our inquiry by comparing those afflicted with the three who were not afflicted. We find that the negative cases, that is, those not poisoned, have alone in common the absence of chicken on their menus. Combining the symbols with the concrete illustration, we have the following:

Positive	Chicken	Potatoes	Bread	Olives	followed by ptomaine poisoning
Instances	A	B	C	D	*pqrs*
	Chicken	Salad	Pickles	Fruit	followed by
	A	E	F	G	*ptuv*
	Chicken	Peas	Rolls	Nuts	followed by
	A	H	I	J	*pwxy*
Negative		Potatoes	Bread	Steak	followed by
Instances		B	C	K	*qro*
		Salad	Pickles	Beef	followed by
		E	F	L	*tuv*
		Peas	Rolls	Duck	followed by
		H	I	M	*wxz*

Hence chicken *A* is casually related to ptomaine poisoning, "*p.*" [20]

As indicated earlier in the separate discussion of these methods, great care must be exercised in the choice of relevant factors. A strict application of the rule requires that the negative instances have nothing in common save the absence of the alleged causal antecedent. If this rule were taken literally, it would be impossible to apply and could lead to ludicrous results. For instance, in the foregoing illustration by Searles there were such factors in common as the roof, the furniture, the kitchen,

[20] Searles, *ibid.*, pp. 202–203.

and so on, but these factors were presumably irrelevant. The method, however, does not tell us what is relevant or irrelevant. The matter of relevancy of factors, both for control and for testing, must be decided by the researcher on the basis of past research facts and a logical application of existing theory in regard to these facts and the problem under consideration.[21]

It would be helpful if the logic of the Joint Method of Agreement and Difference were summarized by means of a 2×2 classification table.

Let us denote the dependent variable by D and its negation by $\overline{D}$, or "not D." The independent variable we will denote by the capital letter I and its negation by $\overline{I}$. If it is helpful to have the D's and I's refer to specific content, then the student might imagine that the independent variable refers to "broken homes" and the dependent variable to "emotionally ill." Suppose we make a hundred observations and apply the logic of the Joint Method of Agreement and Difference. In this case, there would be 50 cases involving the I variable and 50 involving the $\overline{I}$ variable. The table would look like the following:

TABLE 6.11. TABLE ILLUSTRATING JOINT METHOD OF AGREEMENT AND DIFFERENCE

	I	$-$I	Total
D	$50^{(a)}$	$0^{(b)}$	50
$-D$	$0^{(c)}$	$50^{(d)}$	50
Total	50	50	100

If such a distribution were to result from a sample of 100 cases, we would have demonstrated as best one can that the dependent variable D occurs if and only if the independent variable I occurs. It is the assumption in this text that the values in cells b and c will only approach zero but never empirically reach zero. There are at least two major reasons why this is true. First, scientific measurement is never so completely refined or error-free; and, secondly, we are always, in the sense of "all possible" cases, only dealing with a sample population and there is error due to sampling fluctuation. Therefore, on the basis of these two reasons alone we could expect to find positive values greater than zero in these cells.

Assuming that there will always occur values greater than zero in cells b and c, that is, the minor diagonal of the table, then the problem becomes one of determining whether the proportion in the major diag-

---

[21] For a general discussion of the procedures in theory testing, see William H. Sewell, "Some Observations on Theory Testing," *Rural Sociology*, vol. 21 (March, 1956), pp. 1–12.

onal (cells *a* and *d*) is significantly different statistically from the minor diagonal to warrant inferring a relationship between *I* and *D*. In other words, the argument becomes a probability argument.

It should now be easy to see that since we are conceiving of the values in the minor diagonal as representing the "error" in the research (that is, sampling error and measurement error and perhaps error due to inadequate conceptualization), then, if there exists a theoretically exact way to measure this error, this allows a basis for deciding whether a relationship exists between the independent and dependent variables. The argument is very simple, but the mathematical proof is very complex and is not appropriate to be introduced here.

Intuitively, the arguments may be seen as follows. Let us take a boundary case, one where there is complete explanation. Referring to the foregoing table of 100 cases with zero error in cells *b* and *c*, in this case we would have established a "causal" or invariant relationship between the independent variable and the dependent variable, that is, there is no error in this case. Let us now take the opposite extreme in which case there would be zero values in cells *a* and *d*: hence, any implied relationship between the independent variable *I* and the dependent variable *D* would be completely contradicted. In this case, there is nothing but error. Normally, as indicated previously, we find that the actual results are somewhere in between these extreme possibles and, therefore, the evaluation becomes a matter of determining the probability that such a proportion or mean could occur by chance.

Assuming that we have values or frequencies in cells *b* and *c*, then, if we can measure the error that we would expect to occur by chance, we are in a position to state exactly what the probability is that the difference between the two groups under comparison might be the result of chance. Methods for exactly measuring the amount of variation in a research design that is due to random error or chance are given in textbooks on statistics or experimental design and will not be presented here.[22] Here it is only desired to establish the fact that such techniques exist and to indicate in a very simple way their role in experimental designs.

As the foregoing discussion indicates, we are arguing that we have actually established the existence of a relationship when we have successfully displaced chance or experimental error in a research design. Thus, one of the major outcomes of scientific research in a given field is the reduction of error in the establishing of relationships. For example, if we find that the correlation between two variables is .50, this means that the percent of the total variance *accounted for* by the independent variable is 25 percent, that is, r^2, or in this case .50 squared. With 25 per-

22 See, for example, Paul G. Hoel, *Introduction to Mathematical Statistics*, 2nd ed., New York, Wiley, 1954, or Hubert M. Blalock, *Social Statistics*, New York, McGraw-Hill, 1960.

cent of the variance accounted for, the researcher's problem is to explain the remaining 75 percent.[23]

All research decisions in respect to hypothesis testing are fundamentally an elaboration or modification of the logic expressed in the foregoing 2×2 table. The discussion of the 2×2 table was aimed at showing how to establish that a relationship exists. Once it has been established that a relationship exists, the next step is that of determining the *degree* of the relationship, or association, present.

Some Measures of Relationship

There are many measures by which the degree of relationship can be measured in a 2×2 table. The choice of the measure depends upon the theoretical argument and the nature and distribution of the data within the table. It is only necessary to point out this matter here. The student will be confronted with this problem in detail in courses in statistics and research designs.[24]

One measure will be given here, but without consideration of mathematical proof. The measure is Yule's Q. The formula is,

$$Q = \frac{ad - bc}{ad + bc}$$

where the letters a, b, c, and d refer to the particular cells noted in Table 6.11, which illustrated the Joint Method of Agreement and Difference. Substituting the values for the letters, we have,

$$Q = \frac{50(50) - 0(0)}{50(50) + 0(0)} = \frac{2500}{2500} = 1.00.$$

It is clear that we have perfect association. Q would show zero association if the cell frequencies represented a purely random distribution of the table totals. The student should substitute various values in the four cells, being careful, of course, to maintain the same marginal totals, and observe the effect on Q.

Another measure which is more commonly used to measure the amount of association in a 2×2 table is the phi coefficient, or ϕ. One formula for calculating the phi coefficient where a, b, c, and d represent the usual cell frequencies is,

$$\phi = \frac{ad - bc}{\sqrt{(a + b)(c + d)(a + c)(b + d)}}.$$

[23] For a discussion of the statistical basis for this example see any elementary text on statistics, for example, T. C. McCormick, *Elementary Social Statistics*, New York, McGraw-Hill, 1941, pp. 182–183.

[24] For a good discussion of alternative measures see Roy G. Francis, *The Rhetoric of Science: A Methodological Discussion of the Two-by-Two Table*, Minneapolis, University of Minnesota Press, 1961, chaps. 3–7.

Like Q, the statistic ϕ is applicable only to 2×2 tables of true dichotomies that have no scale of values, or to continuous variables that can be logically dichotomized. ϕ does not perform exactly the same as Q under all conditions. If we apply ϕ to the table used for computing Q, we will note that ϕ also yields 1.0. However, Q will also yield a coefficient of 1.0 or —1.0 with only one cell with zero frequency. Under such a condition ϕ will be less than 1.0. To illustrate, suppose we have the following table of results.

From Table 6.12,

TABLE 6.12. DELINQUENCY BY HOME CONDITION
(HYPOTHETICAL DATA)

	Broken Homes	Nonbroken Homes	
Delinquent	30	0	30
Nondelinquent	30	40	70
Total 60		40	100

$$\phi = \frac{1200 - 0}{\sqrt{30 \cdot 70 \cdot 60 \cdot 40}} = \frac{1200}{2245} = .53,$$

and

$$Q = \frac{ad - bc}{ad + bc} = \frac{1200 - 0}{1200 + 0} = 1.0.$$

Q is necessarily unity, or 1.0, since *all* the delinquents come from broken homes. However, the converse that all children from broken homes are delinquents obviously does not hold. Thus it appears that there is a fundamental difference in what ϕ and Q measure. So a ϕ value of 1.0 implies both necessity and sufficiency of conditions in explanation.

If the reader will recall the discussion of the Method of Difference and Agreement as separate methods and then compare them with the Joint Method of Agreement and Difference, then the difference between ϕ and Q becomes clear. The formula for Q does *not* take into account joint or mutual relationships. ϕ is designed to measure the degree of two-way association between two sets of attributes. In a perfect two-way association, where the minor diagonal, that is, cells b and c, add to zero, then ϕ and Q will both equal unity.[25]

The discussion of ϕ and Q is only intended to give a clearer picture

25 Q is not a wholly unambiguous measure. For a technical discussion of its meaning see L. A. Goodman and W. H. Krushal, "Measures of Association for Cross Classification," *Journal of the American Statistical Association*, vol. 49 (1954), p. 750. For an excellent general discussion of measures of association the student should read G. U. Yule and M. G. Kendall, *An Introduction to the Theory of Statistics*, 14th ed., New York, Hafner, 1950, pp. 1–68.

of the ideas involved in research designs which apply the *Joint Methods of Agreement and Difference*. At this point in the student's consideration of research designs it is not necessary to become involved in considerations of which measure to use. In general, where one has a 2×2 table involving true dichotomies the phi coefficient provides a clearer measure than Q of the degree of association. However, where the marginal totals or subtotals are *unlike*, we still have a problem of *evaluating* the degree of relationship present. It has been proposed that an escape from this difficulty is to express the observed or obtained ϕ as a proportion of the maximum possible ϕ under a given set of marginal totals. But as Mueller and Schuessler say, "By that technique, an observed ϕ of .2 and a ϕ_{max} of .2 would yield a 'corrected' ϕ of unity! This would certainly be an overstatement of the existing association.

"In any event, it is not clear whether a low value of ϕ is due to the inhibiting force of the marginal frequencies or to a weak intrinsic relation between the variables as evidenced by cell frequencies." [26]

There are many measures designed to determine the degree of relationship among a set of variables. We shall mention two additional measures since they are also based on the phi coefficient but, in this case, the phi coefficient *squared*.

The first of these measures is Tschuprow's T, which is defined as,

$$T^2 = \frac{\phi^2}{\sqrt{(r-1)(c-1)}}.$$

The coefficient varies between 0 and 1 for any square table, that is, when the number of rows and columns is equal. Rows and columns are designated in the above formula as r and c respectively. All that is necessary to determine T^2 for a 2×2 table is to calculate phi square and then determine the square root of the product of $(r-1)(c-1)$ and divide this result into ϕ^2. Suppose $\phi = .50$ and we have a 2×2 table, what is T?

$$T^2 = \frac{\phi^2}{\sqrt{(r-1)(c-1)}} = \frac{.50^2}{\sqrt{1.0}} = \frac{.25}{1.0} = .40$$
$$T = \sqrt{.40} = .63.$$

When the number of rows and columns is larger than 2×2, ϕ^2 can attain a value larger than unity. Therefore, some other measure for the numerator of T^2 becomes necessary. The general measure for this purpose is χ^2 (chi square), where

$$\chi^2 = \Sigma \frac{(f_o - f_t)^2}{f_t}.$$

To obtain χ^2, we subtract each expected frequency f_t from the correspond-

---

[26] John H. Mueller and Karl F. Schuessler, *Statistical Reasoning in Sociology*, Boston, Houghton Mifflin, 1961, pp. 256–257. For a logical formulation of this problem see Roy G. Francis, *op. cit.*, pp. 97–103.

ing observed frequency f_0, divide the squared difference by the expected frequency, and sum these ratios. Suppose we have the following 3×3 table.

TABLE 6.13. ILLUSTRATING THE CALCULATION OF χ^2 (CHI SQUARE)

		Social Class			
		High (1)	Middle (2)	Low (3)	
Death Rates	High (1)	15 (1)	30 (2)	50 (3)	95
	Medium (2)	25 (4)	20 (5)	30 (6)	75
	Low (3)	35 (7)	10 (8)	20 (9)	65
	Total	75	60	100	235

Table 6.13 provides the observed frequency, or f_0 values and by use of the subtotals from this table and application of certain probability rules we can calculate the needed expected, or f_t values. On the basis of the marginal totals in Table 6.13 the probable or expected value for row (1)—high death rates—and column (1)—high social class—is $\frac{75(95)}{235}$ or $235\left(\frac{75}{235}\right)\left(\frac{95}{235}\right) = 30.32$. For cell (2) or row (1) and column (2) we have $\frac{60(95)}{235}$ or 24.25. Following the same procedure for the remaining seven cells, we come up with the following table of expected frequencies.

TABLE 6.14. EXPECTED FREQUENCIES FOR THE OBSERVED FREQUENCIES IN TABLE 6.13

		Social Class			
		High	Middle	Low	
Death Rates	High	30.32	24.25	40.43	95.00
	Medium	23.94	19.15	31.91	75.00
	Low	20.74	16.60	27.66	65.00
	Total	75.00	60.00	100.00	235.00

It should be observed that if the computations used in calculating the expected frequencies are correct, the marginal totals will sum to the same as the related observed frequencies; otherwise, an error has been made.

To obtain χ^2, we subtract each expected frequency from the corresponding observed frequency, divide the squared difference by the expected frequency, and sum these ratios. These calculations are shown in Table 6.15.

TABLE 6.15. CHI SQUARE (χ^2) TEST FOR TABLES 6.13 AND 6.14

(1) Death Rates	(2) Social Class	(3) f_0	(4) f_t	(5) $f_0 - f_t$	(6) $(f_0 - f_t)^2$	(7) $\dfrac{(f_0 - f_t)^2}{f_t}$
High	High	15	30.32	−15.32	234.70	7.74
High	Middle	30	24.25	+ 5.75	33.06	1.36
High	Low	50	40.43	+ 9.57	91.58	2.26
Medium	High	25	23.94	+ 1.06	1.12	0.04
Medium	Middle	20	19.15	+ 0.85	0.72	0.03
Medium	Low	30	31.91	− 1.91	3.65	0.11
Low	High	35	20.74	+14.26	203.34	9.80
Low	Middle	10	16.60	− 6.60	43.56	2.62
Low	Low	20	27.66	− 7.66	58.67	2.12
				0.00		$26.08 = \chi^2$

It was seen above that the expected frequencies used in Table 6.15 were calculated from the row and column totals of the observed frequencies in Table 6.13. This means that the expected frequencies are the random expectations, given these observed marginal totals; but with different marginal totals one would get different expected values. Therefore, in evaluating the χ^2 of this table, it is necessary to take into account the degrees of freedom, that is, the number of independent cells. In any $r \times c$ table, like Table 6.13, it is clear that if the row totals and the column totals are given, the number of cells that are free to vary are $(c - 1)(r - 1)$ or in this case $(3 - 1)(3 - 1) = 4$, so that a 3×3 table has 4 degrees of freedom. This follows from what we have already learned about the degrees of freedom for a given column with a fixed sum. It will be recalled that, given a fixed sum, there were $N - 1$ values which could be assigned arbitrarily and still add up to the given sum. If we have *both* columns and rows with fixed sums, then the degrees of freedom would be $(c - 1)(r - 1)$.

If the value of χ^2 obtained is 26.08, it is referred to a table of χ^2, such as Table 5.12, in Chapter 5, and the table is entered at 4 degrees of freedom and at the 5 percent level of significance, it is seen that a χ^2 as large as 9.48 could occur by chance 5 times in 100. Our χ^2 is 26.08, which is much larger, and would occur by chance less often than 5 in 100 times. Since it is customary to reject chance as the explanation of an event that can happen by chance no oftener than 5 times in 100, we conclude that one's life expectancy is related to one's social class position.

Now that we have established by the χ^2 test that life expectancy and class position are related, the next question is, to what extent are they related? It was this question which caused us to introduce the notion of χ^2 as a substitute in the numerator of T^2 when the table is larger than a 2×2 table. Since we now have the needed χ^2 value, we are in position to calculate T^2 for the 3×3 table or any other square table so long as we have the χ^2 value for that table. The new formula is,[27]

$$T^2 = \frac{\chi^2}{N \sqrt{(r-1)(c-1)}} = \frac{26.08}{235 \sqrt{(3-1)(3-1)}}$$

$$= \frac{26.08}{235 \sqrt{4}} = \frac{26.08}{235(2)} = .06 \text{ and } T = \sqrt{.06} = .24.$$

T^2 has the defect of underestimating the relationship present for tables that are *not* square. A measure that is free from this defect is preferable. Such a measure has been developed by Cramer, and Blalock denotes it by the symbol V

$$V^2 = \frac{\chi^2}{N \, \text{Min}(r-1, c-1)}$$
$$V = \sqrt{V^2}.$$

Where Min $(r-1, c-1)$ refers to either $r-1$ or $c-1$, whichever is the smaller. In other words, the smaller is chosen as the denominator and is multiplied by N. If they are equal, either is chosen. V and T are equivalent whenever $r = c$; otherwise, V will always be somewhat larger than T. Both measures are the same as ϕ for 2×2 tables.[28]

7. DIFFICULTIES AND PITFALLS IN THE USE OF LABORATORY EXPERIMENTAL DESIGNS IN SOCIAL PSYCHOLOGICAL RESEARCH

One of the major points which we have emphasized is the notion of multiple factors and joint effects in the functioning of social behavior. We have seen in previous parts of this book that human behavior always occurs in a complex network of relationships. This fact produces difficulties for research design formulations. The principal difficulty centers in the ever-present possibility of oversimplifying reality or in combining variables or separating variables in ways which provide misleading results. The principal task is to build a design which allows for a balanced interplay of factors which approximates reality to a determinable degree.

[27] See Blalock, *op. cit.*, p. 229, or Yule and Kendall, *op. cit.*, p. 56, for a slightly different form of this equation.
[28] Blalock, *op. cit.*, p. 230.

The complex analysis of variance designs and the multiple and partial correlation designs are steps in this direction.

Particularly the latter methods, that is, the multiple and partial correlation procedures, can be very effective in establishing joint or separate relationships in a natural context providing that the researcher is sufficiently clever in measuring the variables and in designing the sample or series of samples.

No particular research procedure or strategy is adequate by itself for the disentangling of the matrix of relationships in social and psychological reality. The strategy which I would suggest is one of utilizing interlocking levels of complexity of particular behavior variables in an expanding context of social organization in both laboratory and natural settings. Take the phenomenon of prejudice as an example. Prejudice may be studied as it manifests itself in an interpersonal situation such as in the case of two people or a dyad. Does its manifestation vary as the number of people in interaction increases? What happens when you change interacting partners? The interpersonal situation can be extended to include an organizational context such as a business firm, factory, or the permanent staff of a school system, and so on. The context may still be expanded to include the interlocking organizations and institutions within a community. All the time, we are keeping under observation the same sample of people but under the condition of an expanding context or matrix of natural relationships. Such an approach is complex and is fraught with great difficulties in the control of variables, but if these can be measured they can be controlled mathematically. The probable successes are well worth the efforts.

8. SUMMARY

We have attempted to show that the narrow classical view of experimentation is not only insufficient, but can be misleading in its results. This is true of the behavioral sciences and it was and is also true of the physical sciences.

We speak of experiments today in outer space. Certainly these procedures are not of the classical type of relating an independent variable to a dependent variable while other interfering variables are controlled. The controls are not of a direct form of physical manipulation, but the manipulation is indirect by means of mathematical measurement and symbolic control. The same is true of modern studies on social and psychological behavior. In fact, systems of social behavior are now being simulated on computers and the results checked against empirical situations.

The research endeavor was conceived as beginning with an observation of an empirical regularity either from the laboratory or the field that was not explainable from existing knowledge. Efforts to explain this regularity focused *first* on the establishment of concomitant variations—in other words, the finding of other empirical factors which indicated that they were related to the factor to be explained or the dependent variable. Toward this end, two major methods were presented and analyzed, namely, linear regression and analysis of variance.

Following this a *second* set of considerations was introduced to assist in determining how the variables under consideration were connected. This involved a discussion of Mill's methods and modern modifications and uses of these. It also took into account the question of differing combinations of variables under different contexts and the varying approximations of the outcomes to "reality."

Also, the matter of the degree of relationship was considered and several measures of association were presented. Finally, some of the pitfalls of a too narrow view of the meaning of experimentation were discussed.

SELECTED REFERENCES

Greenwood, Ernest, *Experimental Sociology,* New York, Kings Crown, 1945.

Hoel, Paul G., *Elementary Statistics,* New York, Wiley, 1960.

Yule, G. Udny, and M. G. Kendall, *An Introduction to the Theory of Statistics,* 14th ed., New York, Hafner, 1950.

7
Roy G. Francis

SOME APPLICATIONS OF EXPERIMENTATION IN SOCIOLOGY AND SOCIAL PSYCHOLOGY

1. DEFINITION AND PROBLEM

Social scientists have reacted variously to the word "experiment." Some have retreated, surrendering to the assumptions and formulations of physical sciences; others, stimulated by the social rewards in the form of prestige and monetary support for research, have cast envious glances at the physical scientists. Neither position can properly resolve the issue. Like a third group of social scientists—growing in numbers and influence—we should examine the logical role of experimentation, its place in research, the limitations of the argument, and the conditions under which it seems applicable in social inquiry.

In short, experimentation is here to stay. It has something to offer. It is not the end-all of science; good research is possible without it— astronomy, for example. Yet, under proper conditions, experimentation permits rigorous and convincing arguments. We use it where it fits, and avoid it where it doesn't.

There is nothing mysterious about experimentation. It is simply a part of a general scientific framework. Science attempts to obtain a theory from which hypothetical deductions can be tested; the experiment is simply a way in which a hypothesis may be tested. Contrasted with hypothesis testing by field observations, the experiment is characterized by a maximization of control over the different variables involved in the test.

While a certain amount of trial and error is empirically involved in early attempts at experimentation, trial and error does not define the experiment. Indeed, scientific experimentation tries to minimize the trial and error activities of the scientist. In the place of merely, "seeing what happens if we do so and so," the rigorous experimenter deduces as many potential consequences as his theory allows. He then proceeds to determine the relative likelihood of the various consequences of his manipulations.

Another contrast with observational research is that in observational research one necessarily encounters as many factors as empirically exist. In experimentation, the goal is to vary only the critical variables and to control (hold constant) other variables of theoretical interest. Many experiments, as a matter of fact, are designed to permit the manipulation of a single variable.

The formal structure of the hypothetical proposition, "if A, then B," can be used to characterize the sort of propositions which science, in general, seeks to validate. The A part of the hypothesis is seldom a single factor; rather, it is often a set of conditions. Experimentation seeks to control the variables such that it is first possible to assert that A is indeed present.

Recall that the predictive argument was of the form, if A, then B; create A; hence, I predict B. The creation of A involves all of the operations performed in the experiment.

Notice, however, that nothing is said in this form of the negation of A. If it turns out that one could also say, "if not A, then B," the experiment has not proved anything. Hence the experiment goes beyond a merely predictive hypothesis. Generally, the experiment will, in some sense, include a control group. A control group is one in which the theoretical antecedent is negated. Thus many experiments involve operations identifying the antecedent and operations identifying its negation. When this is so, the if A, then B statement must be amended. The premise then includes the operations identifying both the antecedent and its negation.[1] In this respect, the experiment eptomizes scientific prediction.

Notice one last contrast with observational research. In that type of inquiry one often temporarily begins with a set of observations requiring explanation. The premise is discerned after the problematic consequence is observed. That is, one begins with the B part of the hypothesis, and hopes to be able to connect it with the A part. In experimentation, however, the temporal sequence of knowledge is the same as the logical sequence of the argument. From one's theory, one can deduce what the A conditions must be; these are then re-created under controlled conditions. Through this sequence of time, and with the passage of time, one observes whether or not the predicted consequence occurs.

[1] S. A. Stouffer, "Some Observations on Study Design," *American Journal of Sociology*, vol. 15, no. 4 (January, 1950), pp. 355–361.

This identity between the temporal sequence of knowledge and the logical sequence of the argument gives rise to the power of the experiment as a scientific test of hypotheses. It also raises the central problem— how to secure sufficient control to enable one to infer that the identity exists. How to insure the re-creation of the theoretical premise is the critical issue in experimentation.

2. THE LOGIC OF EXPERIMENTATION

The logic of experimentation is a straightforward extension of the general scientific argument. (This was discussed in the previous chapter.) Adding the fact of manipulating the explanatory variables, one seeks to observe a connection between the explanation and the problem. The traditional terminology is somewhat different (since problematic data and explanatory data are general terms). We often refer to the problematic data, that is, that which is to be explained, as the "consequence"; and we refer to the explanatory data as the "antecedent."

Denoting the antecedent by A, and its absence or negation by $-A$, we will similarly denote the consequent by C and its absence by $-C$. It should be noted that these symbols and expressions are quite general. Thus, A may refer to a single factor, or a set of factors, or a patterning of factors. The same is true of C. In particular, the antecedent refers to the whole set of operations performed in the course of the experiment, including not only the theoretical variable but the process in terms of which it has been identified. Moreover, the consequence may be held to include not only the specific behavior of the objects studied, but may also include the type of relationship (e.g., a linear relation with known values for the constant terms in the equation). Heuristically, however, we may regard the antecedent as defining certain conditions or factors, and the consequence as the behavior we seek to explain.

We may then construct a model showing the general structure of the argument. We first build a 2 $\times$ 2 table:

$$\begin{array}{c|c|c|} & A & -A \\ \hline C & & \\ \hline -C & & \\ \hline \end{array}$$

If the joint outcome, C and $-A$, has no members, this means that the consequent occurs only when the antecedent occurs; this is called, "necessary conditions." This simply means that the antecedent is necessary for the occurrence of the consequent. If the joint outcome, A and $-C$, has no members, it means that while the antecedent will produce the consequent other things will too. We then speak of, "sufficient conditions." If both of these joint outcomes have no members, we speak of, "necessary and sufficient conditions." [2]

As one can imagine, the likelihood of getting zeros in these two cells is remarkably small. For one thing, the operations by which we identify the antecedents are generally not unique. That is, the same antecedent may be identified by more than one operation. But if we allow only one specific operation, then all other possible identifications occur under $-A$, reducing the possibility of obtaining zero frequencies. For another thing, the relationship between the antecedents and the consequent may not be perfect. Hence, some variation explicable by chance is likely to exist. It becomes obvious that a statistical argument is going to be used in experimentation.

Before proceeding to a discussion of the role of statistics in experimentation, one further point regarding the experiment must be established. The description of scientific experimentation in section 1 of this chapter is, obviously, ideal. Researchers have often tried to conduct experiments before their theory was rigorous enough to warrant a precise inference either as to proper identification of the antecedent or the kind of relationship expected to emerge. Hence, we may speak of three types of experiments currently being used.

The first, and most simple, is that experiment which seeks only to answer questions. This is not too far removed from trial-and-error experimentation. In this case, one simply asks, What will happen if I do so and so? Clearly, nothing is being tested in this type of activity. It may give rise to a fruitful hypothesis; it may, on the other hand, involve a great waste of time and money.

The second type of experiment involves the test of an elliptical hypothesis. You recall that the elliptical hypothesis omits certain elements of content, presumably until after the experiment is completed. Quite often the elliptical hypothesis is the null hypothesis which simply asserts that the hypothetical antecedent is no different from its negation in producing the consequent.

The third main type of experiment involves a specific hypothesis. Of course, the amount of specificity varies from one experiment to another. Since this type of hypothesis is the most easily falsified, it is also the most rigorous test. When one can predict within a relatively small range of statistical error, the argument is not only tightened, it is also more convincing.

This third type of experiment is the most desired in scientific re-

2 Note relationship of this argument with Mill's "Canons." See Ch. 6, pp. 138–145.

search. Currently, however, it is engaged in less frequently than the second type. Nonetheless, it is the goal; and the first two types of experiments must be regarded as steps towards the third.

3. STATISTICS IN EXPERIMENTAL DESIGN

The critical experiment in which one spectacular result is completely convincing of the verification of the hypothesis is virtually non-existent. The test of any experiment rests by and large upon the replication of the entire set of operations. The repetition of any test, unless a perfect relationship exists, generally involves the possibility of sampling error. This being so, the statistical rejection of chance as an explanation is fundamental to experimental inference.[3]

At the same time, the statistical argument must be fully considered before the experiments are to take place. Some years ago, the author was asked to give some advice to a physiologist who was engaged in an experiment on cats. The general hypothesis was that electric stimulation of different sections of the brain would result in different reactions in heartbeat and respiration of the cat in question. The preparation of each cat for the test was a tedious job; about one cat a day could be prepared and used in the experiment. By the time the advice was sought, some 400 cats had been exhausted. After the data had been classified, some statistical design was sought.

By then, it was too late to develop a rigorous statistical argument. The categories were not designed to permit statistical analysis. The various controls were lacking in rigor. The basic assumptions of statistical inference were unknown and, hence, ignored. At best, some simple frequency analysis could be safely used. From the point of view of rigorous experimentation, no general inferences could be drawn. Some descriptive statements about a particular group of dissected cats were all that was possible. The moral is quite clear: the statistical design must be incorporated into the general system of operations to be performed.

Recall the argument given in the preceding chapter that a statistical formula represents the solution of some problem. Unless the problem solved is in fact the one faced by the experimenter, gratuitous use of statistics is misleading. This is not to say that there is absolutely no value to the *ad hoc* application of a statistical argument. But it does mean that the chances for meeting the assumptions of statistical inference are minimized if these assumptions are not explicitly a part of the experimental design.

[3] Cf. C. West Churchman, *Theory of Experimental Inference,* New York, Macmillan, 1948.

Perhaps the simplest statistical argument which could fit an experimental design would involve the simple dichotomy of "success" and "failure" regarding the identification of the possible outcomes of the consequent. The antecedent would, of course, be the experimental group which is subject to some experience; its negation would be a control group which is subjected to some experience; the negation of this negation would be a control group not subjected to the experience. If, prior to the experiment, both groups are independent random samples from the same population, the statistical design would be the critical ratio of proportions. Of course, since frequencies of outcomes are involved, a chi-square test of a 2×2 table could be used.

If the consequential behavior varies in amount, a simple experimental design would involve differences in mean amounts before the experiment and after.[4] The control group would be a random sample whose problematic behavior is measured before the experiment. The experimental group would be the same group measured after the experience. A certain amount (though unknown) of correlation will exist since the same people occur in both the control and experimental groups. Hence, the standard error formula would have to take the correlation into account. Formula 24 in Chapter 5, page 93, it will be recalled, does take the correlation into account.

So far the experimental argument has been relatively simple—the comparison of one presumed antecedent against its negation or absence. However, the same problematic behavior could be differentially related to a set of possible antecedents. For convenience, let us call the set of antecedents, "treatments."

The experiment will then proceed in this way. The problematic data are essentially quantitative. Corresponding to each treatment, a random sample is drawn either from a parent population which has not been subjected to the treatments, or from an original sample so drawn. Each sample is then subjected to the treatment designated in the design and each object is measured in respect to the problematic data. If the consequence of each treatment differs from all the rest, the arithmetic means of the several treatments ought to be significantly different from each other. It would be possible to test the difference between all possible pairs of means. Clearly, that kind of analysis would be rather difficult and time consuming.

A more direct approach would be to ask whether the variation of the treatment means around the grand mean estimates the same variance as does the variation of the dependent variable around each treatment mean. If the two sources of variation estimate the same thing, the treatments make no real difference. If, however, the two sources

[4] See Chapter 5.

are estimating different kinds of variance, then the treatments have been differentially effective. This can be tested by the F ratio of analysis of variance. We will proceed to give a numerical example.

It is known that performance level, as identified by measuring the time taken to complete a uniform task, is a variable. The problem is to explain, as much as possible, this variation. The statistical explanation is of the form of reduction of variance. Accordingly, we seek to determine if performance under different controlled conditions results in any explanation of the variation.

The experimental design is simple and straightforward. The problematic data consists of the time taken by school children to solve a relatively simple puzzle. The treatments consist of four conditions under which the puzzle-solving activity is to take place. Group A will consist of those children who have been given instruction on how to solve a similar type of puzzle. This instruction is "treatment A." Group B will consist of those who have simply been asked to solve the puzzle, but no instructions have been given. Group C will consist of those who have been given the instruction in treatment A and, in addition, are promised a reward if they can solve the puzzle. Group D will consist of those who are not only not instructed, but are subjected to certain mild distractions (i.e., doors opening and closing, people talking, etc.). The entire group is a random sample of 28 school children drawn from a class of 156 fifth graders. They are randomly assorted to the 4 groups, each having 7 children.

TABLE 7.1. TIME TAKEN IN MINUTES TO COMPLETE A SIMPLE PUZZLE
UNDER SELECTED CONDITIONS

With Instruction A	Merely Asked to Solve Puzzle B	Instructions Plus Rewards C	Distractions Present D
5	6	3	9
8	10	5	12
10	12	4	12
7	9	7	8
8	10	6	10
5	8	8	11
10	9	5	10

Source: Hypothetical.

The number in Table 7.1 represents the number of minutes taken by each child to complete the puzzle. Notice that the column sums vary, apparently considerably. The legitimacy of analysis of variance seems obvious.[5] To refresh our memory, the computational formulas for analysis of variance are given in Table 7.2. This is simply a reproduction of the table given in Chapter 5.

TABLE 7.2. ANALYSIS OF VARIANCE

Source	Sum of Squares	d.f.	Mean Square	F
Total	$\Sigma X_i{}^2{}_j - \dfrac{(\Sigma X_{ij})^2}{N}$	$N-1$		
Between	$\dfrac{\Sigma X.{}^2{}_i}{n} - \dfrac{(\Sigma X_{ij})^2}{N}$	$M-1$	$\dfrac{\dfrac{\Sigma X.{}^2{}_j}{n} - \dfrac{(\Sigma X_{ij})^2}{N}}{M-1}$	$\dfrac{\dfrac{\Sigma X.{}^2{}_j}{n} - \dfrac{(\Sigma X_{ij})^2}{N}}{M-1}$
Within	$\Sigma X_i{}^2{}_j - \dfrac{\Sigma X.{}^2{}_j}{n}$	$N-M$	$\dfrac{\Sigma X_i{}^2{}_j - \dfrac{\Sigma X.{}^2{}_j}{n}}{N-M}$	$\dfrac{\Sigma X_i{}^2{}_j - \dfrac{\Sigma X.{}^2{}_j}{n}}{N-M}$

To facilitate the computation we will construct a table which will give us the needed information. This is given in Table 7.3 below.

TABLE 7.3. TIME TAKEN TO COMPLETE PUZZLE,
ARRANGED TO FACILITATE COMPUTATIONS

		A		B		C		D	
		X	X^2	X	X^2	X	X^2	X	X^2
		5	25	6	36	3	9	9	81
		8	64	10	100	5	25	12	144
		10	100	12	144	4	16	12	144
		7	49	9	81	7	49	8	64
		8	64	10	100	6	36	10	100
		5	25	8	64	8	64	11	121
		10	100	9	81	5	25	10	100
	Total	53	427	64	606	38	224	72	754
$(\Sigma X)^2$		2809		4096		1444		5184	

Source: From Table 7.1.

Notice that under each treatment we have a column labeled X and X^2. Direct computation gives us the following results:

[5] For a test of homoscedasticity see Wilfred J. Dixon and Frank J. Massey, Jr., *Introduction to Statistical Analysis*, New York, McGraw-Hill, 1951, p. 147.

$$\Sigma\, X_{ij} = 227$$
$$\Sigma\, X^2_{ij} = 2011$$
$$\Sigma(\Sigma\, X_{ij})^2 = 13{,}533$$
$$(\Sigma\, X_{ij})^2 = 51{,}529$$

Since there are four columns, $m = 4$. Inserting these into the equations given in Table 7.2 we find,

TABLE 7.4. ANALYSIS OF VARIANCE, NUMERICAL EXAMPLE

Source	Sum of Squares	d.f.	Mean Squares	F
Between	$\dfrac{13533}{7} - \dfrac{51529}{28}$	3	$\dfrac{92.96}{3} = 30.99$	30.99
Within	$2011 - \dfrac{13533}{7}$	24	$\dfrac{77.72}{24} = 3.24$	3.24

Note that $\Sigma(\Sigma X_{ij})^2$ can be used to denote $\Sigma X.^2_{j}$.

Thus, with the between column mean square in the numerator, and the within column mean square in the denominator,

$$F = 30.99/3.24 = 9.86$$

With 3 degrees of freedom for the numerator and 24 degrees of freedom for the denominator, we find from Table 5.16 page 108, that the probability of obtaining an F-ratio as large or larger than 3.01 is .05. Our formal null hypothesis would be, "If chance explains the differences in means squares, at the 5 percent level of confidence, the F-ratio will be less than 3.01." Since ours is much larger than that, we reject the null hypothesis. This, in turn, implies that the column means differ significantly and, hence, that level of performance varies according to the conditions under which the activity takes place.

4. EXPERIMENTAL DESIGN: THE CONTROL OF VARIABLES

The results in our hypothetical experiment seem quite conclusive. Certainly, the results conform to our expectation. We may, in order to clarify the issue of controlling variables, ask if we did have sufficient control to place any confidence upon the operations performed.

In regards to our problematic data, that is, the level of performance, we may wonder whether recording the data in terms of minutes taken to solve the puzzle was sufficient. Is "time taken to solve the puzzle" a sufficient identification of performance level? Ought we not include the number of false starts, the incorrect solutions tried? Does the person who tries several false solutions quickly have the same performance level as the one who tries only one but who takes as much total time? Have trial and error solutions to the problem been sufficiently controlled, or do we have reason to infer they make no difference to the outcome?

Further, no one is particularly interested in the solution of puzzles as such; we wish to generalize to the theoretical construct, "performance level." In a general theoretical sense, have we properly identified our problems? Keeping the same sorts of treatments, would we get the same results if we changed our identification of performance? All these questions must be carefully considered before we can have any faith in the outcome of the experiment.

In reference to our treatment, we may ask the same general questions: (1) have we properly identified the variables we think are important, and (2) have we properly controlled other variables which might be present? For example, does past experience with puzzles of this type have any effect on performance? Judging from our own experiment (treatments A and B differ by the former having instructions which the latter did not), prior knowledge of the task is exceedingly important. Have we controlled past experience? What about general intelligence? Does this make a difference? We are tempted to say that it *obviously* does. Has it been controlled? Other relevant factors are just as easily thought of; the student should consider as many as he can.

The main principle of control which we employed was that of "randomization." We selected our primary sample by random means and sorted out the four treatment groups randomly. This means that we hoped that the presence of these other factors appear equally in all four groups. This is a rather large order, in view of having four groups with only seven in each group. Moreover, the population from which the original sample was drawn is itself limited. If, for example, past experience with puzzles is partly a function of the social class of the child, and if, ecologically, different schools service different social classes, we would lose control through the sample we took.

Randomization is the fundamental control in experimentation in the social sciences. Whenever we reach the point of being unable to further control the variables in question, we resort to randomization. The main justification is a theorem in mathematical statistics which shows that the means of a large number of samples of a large set of variables tend to be normally distributed even if the original variables were not.[6] This theorem is appealed to when the error is considered a consequence of a large number of uncontrolled factors. The difficulty lies in knowing

[6] This theorem is generally called the "Central Limit Theorem." See Alexander Mood, *Introduction to the Theory of Statistics*, New York, McGraw-Hill, 1950, p. 136 ff.

what a large number of uncontrolled factors really means. Then, too, the possibility of correlation between the factors (as between social class and past experience) rules out randomization, since correlation negates the inference of statistical independence.

Some control exists in *matching* for factors. One way is to select the experimental groups in such a way that each group has the same number of members having past experience with puzzles, certain levels of intelligence, etc. Another way is to match individuals for these characteristics. That is, if a member of group *A* has a high level of intelligence, comes from a certain social class, has a certain amount of past experience, each of the other groups should have a member with the same characteristics. Clearly, this kind of matching is more rigorous than the group matching; it is also more time consuming and more costly. Further, either kind of matching introduces correlation between the several groups and complicates the statistical argument.

If the potentially interfering factors are subject to physical manipulation, we may speak of "equalizing" them. In our example, it might be true that the relative amount of light is a significant variable. This could be controlled by keeping the amount of light constant, that is, the same amount of light for each group.[7] Holding the influence of interfering variables constant is a principle second to randomization in experimental design.

The reason for holding certain variables constant is quite apparent: it reduces the complexity of the design, and clarifies the statement of relationships which can be made. Instead of having to compare the experimental results simultaneously for differing levels of the interfering variable (e.g., differing amount of light) the relationship is described for only one level (e.g., the constant amount of light used). Of course, the generality of the experiment might be reduced; in effect, one buys rigor at the expense of generality.

Thus, one of the main controls in experimental design consists of holding variables constant where possible. If the problem or data are such as to make that infeasible, the objects studied are matched for the several interfering variables. This matching may either be in terms of the experimental groups, or by individuals in the different groups. When the possibility for holding the variables constant, or for matching them, is no longer real—increased rigor may lead to a complex design if a larger number of variables are considered simultaneously—one employs the principle of randomization.

The control of variables in experimental research is a difficult task.

---

[7] An advanced statistical technique for holding variables constant is that of multiple and partial correlation. See Mordecai Ezekiel, *Methods of Correlation Analysis*, 2nd ed., New York, Wiley, 1941.

One must not only have a clear conception of what variables are related to the problem, one must know how to identify the variables empirically. Since there is an element of fadism connected with experimentation, we should be reminded that the operation identifying the variable ought not to be equated with the variable itself.

Two dangers exist in the equating of operational and theoretical definitions. On the one hand, it may lead to over-generalization of the results. If, in particular, the explanatory antecedent is defined operationally by a specific operation but retains a general "name," one might draw false inferences about instances of the antecedent when identifiable by other operations. On the other hand, restricting the argument simply to the operational definition can lead to sterile results. In particular, the operation may properly identify an antecedent, but because of its restricted utility, be of little theoretical importance.

5. EXPERIMENTAL DESIGN: LEARNING THEORY

While most contemporary research in learning theory generally involves highly complex statistical arguments, we will illustrate only the most simple kind of experimentation from learning theory. It will be recalled that an elementary form of experimentation is designed simply to answer a question.

One of the basic tenets of physiological learning theory is the assumption of random behavior on the part of a subject learning some particular type of activity. Indeed, many formulations of learning theory emphasize the reduction of error in the process of learning. Reduction of error, as a measure of learning, makes sense only if the initial stages of the activity were of a trial-and-error sort.

Consequently, it becomes important to know if the amount of random behavior is a function of controllable conditions, or if it is a *constant* force. When the conception of "drive" was introduced to explain "motivation" for the reduction of error, the question was raised, Is the amount of drive related to the amount of random behavior of the subject being studied? If the answer was yes, then the amount of drive would have to be controlled in future experiments.

To answer the question, a relatively simple experiment was designed. The subjects were white rats. The variable "drive" was operationally defined in terms of hunger. Accordingly, 17 white rats were recently fed, and 17 were left hungry. The maze was simply marked off with an equal number of squares; no "goal" (i.e., nothing to reduce the drive) was present. The only behavior possible was random behavior.

The rats were alternatively set in the maze (i.e., a fed rat followed by a hungry rat). The concept random behavior was measured by counting the number of squares the rats entered. Thus, operationally, the more squares the rat entered, the greater its random behavior. It turned out that the average number of squares entered by the fed rat was 26.7; while an average of 42.9 squares were entered by the hungry rats. From this, the conclusion was that the amount of random activity varies with the amount of drive.[8]

Notice the way in which controls were used: (1) the drive was directly manipulated by giving or withholding food; (2) the possibility of drive-reduction as an explanation was controlled through the absence of any goal directly connected with the drive; [9] (3) the alternation of hungry and fed rats randomized the sequence of the activity; (4) a genetic assumption about the intelligence of rats was at least partially controlled by a random sorting of the original 34 rats into the 2 groups.

6. EXPERIMENTAL DESIGN: SOCIAL PSYCHOLOGICAL THEORY

The concept, "frame of reference" has a wide currency in social psychological theory. For the most part, the inference of a frame of reference was an *ad hoc* one—used after the fact to account for certain types of behavior. In other words, the temporal sequence of knowledge reversed the logical sequence of the argument. The logical form went something like this: If frame of reference X, then behavior B. But the temporal sequence was to discern frame of reference X after observing behavior B. To gain a more rigorous foundation for the concept, it was desired to develop a frame of reference under controlled conditions, that is, experimentally.

To control the possibility of potentially intruding factors (e.g., the possibility of a pre-existing frame of reference), the basic condition was to insure an absence of a frame of reference. The knowledge of auto-kinetic phenomena led to the experimental design. It was long known that a fixed light in an otherwise darkened space gave the appearance of

8 J. F. Dashiell, "A Quantitative Demonstration of Animal Drive," *Journal of Comparative Psychology*, vol. 5, 1925, pp. 205–208.
9 Had the subjects been human beings, the amount of random activity may have been a type of drive-reduction, i.e., in certain situations a social value, and hence a drive, to "do something" exists. This implies a conviction that some activity is better than none, even if the activity is logically unrelated to other goals or wishes. An example may be found in the experience of many soldiers during World War II who, in critical front-line actions, preferred to be doing something to relatively pure idleness. This preference was made even if the only inferential result was the reduction of tension. In other words, human beings might not always behave like white rats in essentially the same experimental set-up.

motion. Since no physical position could be attached to the space of motion, no ordinary frame of reference could be employed.

Three hypotheses occurred to Professor Muzafer Sherif.[10] One was that an individual, after a number of trials, would eventually hit upon a projected norm of the amount of movement, and that this norm would result from a basis of judgment subjectively defined. That is, in the absence of an external frame of reference, a subjective one would be evolved. The proof would lie in the existence of a consistent pattern of estimation of motion; erratic judgments would falsify the hypothesis.

The second hypothesis was that a group of individuals would not give a hodgepodge of individual judgments, but would show a group consensus. If the latter were true, and we could argue that a group norm had been established, what would be the effect of the group norm on individual judgments?

The third hypothesis was that the group norm would persist and become the frame of reference for the individual judgment. The verification of this hypothesis warrants the inference that a frame of reference had been produced under controlled conditions.

Accordingly, a darkened room was chosen, and the stimulus light (five meters from the subjects) was a tiny point of light controlled by a shutter operated by the experimenter. One group of individuals were first tested for individual judgments. A second group consisted of individuals without previous experience who were to arrive at a group judgment. Later, some of these were to make individual judgments. A third group consisted of those who had made individual judgments and who later made group judgments.

Briefly, the data tended to verify the major hypotheses. To be sure, there were considerable fluctuations. In the group situations, however, much of the fluctuation was a group phenomenon; the norms differed for each session, but it was the group which fluctuated.

Despite the schematic presentation of this design, it is possible to discuss ways in which one could increase the amount of control over the behavior of the subjects. For one thing, in the group situation, the personalities of the subjects were uncontrolled. If personality can be typed along a leader-follower continuum, the composition of the groups in terms of this variable could conceivably result in changes of the resultant norms. That is, if a group consisted of followers, the emergent norm might have a different pattern than if the group consisted of both leaders and followers.[11] As an exercise, the reader should consider other possible

[10] Muzafer Sherif and Hadley Cantril, *The Psychology of Ego-Involvements*, New York, Wiley, 1947, p. 52 ff.

[11] At the time this was being written further research in this problem area, particularly in an attempt to be more rigorous statistically, was being pursued by the staff of the Urban Life Research Institute at Tulane University. It is not, obviously, a dead problem.

variables and decide how these may be controlled in future research designs.

A well-known statistical proposition holds that a single dimension measured by two different metric systems will generate a high degree of linear correlation. Deviation from perfect correlation can be accounted for by random measurement error. We can make use of this proposition in specifying an experimental design.

Theoretical propositions are, of course, general. They are far more general than any specific test. In some sense, this makes it impossible to refute a perfectly general statement on a single test; failure in a single instance could simply result in explicating a limiting condition of the hypothesis. But consider that the concepts making up a general proposition can in some instances generate different operational specifications. Since operational specifications can be thought of as behavioral specifications, we may create a situation in which we propose to correlate in some sense two behavioral consequences implied by one general concept. If our argument flowing from the concept is sound, a predictable pattern of association should be manifest in our data.

Consider, then, the general Durkheimian notion that a major social dimension required to explain, "what keeps social relations going," is that of solidarity. Now, it seems to make sense to think that groups manifesting high solidarity should be attractive to its members—and the converse should hold, too. Moreover, groups of high solidarity should impose sanctions upon those who would deviate from critical values of the group. The point here is that the idea of solidarity encompasses both attractiveness and sanctions.

If these two dimensions could be measured quantitatively, the design would be a simple linear correlation. However, we may not be as precise in our operational specifications as is required for quantitative expression. Accordingly, some sort of categorization of at least one dimension in the problem is needed.

At this point we can borrow from the well-developed strategies in small group research. We can (in principle, at least) secure a randomly selected sample which we shall partition in two or more kinds of groups. For convenience, we will think in terms of two kinds; class *A* will be those experimentally designed to have a high degree of attractiveness and class *B* will be those designed to have a low degree of attractiveness. This may be manipulated by specifying its reputation and the difficulty in obtaining membership. The subjects will be told that one type is "better" and more highly sought after than the other. One interpretation of all such research is that people are being tested on their ability to obey instructions.

Each group of both classes will have one member whose behavior is controlled by the study. That is to say, one member will, upon signal from the research team, engage in deviant behavior. The point of the research is to observe the sanction-like response of the group members. In the class A groups there should, by the hypothesis, be more evidence of efforts to get conformity than in the class B groups.

The statistical test would depend upon how the sanction behavior has been measured. If one could only define categories (e.g., sanction, non-sanction), then a critical ratio of proportions would be used; if some sense of quantification were possible, then a critical ratio of means would be appropriate. The N in either case would be the number of groups created in each class. If the N is less than 30, then a small sample argument (the t-test) is required.

The t-test is similar to the critical ratio except that the shape of the curve, and hence the critical point, varies according to the number of degrees of freedom. Moreover, it depends upon homogeneity of variance. Rather than shrinking from such a test, it should be welcome for the real difference may be in the magnitude of variance. One would infer that the variance in class A groups should be smaller than in the class B groups. This may be assessed by the F-test which is a ratio of two unbiased estimates of variance.

The larger of the two estimates is always put in the numerator and the smaller in the denominator. Its interpretation depends upon the number of degrees of freedom in both the numerator and the denominator. Tables of F, found in books of tables for statisticians, usually specify the $d.f.$ of the numerator as column headings and the $d.f.$ of the denominator as row headings. The cell entries are the critical values; these are presented in differing kinds of type. For instance, bold face may represent the value of F for a given pair of degrees of freedom that is exceeded 5 percent of the time by chance. Any F equal to, or greater than, that number would be significant and would justify a rejection of the hypothesis that the variances are equal.

The point of this discussion is to emphasize the general need to compare variances. It is interesting to note that the engineering sciences used to refer to variance as "precision." That it, too, could signify something of cohesion—or solidarity—should occur to the experimentally minded sociologist. In other words, an experimental comparison of variances constitutes an important research design for sociological research.

7. EXPERIMENTAL DESIGN: SOCIOLOGICAL THEORY

If group A believes that group B is interfering with the attainment of its goals, are hostilities likely to break out between them? Admitting the possibility of a precipitating factor, most sociologists would agree that hostilities are likely. Can this point be experimentally demonstrated?

To demonstrate the correctness of the statement, several things must be experimentally created. The individuals selected to comprise the groups must not merely be a congregation of discrete personalities, but must be members of a social group. There must be some structure, some identity of self, and a "consciousness of kind." Further, the belief that *B* is interfering with *A* must be subject to experimental control. In other words, the members of group *A* ought not begin with the notion that group *B* is against them. Finally, the precipitating factor must be subjected to control by the experimenter. Granting the experimental creation of the two groups and the experimental creation of inter-group tensions, it is possible that hostilities could begin without the intervention of the experimenter. In this case, however, the precise situation leading to hostilities would not be well enough known to permit rigorous inference.

To determine whether or not such an experiment was feasible, Sherif made a study on a group of 24 boys from the lower-middle class income group in the New Haven area.[12] The deliberate attempt was made to secure a homogeneity of background: similarity of religious affiliation (19 belonging to the same denomination), educational experience and family backgrounds. None were behavior problems, all more or less "normal," with about average IQ. The boys were enrolled in a summer camp.

The initial stage of the experiment allowed the boys to develop their own friendship patterns. In the second stage, when the two groups were to be created, the friendship patterns were deliberately broken; 65 percent of those who were put in the "Bulldogs" group preferred friends who were put in the "Red Devils" group, and vice versa. Thus, later hostilities between the two groups would have to overcome those friendship feelings which had not been controlled in any way. Later on, some 95 percent of the Red Devils were to prefer boys from that group for friends; this compares with the 35 percent at the beginning of stage 2.

Stage 2, then, can be called the stage of in-group membership and identify the group as such. Opportunities were created in which the individual participants could "show their stuff," and in that way be accepted as worthwhile members of the groups. Rewards were made on a group basis, rather than to individual stars. In this period leadership patterns emerged, and data were carefully recorded which permitted the inference of group solidarity.

In stage 3, open competition between the groups was fostered. Ball

[12] Muzafer Sherif, "A Preliminary Experimental Study of Intergroup Relations," chapter 17 in John H. Rohrer and and Muzafer Sherif, eds., *Social Psychology at the Crossroads,* New York, Harper & Row, 1951.

games and tugs-of-war were engaged in. While the Bulldogs tended to win, the Red Devils developed group rationalizations for their losses. A general pattern of prejudice developed, and the conception of the Bulldogs as "cheaters" typified the attitude of the Red Devils.

Certain frustrating experiences were carefully manipulated by the experimenters, so designed that the blame would fall on the other group. Towards the end of the experiment a big party was held for the two groups. Half of the food was slightly damaged (e.g., the cake crushed), and the Red Devils, being allowed to eat first, were told to take their share. They took the good food. When the Bulldogs entered they saw the damaged goods, and attributed it to the other group. Some wanted to fight immediately, but they decided to eat what they could. They retired to a corner and began to hurl insults at the Red Devils. When the Red Devils went to leave, one Bulldog was seen putting an empty ice cream carton on the Red Devils' table. This led to physical contact, and one Bulldog opened a knife and had to be restrained.

A series of raids and fights between the two groups followed. Though the experiment had ended with the production of open hostilities, those in charge of the study then attempted to minimize the extent of the conflict. To a degree, they were successful. But on the last night, the two groups wanted to be by themselves, "for the last time."

This study shows quite clearly that by careful manipulation true social groups can be formed. It is also possible to instill beliefs in the minds of group members antagonistic to members of the out-group. Moreover, open hostilities can be produced under controlled conditions.

One striking thing about the study is the attempt at control over variables. Notice, for example, that none of the boys were behavior problems; yet the pattern of physical fighting and even drawing a knife resulted from the hostile attitudes. Note, also, the careful ways in which a potentially interfering variable was put to good use in the design. The original friendship patterns were broken and surmounted. Despite earlier feelings of friendship, *group* antagonism was indeed possible. Had the two groups been originally composed of these natural friendships, the strength of the experiment would have been weakened.

Of course, some basic elements were not controlled. As Sherif points out all of these boys came from a culture which accepts and emphasizes the competitive role in society. Whether the same results could have been obtained from a sample of boys drawn from a noncompetitive culture could not be answered by this experiment.

8. EXPERIMENTAL DESIGN: COMMUNICATION THEORY

Does the pressure of members of a group to communicate to other members of the group about some item, say x, grow with increases in the cohesiveness of the group? Assuming, for the argument, that all other factors are either constant or irrelevant, the answer seems to be, yes. Insofar as the item x is concerned, it may be such an irrelevant item that there never is any pressure to communicate. Or, the mores of the group may be such as to exclude communication about the item, irrespective of the amount of cohesiveness. In some cases lack of cohesiveness might bring about discussion. An example of this is "sex" in the Victorian family group.

Limiting our concern, then, to topics which are of generic interest to the group, we might wish to demonstrate the affirmative answer to our question. That is, we may phrase the question as an hypothesis and strive to test it experimentally. This was done by members of the Research Center for Group Dynamics, Institute of Social Research, at the University of Michigan. They defined "cohesiveness of a group" as "the resultant of all the forces acting on the members to remain in the group." They further identified the significant forces as the attractiveness of the group in terms of the prestige of the group, the personal attraction of the members, and the activities engaged in. In any experimental test of their hypothesis, these forces must be controlled and, if possible, measured in some way.

The action to be engaged in by the participants consisted of looking at a set of pictures. The participants were paired, and each pair member got a slightly different set of pictures. They were separately to write a story about these pictures and, subsequently, were to discuss their story with their pair partner for possible revisions. The experimenters were then to trace the patterns of agreement and directions of influence which occurred.

The operational definition for the three measures of cohesiveness are essentially these: (1) The personal attractiveness of the members was dichotomized into low and high cohesiveness. Those in the low category were given the usual instructions and then some comment on how they had tried to match group members to get compatible people together, but in this case they could only get the main points. Those in the high category were told that the pair matched very high and that the two would like each other a lot.

(2) The attractiveness of the activity of the group was also dichotomized into low and high categories. Those in the low cohesiveness category were told they were to use their imagination and to strive for a high score. Those in the high cohesiveness category were promised a reward. Both groups were told that they could not be matched on personality factors, but that the main objection had been met. The third force, (3), the attractiveness of the prestige of the group, was also dichotomized into

low and high categories. In the low category, the comments were of the order that their lab instructors had said they would be particularly suited material for a good group. For the high category they were told that they had all of the qualifications which were needed for success in the task and that this pair should be the best group, and could be used as a model in subsequent instruction.

Table 7.5 gives the mean number of changes in the stories which were influenced by the partner. It is seen that, in each type of force there were more changes in the high cohesiveness category than in the low one, just as one would expect by the hypothesis. The question becomes, Is this a significant finding, or is this a chance relationship? The question was answered by use of analysis of variance. These means were different at about the 10 percent level of significance. This implies that if we were using the 5 percent level, we could not reject chance.

TABLE 7.5. MEAN NUMBER OF CHANGES IN STORIES WHICH WERE INFLUENCED BY THE PARTNER

	Nature of Attraction to Group		
	Personal Attraction	Task Direction	Group Prestige
Low Cohesive Pairs	7.9	8.9	6.7
High Cohesive Pairs	10.5	11.0	8.3

From: Kurt W. Back, "Influence Through Social Communication," *Journal of Abnormal & Social Psychology*, 46, no. 1, 1951, p. 18. Copyrighted 1951 by the American Psychological Assn., and reproduced by permission.

We are not so much interested here in the fact that the significance level in support of the hypothesis was not reached as we are in an assessment of the operations performed. We might first question the existence of a group in a sociological sense. The simple fact of taking two people into the same room and having them talk about a common subject does not necessarily imply that a group exists. One might arbitrarily define a group to include such a situation; but science is public and the term group must be defined in other than idiosyncratic fashion.

We might also question the validity of the operations defining the various forces resulting in the members remaining in the group. It might well be that the variable which the experimenters were really measuring was the psychological dimension of suggestibility rather than the sociological one of group cohesiveness. Certainly, one could argue just as plausibly in favor of suggestibility as one could for cohesiveness. The alternative arguments appear equally strong. As a result, we must admit that the results from this experiment are not very conclusive. Insofar as the operations do measure the variables in question, we can have confidence in the direction of the findings. But, on the contrary, insofar as the operations fail to measure the variables in question, we must question the findings.

The purpose of the criticism is not to suggest the fundamental inadequacy of the experimental method in testing hypotheses such as these. The logic of experimentation is untouched by the criticisms offered. Rather, we seek to point out that experimentation is a difficult task. Particularly difficult is the development of a set of operations upon which general agreement is not, methodologically, a deterent to future experimentation. One can, if not ego-involved in the particular experimental design, learn much from failure and criticism. The subsequent experimenter, at least, can face up to some of the criticisms of which the original experimenter was unaware.

9. SOME FURTHER EXAMPLES OF CONTEMPORARY EXPERIMENTATION

Contemporary experimentation in sociology continues the strategy of isolating one dimension for precise manipulation. The argument often becomes an analogous one in that the dimension manipulated is an analogue of a real dimension.

Consider the problem of studying the impact of value-conflicts on interpersonal relations. This sort of issue is critical in the family; but experiments often seem to have a "let's play house" atmosphere. Accordingly, it is necessary to insert a dimension which is germane to the task of the experimental group and which is similar to those encountered in the family. In the case of value-conflicts, simply telling the player of role A that his value is such and such and then telling the player of role B that her value is such as to be in conflict with the former does not test out the issue—it is little more than asking the question whether or not people can follow instructions.

If one considers the characteristics of value commitments, however, he finds that they are not empirically demonstrable. Those holding to the value know that the value is true, and no proof to the contrary is possible. Suppose, then, that two people are to act out a relationship each given contradictory information. Let them have the task of playing a game but one be given one rule for moving ahead and the other is given another rule. Let them both be on the same team and then let an observer watch their behavior. Note that here each had knowledge which is not empirically demonstrated, but the truth of which cannot be doubted. Any resulting bickering can, in part at least, be regarded as similar to the consequences of team-members sharing different values.

Modifications of this strategy are many. They can be given more or less the same rules, but different ideas of how to score or win. One may be told that to score, one must get a marker over a box and the other to get it in the box.

A common procedure, since many subjects are college students who are test wise, is to con them into participating in an experiment. They are told what the experiment is all about—they are let in on the idea of the experiment. For example, some of the subjects may be told that the other subjects are people with a low threshold to frustration and that they may become quite violent. The idea is that the subjects are to be motivated to perform some task. They, as part of the experiment, are to act unaware and pretend not to understand the other subjects. Of course, if the experiment goes well, the naïve subjects will get quite angry. They are being manipulated, the subjects are only acting anger and the point of the experiment is to see how much anger the students will tolerate before they inform the subjects that it is all a part of the study.

This "double-dealing" is easily proliferated, too. One may question the ethical propriety of the procedure since it requires deliberate falsification of the situation. What is interesting is that few social scientists who utilize this sort of trickery ever suspect that their subjects can deceive them.

For example, a study has students go out and interview. The dependent variable is the number of completed and usable schedules. The manipulation is to instill in one group a sense of need, other than an economic one, to do a good job. They are given a pseudo-personality test and told that they are the kind who simply must succeed or they feel guilty. After the experiment is over, they are told that the test was a phoney and that they are normal. But the point is the experiment proceeds to test out the hypothesis that those who are anxious over success will go out and do a better job than a control group. That they may be induced to falsify data, not really interviewing but merely appearing to, seldom occurs to the researcher.

There are two points to this anecdote. One is to raise the ethical question of morality (and the student must understand that the raising of the question does not imply a negative answer). The other is to point out the need to control the possible alternatives to the behavior. Most experiments proceed on the assumption that only two alternative courses of action obtain—that which is most likely for the experimental group and that which is most likely for a control group.

The following experiment is based on a large body of experiments growing out of small group research.[13] Rather than appealing simply to the language of social psychology, we can appeal to Durkheim's argument on the significance of social solidarity or cohesiveness. Recalling Durkheim's observation that suicide is more acceptable in low cohesive groups, one may propose the hypothesis that a person expressing a deviant opinion would be rejected more frequently in a highly cohesive group than in a low cohesive group.

Notice that an hypothesis has been drawn from a body of theory. To determine its truth value we must not only be able to control the expression of deviant behavior, we must also be able to specify a degree of cohesiveness. Moreover, this cohesiveness must be either measured independently of expressions of deviance or in terms of rejection-acceptance of its members. All groups used in such a study will be *ad hoc* groups created by the researcher. It is conceivable that one could find groups of high and low cohesiveness, but then the problem would be to induce some members to express deviant opinions.

It is not enough to tell groups that they are highly cohesive; the experiment becomes simply a test of following instructions. If one cannot create the conditions directly, he must make them indirectly. This requires developing a dimension which is known, or presumed, to be highly correlated with cohesiveness. It happens that some research indicates that group attractiveness is related to cohesiveness. Then if one can indicate that membership in one set of groups is prestigious while other groups are not, cohesiveness is theoretically being manipulated through attractiveness. The entire experiment hinges on such a connection.

Since all groups are easily defined by the researcher, he can also control the members and plant one person who will deviate from the norms of the group. This will be done in both the low cohesive and high cohesive groups. To measure acceptance or rejection, one could simply require that group members rate each other and see if the deviants are ranked as low in the high cohesive group as the hypothesis would require.

This type of experiment identifies the main structural features—and hence the weaknesses as well as strengths—of this kind of research. The basic theory generates an hypothesis. The conditions required by the hypothesis are then created. If they cannot be done directly, then a theoretical argument (supported, if possible, by independent research) allowing an indirect control is required. Finally, the behavior predicted by the hypothesis is operationally specified. A simple statistical argument

[13] It was designated primarily by Donald D. Peterson for use in explaining a statistical problem. See Roy G. Francis and Donald D. Peterson, *Lecture Notes for Elementary Statistics,* Minneapolis, Burgess, 1966, pp. 109–111.

will normally follow and permit, within the rules of probability inference, a decision regarding the soundness of the argument.

Frequently a charge against experimentation is that the alternative explanation "the subjects simply followed instructions" is better than the scientific one. The reason for such a charge is that most experiments are culture-bound, if they work at all. If an experiment is culture-bound, it could also be bound to a particular class of that culture. Hence, considerable effort has been directed towards creating culture-free experiments. It is quite likely that an experiment absolutely free from cultural limitations is not possible. However, some steps in the direction of reducing the effects of culture have been made.

The idea is quite simple; but its simplicity leads to difficulty. Simply require a decision in a situation whose elements violate a cultural pattern. Rokeach devised a game in which the subjects were told of a jumping bug which acted in a way not consistent with our cultural expectations.[14] For example, it could take leaps of any magnitude but having taken one, it had to take a second one. The task was to determine how many jumps it would take to be in a position to eat some food. Another difficulty lay in its not eating in a way consonant with our culture. The intent was to determine the extent to which minds were closed. This was measured, in part, by the refusal to continue the game.

10. SOME LIMITS ON EXPERIMENTATION

The experiment is a very convincing argument. The logical sequence and the temporal sequence of the argument are the same. A temporal fact is built into the design; first one creates the antecedent and then one observes the consequent. This temporal sequence serves to distinguish relationships which can be called "associational" from those which can be termed "causal." By illustration, the relationship between hair color and eye color is associational; presumably, both are a function of the same underlying genetic variable. The relation between hostile attitudes towards an outgroup and subsequent hostilities is not merely associational. The time sequence makes a difference.

However desirable experimentation may be, we must be careful not to define scientific method as experimentation. As we have indicated time and again, the critical point is the problem and the type of data necessary to solve the problem. If these are not amenable to experimentation, then other research designs are necessary.

[14] Milton Rokeach, *The Open and Closed Mind,* New York, Basic Books, Inc., 1960.

Whether or not a problem is suited to experimentation is not merely a theoretical issue. There are many practical considerations which are involved. The data necessary to any research design must be available before the design can be carried out and if research is carried out in a social situation, that situation may prevent the acquisition of the necessary data.

In a recent study direct observation of members of a bureaucracy led to the inference that the bureaucrat *individualized,* rather than *personalized,* his relationships to his clients.[15] Since the clientele proved to attach no significance to this type of behavior, the hypothesis was suggested that this behavior was a political buffer against negative public reaction. The hypothesis could have been tested experimentally. It is conceivable that the bureaucrats could have acted indifferently and even churlishly towards the clientele. Had the hypothesis been correct, a negative reaction should have been evidenced (perhaps by letters to editors of the local papers). However remote or likely that eventuality would have been, the manager of the office could not take that risk. A negative public reaction was precisely what he sought to avoid, even if the hypothesis had been wrong. It would have been impossible to put the claims of scientific method ahead of the claims of the office manager.

The social limitations to experimentation must be taken into account in research design. In addition to the difficulty of deducing manipulable variables, which itself limits the possibility of sociological experimentation, the social situation in which the research must take place needs to be taken into account. Moreover, the social situation is not always as specific as the cited. Suppose, for example, a psychologist had an hypothesis which, if true, would render a person permanently insane. Would the social values of the American culture permit an experimental test of the hypothesis? Obviously not; the consequences to the individual compete with norms which are more basic to our culture than the norm for scientific knowledge. In contrast, perhaps, we should point out the kind of experiments on human beings which were permitted during the Nazi regime in Germany. At the same time that the Nazi government permitted deprivation studies to be conducted on interned Jews, other experiments which would, if successful, contradict the ethic of racism could not be conducted.

The ethical problems underlying experimental research have other connotations. One fundamental issue is whether or not the subject has a moral right to know that he is the subject of an experiment. One byproduct of the Western Electric studies is the knowledge that an experi-

---

[15] Reference is made to a research on bureaucracy conducted by Roy G. Francis and Robert C. Stone, under the auspices of the Urban Life Research Institute of Tulane University.

mental group will often behave differently simply because it is known to be an experimental group. The study cited indicated that the experimental group had higher production levels simply because the participants knew they were "special." [16] Thus, the knowledge that one is the subject of an experiment tends towards a bias in the results obtainable. This is not particularly surprising, but the problem it raises is not easily resolved.

There is no unique solution to the problem. Whatever answer one gives is contingent upon his own system of values, and the relative hierarchy of claims of science and other considerations. We should not expect a categorical solution, nor even a pragmatic one; the pragmatic solution is acceptable only in terms of a pragmatic ethic. It is simply an issue which the individual scientist, operating in his own social context, must work out. The solution he arrives at, however, will determine largely whether or not certain types of experiments are possible.

One of the difficulties with sociological experimentation resides in the degree to which legitimate doubts can be attached to the designation of controls. In a typical experimental situation, the researcher assembles an aggregate of people and tells them they are to carry out a certain activity. Thus, a group is formed. The current language refers to groups created for the purpose of research as *ad hoc* groups, to distinguish them from natural groups (i.e., those which arise out of the general social process).

When a natural group is transformed into an experimental one, as is sometimes done to test organizational ideas in a factory, hospital, or other situation involving assemblages of people, those in the experimental group may display the "Hawthorne effect." This refers to a study done in an electrical company in which the experimental group always outperformed the control group because they knew they were special. Hence, although statements are ultimately to be made about the natural group, the fears of a Hawthorne effect are great enough to push social scientists into the *ad hoc* situation.

In any case, there is a current tendency not to tell the experimental group what the study is about. Indeed, the strategy often is to lie to the subjects so as to minimize any contamination of the study. Of course, no scientist would dare assume that his subjects lie to him; he must take all of their statements at face value. A number of scientists have questioned the ethics of misrepresenting an experiment to the subject. In the case of personality studies the falsification may involve some sort of "psychological clobbering," for example, telling a person that a personality

---

[16] For an account of Elton Mayo's findings in this regard, see F. J. Roethlisberger and William J. Dickson, *Management and the Worker*, Cambridge, Harvard University Press, 1939.

test he just took demonstrates that he is really a psychopathic deviate. The admission at the end of the study that the diagnosis was a phoney is supposed to undo any psychic damage that was done to the subject. There is no real systematic evidence that such is the case. This may be because no damage does occur, or it may be due to a lack of concerted inquiry (no scientist has yet reported a study in which the existence of psychic damage was the point he sought to establish). Those who fear these outcomes are not likely to engage in that kind of experiment; those who wish to prove no ill effects are, to a degree, open to suspicion because of their desire to report no serious consequences.

Consider the possibility of experimentally induced suicide. Here the value problem is enormous. One would hesitate to argue that it is proper, strictly in the interests of science, that a person should be provoked into ending his own life. Most of our values are in the other direction, that of doing all we can to prevent such an event. It has been argued, however, that such an experiment might result in the subsequent saving of many more from suicide—the experiment may have failed. The point is that the normative and moral problems are vexing. In particular, one must not think that just because an issue involves a moral choice, the answer is immediate—Don't do it! Each day many individuals face the moral issue of whether or not they should enter into a monogamous relation with another.

Despite this point, I wish to emphasize the problem of reconciling deceit in the name of science and the moral basis of academic freedom—integrity. We ought not confound the issue by pointing out how others act. It is, after all, a decision which we must individually face; often despite the groups to which we would like to be loyal.

The limitations to social experimentation have not been exhausted in this brief summary. The student can easily discover other limitations for himself. He may also find comfort in the position that experimental designs do not exhaust scientific methodology. The old saying that astronomy has done well without experimentally producing a universe is well taken.

11. EX POST FACTO DESIGN

Ultimately, all experiments become reduced to propositional form. The theoretical antecedents are stated propositionally. The operations by which empirical members of the theoretical antecedents are identified are similarly reduced to propositions. Propositions about the basic data are made. The conclusion is presented as a proposition. These are made a part of a logical form, and the correctness of the proportions may be communicated to other scientists, and the correctness of the inferences may be judged.

Many before-and-after events take place in the world about us. In particular, in the social world, a certain set of conditions is defined as a "social problem" (e.g., slum conditions after having shown to be associated with delinquency). A social policy is adopted purporting to change some of the undesirable conditions, in the hope that the problem is reduced. An example is low-cost housing to reduce delinquency. If the necessary data could be recaptured, this could also be reduced to propositional form, and conclusions about the effectiveness of the policy could be reached. If the policy did indeed manipulate relevant variables, the result is quite similar to a description of an experiment.

These considerations prompted Professor F. Stuart Chapin to design what he called, "ex post facto experiments." [17] The term "ex post facto" indicates that the experiment has already taken place. The consequence is immediately knowable, and the problem is to determine the antecedents which gave rise to the consequence. The manipulation, performed by others than the social scientist, has already taken place. But some manipulation has occurred: a time dimension is certainly present and if any relation between the manipulated variable and the consequence can be discerned, the argument is more than merely that of association.[18]

The initial phase in the ex post facto design would be the identification of the experimental group, e.g., the group which had been admitted to a housing project. The next phase would be the identification of a control group. The control group would have to be equatable with the experimental group prior to the experiment. Formally, this means that both groups must be random samples from the same universe. It happens, however, that the administrators of a housing project are not likely to draw subjects randomly, but will use a set of criteria which, practically, is defensible but which, scientifically, is biased. Thus, they may have some criterion of need, with the result that only a small portion of the population of which the control group is a random sample is taken. The experimental design will have to overcome such biases.

It takes a certain amount of time for a social experiment to have an effect. Consider the problematic data as, "amount of delinquency": if better housing results in lowering the amount of delinquency, it may take years before the difference is significant. During this time a certain amount of "mortality" occurs, that is, people leaving both the project and the control group by death, migration, refusal to cooperate further in the study, etc. It also happens that the effect of mortality differs for the

[17] F. Stuart Chapin, *Experimental Designs in Sociological Research,* New York, Harper & Row, 1947.

[18] The use of the word "experiment" has been challenged since direct manipulation by the scientist is not possible. Without clouding our thinking by introducing semantic issues, we should recognize that the same type of problem is pursued by "experimentation" and the ex post facto "experiment," namely, the addition of the time factor between the antecedent and the consequent.

two groups, and that the reasons for mortality also differ. Hence, a practical problem exists in maintaining a constant equatability for the two groups.

In addition to the "gross mortality," this simply means that out of an initial number of subjects, with increasing rigor in the design, the number studied in the final analysis is sharply reduced. The problems of ex post facto design, in particular reference to "effective mortality," can be illustrated by citing a well-known experiment of this type.

One of the justifications for increasing expenditures for the school system of any locality is that the high school graduate is better prepared for economic success than those without high school training. There are other reasons, of course, but this is a particularly critical one—its consequences are practical. We can restate this as a formal hypothesis or, for the sake of consistency with a statistical terminology, as a null hypothesis.

Prior to stating the hypothesis, we must clearly identify what we will mean by economic success. Simplicity, at least, would require the single most meaningful measure obtainable. The measure of success was to be taken in the year 1935; the impact of the depression had been fully appreciated. Since this was a critical depression year, the measure of success would be the percent of job shifts from 1926 (the year the high school graduates graduated) to 1935, that involved either an increase in salary or no change in salary as contrasted to the percent of shifts that did involve a decrease in salary. This measure of success might not be as meaningful in a period of economic growth and inflation as it was during the depression years. Whether or not a different operation identifying success during periods of inflation would give different results is a matter of further research. One persistent problem in the ex post facto design is the possible limitation inherent in the time-space matrix within which the experiment takes place.

The null hypothesis would be that, other things being equal, there is no significant difference in economic success as measured between those who graduated from high school in 1926 and those who dropped out of high school in 1926 (in St. Paul, Minnesota, at least).

Out of a total group of 2127 students, 1130 graduated and 997 dropped out of school in 1926. In 1935, 1194 were interviewed; the gross mortality amounted to 933 students. The hypothesis postulated an equality of conditions other than high school graduation. If the reasons for dropping out of school are correlated with economic success, then nothing new has been added by the hypothesis being tested. Accordingly, background factors known to be related to economic success must be controlled, lest interfering variables hide or otherwise change the results.

When the experimental group and the control group were matched (on a group percentage basis) for five controls (father's occupation, parental nativity, neighborhood, age, and sex), the total number of usable cases was reduced from 1194 to 400. When a sixth control, average high school grades, was added the number of usable cases was reduced to 290. When the background factors were matched individually, 23 graduates were matched with 23 non-graduates. Evidently, effective mortality of matching takes a big toll.

When the experimental and control groups were matched proportionately for the six control factors, 88.7 percent of the graduates had either an increase in salary or no change, while 83.4 percent of the non-graduates were similarly judged to have had economic success. When the experimental and control groups were individually matched for the six control factors, 92 percent of the high school graduates had a successful economic adjustment while only 58 percent of the non-graduates were similarly successful. In this case, the additional labor seems to have been repaid in greater precision. However, it must be pointed out, that the relationship between high school education and economic success might have been shown to be smaller with more control. As Chapin comments, "Whether the analysis confirms the hypothesis or disproves it is a consideration entirely irrelevant to the experimental method." [19] The important fact is that increased precision allows us to get closer to the underlying relationship.

12. SUMMARY

Experimentation does not define science; it is possible to obtain rigorous results without it. However, experimentation seems to carry strong conviction along with rigorous proof.

Experimentation is possible when variables are amenable to control; it is desirable when time is an important dimension in the proof. Indeed, the power of experimentation resides in the correspondence of the temporal sequence of research and the logical sequence of the argument.

We have noted some elementary forms of experimentation in psychology, social psychology, sociology, and communication theory. We can notice the difficulties surrounding the ways in which theoretical variables may be operationally defined. Despite the limitations known to adhere to the examples given, the difficulty of conducting an experiment should not be used to exclude experimentation from social science.

At the same time, we must be aware of certain extra scientific limitations to experimentation. Science is conducted in a social situation, and in the social sciences the values of the broader culture prevent the utilization of many known techniques. Hence, to continue to do rigorous research we must look for ways to use the logic of experimentation without being able to use direct manipulation of our variables.

The fact that much control stems from randomization as well as

19 Chapin, *op. cit.*, p. 107.

manipulation led to the development of the ex post facto design. To be sure, this is not a perfect substitute for experimentation, but it is a completely honest recognition of the social situation in which much of social science is currently being conducted.

SELECTED REFERENCES

Churchman, C. West, *Theory of Experimental Inference,* New York, Macmillan, 1948.

Fisher, Ronald A., *The Design of Experiments,* Edinburgh, Oliver & Boyd, 1935.

Greenwood, Ernest, *Experimental Sociology,* New York, King's Crown, 1945.

Lacey, Oliver L., *Statistical Methods in Experimentation,* New York, Macmillan, 1953.

8
Roy G. Francis

SCALING TECHNIQUES

1. INTRODUCTION

Sociologists are not only in the "if *A*, then *B*" sentence building business, they also seek to test statements of that kind. Sociologists, as do all scientists, seek to establish *veridical* propositions in forms such as that.

We must remember that the hypothetical form is one of many types of statements of relationship. A major class of relations are mathematical in form, i.e., $Y = f(X)$. Sometimes, as we saw in our work in statistics, the assertion is simply, "The mean of group *A* is larger than the mean of group *B*." To determine the empirical truth-value of such statements, we need to be able to assert the quantitative variation required in each of them. That is to say, in order to test out the truth-value of certain statements, we need to measure the dimensions asserted to vary according to some rule.

Measurement, then, is instrumental to science, it is not the goal of scientific activity. We measure to test certain hypotheses. Attempting to make the precision of measured units the ultimate goal of our activity is to commit the age-old fallacy of elevating means to ends. Nonetheless, a critical part of scientific activity is the development of meaningful measures.

Measurement is often defined as the "assignment of numbers according to some rule." It must be understood that the conception of a varying dimension is a theoretical one. The conception of the variable is logically prior to its measurement. In general, we will refer to the theoretical definition of a quantitative dimension as a variable and its operational specification as a measure. We do our empirical work with measures and our thinking, or theoretical work, with variables.

From our point of view, a science can have more than one measurement of the same variable. Indeed, some measures are better than others. To assert this is to deny the admissibility of the naïvely put assertion that, for example, intelligence is what an intelligence test measures. We will require that our operational procedures must be consistent with our theoretical positions. It would be preferable to require that our theory imply our measuring procedures. Unfortunately, we have not achieved that rigor; we must be content with logical consistency where logical necessity is lacking. What this means, obviously, is that our measures ought not contradict our theoretical assumptions.

Even the most anti-statistical sociologist frequently asserts something of quantitative variation. One will generally feel he knows what is being asserted when he reads, "Country X is more urbanized than is country Y," or "Those procedures were more bureaucratic than the earlier ones." The notion that something is more than another thing, in respect to a theoretical dimension, is common enough. Being able to develop a set of specifications to test assertions containing such notions is quite another matter.

Yet, it must be admitted, there are some good theoretical grounds for being concerned with a simple-minded, theoretical approach to measurement. The degree to which a measure corresponds to a variable is indeed an important one. The naïve operationalist assumes that, by fiat, measures and variables stand in 1:1 correspondence. If we use a mathematical notation, with M denoting the measure and V the variable, this naïve notion asserts, $M = V$. There is not a priori reason to suppose that such a simple linear relation always obtains. One can imagine a number of differing types of relations existing, some implying greater variance at certain segments of the variable, others greater precision.

Thus, a scientist may have good reason to believe that in such a case of attempted measurement as attitude analysis, one ought not simply add up scores—that beliefs are too complicated for that. Yet such a person, facing a typical situation, may well be motivated to scaling for purely pragmatic reasons. Consider the plight of such a researcher if he had a sample of 2,000 each of whom completed an instrument containing 50 bits of background information, and responded to 250 items the content of which is clearly appropriate to the topic being studied. This generates 300 bits of information per person or a total of 600,000 bits of information. Just for the sake of summarizing data, for reducing enormous amounts of data to a fewer number, the scientist may well accept scaling procedures. If he is to speak empirically at all, he has little choice.

Thus, we find two major justifications for attempting to measure sociologically relevant dimensions. The major one is theoretical—one measures in order to test ideas. The other is pragmatic—one measures simply to summarize data and permit the handling of a large amount of otherwise unmanageable materials. In general, one would suppose that the theoretical justification is better than the pragmatic one. Yet we ought not overlook the practicalities of research. They can make a difference.

2. *SOME POSTULATES OF MEASUREMENT*

The definition of measurement as "the assigning of numbers according to a system of rules" does not warrant an arbitrary system. If the numbering system we use in our world of mathematics is to be of any analytic use to us, then these rules we develop must be consistent with the postulates of various kinds of numbers as reflected in mathematical operations.

A complete philosophical and operational system of mensuration would recognize a complicated differentiation of various types of numbers. We will limit ourselves, in this text, simply to three: nominal numbers, ordinal numbers, and cardinal numbers. Everyone will recognize that by cardinal numbers we have in mind the kind of numbers most of us intuit when we think of quantification.

Nominal Numbers. The nominal assignment of numbers is simply that of *naming* categories. No one seriously thinks that a tackle in football with the numeral "77" on his jersey is anything like "7 times a quarterback" who happens to wear the numeral "11." We recognize that the number is mapped uniquely with a name, plus the possibility that the first digit may indicate the position (70's for tackles, 60's for guards, etc.) and the second digit, by being odd or even, indicating whether the person normally lines up on the right or left side of center.

Formally, the assumptions for a nominal assignment are the following:

(1) $a = - - a$

(2) $(b) [(b = a) \ V \ (b \neq a)].$

The first postulate may be read, "*a* is equal to not not *a*." Thus, a minimal requirement is a dichotomy. The second postulate asserts, "**For any** *b*, either $b = a$ or *b* is not equal to *a*." Note that no amount of difference is required for this assertion.

Those statistical operations which are consistent with a *counting* operation are permissible on data such as these. Thus, any frequency analysis is legitimate, as is percentage, proportion, probability, and related arguments. If we have a dichotomy and assign a 1 to the outcome we are interested in (the success), and a 0 to the other (the failure), the operations of obtaining a mean and variance flow from either the statistics of proportions or the usual $\overline{X} = \dfrac{\Sigma f X}{N}$ and the related formula for variance.

Ordinal Numbers. Many sociological assertions imply the ability to rank people objectively along some presumed dimension—he has more status than someone else; this city is more gemeinschaft than some other;

he is more radical than she is; and so on. For such data, the following assumptions are required:

(3) $a \neq b$

(4) $(a > b) \supset (b < a)$

(5) $[(a > b) . (b > c)] \supset (a > c)$.

The third postulate differs from the second in that the second merely asserts that two objects are either equal or not equal. However, if one claims to be able to rank objects, the initial claim is that one is more or less than a specified other. The fourth postulate asserts an intransitive relation—"If a is greater than b, b is less than a." This is neither obvious nor redundant. It not only excludes comparisons on other dimensions than the one under discussion, it enables one to incorporate the argument of "more than" and the argument of "less than" into one system. Thus, the algebra of inequalities is legitimate. The fifth postulate simply extends the concept of order to the entire listing. It may be read as, "If a is greater than b, and if b is greater than c, then a is greater than c."

All of the operations of the nominal case are permitted, with the reminder that the dichtomous relation is a very special relation in both cases. But in addition to those associated with nominal numbers, the statistics of rank-order analysis—as Spearman's rank-order correlation, the Mann-Whitney U test, and the like—are admissible.

Note that with ordinal numbers, there is no postulate which justifies the operation of addition or related arithmetic operations. Hence, multiplication does not make sense. To assert that a is greater than b does not enable us to assert that the product of a and b is a specific number;

$$[(a > b) \supset (ab = c)]$$

is nonsense. There will be times when a researcher will be troubled by this point. He may develop measurements from which he can confidently assign ordinal positions, but his intent may be to get numbers which he would like statistically to treat as though they were cardinal.

Cardinal Numbers. To use the ordinary mathematical rules of algebra, to legitimize the additive operations and the like, an extensive set of postulates is in order.

(6) $a + b = b + a$

(7) $ab = ba$

These are the *commutative* laws of addition and multiplication. They simply assert that these operations may be performed in any order with the same result obtaining.

(8) $(a + b) + c = a + (b + c)$

(9) $(ab)c = a(bc)$

These are the associative laws. They assert that the numbers for which successive multiplication or addition is to be done can be variously grouped.

(10) $a(b + c) = ab + ac$

This is the *distributive* law. It connects rules of addition and multiplication. Together with postulates (8) and (9), the basic rules for manipulating parenthetic statements in algebraic derivations are provided.

(11) $a + 0 = a$

(12) $(a)(1) = a$

Number eleven asserts the positional character of 0—if 0 is added to a number, the number remains the same. For those who recall the suggestion that our real numbers can be identified with points on a line so that adding implies movement to the right (subtracting, not yet defined by our postulates, would mean moving to the left), (11) says that if you do not move at all, you remain in the same place as before. Postulate (12) defines, in part, the meaning of 1, i.e., a number multiplied by 1 is the number itself. These two postulates generate "identity operations" (one for addition and one for multiplication). With the next two, the system will be complete for our purposes.

(13) $(a) (\exists b) (a + b = 0)$

(14) $(a).(b) [(b \neq 0) \supset (\exists c) (bc = a)]$

Read postulate (13) thusly: "For any a, there is a b such that a plus b equals 0." This postulate defines subtraction. It is particularly important in many mensuration problems as the conceptualization of subtracting may be quite difficult. It is not clear, for example, how one would subtract so many units from a's status in one group to arrive at an equivalent status position elsewhere. Postulate (14) is to be read, "For any a and for any b, if b does not equal 0, then there is a c such that the product of b and c equals a." This postulate sets up division.

Reviewing the entire set of postulates, we can see that by surrendering some information from cardinal measurement, we can reduce our data to ordinal ones. That is, if we knew people's ages, by ignoring the number of units distinguishing them from each other, we could retain the same order from younger to older. By surrendering more information, we could translate ordinal into nominal categories (age categories a, b and c). One may arbitrarily move from cardinal to less precise data though the converse is not possible. One cannot, by fiat, move from nominal to cardinal data.

Yet, in essence, that is pretty much the problem of social measurement. Can we create a set of operations such that we can move from dichotomous responses to questions and, then, into a numbering system which justifies the operations of addition, subtraction, multiplication, and division that adhere to cardinal numbers? Only when justified can we assert a solution to the problem of measurement or scaling.

3. THE GENERAL PROBLEM OF SCALING OPERATIONS

In general, the operation of scaling reduces to these two questions: Of all the items that could go into the scale, which ought to be retained? What weight ought to be assigned to a response to a particular item? The theoretical problem is, of course, that generally discussed under the topic of validity, namely, what theoretical dimension is this set of operations proposing to measure? The question of reliability is the determination that this set of operations always gives the same results.

In respect to the operational problem of scaling, a limiting condition is necessary to provide a basis for judging among contending operations. Ideally, the assignment of numbers would reflect some correspondence between the magnitude of the dimension and our numbering system. Unlike the simple physical situation in which some sort of ruler can be shown to be isomorphic physically to the object being measured, the situation in the social sciences becomes quite complex. Ideally, the number assigned should be a function of the size of the object to be measured by the particular metric in terms of which members are associated with size.

In the case of social science, the number assigned can be a function of many more factors and conditions than just the size of the object being measured and the numbering system. Consider an attempt by an assemblage of people to measure a table in the room they are currently occupying. Each is standing at a different spot in the room, at varying distances from the table. The measuring rules require them not to move, and to use whatever unit they may have on their person. Some would use a pen, some a cigarette, some a comb, or whatever object possible. The angle of vision, the distance from the table, the eyesight, the skill and imagination of the person, all contribute to what final number each asserts.

The point is, some ways of assigning numbers involve so many factors other than the thing to be measured that bias in measurement may well exceed any simple variation caused by sampling. The point is a general one that must be well appreciated. There are many conceivable systems of assigning numbers in the social sciences. However systematic they may be, it is always possible that the "first order of approximate measurement" may contain so many sources of error that no comparisons can meaningfully follow.

To argue, as does the operationalist, that my operations give me my concepts, is to deny a much more responsible response. One can, in recognizing the operational limits of a given procedure, stay oriented to the problem of trying to measure some theoretical dimension, thereby justifying continued work to improve the measure. The concept of improving the measure doesn't make sense if the operation generates the concept being measured.

The rules that result in answers to our operational questions are many. One recurring scheme for deciding whether an item should be included in the final battery involves correlating it with some criterion. Yet, it is possible to have a set of items correlated sufficiently high with the criterion so large in number that the set must be further reduced by some scheme. For example, one may end up with 5,000 items each of which is statistically associated with the criterion measure. Obviously, few tests can require a person to respond to so many items. That one may choose a random sub-set, or some other kind, is clear enough. We cannot assume, then, that the statistical argument alone provides the answer.

4. SCALING TECHNIQUES IN SOCIAL RESEARCH

Scaling techniques belong to that general field of science dealing with the definition of concepts. A basic problem in any research project is how to define the variable being studied. Measurement can proceed only after one has solved this problem of definition. Scaling techniques provide a valuable tool for help in *deriving definitions* and *permitting measurement* in terms of these definitions.

Let us suppose that one is faced with the problem of determining the reliability and validity of such statements as, "Most factory workers are satisfied with their jobs," "Pretty girls are not very intelligent," and "Intergroup contact decreases prejudice." One cannot proceed very far in research on these hypotheses without facing the problem of defining such concepts as "job satisfaction," "beauty," "intelligence," and "prejudice." Certainly one cannot hope to measure until the problem of definition has been satisfactorily solved.

How, then, do scaling techniques attempt to solve the problem of definition and measurement? Like most problems of definition, they proceed first by listing the characteristics of the object to be defined. This list of characteristics must then be analyzed for reliability and validity; this is where scaling techniques are needed. Through the analysis of the *interrelationship* of the proposed list of defining characteristics, scaling techniques attempt to do four main things: (1) eliminate irrelevant items, (2) eliminate confusing items, (3) separate and classify items according to different dimensions, and (4) assign relative weights to the different items.

The successful operation of a scaling procedure, therefore, should produce for the researcher a series of items each of which has been tested for relevance to the concept being defined and for clarity of understanding. Furthermore, the various items will have been grouped or classified according to the different dimensions involved in the definition of the concept, or if it proves to contain only one dimension, the unidimensionality of the concept will be established.

A. Basic Concepts of Scaling

At this stage it is important to understand three basic concepts of assumptions involved in most scaling procedures: (1) There exists for any object being defined or measured an unlimited number of possible characterizing or defining items. This is often referred to as the "universe of content." (2) Any definition or measurement of this object will be based on only a selected sample of items from this total universe. (3) A definition to permit quantitative measurement must consist of a unidimensional continuum.

The above three restrictions force the researcher to consider such questions as, How shall I find items which belong to the universe of content in which I am interested? How broad or narrow should I make this universe of content? Will other social scientists accept the items I have selected as defining the concept in which I am interested? Do the manifest or actual items I am using represent the latent concept in which I am interested? Am I using enough items and a representative sample of items to permit me to test the reliability and validity of the proposed scale? Am I combining only those items that have the same meaning so that I can order along a single continuum? Should I subdivide these items into separate dimensions or factors?

Until one has answered the above questions, one cannot proceed with assurance to measure individuals or objects. A ranking of individuals which is not based upon answers to the above questions may be both unreliable and invalid. To be sure there are different degrees to which one can satisfactorily answer these questions. In some cases one may not be able to answer all of them due to practical research considerations, or one may be forced to assume that the answers would be forthcoming satisfactorily if one had additional data. But, certainly, the further one proceeds to actually offer evidence in answer to these questions, the better one will have solved the problem of measurement. The systematic analysis of a series of items in an attempt to answer these questions permits one to state with greater confidence that the concept is being defined in terms of the inherent structure of the natural phenomenon, and is not the result of an arbitrary and artificial classification or ordering.

B. *Relation of Scaling to Other Forms of Measurement*

The analysis problem one is faced with when one contemplates using scaling techniques is how to analyze simultaneously a series of observations or answers to several questions. There are three basic approaches one can use in order to analyze a series of items.

First, one can attempt to secure a uni-dimensional scale which would permit us to rank or order people according to their response on the several items involved. This problem of rank order measurement is the basic motivation for making a scale analysis. If the items form a scale, one can then score people as indicated by the scale analysis and rank them from more to less along a single continuum of meaning.

Second, one may find that the items do not fit into a single dimension, but rather consist of two or more dimensions. In such a case it is impossible to rank individuals and one proceeds to form types or classes. These procedures are discussed in a separate chapter on typological classification.

Third, one may proceed to analyze the various items in terms of some arbitrary index or summary score. Such an index is usually a custom-made formula which permits one to summarize the responses of individuals to a series of items. Such indices usually are not based upon a logical attempt to test dimensionality as in the previous two measures.

Scale analysis, then, represents a decision on the part of the researcher to analyze his data in terms of logical dimensions. Usually the basis for this decision is the desire to secure a rank ordering of individuals or objects along some simple continuum. The purpose of this chapter is to indicate the major forms of scaling techniques and to discuss their relative value.

C. *Units of Scaling*

While the greatest amount of attention in the development of scales has been devoted to the determination of a rank order for individuals, it is important to remember that these techniques are not limited by the type of object being measured. At the present time most of the problems in scaling are limited to the ranking of people. However, there is good reason to believe that an extension of scaling techniques to other aspects of measurement would also be beneficial.

We may classify all aspects of social existence into three general categories—people, situations or occasions, and concepts or variables. We are concerned either with the study of individuals, in which case we attempt to classify or rank people. Or we may be interested in the study of situations or occasions involving a comparison or analysis of different occurrences, or, finally, we may be concerned with the analysis and comparison of different variables or concepts. *Any one of these three forms of measurement may constitute the focus of a scale analysis.*

Scale analysis is one form of multivariate analysis. That is to say that whenever we are faced with the problem of analyzing simultaneously a number or series of measurements (either of people, situations, or concepts), we must determine some technique for studying the interrelationships of the different measures.

We may summarize the various types of measurement problems by looking at the interrelationship between the three basic aspects of measurement. First, holding our situation constant, we may scale people for a series of variables. Given a population of people who respond to a series of items, we attempt to determine the dimensionality of the items and then to rank the people according to this dimension. These are the "Q-scales" and represent the most common type used today.

Still keeping the situation constant, we may also attempt to scale a population of variables for a collection of people. In this case our main emphasis is to rank the different variables or objects by analyzing the order they have for a group of people. The best examples of this to date are the "object scales" developed by Riley at Rutgers. These scales are commonly called "R-scales."

Secondly, we may hold the variable constant and study either scales of people for a population of situations, or scales of situations for a population of people. The former may be called "S-scales" and have recently been studied by Stouffer in an attempt to define and measure role behavior. Since roles may be defined as the behavior of an individual in different situations, this seems to be a promising development. Using a series of different situations, we now attempt to scale people according to some uni-dimensional aspects of role behavior (if the test succeeds in indicating such uni-dimensionality).

The scale of situations for a population of people may be called a "T-scale" and represents, on a non-conceptual level, the common measure of test-retest reliability. Holding the variable constant, we attempt to study the dimensionality of different situations for a population of people. Where this situation is a repetition of a previous one, we have the common test of reliability. However, this is a rather unimaginative and limited use of such comparative situation tests. It would be much more interesting to test a series of situations in terms of conceptual stability or dimensionality rather than purely methodological reliability. This statement of the problem seems to make better sense out of some of the current problems revolving around a distinction between reliability versus meaningful change.

Finally, we may hold the people constant and study the scalability of situations for a population of variables and the scalability of variables for a population of situations. The former are commonly called "O-scales" and involve the problem of situational analysis, wherein our concern is with the ordering of situations based upon the arrangement of variables observed in the situation. The second type, called "P-scales," involves the ranking of variables based upon the measurement of these variables in different situations. These have traditionally been called trait or personality scales; the emphasis is upon the internal organization within a single individual of different variables under different situational conditions. This is a clinical concept implying a measure of the dimensionality of the individual's personality organization.

5. SCALE PROBLEMS

A. Scaling Techniques

There are four main ways in which a scale problem can be attacked. Each of these methods, while aimed at the same general problem of developing a uni-dimensional rank order, does have a fairly different approach to the problem. It is important to recognize that these methods are all operational and subject to revision depending upon the specific problem one is attacking. If one can master the basic procedure for each of these four methods, one will be in a position to improvise a scaling technique most adequate to a particular problem.

1. Judgmental Scales

Arbitrary Scales. Before discussing these methods it might be worthwhile to describe very quickly the many variations of scaling that are based upon arbitrary counting or weighting procedures. Quite often one will find that a scale is being used which consists of nothing more than an arbitrary addition of responses to a series of questions or items. This procedure does not constitute an adequate test of a scale, but rather provides an arbitrary index which tells little about the underlying structure of the items being analyzed. Such scales are really nominal scales and do not provide any test for an underlying single continuum. This means that the researcher has no assurance that the rank order, determined by the arbitrary counting procedure, has reliability. Changing the weights of the items can completely change the rank order. Adding new items may have the same effect.

This does not mean that scales constructed by arbitrary counting procedures are all bad. What it does mean is that until one has studied the internal structure of the items one does not know how good or bad the scale is.

Consensus Scales. By this technique, items are retained or eliminated depending upon how they are rated by a group of judges. If the judges agree that the item which belongs to the area being studied is unambiguous, and if there is further agreement by the judges in their estimate of how positive or negative the item is, then the item is retained. Items are weighted according to the average of the judge's ratings.

2. Complex Operational Scales

The basic existing methods for scale analysis may be grouped into one of the following three major techniques: (1) Cumulative Scales; (2) Item Analysis; and (3) Factor Scales. The basic logic and procedures for these three methods are quite different. Before proceeding to study each method individually, let us briefly summarize the major differences between them.

Cumulative Scales. Cumulative scales provide a test of unidimensionality based upon a dependent relationship between the items being analyzed. If the items being analyzed are ranked in order of ascending positive frequencies and descending negative frequencies, and if individuals are ranked in order of descending positive scores, the resulting pattern of responses forms a parallelogram. The presence of this pattern indicates that endorsement, or presence, of an item indicative of an extreme position should be accepted by endorsement of all items indicative of less extreme position. Furthermore, people or objects occupying the same scale position should have the same response characteristics. This means that one can reproduce all responses of an individual given his scale score.

The cumulative nature of this scale is indicated by the fact that people in higher scale positions have all of the characteristics of people in lower scale positions plus at least one additional positive response. We will study this pattern in more detail when we take up the specific computational procedures.

Item Analysis Techniques. According to this technique, items are selected for inclusion in this scale dependent upon their relationship to the total score of the scale. If an item discriminates between individuals with high and low scores, the item becomes a part of the final scale series. Sometimes these items are given different weights depending upon the size of their relationship to the total scale.

Factor Scales. If it can be shown by a study of the intercorrelation of the items that a common factor is present which accounts for the existence of the relationship between items, then the items are said to contain a common factor. By a study of the manifest relationships between items it is possible to determine the probability with which any series of items will fit a predetermined, latent structure.

These three methods constitute the basic forms of scale analysis existent today. While each of them attempts to solve the same problem, that is, to rank individuals along a continuum depending upon their responses to a series of questions, each of them proceeds by rather different logic and technique. We will now examine each of these techniques briefly.

It is impossible in a preliminary text book to present the step by step details for each of these techniques. The student is referred to the references at the end of this chapter for computational procedures. We will present below the basic steps involved in each of the methods but cannot give enough detail to cover all specific problems.

B. Operational Procedures

Cumulative Scale. Let there be n items to which the s subjects can dichotomously respond, positively, and negatively (n and s both being integers). If these items can be ordered in such a way that the positive response to the ith item implies a positive response to all succeeding items while a negative response to the ith item implies nothing about response to subsequent items, a cumulative scale may be said to exist.

The problem of arriving at the proper sequence or order of items can be approached two ways. It may be hypothesized *a priori* that the items will fall into a certain sequence. This hypothesis is most easily rejected and depends for its utility upon a strong body of theory and previous research. There are no existent examples of this kind of scale.

The second approach is an *ad hoc* one. In this case, one simply tries to get the best possible ordering out of all the response patterns which exist. This activity requires a criterion before one can agree that the best ordering has been found. Currently, this criterion is the "Coefficient of Reproducibility" and will be explained below. Right now, however, we should point out that no theoretical reason for this criterion exists. It is simply a convenient empirical rule of thumb.

If there are n items, each having two possible responses, 2^n possible response patterns can emerge. Out of this we want only $n + 1$ patterns. These we will call "scale types" and all other we will call "non-scale types." We will describe a simple way of obtaining the best possible scale if n is small, say five or fewer.

If n is large, the operations are more complex and can become quite tedious. The student is referred to chapters two through nine in *Measurement and Prediction*.[1] Those chapters were written by Louis Guttman, for whom this type of scale is often named. In it the use of "Guttman's scalogram board" is described. Dr. Marvin Taves of the University of Minnesota has developed a "Simplified scalogram board" in which items and respondents can be treated freely and in any sequence.

[1] Samuel A. Stouffer *et al., Measurement and Prediction,* Princeton, Princeton University Press, 1950.

Returning to the problem of developing a scale, suppose one wanted to scale "school spirit" at a hypothetical college and asked the following questions:

1. Do you regularly attend intercollegiate debate sessions when held on this campus?
2. Do you regularly attend theatrical performances given by the Speech Department?
3. Do you regularly attend the concerts given by the Music Department?
4. Do you regularly attend intercollegiate sporting events (e.g., football and basketball)?

The first step would be to determine the proportion of affirmative responses to these questions. The next step is to create the initial sequence by ordering these questions from least to greatest proportion. These are shown in Figure 8.1.

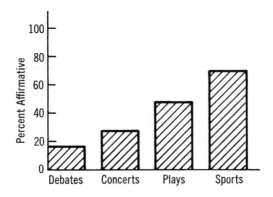

Figure 8.1. Items arranged in initial sequence of percent of favorable response.

The next step is to determine the existing response patterns and the number of members of each. "Fixing" the sequence as above, and denoting an affirmative response by + and a negative response by —, we obtain the results in Table 8.1, below.

The task is now simply to fit the non-scale types into the scale types in such a way that the amount of error is a minimum. For example, if the type + — + + were classified as belonging in type + + + +, an error would be made in response to the second item, but none of the others. Had the same type (+ — + +) been classified as — — + +, there would have been an error in the first item only. Although some effort has been directed toward a unique solution to the issue of which alternative classification is right, no completely satisfactory rule exists. However, had the type (+ — + +) been classified as — — — +, there would have been two errors. Clearly, if we hold as our criterion the

TABLE 8.1. DISTRIBUTION OF RESPONSE PATTERNS
HAVING EMPIRICAL MEMBERS

Scale Type	Frequency	Non-Scale Type	Frequency
+ + + +	5	+ − + +	2
− + + +	8	+ + − +	1
		+ − − +	5
− − + +	22	− + − +	3
		− + + −	2
− − − +	23	− − + −	10
		− + − −	6
− − − −	11	+ − − −	1
	Total 69		Total 31

minimization of error this would not be an admissible classification. Note, that in any event, one assumes that the proper sequence of items exists. In our example, the single criterion of minimum error can be safely appealed to. But if there had been as many members of type $+ - + +$ as of type $- + + +$, the argument would be strained.

TABLE 8.2. THE COMPUTATION OF ERROR IN NEW CLASSIFICATION

Scale Type Includes		Frequency Total for Type	Types with Error	Error
+ + + +		9		
	+ − + +		3	3
	+ + − +		1	1
− + + +		13		
	− + − +		3	3
	− + + −		2	2
− − + +		22	0	0
− − − +		28		
	+ − − +		5	5
− − − −		28		
	− − + −		10	10
	− + − −		6	6
	+ − − −		1	1
	Total 100			Total 31

In Table 8.2, the non-scale types are classified to the nearest scale type. Column one denotes the scale type including the former non-scale type, column two denotes the new frequency, and column three denotes the number of predictive errors. The number of errors is the result of the following operations—The number of predictive errors in each new classification of scale types is determined as before. These are multiplied by the frequency of the old non-scale type, e.g., putting $+ - + +$ into $+ + + +$ involves one error; $+ - + +$ had 3 members. Hence 3 predictive errors occur.

Summing the total number of errors gives us 31 misclassifications of item responses. Since each of the 100 individuals made 4 judgments, the proportion of error is 31 divided by $4(100) = 31/400 = .078$. The coefficient of reproducibility is simply this number subtracted from 1, i.e., $1 - .078 = .922$. By convention, a coefficient of reproducibility above .90 is regarded as being acceptable. Note, however, in the above, that 31 percent of the respondents were non-scale types.

Note also that, in Table 8.2, we could have classified some non-scale types differently and obtained a different frequency distribution with the same coefficient of reproducibility. Thus, type $- - + -$ which was classified as $- - - -$ with one error, could have been classified as $- - + +$ with one error. Clearly the frequencies would have changed but the number of errors would remain constant. This means that, upon using a scale distribution in correlation with other variables, one can obtain various results depending upon how the non-scale types were classified. The lack of a unique solution renders difficult the use of this scale to define a concept.

Item Analysis. It should not be imagined that reproducibility is a necessary aspect of measurement. Suppose one wanted to measure height by obtaining the lengths of the head, neck, trunk, and legs. The sum of these would presumably give total height. Now a knowledge of total height does not imply a knowledge of the length of the separable parts. For most purposes this is an irrelevant consideration. The point, however, is clear. Reproducibility is not a necessary characteristic of measurement. Hence, we are justified in assessing other types of scale construction.

One popular technique is item analysis. The argument is simple and direct. If any item has no correlation with a problematically relevant outside criterion it is rejected. For example, suppose that a scale was being developed for a study of marital adjustment. Suppose further that an item of the kind, "Did you window-shop with your fiancé before marriage?" was not correlated with divorce. Clearly, it would add no useful knowledge.

After a battery of items has been tested the question becomes, How much weight should a given item have? This rests on the plausible grounds that the items most highly correlated with the problematic data are more important. Note that the question of weighting was irrelevant to the cumulative scale since any weighting system would have left the sequence of items unaltered. In this case, however, weighting is important.

The importance of weighting items is seen in a review of the issues involved in measurement itself. Recall that the idea of measurement is the assignment of a score according to some rule. Recall, further, that the score assigned should be a function of the variable. That is to say, a pure measurement finds each item "loaded" entirely with the variable. However, in social measurement this is not the case. Any item may be correlated to more than one variable; hence one must know the extent to which the item reflects the variable in question. Part of the scoring system may be random error which would only inflate an estimation of variance; it may be a bias, or it may be some effects from other variables. The issue of weighting revolves around the attempt to indicate the extent to which each item making up the operational scheme reflects the variable in question. To give each item equal weight is to claim that each item equally reflects the underlying dimension. This condition is only rarely true in social sciences. Hence, weighting is critical in most instances of scale construction.

One way of weighting items is to first obtain the proportion of variance explained by a given item which is also equivalent to the square of the coefficient of correlation, namely r^2. Then subtract this number from 1, and take the reciprocal of the result (i.e., divide it into 1). Symbolically, a weight would be obtained by $w = \dfrac{1}{1 - r^2}$. As r^2 approaches 1, w approaches infinity. This implies that if a single item is perfectly correlated with the problematic data, further items are redundant—as r^2 approaches 0, w approaches 1. If $r^2 = 0$, $w = 0$ by definition. w takes on the algebraic sign of r. Then, if an individual agrees with the item in question he is given a score which equals w. If he disagrees with the item he is given a score which equals $(-1)(w)$. Thus, if w is negatively correlated with the criterion and he agrees with the item, he obtains a negative score; but if he disagrees with the item, he obtains a positive score. One's total score is the sum of the scores for the n items which have been retained.

For the most part, one cannot compute a Pearsonian product, i.e., moment r for item analysis. The reason is that the responses to the item are usually dichotomous. A convenient way out is to compute ϕ^2. This is found by dividing χ^2 by N, i.e., $\phi^2 = \dfrac{\chi^2}{N}$. For a 2×2 table (where the item and the outside criterion are both dichotomized), χ^2 can be found by

$$\chi^2 = \frac{(ad - bc)^2 N}{(_1n \; _2n)(n_1 \, n_2)},$$

where the letters are those found in Table 8.3 below.

TABLE 8.3. A SHORT CUT–x^2 TABLE

	Item		
	Yes	No	
Outside +	a	b	n_1
Criterion –	c	d	n_2
	$_1n$	$_2n$	N

To illustrate with the previously mentioned example. Let the item be, Did you discuss child-raising with your fiancé before your marriage? Suppose that the relation between the responses to that question and divorce was as given below (Table 8.4).

TABLE 8.4. ANALYSIS OF ILLUSTRATION

	Item		
	Yes	No	Total
Divorced	10	40	50
Not Divorced	90	60	150
Total	100	100	200

Then χ^2 would be,

$$\chi^2 = \frac{[(10)\,(60) - (40)\,(90)]^2\,200}{(100)\,(100)\,(50)\,(150)}$$

$$\chi^2 = \frac{(600 - 3600)^2\,200}{(100)\,(100)\,(50)\,(150)}$$

$$\chi^2 = \frac{(-3000)\,(-3000)\,(200)}{(100)\,(100)\,(50)\,(150)}$$

$$\chi^2 = 24.$$

This is clearly significant.

$\phi^2 = \dfrac{24}{200} = .12$, indicating low correlation.

$$w = \frac{1}{1 - .12} = \frac{1}{.88} = 1.13.$$

Since the table was constructed such that the correlation is negative, $w = -1.13$. Thus a note of caution must be sounded. The direction of correlation in 2×2 tables is largely a junction of the organization of the table which, in turn, is a junction of the wording of one question. Those using this technique to create a score should ensure themselves that an affirmative response implies the direction of correlation which their hypothesis requires.

There are other bases for item analysis. One such is the correlation between the response to a single item and the total score. Another involves the use of the critical ratio.[2] The student might try to devise one of his own. In any event, each such score includes only those items which have a discriminatory power. These items are subsequently weighted according to some logical scheme.

Scale Construction with Factor Analysis.[3] Suppose the solution of a research problem involved a theoretical variable, "religiosity." The question is, How can I identify objects having different amounts of this variable? Thus, one could argue that each of the following measures impart the same thing. That is, one could assert the:

1. amount of *religious behavior* (church attendance, office holding, contributions, etc.) is in some sense a measure of religiosity—and some irrelevant items as, say, prestige in church attendance, etc.

2. attitudes about the church as a social institution are measures of religiosity—plus some irrelevant items as general conservatism, liberalism, etc.

3. beliefs about theological questions could also generate a scale of religiosity along with such irrelevant items as the negative reaction to a disliked minister, etc.

If these operations do involve the measurement of the same underlying variable, plus things more or less unique to the operation, one could obtain the amount of the basic variable in each measurement through factor analysis. We will accept, without proof, the steps involved in factor analysis and the argument that the first factor will be the underlying variable in question.

Denoting the measurements as,

$x_1 =$ religious behavior
$x_2 =$ attitudes about the church
$x_3 =$ theological beliefs,

we first obtain the intercorrelations between these measures. Assuming, for the illustration of factor analysis, that these measures were essentially quantitative, the correlations are Pearsonian product-moment r's.

We will perform a set of operations upon this "matrix" of correlation ratios to obtain the required factor loadings of each measure. Clearly

[2] See Chapter 5.

[3] The author thanks Dr. Marvin Taves for the use of the following data and the arithmetic computations included. The materials, but not the arguments, are found in "A Study of Factors Associated with Religiosity" by Dr. Taves, Unpublished Doctoral Dissertation, University of Minnesota Library, 1954.

TABLE 8.5. INTERCORRELATIONS BETWEEN THREE ITEMS
MEASURING RELIGIOSITY

	1	2	3
1	–	.54	.66
2	.54	–	.71
3	.66	.71	–

a variable is perfectly correlated with itself. Hence, we will insert 1's in the main diagonal.

After revising our matrix, we then sum the columns to obtain the results denoted by $\Sigma 1$. Divide each of these sums by the largest sum in that row. These are entered as the first weights, i.e., w_1 for variable (1) is $2{:}20/2.37 = .93$. Multiply column (1) by the corresponding entry in w_1 and sum to obtain $\Sigma 2$, viz., $(.93)\,(1.00) + (.95)\,(.54) + (1.00)\,(.66) = 2.10$. Repeat for column (2), viz., $(.93)\,(.54) + (.95)\,(1.00) + (1.00)\,(.71) = 2.16$. Repeat for column (3) and all remaining columns. (d) Divide each entry in $\Sigma 2$ by the largest single entry to obtain w_2.

TABLE 8.6. ILLUSTRATION OF OPERATIONS IN FACTOR ANALYSIS

		(1)	(2)	(3)	w_1	w_2	w_3	w_4
	(1)	1.00	0.54	0.66	.93	.92	.92	.92
	(2)	0.54	1.00	0.71	.95	.94	.95	.95
	(3)	0.66	0.71	1.00	1.00	1.00	1.00	1.00
Successive	$\Sigma 1$	2.20	2.25	2.37				
Summing	$\Sigma 2$	2.10	2.16	2.29				
	$\Sigma 3$	2.09	2.15	2.27				
	$\Sigma 4$	2.09	2.16	2.28				

The heading "Successive Weights" spans the w_1, w_2, w_3, w_4 columns.

From this point on, one successively repeats the operations to obtain the new sums (e.g., $\Sigma 3$), and the new weights, until "stability" is reached. Normally one continues the process until a column of weights (w_{i+1}), is either identical or within .001 of w_i. This procedure is widely used.

The weights in w_{i+1} are proportional to the correlation coefficients of the underlying variable and these 3 measures. To obtain these coefficients one multiplies each weight in w_{i+1} by,

$$\sqrt{\frac{\text{largest sum of the final summations.}}{\text{sum of the squares of } w_{i+1}}}$$

In this case,

$$a = w_{i+1}\left(\sqrt{\frac{2.28}{(.92)^2 + (.95)^2 + (1.00)^2}}\right)$$

$$a = w_{i+1}\,(.9107).$$

To complete the scale of religiosity, one computes the *a* values for each of the measures. The scale of religiosity is assumed to be a linear function of the 3 separate measures and is obtained by,

$$R = \frac{a_1 (X_1 - \overline{X}_1)}{\sigma_1} + \frac{a_2 (X_2 - \overline{X}_2)}{\sigma_2} + \frac{a_3 (X_3 - \overline{X}_3)}{\sigma_3}.$$

Since X_j and σ_j will be obtained for each measure and are arithmetic constants, R can be written as,

$$R = \frac{a_1 X_1}{\sigma_1} + \frac{a_2 X_2}{\sigma_2} + \frac{a_3 X_3}{\sigma_3} - \frac{a_1 \overline{X}_1}{\sigma_1} + \frac{a_2 \overline{X}_2}{\sigma_2} + \frac{a_3 \overline{X}_3}{\sigma_3}.$$

The term in parentheses degenerate to a single constant in any empirical case; of course, if more than 3 measures were used, R would involve more terms, but the general form would persist.

6. THE LIKERT SCALE: AN ILLUSTRATION OF A COMMON PROBLEM

The Likert scale is such a commonly used research strategy that it justifies a single section. Most of the issues of measurement appear here. In this section we will discuss the creation of such measuring instruments. We will also develop a set of scaling procedures.

One can suppose that nearly everyone has experienced a Likert-type scale. The subject is given a set of items to respond to; his choices are limited, usually of the order "strongly agree," "agree," "disagree," "strongly disagree." The test, then, is made up of a body of statements about which restricted choices are made. Ordinarily, each alternative is given some arithmetic value and these are totaled to arrive at the individual's score. Such scores are refined according to some statistical strategy—they are often converted to z-scores and reconverted to a common scale by a linear transformation which will control the range and limiting values. Often the transformation (of the form, "50 ± 10z") is chosen to make the results range between 0 and 100—or any other desired numerical values.

Clearly, the researcher has a number of questions which must be systematically answered. The important ones are:

1. How many items ought to be included in the final test?
2. Which particular items should be included?
3. How many alternative choices ought the respondent have, and what content should those choices have?
4. What weight should be given to each item (or set of alternatives)?

There are a number of things to be considered in answering each. And the logic of the answers is not always the same—not all decisions are or should be statistically based. We will consider each question in turn.

A. How Many Items Ought to Be Included in the Final Test?

The answer to this involves the resolution of the tension between theoretical preference and pragmatic considerations. One may devise a test which no one would take the time to answer—scarcely a worthwhile task. Thus, we cannot at the onset say that theory alone sensibly answers the question. But, neither can expediency be the final arbiter of scientific decisions. It takes a certain maturity to face up to this question; nonetheless, some principles can be pointed out.

Many times the research demands are such that one deliberately includes a number of sub-scales. Thus, in measuring "economic liberalism," one may wish to include sub-scales on "female employment," "indebtedness," "economic policy," and the like. If one is serious about having sub-scales, he must have in mind some use for them, and this seems to require some idea about the range in scores one expects on each sub-scale for only if there is reasonable variation can a scale expect to differentiate meaningful cases. Though some sub-scales are reportedly using as few as two items, we cannot recommend that. Indeed, we doubt if fewer than ten items makes sense, especially when the initial judgment is based on "face-validity," that is, the scale is made up of those items which seem, on reading, to be related to a common dimension. A more rigorous procedure would be some factor-analytic technique to see if a whole set of items could be made up of sub-scales.

Another recurring point is the element of time. Hence, one must judge the attention span of his respondents and have the scale short enough to be completed in a reasonable amount of time. It is difficult to decide how many items make up a good test. Some tests run over 500 items; some good ones as few as 50. Between theoretical and practical problems, one must decide the total number. It is best if this be the first decision made in developing the scale (after the dimension has been agreed to, of course). The time of day, day of the week, and the subject matter also play a part in these decisions. Explosive (emotionally charged), and controversial, items seem to permit a shorter instrument than others. Invasion of evening hours sometimes precludes lengthy instruments. Obviously, it is impossible to specify a magic number.

B. Which Particular Items Should Be Included?

To pretend that the items one selects represent, in a meaningful way, a *sample* randomly drawn from a specified universe, is dangerous. That simply is not true. It is true that in a universe of discourse, one can specify virtually an infinite number of possible items. Yet those that occur to any individual can scarcely be thought of as random. One item tends to suggest another; the researcher tends to have a point of view—to favor some segment of the spectrum—and, therefore, associates with similarly oriented colleagues.

A recurring proposition holds that the items finally selected should reflect, as nearly as possible, positions all along the continuum. It should not be subtly biased to insinuate a preference for one type of position. This results, ordinarily, in selecting items such that the direction of the response varies. For example, sometimes the liberal will strongly agree and sometimes he will strongly disagree.

As nearly as possible, the item ought not to be a time-waster. Its responses should enable one to differentiate distinguishable respondents. Thus, if one *knows* that certain groups are (to continue the example) more liberal and that others are more conservative, then each item ought to distinguish between these groups. Moreover, neutral groups should appear as neutral on the items.

Most frequently the decision is made in terms of a significance of difference test. This is also a type of validation, at least, if criterion groups can be established. If an outside criterion is lacking, against which to test each item, then an internal consistency principle can be used. Ordinarily this is accomplished by tentatively assigning scores to each item on the basis of face-validity (this operation also indicates the dimensional direction of the response). Then the totals are obtained for each individual. Since the dimensional direction will specify the meaning of the large score, each item can then be tested against the total scores. The respondents with the largest scores—"the top n cases"—and those with the lowest scores—"the bottom n cases"—are then used as criterion groups. Good and, hence, acceptable items are able to distinguish between these groups. Whether the items are valid is still questionable, but the test is at least internally consistent.

C. How Many Alternative Choices Ought the Respondent Have, and How Should Those Choices Be Designated?

The most common set of alternatives are either four or five choices. The four would be "strongly agree," "agree," "disagree," "strongly disagree," and the fifth would be some neutral point. Some researchers prefer the even number to force the respondent to a choice. This is based on the supposition that the really neutral ones will randomly be assigned to the two middle choices. It is also based on the notion that many people choose the neutral position, not because that represents their point of view but because of shame, fear, or improper motive. Those who prefer the neutral alternative argue that there are those for whom the neutral position does indeed describe their sentiments, and that the researcher has no right to force him into a choice that does not represent his sentiments. That is to say, if any distortion of feeling is made it should result from the respondent's, not the scientist's, action.

Sometimes the alternatives are increased from five (or four) to seven (or six)—and sometimes even more. One justification for this extension of alternatives is to permit a wide range of choices. Another is that people (at least on certain types of content items), seem to avoid appearing extreme. So a set of "dummy extremes" are given in anticipating that they will be avoided and a real set will be used.

Sometimes a scale is given with the extremes and, on occasion, a mid point identified. The respondent is asked to identify where on the scale he fits. Thus: On the following items, identify a point on the scale most nearly representing your position on each item.

Catholics make good neighbors.

Strongly disagree _____ Strongly agree

This is sometimes modified so that the scale appears as a thermometer with a freezing and a boiling point identified.

These latter comments suggest that the Likert strategy can be used with a variety of items not all of which could use the "strongly agree," etc., type of response. "Always," "frequently," "sometimes," and "never" are verbalizations of choice that may fit certain kinds of sentences. If the question had to do with, say, personal characteristics of ethnic groups, the choices could include "always reliable," "sometimes reliable," etc., and related alternatives. The limit to the kinds of alternatives is imposed by the originality and cleverness of the researcher.

In making the choice, one must remember that the respondent is being asked to make a decision. The content of the items most frequently suggests what the alternatives should or could be. Clearly, the choices must appear meaningful to the respondent, both in distinguishing between sensibly different categories and the number of choices. Some populations are not able to distinguish between five categories; some may be able to respond only to dichotomies. One must have some prior knowledge of his population before he can commit himself to this kind of choice.

D. What Weight Should Be Given the Item?

In most cases each item is given equal weight, though other possibilities exist. In the previous section, we discussed some of these possibilities. The best reason for assigning equal weights is the following: the cost in time and money to adjust the weights seldom adds to the precision of the final result. Certainly, if any refinement affected only the third decimal of a correlation coefficient, one could scarcely justify great costs of limited resources.

More important is the issue of assigning numbers to the different alternatives. The most frequently used scheme is to assign the number 1 (or 0) to a terminal point indicating some origin of the dimension ("least cosmopolitan" or "most cosmopolitan," or whatever) and then the integers in sequence for each alternative. If a large number of alternatives are given the middle point is given a 0, and plus and minus values are given to the alternatives.

There are many ways in which one could refine these weights. But research has shown that they are seldom worthwhile. For initial research work, at least, the arbitrary assignment of integers makes sense. Moreover, they have the virtue of simplicity. It may be true that the assignment of "1.60309114" is no more arbitrary than assigning "1," but one finds it difficult to believe that the addition of mysterious values to the right of the decimal has any merit at all.

If the scale is given and the respondent asked to indicate the position he holds, one can actually measure the distance from an origin to the point (in millimeters, inches, or whatever) and use these numbers. They *appear* precise, whether they are or not. Moreover, a sort of built-in pattern of variability is assured. People may, in cowardice, choose a moderate alternative; but it hardly follows that they will, in equal frequencies, choose exactly the same point. One cannot argue that it is impossible for this variation to have meaning. At any rate, this strategy for assigning weights is sometimes used.

7. SUMMARY

Scaling operations have a twofold contribution: (1) By forcing one to connect concepts with the real world, they aid in arriving at precise definitions. (2) The scale then allows for a justifiable ordering in some sense of measurement.

While a naïve operationalism will permit the construction of arbitrary scales, largely through circular reasoning, a type of *a priori* defense of scaling may be found in,

1. The cumulative scale. The fact that weights are irrelevant makes this a desirable type for certain problems.
2. Item analysis. This is particularly helpful in an *ad hoc* design, or other circumstances of outside criteria; the scoring system based on weights deduced from the correlation ratio and other statistical concepts gives this type of scale a defensible base.
3. If several measures or scales involve a single underlying variable an index or scale of this variable can be obtained through the use of factor analysis.

SELECTED REFERENCES

Cattell, Raymond B., *Factor Analysis,* New York, Harper & Row, 1952.

Edwards, Allen, *Techniques of Attitude Scale Construction,* New York, Appleton-Century-Crofts, 1957.

Hagood, Margaret J., and Daniel O. Price, *Statistics for Sociologists,* rev. ed., New York, Holt, Rinehart and Winston, 1952.

McNemar, Quinn, "Opinion-Attitude Methodology," *Psychological Bulletin,* vol. 43, no. 4 (July, 1946).

Riley, Matilda White, John W. Riley, Jr., Jackson Toby, *et al., Sociological Studies in Scale Analysis,* New Brunswick, Rutgers University Press, 1954.

Stouffer, Samuel A., *et al., Measurement and Prediction,* Princeton, Princeton University Press, 1950.

Torgerson, Warren S., *Theory and Methods of Scaling,* New York, Wiley, 1960.

9
John C. McKinney

CONSTRUCTIVE TYPOLOGY: EXPLICATION OF A PROCEDURE

The realm of science, including social science, is composed of that which is common to various observers: the world of common experience as it is symbolically formulated. The experienced world consists of a realm of natural events which are no more the property of the observer than they are of the things observed. There is a necessary relationship between observer and observed; therefore the fundamental factor is the direct and common accessibility of both observer and observed. The completeness of the accessibility will vary, both with reference to object and observer; but the fact that it must be common is essential to the method of science and goes unquestioned.

The pragmatically inclined have been impressed by the fact that the scientist has no generalized problem of knowledge, despite the fact that it is his particular business to know.[1] Knowing is not a matter of proceeding from the uncertain effects in the individual to the world beyond which is supposed to cause those effects—scientific research always posits an unquestioned world of existence within which its problems appear and are tested. Any part of this world may become problematic and, therefore, an object of the knowing process. For the researcher, to know is not to have existences and meanings given. It is the initiation of an inquiry into some parts of the common world that has become problematic, an inquiry that necessarily proceeds through the formulation of hypotheses and their testing in the unquestioned world surrounding the problem area. For the purposes at hand, the instruments, the controls, the laboratories, the fellow scholars (the verifiers) are a part of the unproblematic world that is "there" as a world of objects in which theories can be

The material contained in the next two chapters has been extracted from a more comprehensive statement on constructive typology with special reference to social theory. See John C. McKinney, *Constructive Typology and Social Theory*, New York, Appleton-Century-Crofts, 1966.

[1] G. H. Mead, *The Philosophy of the Act*, Chicago, University of Chicago Press, 1938, pp. x–xi.

tested. Knowledge in a scientific sense is not contemplation, but discovery through hypotheses tested in action by things which are for the moment unquestionably real, although in other situations they can be a part of the problematic area.

An external world (see Chapter 1, pages 4–5), is objectively assumed by scientists to be independent of their experiencing it. Expressed differently, research work is the work of discovering, and we can only discover what is in existence. Although external objects exist independently of the experiencing individual, they possess certain characteristics by virtue of their relations to his experiencing of them that they would not otherwise possess. These characteristics are the *meanings* they have for us. The independence of data, as suggested here, is frequently interpreted as a metaphysical affirmation of a real world independent of observation and speculation. There is no such necessary implication in scientific methodology. A metaphysical affirmation is of a reality that is final whereas in the scientist's procedures no such finality is contemplated. On the contrary, his procedures contemplate continued modification and reconstruction in the light of facts and events emerging in ceaseless novelty. Data are isolated elements in a world of things, and their isolation is overcome by the scientist's hypothesis. He cannot stop with the data. They do not speak for themselves, but are a phase of the investigation involved in his cognitive advance. The problem for the scientist is not simply a matter of "seeing" what is "out there." Seeing in any meaningful sense depends upon looking, and looking will inevitably reflect a whole system of interests, theories, and purposes that will lead him to seek one character rather than another in the object or matter under consideration. For the researcher, data are always taken rather than given. Observation is not merely a matter of opening one's eyes or ears, or turning on one's instruments; rather, it is always directed in terms of some sort of problem and expresses some sort of an interest. However tentative and uncertain he may be of its reliability and validity, the scientist persistently will effect a relationship between data, bringing them into some sort of an ordered whole. This gives them at least a provisional reality, a meaning not attached to them as mere data.

In creating this ordered whole, even provisionally, the scientist is postulating a uniformity of nature. On a pragmatic basis we can continue to explain the world in terms of uniformities, and to do so with confidence because the assumption has always worked.[2] As an aspect of explanation, the results looked for by science are uniformities and it states them in terms of probabilities. As an aspect of this pragmatic view and probabilistic approach, we have the "process of typification" and the "production of typologies."

2 G. H. Mead, *Movements of Thought in the Nineteenth Century,* Chicago, University of Chicago Press, 1936, pp. 6–7.

The clarification which typological procedure has attained to date, however unsatisfactory, must be attributed primarily to the persistent empirical and theoretical labors of a small but active aggregate of sociologists. All of these scholars are of course greatly indebted to Max Weber for his ambiguous but highly provocative explication of "the ideal type." It must be noted, however, that the reduction of the ideal type as a special case of the generic constructed type, represents a peculiarly American contribution. In the United States, Becker has unquestionably played the major role in developing the logical character of the type as well as in demonstrating its empirical utility. Tracing his writings, beginning in 1932 with those parts of *Systematic Sociology* which came directly from his pen, gives one the best single insight into the gradual transfer of attention from the ubiquitous ideal type to the more fundamental process of type construction.[3] The theoretical work of Abel, Barton, Bendix, Goode, Grimshaw, Hempel, Kolb, Lazarsfeld, Loomis, Parsons, Redfield, Rose, Shuetz, Sorokin, and Winch must also be cited with reference to the development of typology in the past three decades.[4]

There has also been a gradual increase in competent empirical and analytic adaptation of typology. Hughes studied the relation of personal-

---

[3] See Howard Becker and Alvin Boskoff (eds.), *Modern Sociological Theory*, New York, Holt, Rinehart and Winston, 1957, pp. 308–332, for key Becker bibliographic references.

[4] Theodore Abel, *Systematic Sociology in Germany*, New York, Columbia University Press, 1929; Allen Barton, "The Concept of Property-Space in Social Research," in P. F. Lazarsfeld and Morris Rosenberg (eds.), *The Language of Social Research*, New York, Free Press, 1955, pp. 40–53; Reinhard Bendix, "Concepts and Generalizations in Comparative Sociological Studies," *American Sociological Review*, vol. 28 (August, 1963), pp. 532–538; Reinhard Bendix, and Bennett Berger, "Images of Society and Concept Formation in Sociology," in Llewellyn Gross (ed.), *Symposium on Sociological Theory*, New York, Harper & Row, 1959, pp. 92–118; W. J. Goode, "A Note on the Ideal Type," *American Sociological Review*, vol. 12 (August, 1947), pp. 473–474; A. D. Grimshaw, "Specification of Boundaries of Constructed Types Through Use of the Pattern Variables," *The Sociological Quarterly*, vol. 3 (July, 1962), pp. 179–195; C. G. Hempel, "Typological Methods in the Natural and Social Sciences," *Proceedings*, American Philosophical Association: Eastern Division, vol. 1 (1952), pp. 65–86; W. L. Kolb, "The Peasant in Revolution: A Study in Constructive Typology," unpublished Ph. D. dissertation, University of Wisconsin, 1943; P. F. Lazarsfeld, "Some Remarks on Typological Procedure in Social Research," *Zeitschrift fur Sozialforschung*, vol. 6 (1937), pp. 119–139; P. F. Lazarsfeld, and A. H. Barton, "Qualitative Measurement in the Social Sciences," in Daniel Lerner and H. D. Lasswell (eds.) *The Policy Sciences*, Stanford, Stanford University Press, 1951, pp. 155–192; C. P. Loomis, "The Nature of Rural Social Systems: A Typological Analysis," *Rural Sociology*, vol. 15 (June, 1950), pp. 156–174; Talcott Parsons, *The Structure of Social Action*, New York, Free Press, 1949, in particular, see chaps. 14–17; Robert Redfield, "The Folk Society," *American Journal of Sociology*, vol. 52 (January, 1947), pp. 293–308; Arnold Rose, "A Deductive Ideal-Type Method," *American Journal of Sociology*, vol. 56 (July, 1950), pp. 35–42; Alfred Shuetz, "Concept and Theory Formation in the Social Sciences," *Journal of Philosophy*, vol. 51 (April, 1954), pp. 257–273; P. A. Sorokin, *Social and Cultural Dynamics*, New York, American Book, 1941, *passim*; and R. F. Winch, "Heuristic and Empirical Typologies," *American Sociological Review*, vol. 12 (February, 1947), pp. 68–75.

ity types to the sacred and secular aspects of the division of labor; Hiller examined the "strike cycle" as it appeared in distinctive patterns; Redfield introduced the folk-urban continuum as a basis for the comparative examination of empirical cultures; Schmid intensively examined the German youth movement; Becker analyzed this movement and traced its ultimate perversion to Hitlerism; Foreman reported on the Negro lifeways in the South; Yinger analyzed the sociological significance of religion in the struggle for power; Young studied the secularization accompanying the acculturation of a Russian peasant group in an urban setting; Eister investigated the factors inducing and supporting the movement for Moral Rearmament; Loomis began the work of typing and comparing "social systems"; Merton developed his typology of modes of individual adaptation in approaching the problem of formulating a general theory of deviancy; Goode undertook an analysis of religion from a functionalist viewpoint through the use of types; Fichter developed a typology of religious orientation in examining the involvement of individuals in the life of the church; Gouldner developed a typology of bureaucratic structure in the attempt to break away from the traditional Weberian model; Riesman developed his typology of societal and personality types in his analysis of American social and cultural life; Landecker delineated a typology of social integration; Bellah posited and described five idealtypical stages in the evolution of religion; Dynes undertook the task of operationalizing Troeltsch's typology in an empirical study; Freeman and associates developed a typology of leadership in assessing the problem of locating leaders in a community; Gordon and Babchuck developed a typology of voluntary associations along an instrumental-expressive continuum; Hillery constructed a typology for more adequately differentiating among various human groupings often lumped together under the term "community"; Horowitz made an effort to systematize the sociology of knowledge by means of a typology; Mack proposed a typology for describing occupations and occupational roles based on the degree of determinateness found in the occupation or role; Mizruchi and Perrucci in examining data on drinking pathology used them to construct an eight-fold typology of norms along a prescriptive-proscriptive dimension; and Peterson developed a four-fold typology encompassing both internal and external migration.[5] The preceding citations are in no sense meant

[5] E. C. Hughes, "Personality Types and the Division of Labor," *American Journal of Sociology*, vol. 33 (March, 1928), pp. 754–768; E. T. Hiller, *The Strike Cycle*, Chicago, University of Chicago Press, 1928; Robert Redfield, *Tepoztlan: A Mexican Village*, Chicago, University of Chicago Press, 1930, and Redfield's *The Folk Culture of Yucatan*, Chicago, University of Chicago Press, 1941; Robert Schmid, "German Youth Movements: A Typological Study," unpublished Ph.D. dissertation, University of Wisconsin, 1941; Howard Becker, *German Youth: Bond or Free*, New York, Oxford University Press, 1946; P. B. Foreman, "Negro Lifeways in the Rural South: A Typological Approach to Social Differentiation," *American Sociological Review*, vol. 13 (August, 1948), pp. 409–418; J. M. Yinger, *Religion in the Struggle for Power*, Durham, Duke

to exhaust the great amount of typological activity that has been, and is being, carried on. It represents a mere skimming off of some of the work as an indication of the range of typological activity. In a pragmatic sense, American sociology has extensively utilized typological procedures in its advance toward a greater knowledge of social behavior.

All typification consists in the pragmatic reduction and equalization of attributes relevant to the particular purpose at hand for which the type has been formed, and involves disregarding those individual differences of the typified objects that are not relevant to such purpose. *There is no such thing as a type independent of the purposes for which it was constructed.* This purpose resides in the theoretical or practical problem which, as a result of our selective interest, has emerged as questionable from the unquestioned world in the background. Typologies are subordinate to the aims of research, namely the establishment of uniformities of explanatory value. Typologies are *instrumental* in the research process; they are fictional in the sense that they have been constructed to be useful in the research process. The reference of the type to the problem for whose solution it has been constructed, its "problem relevance," constitutes the meaning of the typification. Thus typologies should be constructed to aid in the analysis of specific bodies of data. The extension of the area of applicability of the type simultaneously involves the extension of problem relevance and the analysis of relevant data. Typologies must

University Press, 1946; Pauline Young, *Pilgrims of Russian Town,* Chicago, University of Chicago Press, 1932; A. W. Eister, *Drawing-Room Conversion: A Sociological Account of the Oxford Group Movement,* Durham, Duke University Press, 1950; C. P. Loomis, and J. A. Beegle, "A Typological Analysis of Social Systems," *Sociometry,* vol. 9 (August, 1948), pp. 147–191; R. K. Merton, "Social Structure and Anomie," in his *Social Theory and Social Structure,* New York, Free Press, 1949, pp. 125–133; W. J. Goode, *Religion Among the Primitives,* New York, Free Press, 1948; Joseph Fichter, *Social Relations in the Urban Parish,* Chicago, University of Chicago Press, 1954; A. W. Gouldner, *Patterns of Industrial Bureaucracy,* New York, Free Press, 1954; David Riesman, *et al., The Lonely Crowd,* New Haven, Yale University Press, 1950; Werner Landecker, "Types of Integration and Their Measurement," *American Journal of Sociology,* vol. 56 (January, 1951), pp. 332–340; R. N. Bellah, "Religious Evolution," *American Sociological Review,* vol. 29 (June, 1964), pp. 358–374; R. R. Dynes, "Church-Sect Typology and Socio-Economic Status," *American Sociological Review,* vol. 20 (October, 1955), pp. 555–560; L. C. Freeman, T. J. Fararo, Warner Bloomberg, and M. H. Sunshine, "Locating Leaders in Local Communities: A Comparison of Some Alternative Approaches," *American Sociological Review,* vol. 28 (October, 1963), pp. 791–798; G. W. Gordon, and Nicholas Babchuck, "A Typology of Voluntary Associations," *American Sociological Review,* vol. 24 (February, 1959), pp. 22–29; G. A. Hillery, "Villages, Cities, and Total Institutions," *American Sociological Review,* vol. 28 (October, 1963), pp. 779–791; I. L. Horowitz, "A Formalization of the Sociology of Knowledge," *Behavioral Science,* vol. 9 (January, 1964), pp. 45–55; R. C. Mack, "Occupational Determinateness: A Problem and Hypothesis in Role Theory," *Social Forces,* vol. 35 (October, 1956), pp. 20–25; E. H. Mizruchi, and Robert Perrucci, "Norm Qualities and Differential Effects of Deviant Behavior: An Exploratory Analysis," *American Sociological Review,* vol. 27 (June, 1962), pp. 391–399; William Peterson, "A General Typology of Migration," *American Sociological Review,* vol. 23 (June, 1958), pp. 256–266.

be understood as representative of a pragmatic research methodology and thus subject to evaluation in terms of the accuracy of predictions which result from their utilization. An empirical error criterion is as fundamental in typological procedure as it is in research methodology generally. It is clear that some particular typology can be used in the study of several different social systems or processes. This requires, however, that the goodness of fit of the typology to each set of data must be evaluated. Typologies, by the very nature of their construction, cannot have a perfect fit to any set of data. The better the fit, however, the greater the probability that the typology will be useful in the subsequent analysis.[6]

The construction of types is an aspect of scientific methodology generally and is not confined to any particular science; it is a procedure applicable to the data of any science, although obviously more characteristic of some than of others. This device has played an undeniable role in the growth of social scientific knowledge despite the fact that it retains many of its methodological ambiguities. The literature abounds in types; yet whatever standardization exists in their construction is largely implicit. Despite the almost universal use of types within the social sciences, the problem of standardizing the procedures for their construction remains largely untouched.

Controversy has swirled around the concept of type since the time of Weber, and we continue to have excellent, although invariably ambiguous, discussions of typology in the literature.[7] These discussions continue to focus primarily on the ontology of types rather than the development of their pragmatic utility as tools.[8] Whatever else a constructed type may be, it is clearly a conceptual tool. Despite its varied use over the years, it is possible to discern an underlying consensus which has enabled us to define the constructed type as a *purposive, planned selection, ab-*

[6] The emphasis which Weber placed upon the "fictionality" (comparable in meaning to "abstract") of typologies can be interpreted as evidence of a pragmatic orientation and should not be permitted to obscure the fact that the ultimate criterion in his methodology is an empirical error criterion. See Max Weber, *The Methodology of the Social Sciences*, E. A. Shils and H. A. Finch (eds.), New York, Free Press, 1949, p. 93, *passim.*

[7] Among the more provocative recent discussions are: Paul F. Lazarsfeld, "Philosophy of Science and Empirical Social Research," in Ernest Nagel, Patrick Suppes, and Alfred Tarski (eds.), *Logic, Methodology and Philosophy of Science*, Stanford, Stanford University Press, 1962, pp. 463–473; Don Martindale, "Sociological Theory and the Ideal Type," in Gross, *op. cit.*, pp. 57–91; C. G. Hempel, "Typological Methods in the Natural and Social Sciences," *Proceedings*, American Philosophical Association: Eastern Division, 1, 1952, pp. 65–86; and J. W. N. Watkins, "Ideal Types and Historical Explanation," *The British Journal for the Philosophy of Science*, vol. 3 (May, 1952), pp. 22–43.

[8] Recent exceptions would include Barton, in Lazarsfeld and Rosenberg, *op. cit.*, pp. 40–53; A. D. Grimshaw, "Specification of Boundaries of Constructed Types through Use of the Pattern Variable," *The Sociological Quarterly*, vol. 3 (July, 1962), pp. 179–194; and Milton Bloombaum, "A Contribution to the Theory of Typological Construction," *The Sociological Quarterly*, vol. 5 (Spring, 1964), pp. 157–162.

straction, combination, and (sometimes) accentuation of a set of criteria with empirical referents that serves as a basis for comparison of empirical cases.[9] The elements and relations actually found in historical and contemporary social life supply the materials out of which the conceptual tool is constituted. These are identified, selected, articulated, and simplified into the constructed type on the basis of some idea of the social scientist as to the nature of social reality and on the basis of the purposes of his inquiry. The question remains as to *how* this is done. An exploratory approach to this problem will be made here by means of a demonstrational analysis. This analysis consists of an explication of a procedural sequence in type construction. It is not implied that this particular sequence encompasses the range of typological procedures. On the contrary, the implication is that other procedures and sequences will have to be similarly explicated if the general process of type construction and utilization is to be properly delineated and recognized.

Unfortunately, it is not possible to turn to the work of those who have used typologies in the past to gain a clear idea of the steps involved. There is no standardized procedure used by all typologists. However, given the work of the past and an extension of this work in the light of relatively simple sociological methods, it is possible to develop a series of typological operations or procedural steps that may help to make explicit both the utility and the limitations of constructive typology in sociology and the social sciences in general. In order to make the set of operations explicit, a single illustrative case will be used throughout.

Delineation of the Problem Situation. The typologist, as all social scientists, works with some substantive area of inquiry. He faces an em-

---

[9] With this definition as our bench mark, it is possible to assert that *all* types are constructed, and that moreover the scientist typically constructs the units with which he operates. This is true of the physical as well as the social sciences. One only has to glance at any of the special sciences to realize the tremendous importance of constructs to their endeavor. For example: the perfect lever, perfect gas, frictionless motion, perfect vacuum, perfect surfaces, straight cylinders and spheres, and other similar constructs have contributed heavily to the physicist's knowledge in his problem domain. Economics is deeply indebted to its "economic man" from which the classical economic theory was derived. The essential concepts of perfect competition, the perfectly mobile factors of supply and demand, the perfect monopoly, or such classificatory labels as capitalist and socialist systems, money, credit, or barter economies are all constructed types. The sociologist is dependent upon such notions as competition, conflict, accommodation, assimilation, socialization, superordination, subordination, institutionalization, community, society, caste and class, sacred and secular, rural and urban, democracy-autocracy, bureaucracy, the deviant, solidarity, primary group; these and many more may be constructed types. Even the ideographic historian, whose aim is different than that of the scientist and who is legitimately concerned with the unique and individual, constantly utilizes constructed types. When he talks of epochs, eras, and periods, he has constructed them. When the historian speaks of the Greek city-society, the feudal system, the manorial system, early Protestantism, the medieval Papacy, the Calvinistic ethic, the estates within the state, and countless other things, he is utilizing, usually without awareness, the procedure of constructive typology in his own particular way.

pirical as well as a theoretical problem. For the purpose of developing an illustration, let us pose the very broad sociological problem of assessing the degree of war guilt of various segments of the German society during World War II. Let us further pose the more limited problem of the typologist as the following: What was the role of the German intellectual in the conduct of the aggressive acts of World War II? This is an empirical question, but in an effort to answer it the typologist will pose, and be largely concerned with, more abstract and more theoretically relevant problems. First, however, he will concern himself with other steps.

Familiarization with the Relevant Available Data. In our example, the typologist would immerse himself in the particularities of the German situation. The facts and interpretations provided by the historian give a descriptive account of this situation. Some knowledge of German traditions, recent German events, and modern German behavior patterns is essential before proceeding further.

Since the literature implied by the breadth of the problem (its scope of relevance) is vast it would, of course, be necessary to seek salient leads. For example, some of the work done in studying the German youth movement would be relevant. With a small number of basic types Becker carried out a penetrating study of the movement.[10] The basic concepts were sacred-secular, cult-sect-denomination-ecclesia, and charisma.

Becker hypothesized that the German youth movement came into being because the ends and prospective life situations of its adherents had been defined by adults in patterns which were in sharp and observable contrast with the things adults actually did. There was a readily distinguishable difference between what parents said should be done and their actual deeds. Parents were seen to practice expediency under the guise of sanction and tradition. They visibly utilized affective outlets that they verbally condemned. Youthful idealism, fed on idealized patterns of the past, was rudely shaken by the harsh reality of adult deviousness. This demanded a redefinition of life by confused youth.

This dissent and rejection of adult values and standards gave rise to like-mindedness, and resulted in the emergence of youth conventicles which later fused into sects. It became possible for rebels to join forces against a despised way of life. There was an emotional and collective youth reaction against the insincerities of rapid secularization. The emergence of hundreds of groups manifesting certain basic similarities of conduct was typed as the German youth movement.

Becker then delved into the important relationship between the youth movement, youth tutelage, Hitler youth, and ultimately the Nazi movement itself. He was able to show very clearly how the youth movement was perverted by the Nazis. The loose framework of fellowship (conventicles and sects) was eventually converted into a highly organized

[10] Becker, *German Youth: Bond or Free,* New York, Oxford University Press, 1946.

ecclesia. This was in direct contrast to the avowed aims of the early leaders and participants. Youth movement became youth tutelage, and a huge paramilitary organization emerged that was in sharp contrast to the early romanticism and anarchism. The external manifestations of the youth movement such as the dress, the "roaming," the "nest," the "camp," the "leadership principle," and the songs were borrowed by the Nazis, but they were utilized as means to the accomplishment of specific ends. These were the Nazi ends of converting and utilizing youth in their system of control and expansion.

The phenomenon of perversion of a movement, the invidious use of tutelage for doctrinaire purposes, the buttressing of a movement by depicting it as the ideal realization of a powerful folk movement, the erection of a devised sacred society are all of significance for the understanding of the Nazi movement and the continued strength and appeal of its ideology. Contrasting interpretations of this same phenomenon and analyses of other salient features of German society should be absorbed before attempting an approach to the specific problem.

Derivation of Hypotheses About Relationships and Sequences. On the basis of this knowledge of twentieth-century German characteristics and the Hitlerian movement, the typologist might be led to hypothesize that there was a very limited involvement of the German intellectual in the Hitlerian regime and its aggressive acts. In order to arrive at this hypothesis, it will be necessary for him to turn to a more abstract level of analysis, at the same time keeping in mind the specifics of the historical situation with which he is dealing. When he turns to the sociological conceptual framework for the analysis of social systems and the role played by particular segments of populations in social systems, he develops a more abstract statement of his original problem. In so doing, he is able to generate a specific hypothesis relevant to his original empirical problem and at the same time make a more general statement, only one example of which is represented by his empirical problem.

In the particular example we are using, for instance, he may define the intellectual as "the professional man of knowledge," with further specification of the kinds of individuals included in the class.[11] He will also classify the Hitlerian social system according to some scheme such as the following: charismatic, affectual, traditionally-oriented, prescribed-

[11] For an example of the type of materials of relevance here, see Florian Znaniecki, *The Social Role of the Man of Knowledge,* New York, Columbia University Press, 1940. Znaniecki's study of the types of men of knowledge asks the broad question: What social function does the man of knowledge perform in all cultures and at all times? Znaniecki arrived at four types of men of knowledge who function under certain typical cultural conditions: technologists, sages, schoolmen, and explorer-creators. Each survive and serve their times with a specific type of knowledge. The Znaniecki formulation of course has no direct applicability to the problem in question here, but would constitute a part of the essential background. See also Logan Wilson, *The Academic Man,* New York, Oxford University Press, 1942.

sacred, and antirationalistic.[12] At this higher level of abstraction, he would hypothesize that in such a social system there would be relatively little emphasis on the general role of knowledge, and consequently the intellectual, as the professional man of knowledge, would probably be relegated to a minor and passive role in the social system.[13] The hypothesis at the general level would thus be: "In a charismatic, affectual, traditionally-oriented, prescribed-sacred, and anti-rationalistic social system, intellectuals will play a relatively minor and passive role in the central activities of the social system." At the more specific empirical level in which the typologist is originally interested, he would state his hypothesis as follows: "The intellectual was an impotent factor in the Hitlerian order."

Delineation of Empirical Uniformities and Pragmatic Reduction to Type. The class of intellectuals having been roughly blocked out as consisting of professional men of knowledge, the typologist then attempts to define the attributes of this class. These attributes are empirical uniformities of the class, but they are chosen so as to be most *significantly representative* of the intellectuals' behavior with respect to the social system. He chooses those attributes which stand out as being the most obvious or the most crucial with respect to this relationship between the class of intellectuals and the type of social system being dealt with.

You will find that you often get the best insights by considering extreme types, or from thinking of the opposite of that with which you are directly concerned. If you think about despair, then also think about elation; if you study the miser, then also the spendthrift. That is also a general characteristic of anchor projects, which, if it is possible, ought to be designated in terms of "polar types." The hardest thing in the world is to study one object, but when you try to contrast objects, you get a sort of grip on the materials and you can then sort out the dimensions in terms of which comparisons are made. You will find that the shuttling between attention to these dimensions and to the concrete types is very illuminating. This technique is also logically sound, for without a sample, you can only guess about statistical frequencies anyway: what you can do is to give

[12] A summary statement such as the following one by Mühlmann can be very revealing: "We Germans have a barely concealed inclination for a romantic espousal of the cause of *Gemeinschaft* (culture, feeling) against *Gesellschaft* (civilization, intellect)." W. E. Mühlmann, "Sociology in Germany: Shift in Alinement," in Becker and Boskoff, *op. cit.,* p. 662.

[13] It would be of some importance here to check materials in the pre-Hitler period. In this regard Paul Honigsheim, as early as 1926, discerning a crisis in German higher education had related it to the diminution of *Gemeinschaft* and its replacement by an undesirable *Gesellschaft.* He developed a typology of individuals involved in the educational process. The types of professors—savant, aristocratic state employee, industrial capitalist, *literatus* or journalist, prophet, and the organizer—are discursively related to characteristic backgrounds, followers, and to the trends in the educational process. Paul Honigsheim, "Die Gezenwartskrise der Kulturinstitute in ihrer soziologischen Bedingheit," in Max Scheler (ed.), *Versuche zu einer Soziologie der Wissens,* Leipzig, Duncker und Humblot, 1926, pp. 426–450.

the range and the major types of some phenomenon, and for that it is more economical to begin by constructing "polar types," opposites along various dimensions. This does not mean of course that you will not strive to gain and to maintain a sense of proportion, with the hope of obtaining some lead on the frequencies of given types. One continually tries, in fact, to combine this quest with the search for indices for which one might find or collect statistics.[14]

He defines those attributes in pure, possibly even exaggerated, form and then imputes to them the character of system.[15] In other words, he assumes for the purposes at hand that they belong together and hence are representative of the system of behavior called intellectual under the type of social conditions postulated. The type then is an hypothesized compound of empirically observed, but selected and purified attributes of the class being studied.

The attributes included within the construct "impotent German intellectual" in the present example might be (1) strong nationalism, (2) great respect for the traditions of the German armed forces, (3) fear of Russia so great that the Nazis appear to be the lesser evil, (4) the view that the outside world and not German docility is responsible for the rise of Hitler, (5) political inactivity, (6) opposition to the Nazis expressed only in verbal grumbling rather than in more determined ways, (7) rejection of collaboration with working-class groups which oppose the Nazis, (8) pride in intellectuality as an end in itself, and (9) self-pity.[16]

The question might legitimately be raised at this time as to whether or not this type of intellectual might actively collaborate in Hitler's programme. The working assumption here is that they would not. Intellectuals who actively collaborated in the Nazi movement could easily possess *some* of the attributes of the type since these same attributes (as individual attributes) could characterize other types of intellectuals or the intellectual as a general type. As a *composite,* however, it is assumed that this set of attributes manifest in intellectuals would be conducive to inactivity rather than activity and nonparticipation rather than participation. Such an assumption is necessary at this stage of the inquiry but is subject to empirical check. The check should be made prior to the final or interpretive phase of the inquiry.

It should be noted, of course, that if the type is to be constructed at a

---

[14] C. W. Mills, "On Intellectual Craftsmanship," in Gross, *op. cit.,* p. 43.

[15] For a criticism of the tendency of users of typologies to "slide" from *nominal* to *real* definitions without empirical testing, see Hans Zetterberg, "On Axiomatic Theories in Sociology," in Lazarsfeld and Rosenberg, *op. cit.,* pp. 539–540.

[16] This type is "borrowed" from Howard Becker, "Propaganda and the Impotent German Intellectual," *Social Forces,* vol. 29 (March, 1951), pp. 273–276. The type is used *illustratively* here. The intent is to clarify the procedural steps of typology, and the substantive material involved is purely illustrative.

more abstract level so as to be relevant to the more general hypothesis stated earlier, some of the nine attributes specified would either be dropped or be stated in a less idiosyncratic form. For instance, "great respect for the traditions of the German armed forces" might be deleted or restated as, "great respect for all traditions of the national state." Such an abstract definition of the type would tend, in most instances, to increase the general utility of the type in a number of empirical cases at the cost of its degree of precision in any one case. Before considering the matter of utility, however, there are two other typological steps to be taken.

Simplification of the Type with Regard to the Attribute Sphere from Which It Is Drawn. It is evident that, given the ideal nature of the constructed type and the usual diversity of empirical cases, there will be less than complete correspondence between the constructed type and the empirical class to which it refers.[17] In fact, the degree of deviation from the type (and the distribution of that deviation in the class population) is as important as any other data in the ultimate evaluation of the utility of the type. However, given this deviation, there are certain to be *at least* 2 kinds of empirical cases—those which fit the type and those which do not. In fact, in the case under discussion, if we assume that each of the 9 attributes used in defining the type is a dichotomy, there is the logical possibility of 29 kinds of empirical cases, or 512 kinds of intellectuals, only 1 kind of which is the constructed type. Of course, if the attributes are actually variables assuming more than 2 values each, the number of kinds of intellectuals, so defined, is much greater.

Thus, before going to the empirical data for a rigorous examination of the correspondence between the type and the actual intellectuals, it is well to decide on the basis of a general knowledge of the relevant data and a limited number of complete cases whether all of the attributes included in the type are needed. Of course, it is also possible at this stage to locate additional crucial definitive attributes not originally included in the type. If it appears that two or more of the attributes are very highly correlated, some may be dropped. For instance, if all those who exhibit pride in intellectuality as an end in itself also exhibit self-pity, there is no need to carry both attributes in the type definition. Also, if it is found that some attribute included in the type on rational rather than empirical grounds is not found in the empirical cases, it can be dropped. Of course, this sort of simplification of the type definition can also take place after the empirical data have been more rigorously examined, but much effort will be saved if simplification can take place at this time.

Adaptation of Available Theories and Principles to Give a Tentative

---

17 The discussion by P. F. Lazarsfeld in "Some Remarks on the Typological Procedures in Social Research," *Zeitschrift fur Sozialforschung*, vol. 6, Alcan, Paris, 1937, pp. 119–139, is relevant here. See also Barton, in Lazarsfeld and Rosenberg, *op. cit.,* pp. 40–53.

Explanatory Accounting of the Type. The original definition of the type was based on a consideration of the current state of knowledge and existent theory in the relevant areas of inquiry.[18] However, it is both possible and highly desirable to go beyond the level of asking what role a particular type of person is likely to play in a particular type of social system. It may be possible, for instance, to develop a *series* of hypotheses on the basis of a more rigorous examination of the role of various types of occupations and professions in different kinds of Western social systems. Such an examination might lead us to hypothesize, for instance, that intellectuals placed in different segments of the social system would behave somewhat differently. Thus we would be led to stating hypotheses about the "degree of approximation" of various types of German intellectuals to our constructed type of impotent German intellectual.

It will be seen from the above that there is necessarily a constant interplay between the fifth and sixth steps in the type construction process, between "simplification of the type with regard to the attribute sphere" and the "adaptation of available theories and principles." When these two steps have been completed, the next step is obvious.

Empirical Verification of the Type: Examination of the Rate of Incidence and Degree of Approximation. It is at this point that the often acknowledged and more often implicit split between those sociologists who are primarily methodologically oriented and those who are primarily substantively oriented comes to light. It is also unfortunately true that it is at this crucial point that many of those who have used constructed types become rather vague and elusive. Let us examine what this step involves.

We have noted that, given the 9 attributes used in our example, and assuming that each is a simple dichotomy, there are 512 kinds of intellectuals logically possible. We have also suggested that, where possible, this list of attributes should be reduced in number. But even if it is reduced to 6, there are still 64 possible kinds of intellectuals. Let us assume that we have reduced the number to 6, and let us further assume that we have found empirical cases of only half of these, or 32 kinds of intellectuals, one of which is our primary constructed type. In order to get this far, of course, we must also assume that we have adequate measures of the attributes for an adequate sample of intellectuals.

One of our first tasks will be to record the relative incidence of the constructed type. Since we have purposely made the definitive attributes of the type rather extreme, there is unlikely to be a high proportion of intellectuals who will be the pure type of impotent intellectual. Whether we have retained only our simple original hypothesis that German intel-

---

[18] The difficulties involved in relating types to generalized analytical theory are explored in detail by Talcott Parsons in *The Structure of Social Action*, 2nd ed., New York, Free Press, 1949, pp. 601–639.

lectuals would be found to be impotent, or whether we have developed
more refined hypotheses about different kinds of intellectuals, we are
immediately faced with the problem of measuring the degree of approximation to the constructed type.

It is not sufficient simply to indicate that so many of the empirical
cases fit the type and so many do not. One of the advantages of following
the earlier steps is that one is able at this point to go beyond such a gross
statement to a more refined analysis of the data. If the attributes of the
type are adequately defined, we will know at this point how many cases
exhibit *each* of these attributes, and we will thus be able to examine the
total distribution of attributes within our sample of cases. It will then be
possible to indicate not only how many cases do not fit the type precisely,
but also the degree to which they deviate from it *(how many* attributes
they do not exhibit) and the pattern of these deviations *(which* attributes
they do not exhibit). Given this information, it is possible to use the logic
of scaling procedures to gain added insight into the relationship between
the type and the empirical data. Using the attributes as items in a scale,
we can then analyze these items with respect to their interrelationships.

There are, in effect, six items in our scale, or seven points or scale
values. It is rather clear that here we have a scale of no higher order than
an ordinal scale. Thus, there would be limits on the kind of analysis we
can utilize. But either of the familiar techniques devised by Likert and
Guttman could be used, and they would contribute much to our understanding of the type and the data. Using the Likert criteria, for instance,
we would be able to see if all of the attributes "hang together" in the
sense that each is related to the total configuration in a linear fashion. It
should give us pause if we found, for instance, that there was more pride
in intellectuality in those intellectuals who exhibited few or none of the
other attributes than there was in those who exhibited many of them.

It is highly probable that we do not have a uni-dimensional scale in
the Guttman sense, but it might be very valuable and revealing to investigate this matter. For instance, is it true that *all* those who exhibit self-pity
also exhibit strong nationalism and great respect for the traditions of the
German armed forces, but only *some* of them are politically inactive? Is
it possible that there is not only a rank ordering of intellectuals with respect to their approximation to the constructed type, but also a related
rank ordering of the attributes of the type according to their incidence
in the population of intellectuals? Is it possible that different kinds of
intellectuals (differentially placed in the social system) tend to be particular scale types—that is, do they systematically exhibit some of the type
attributes, but not others? These are exciting and intriguing questions,
but they are not very often considered by the typologist. To do so would
indeed be difficult, but to fail to do so leaves all too many questions
unanswered and much of the utility of typology untapped.

Even if the typologist must settle for a simple score computed by assigning a plus one to all type attributes and a zero to their lack, the problem of degree of approximation must be faced. In using this type, Howard Becker interviewed approximately 600 intellectuals and never found 1 that manifested all 9 attributes contained within the type.[19] As suggested above, such a finding raises a question regarding the adequacy of the original type attributes. It also opens the possibility of reducing the number of attributes in the original type and/or constructing other types, thus taking into account different kinds of intellectuals. Moreover, it must be acknowledged that the adequacy of the measure of approximation is an important factor in determining the utility of the typology. It is also important to recognize that a careful consideration of the problem of degree of approximation is crucial for the final step of type construction.

Interpretation. If the typologist has found that the type occurs with great frequency, he may conclude that the German intellectuals played only a minor role in the aggression, and that no other types representing the class need to be constructed or examined.[20] However, it was suggested earlier that it is probable that the type incidence will not be sufficient to warrant any general statements on the basis of this type alone. As has been suggested, it may be that a number of clear-cut "scale types" have been isolated representing degrees of approximation to the pure constructed type. It is equally (or more) probable that a number of "non-scale types" will have appeared. A careful examination of these may disclose that they are actually cases of a qualitatively different kind of intellectual rather than being quantitative approximations of the original constructed type. It may be that one or more additional types will have to be constructed using other attributes not included in the original type. Thus a series of types of intellectuals might be formed, each of them emphasizing certain aspects which the intellectual has in common with other intellectuals because these aspects each have some relevance to the problem at hand. Numerous types can be formed and frequently have to be formed in connection with one particular problem. Conversely a particular type, after construction, can be found to be relevant to a whole series of problems. In this way a type becomes established and is utilized as a referent in widely varied interpretive activity. In each instance, however, the relevance of the typification to the problem under consideration has to be demonstrated rather than taken for granted.

It must be noted here that the interpretive phase of the inquiry is of crucial significance in the inquiry. The breadth of latitude here is in part responsible for the controversy that surrounds the usage of

---

19 See his "Propaganda and the Impotent German Intellectual."

20 This would be true if it had been empirically established that representatives of the type had in fact been inactive in the Hitler programme.

types. Conversely it is this breadth of latitude that gives typologies their frontier-breaking quality in inquiry. Conclusions with regard to the initial hypothesis must be handled with care and with special attention to counter-argument. In general, typological formulations can give one a compelling rather than conclusive case. It is unlikely that other interpretations of the hypothesis will have been eliminated by the mere establishment of the typology. Such a case, however, is not at all unusual in social research. Indeed, it may be thought of as "typical."

The important point to be made here is that the construction of the original type, involving the collection of data making possible the comparison of empirical cases with this type and the evaluation of the degree of approximation of these cases with the type, has shed additional light on the class of objects being studied (in this case, German intellectuals). It has indicated the degree of adequacy of the generalization (or hypothesis) implicit in the original constructed type, and it has pointed the way toward a clarification of the deviations from this type. In so doing, the process has helped to give system to a body of historical data, thus making it pertinent to the sociological enterprise.

In Sum. It would seem evident that the primary function of types is to identify, simplify, and order the concrete data so that they may be described in terms which make them comparable. They function in this way at any level of abstraction, and hence can be utilized with respect to problems varying from limited to great breadth of scope. In effect, a type constitutes a reduction from the complex to the simple; hence, the careful construction and use of types, as an intermediate procedure, can potentially make many large-scale problems accessible to more refined methodology and technique. The construction of a type or series of types helps us to know more precisely what mechanisms or structural relations are being postulated with respect to a problem area, sometimes calling attention to the need for further clarification of the operational meaning of relevant definitions and statements. The type assists in the discovery of inconsistencies between the empirical data and the theories used to explain them. It thus lays the basis for the further elaboration of theory and frequently suggests further empirical studies in a problem-complex. The type aids in handling complicated, simultaneous interrelations among a relatively large number of variables in a *preliminary* way, prior to the development of the operational possibility of handling them more rigorously with respect to any particular problem. Typologies are always subordinate to the aims of research. As such they are at the service of the social research process and have no relevance except that of a problem relevance within that context. It is for this reason that typologies can be viewed as natural tools within a pragmatically-oriented social research process striving continuously for increments or limited advances in knowledge with respect to social behavior. Indeed, a primary role of the constructed type would seem to be that of a "sensitizing device." Its use allows social scientists cognitively to map broad areas of social phenomena through the systematic tapping of historical and secondary data. This can quite conceivably result in increased precision of analysis in many areas in the social sciences, particularly in such areas as macro-sociology where the problems are currently often beyond the scope of the more rigorous experimental and quantitative techniques.

SELECTED REFERENCES

Barton, Allen H., "The Concept of Property Space in Social Research," in P. F. Lazarsfeld and Morris Rosenberg (eds.), *The Language of Social Research*, New York, Free Press, 1955, pp. 40–53.

Becker, Howard, "Constructive Typology in the Social Sciences," in H. E. Barnes, Howard Becker, and F. B. Becker (eds.), *Contemporary Social Theory*, New York, Appleton-Century-Crofts, 1940.

Bendix, Reinhard, "Concepts and Generalizations in Comparative Sociological Studies," *American Sociological Review*, vol. 28, no. 4 (August, 1963), pp. 532–539.

Bloombaum, Milton, "A Contribution to the Theory of Typology Construction," *Sociological Quarterly*, vol. 5, no. 2 (Spring, 1964), pp. 157–162.

Grimshaw, Allen D., "Specification of Boundaries of Constructed Types Through Use of the Pattern Variable," *The Sociological Quarterly*, vol. 3, no. 3 (July, 1962), pp. 179–195.

Hempel, Carl, "Typological Methods in the Natural and Social Sciences," *Proceedings*, American Philosophical Association Eastern Division, vol. 1 (1952), pp. 65–86.

Lazarsfeld, Paul F., "Philosophy of Science and Social Research," in Nagel, Suppes, and Tarski (eds.), *Logic, Methodology and Philosophy of Science*, Stanford, Stanford University Press, 1962, pp. 463–473.

Lazarsfeld, Paul F., and Allen Barton, "Qualitative Measurement in the Social Sciences: Classification, Typologies, and Indices," in Daniel Lerner and H. D. Lasswell (eds.), *The Policy Sciences*, Stanford, Stanford University Press, 1951, pp. 155–192.

Shuetz, Alfred, "Concept and Theory Formation in the Social Sciences," *Journal of Philosophy*, 51 (April, 1954), pp. 257–273.

Weber, Max, *The Methodology of the Social Sciences*, translated and edited by E. A. Shils and H. A. Finch, New York, Free Press, 1949.

10

John C. McKinney

CONSTRUCTIVE TYPOLOGY: STRUCTURE AND FUNCTION

An examination of the process of concept formation leads inexorably to the conclusion that all concepts are constructs which have been *developed* out of experience. Clearly, raw experience is never really raw even at the moment of perception. As a consequence of having become human through symbolic interaction, human beings naturally and necessarily categorize and structure their experience in terms of concepts.

All phenomena are unique in their occurrence in space and time; therefore no phenomena actually recur in their concrete wholeness. In order to make these phenomena intelligible and explicable they must be *reduced* through conceptualization. When science begins to classify and analyze its data, it is taking a definite and formal step away from reality at the level of direct experience. To comprehend is to introduce order into our experiencing of phenomena. This requires that phenomena be treated *as though* they were identical, recurrent, and general. The meaning of identity, however, is always *identical for the purpose at hand*. The construction of classes, categories, or types is a necessary aspect of the process of inquiry by means of which we reduce the complex to the simple, the unique to the general, and the occurrent to the recurrent. To introduce order with its various scientific implications (including prediction), the scientist necessarily rises above or ignores the unique, the extraneous, and the non-recurring and thereby departs from perceptual experience. This departure is prerequisite to the achievement of abstract generality, which in turn constitutes the basis of our ability to comprehend the world of concrete experience. To conceptualize means to generalize to some degree. To generalize means to reduce the number and variety of objects by conceiving of some of them as being identical in certain ways or for certain purposes. The reduction of the object world reduces the number and variety of relations to be examined and explained. It is on the specification of these relations that our comprehension of the world of phenomena is based.

Scientific concepts never exhaust perceptual experience for they always involve selection. Concepts do not reflect the totality of raw experience in all its diversity and complexity and are, therefore, in a sense, unreal. In brief, all concepts are generalizations and all generalization implies abstraction and reduction. One aspect of this may be described as the process of typification. Within the realm of formal inquiry this process is manifest in the construction of types and typologies.

A great many varieties of types have been described in the literature of the social sciences. Reference is frequently made to ideal, pure, extreme, heuristic, polar, empirical, real, classificatory, and constructed types. Unfortunately, the emphasis has largely been upon the assumed or actual differences between these types and the accompanying assertion of superiority of one version of typing over the others. As a result, the common qualities of *all* types and typing have been largely ignored, and the basic fact that all types are constructed has not often been considered.

The writer has no quarrel with the above type labels, and feels that their delineation and usage has made some contribution to the clarification of typological procedure. But many ambiguities and obscurities remain. As descriptive labels, some of the above reflect purpose (the heuristic type), serial order (the polar type), character of attributes (the pure type), function (the classificatory type), or developmental procedure (the constructed type). Such contrasting bases for labeling have tended to obscure the fundamental qualities shared by all types. From a methodological point of view these qualities center around how types are conceptually developed. When one looks closely at the variety of types extant in any substantive field, it is impossible to avoid the central fact that the development of each of them involved a task of construction. This is not to assert that all types are alike in their construction; it is merely a way of saying that all types are constructed around certain persistent variables. In surveying a broad range of major typologies it would appear that the major variables are (1) the relation of type to perceptual experience, (2) the degree of abstraction involved in the types, (3) the purpose of the type, (4) the temporal scope of the type, (5) the spatial scope of the type, and (6) the function required of the type.

When these variables, which are either explicitly or implicitly present in any type, are viewed as the axes around which types are constructed they appear as the main dimensions of types in general. They are seen as a series of continua which serve to delineate the structure of types. For purposes of analytic convenience and description we will label the polar points of these continua and thereafter treat them as the "polar variables of type construction." We then have the following variables: (1) ideal–extracted, (2) general–specific, (3) scientific–historical, (4) timeless–time-bound, (5) universal–local, and (6) generalizing–individualizing.

It is possible to analyze any given type in terms of its tendency to conform to the requirements of one pole or another on each of the above continua. It is important to note, however, that these continua are not mutually exclusive and do not reflect the same level of abstraction. On the contrary, they are mutually implicated, overlap to a certain unavoidable extent, and reflect methodological relevance rather than logical purity. In other words, these continua represent the empirically persistent points of methodological concern in the development of substantive types. We shall use them as the basis for the construction of a "typology of types." The primary purpose is to indicate the attribute sphere within which types are developed and the bases on which they vary in terms of their construction. The assumption is that the function of a type or typology is dependent upon its structure. The structure of any particular type or typology is made visible by locating it in the attribute sphere of the general process of typification. Our typology of types is presented as a rough cognitive map of that attribute sphere and hence is designed to differentiate between primary modes of type construction.

Ideal–Extracted. The name invariably linked with the "ideal type" is that of Max Weber, its most famous proponent. A comment made by Paul Lazarsfeld should be called to attention here since in effect it constitutes a serious methodological challenge in social research.

Max Weber did spectacular work in historical sociology, a field badly neglected in recent years. But he also wrote a few pages on what he thought he did, calling his procedure the construction of ideal types. These self-declaratory statements contradict each other at many points; they have no visible relation to the actual content of his studies, and they have led to endless and confused literature which is concerned mostly with terminology and, as far as I can see, has resulted in no new investigations. No one has explicated what he did in his actual studies, which has contributed to the difficulty of emulating his skill.[1]

Ideal types are, of course, common in all the sciences as well as the discipline of history, but it was Weber who made us most conscious of this kind of type.

In Weber's generalizing procedure he was looking for order in behavior, and his approach led him to the formulation of the "typical" in its ideal or pure form. To Weber these conceptual formulations were merely expedient heuristic devices useful in understanding the phenomena under consideration. Weber's conceptual system was essentially elastic and readily modifiable in terms of empirical necessity and interest.

Weber conceived of the ideal type as being both abstract and general. For instance, his types did not describe or directly represent concrete courses of action, but instead were representative of objectively

[1] See "Philosophy of Science and Empirical Social Research," in Ernest Nagel, Patrick Suppes, and Alfred Tarski (eds.), *Logic, Methodology and Philosophy of Science,* Stanford, Stanford University Press, 1962, p. 464.

possible modes of action. This would be a course of conduct assuming certain ends and means to be in consistent usage by the individuals involved. Further, this would be a typical course of action not necessarily duplicated in concrete situations by individual modes of behavior, but would be normative in character. The ideal type would logically contain within its structure all the essential properties or elements of a concrete course of action, but not necessarily in the proportion or relationship pattern of any given empirical occurrence. These properties or elements constituted the variables within this type and were held in fixed relationship with each other for theoretical purposes.

As abstractions, Weber's ideal types were conscious deviations from concrete experience. They were structured in such a way as to accentuate some attribute or group of attributes relevant to his research purpose or interest. In a sense, they were a distortion of the concrete, in that all empirical occurrences appeared as deviations from the theoretically conceived ideal type. This is the real core and basic significance of the ideal type. The observations of empirical occurrences yielded nothing but deviations when compared to the ideal type, but these deviations were relative to each other and to the ideal type. Hence, the ideal type served as the model or basic comparative unit. In the light of this, it is obvious that Weber conceived of ideal types as being merely necessary logical expedients. They were not in themselves empirically valid, and were theoretically not subject to reification. They did not directly represent any concrete reality or constitute an essence of actuality. They merely served as consciously devised and delimited conceptual tools in the analysis of the empirical world. In Weber's view, typologies were subordinate to the aims of socio-historical research, namely, the causal analysis of historical events.

At the opposite end of the continuum and from the pole represented by the ideal type, we have the "extracted type," which is often called the "empirical type." [2] These types are definitely not exclusive of one another; on the contrary, they grade gradually into each other. It must be pointed out that even though the ideal type is theoretically derived, it must still have empirical referents, for it is based upon the particularities of actual occurrence. Weber made this very clear in terms of what he did, rather than in terms of what he said about the ideal type. Conversely, the extracted type, no matter how empirical its base, involves a certain amount of problem- or theory-oriented selection and, hence, construction. Both types serve the purpose of simplifying and identifying the object world. Their differences lie primarily in their formulation and the way

---

[2] For substantial reasons this writer prefers the label "extracted type." Part of the negative attitude extant toward ideal types is based upon the mistaken notion that they are anti-empirical types. Consequently it seems inadvisable to contribute in any way to the perpetuation of the impression that there is an ideal-empirical dichotomy.

in which they represent the object world; this, of course, has implications
for what they can do in research.

Kretschmer's description of how he arrived at his two general bio-
types, the "cyclothymic" and "schizothymic," is a classic example of the
extractive method:

The types are no "ideal types" which have emerged, consciously created in
accordance with any given guiding principle or collection of pre-established values. They are, on the contrary, obtained from empirical sources in the following
way: when a fairly large number of morphological similarities can be followed
through a correspondingly large number of individuals, then we begin measuring. When we compute averages the outstanding common characteristics come
out clearly, while those peculiar marks which only occur in isolated cases, disappear in the average value. In exactly the same way we treat the remainder of
the characteristics which can only be described from mere optical observation.
So we proceed as if we were copying at the same time the picture of one-hundred
individuals of a type on the same picture-surface, one on top of the other, in
such a way that those characteristics which cover one another become sharply
outlined, while those which do not fit over one another disappear. Only those
characteristics which become strongly marked in the average values are described
as "typical." [3]

The types arrived at by Kretschmer throw the average and common traits
into bold relief; these are not necessarily the crucial or significant ones.

The role of interpretation is much greater in the method of ideal
typing. The ideal type involves comparison from the ideal limits of the
case, whereas the extracted type involves comparison from central tendencies. The extracted type is based upon the notions of average, common, and concrete rather than upon those of accentuation and
abstractness. Nevertheless, a certain amount of essential ideation is involved in the establishment of extracted types, as for instance in the
delineation of the traits involved (a case of abstraction), and the treatment of a combination of traits as a composite whole (a case of simplification based upon elimination of the seemingly irrelevant and, hence,
again a matter of abstraction). As one views the various typologies extant,
it is easily recognized that not one of them is ideally or empirically pure;
in actuality they are representative of tendencies to emphasize one pole
or the other. In this connection it might be mentioned that the Becker-
McKinney model of type construction is a conscious and purposive attempt to combine aspects of ideal and extracted types in order to
capitalize on what they both have to offer and to avoid their limitations. [4]

[3] Ernest Kretschmer, *Physique and Character*, New York, Harcourt, Brace &
World, 1925, pp. 18–19.

[4] Much of the work of Howard Becker over a period of approximately 30 years
was oriented toward this problem. One gets a sense of development and considerable
change in contrasting his approach in *Systematic Sociology on the Basis of Bezie-
hungslehre and Gebildelehre*, with Leopold von Wiese, New York, Wiley, 1932, with

In this view constructive typology is seen as the generic procedure encompassing all type formation. The ideal type, the extracted type, and the Becker-McKinney model of constructed type are all merely special cases or modes of typification within the general process.

General–Specific. Types can also be distinguished by their relative generality or specificity. Cognizance must be taken of the levels of abstraction involved in the formulation of types. The more general a type is, the greater the simplification of the empirical attributes, and the more specific a type is, the greater the number of general characteristics obscured by the mass of ideographic detail. Empirical generalization made through the use of the more general constructed types must necessarily remain relatively indefinite in the sense of being highly general. Generalization means omission and simplification of particularities. Consequently, as a type effects wide coverage, its adequacy in accounting for specific variations is lessened. This is not to say that general types are not useful; it is merely to take account of the fact that more specific types must be used in conjunction with them for many explanatory purposes.

Such types as *Gemeinschaft, Gesellschaft,* sacred, secular, communal, associational, rural, urban, folk, state, familistic, contractual, primitive, and civilized are obviously "sponge types" as they stand; nevertheless, they have been extremely useful. Numerous sub-types are necessarily involved in their extensive application, but it is the general type that makes the sub-types possible, and furthermore gives them an interpretive context or coherence within a schema.[5] Moreover, for empirical purposes, one can undertake the *ad hoc* construction of types of leadership, occupation, family, association, law, social movement, leisure, participation, enterprise, production, or whatever else constitutes the base of interest in the inquiry. The types can be formulated to be as specific as necessary to accommodate the domain of relevance of the inquiry. The degree of generality-specificity involved in the construction of a type is unalterably related to the purpose at hand and the predictive task it must perform. An extracted type can be general, but tends to be specific due to the nature of its distillation. An ideal type, on the other hand, can fall freely at various points on the general-specific continuum.

Scientific–Historical. Construction of types may proceed in terms of

that in *Through Values to Social Interpretation,* Durham, Duke University Press, 1950. The first analysis relevant to this problem by McKinney was in "The Role of Constructive Typology in Scientific Sociological Analysis," *Social Forces,* vol. 28 (March, 1950), pp. 235–240. The first published reference to the Becker-McKinney model was contained in J. C. McKinney, "The Polar Variables of Type Construction," *Social Forces,* vol. 35 (May, 1957), pp. 300–306.

5 For illustrations of the use of sub-types, see Howard Becker, "Sacred-Secular Societies," in *Through Values to Social Interpretation,* pp. 248–280; C. P. Loomis, "The Nature of Rural Social Systems—A Typological Analysis," *Rural Sociology,* vol. 15 (June, 1950), pp. 167–174; and C. P. Loomis and J. C. McKinney, "Systemic Differences Between Latin American Communities of Family Farms and Large Estates," *American Journal of Sociology,* vol. 61 (March, 1956), pp. 404–412.

the purposes of the scientist or in terms of the purposes of the historian. It must be recognized that they can and do use the same data, for all data are, in a sense, historical. The scientist, however, is in search of the general and recurrent, and the historian is primarily interested in the actual sequence of unique events. Both use constructed types to achieve their objectives. In typological terms, the research task of the scientist is to generalize and that of the historian is to individualize. Both are legitimate enterprises and play important roles in the accumulation and interpretation of knowledge. No confusion need exist between them at the level of typification of their procedural styles, although it seems inevitable that there should be considerable overlap at the level of addressing particular problems.

No serious quarrel can be made with the proposition that all objects or events are unique in time and space. Such a thesis need not involve the argument that objects or events are merely temporal and that they can be known only in their uniqueness, with their time and space markings clearly evident.[6] On the contrary, it is possible through the use of conceptual constructs to conceive of the identical, recurrent, and typical. History is "event-structured" for both the historian and the social scientist, and events not only can be viewed chronologically and individually, but can be viewed as relationship series involving necessary and sufficient antecedents of consequents. Such conditions and consequents can be categorized, and types and the relations involved can be abstractly stated as general relations. It is thus the perspectives of the historian and social scientist that differ.[7]

[6] There is, of course, a long standing tradition, based primarily in German historicism stemming from the idealistic mode of thought, which resists any generalizing due to the uniqueness and individuality of actual history. For modern expressions of this perspective, see K. R. Popper, *The Poverty of Historicism,* London, Routledge, 1957, and Isaiah Berlin, *Historical Inevitability,* London, Oxford, 1954.

[7] Max Weber used two different kinds of constructs in his historical and sociological work. His construct of modern capitalism, for instance, is a unique or historical conception. It is an ideal type construct of behavior, but it is not generally applicable. Its sole referent as a type is to a particular time and place. It does not make empirical sense to speak of modern capitalism as being existent prior to the seventeenth century. Further, it cannot be appropriately applied anywhere outside of the Western world. Nevertheless, it is a construct in that it does not contain within it all the behavioral minutiae of the epoch. The reference of modern capitalism is individual and historical, not analytical and general.

Max Weber's sociological usage of typology was in line with scientific purposes. His second kind of type dealt with recurrent and prevalent phenomena which typically appeared as constituent elements in repetitive social occurrences. Among his concepts that had general application in a variety of historical contexts are those such as his four types of action: purposive rationality, valuational rationality, affectual, and traditional. The concepts of legitimacy, routinization, charisma, sect, and numerous others ought also to be included here. See Max Weber, *The Theory of Social and Economic Organization,* translated by A. M. Henderson and Talcott Parsons, New York, Oxford University Press, 1947; and from *Max Weber: Essays in Sociology,* H. H. Gerth, and C. W. Mills (eds. and trans.) New York, Oxford University Press, 1946.

The field of the historian is the whole range of human activities. The social sciences in their division of labor cover the same range. But whereas the historian is concerned with processes and structures that are singular in their space-time occurrence and does not conceive of them as being repeatable, the social scientist adopts the opposite perspective. The social scientist is concerned with the repetitive and constant factors, or tendencies of regularity of human society. For example, a sociologist may try to determine and state the recurrent aspects involved in the process of urbanization; the historian, on the other hand, will try to state the specific course which urbanization has taken in a given place over a given period of time. This is another way of saying that the sociologist attempts to extract whatever is universal from the phenomenon, whereas the historian attempts to expose the relevant particulars of one case of the phenomena. Constructed types of historical value tend to be highly complex, time-bound, and localized, whereas those of scientific value tend to be *relatively* timeless, universal, and simple, containing a limited number of criteria, and including so limited a content that they are applicable in many diverse historical situations. The historical construct is general in the sense that it does not depict the full concrete reality in all of its concrete manifestation, and the scientific construct is historical in the sense that the behavior it symbolizes necessarily bears a resemblance to that which has historically occurred. The differences in the constructs answer to the purposes for which they are formulated.

Timeless–Time-bound. This axis is very closely related to the one just treated, in that the scientific universal is the closest approximation to the timeless pole of the continuum and the historical construct is the closest approximation to the time-bound pole. Nevertheless, it is important to treat it separately to reveal the *relative* timelessness of the scientific construct. It must be recognized that scientifically useful constructs vary enormously in the extent to which they are timeless. They stand in different relative positions on the timeless–time-bound continuum.

The concept of *Gemeinschaft* as Tönnies used it is unquestionably as timeless as the sociologist can make a concept. Tönnies regarded all social relationships as the creations of human will. He designated two types of will, *Wesenwille* (essential will), and *Kurwille* (arbitrary will). *Wesenwille* refers to any process of willing originating in the traditional adherence to beliefs and sentiments common to the group. *Wesenwille* is responsible for the *Gemeinschaft* relationship and makes it as timeless as the natural behavior of man. On the other hand, *Gesellschaft,* the presumed antithesis of *Gemeinschaft,* is not timeless to the same extent. Being the product of *Kurwille,* the arbitrary will, and involving the expedient adaptation of means to ends, it necessarily is restricted to a more particularized behavioral development, and, hence, in point of time must be a development out of *Gemeinschaft*. Consequently, it is timeless to a lesser degree.[8]

To use another illustration, the concept of superordination-subordination appears to be quite timeless in view of the fact that some type of hierarchical relationship can be found even in the most primitive of contemporary societies. It is not necessarily entirely timeless, for if there were ever such things as hordes or conditions of completely mechanical solidarity it would not have been applicable. As a principle, however, it seems to be a close approximation to the timeless pole. In contrast, the sociologically significant concept of class appears closer to the time-bound pole of the continuum than the concept of superordination-subordination does. Most of recorded history is immune to analysis by many types which are quite useful within a limited temporal span. For instance, it does not make sense to talk of "economic man" (and the presumptions entailed) with reference to typical behavior prior to the emergence of capitalism. It is likewise nonsense to speak of "scientific man" with reference to primitive societies, or of "academic man" prior to the emergence of the occupational role upon which it is based. Constructs cannot ignore facts. On the contrary, they must account for facts, and these include temporal location.

It is important to note that scientifically useful constructs are only relatively timeless. It is the task of the scientific researcher to remove the time-markings from the phenomena under analysis in order to uncover the general and recurrent, but his success is always a relative one. Time will still leave discernible markings on many of the most useful scientific social types.

Universal–Local. The spatial counterpart of the timeless–time-bound continuum is that which we call universal–local. Just as the former deals with the temporal scope of the type, the latter is concerned with its spatial scope, and together the two axes determine the area of applicability of any given type. Constructs vary as to where they fall on the spatial continuum. When a type is applicable anywhere that the particular class of phenomena it deals with is available, then it may be said to be universal. If a type is applicable only to a very limited and specific locale, and is not approximated anywhere else, it may be called localized.

The "sacred" type of relations may be cited as an example of the universal type. Sacred relations are discernible in any society. Although the objects and content will vary, the attitude of sacredness with resultant behavior can be found among all peoples. In contrast, the sacred type of society tends to be considerably more localized. There are many societies that must be characterized as secular rather than sacred, although they have some sacred relations within them. The prevalence of secular societies

---

[8] Ferdinand Tönnies, *Community and Society (Gemeinschaft und Gesellschaft)*, C. P. Loomis (ed. and trans.), East Lansing, Michigan State University Press, 1957.

obviously limits the scope of the sacred societal type, although the sacred type relation remains universal. Additional spatial limitations are imposed when one starts to derive sub-types from the generic types. When Becker speaks of a "prescribed sacred society," for example, he is sharply delimiting the locale of applicability of the type because there simply are not many actual societies that approximate it; hence, it is a much more localized type than its generic parent.

To illustrate further, a "German peasant" type is localized by deliberately restricting it to German culture. This is accomplished by using criteria (attributes) within the type that are supposedly idiosyncratic to German social structure. A "Russian peasant" type could also be constructed that would differ from the former in that it would contain within it certain traits peculiar to the Russian locale. If one wishes to speak of a "peasant" type that accounts for the relevant behavior in the two areas, or indeed if he wants to broaden the type to account for similar behavior in France, England, Latin America, China, and elsewhere, he must focus upon what they have in common as the basis for the type. This can only be accomplished by dropping out the type criteria that are localized within a given area, and retaining those criteria common to all the cases dealt with. Thus, it is legitimately possible to speak of the peasant type. But when one wants to be more specific he has to localize the type, which means again including behavioral attributes relevant only to a given area.

In his scientific orientation, the sociologist is driven to search for universal types—those which are applicable across the board in society and culture. In actual practice and as a function of the research process, however, most of his types tend to be localized, for spatial markings are difficult to remove from socio-cultural types. Indeed, for purposes of most research, it is not even desirable to extend the applicability of the type beyond a given area. In the long run, however, our normative orientation toward science and comparative study demands that we universalize as many types as possible.

Generalizing–Individualizing. Constructed types may be conceived of as being primarily either generalizing or individualizing. They are not unrelated. Indeed, numerous generalizing constructs are usually required to support an individualizing concept and, conversely, through modification an individualizing construct can frequently be adapted to more general use.

Max Weber used the individualizing construct as a means of delineating what he called the "historical individual," i.e., the thing to be explained. The impossibility of handling all the data and determining their relevance made it necessary to construct the individual unit for examination. For instance, the construct of "modern capitalism" was woven out of the particularities of an historical epoch, but it was obviously simplified, selective, and limited.[9] It contained what appeared to be the crucial characteristics of the capitalistic form that distinguished it from other economic configurations. To describe this complex historical individual, however, it was necessary for Weber to imply numerous *generalizing* constructs such as rationality and bureaucracy which have a range of applicability far beyond the particular case of modern capitalism. It is only through the use of such explanatory generalizing constructs that the historical individual is made comparable in any respect. The construction of the historical individual has the function of preparing and organizing the mass of concrete data for analysis in terms of general constructs and ultimate predictive statements of relationships.

The way in which an individualizing concept may be adapted to more general use can be illustrated by the construct of caste. The Indian caste system is certainly an individualizing construct representing extraordinarily heterogeneous phenomena. There is only one Indian caste system and even as an historical individual it has to be enormously simplified in order to be comprehended at all. It is possible, however, to extract from this heterogeneous pattern a number of essential elements whose presence justified the attachment of the label, "system." When such elements are extracted it is possible to drop the prefix Indian and talk about caste as a general phenomenon.

These elements can be conceived of as constituting caste as a general construct: (1) rigidly endogamous groups, (2) arrangement of hereditary groups into a superiority-inferiority hierarchy, (3) group relationship to the division of labor in the form of hereditary occupations, and (4) the maintenance of ceremonial barriers. This abstracting process makes it possible to observe a caste relationship in parts of the world other than India. For instance, only a procedure of this sort justifies the use of caste with regard to the Negro-white relationship in the American South. Through adaptation from the historical individual it becomes possible to conceive of a phenomenon that otherwise might be neglected.

In this context a brief commentary on the "case study" seems appropriate. The study of cases is an essential aspect of inquiry and is preliminary to the formulation of types and generalizations. The case study is a way of ordering social data with the view toward preserving the unitary character of whatever is being studied. It merely selects and treats some socially defined object or act as a *whole*. This whole constitutes the case unit, and the case unit may involve any level or base of

---

[9] Weber followed Marx in believing that capitalism (or rational bourgeois capitalism at least, as he described it) as a system of profit-making enterprises based on rational capitalistic organization of formally free labor was an unprecedented system. Capitalism solely in the sense of pursuit of profit by the utilization of opportunities for exchange but without the market organization of free labor, however, was an ancient system. See Max Weber, *The Protestant Ethic and the Spirit of Capitalism,* Talcott Parsons (trans.), London, Allen & Unwin, 1930, pp. 20–24.

abstraction. The case may be a person, an episode in a person's life, a group, a concrete set of relationships, a specific process, or a culture (any aspect of the empirical world reacted to as a unit). The function of the case study is to describe the case in terms of the particularities that are observable. This means the intensive examination of the specific factors implicated in the case.

The wholeness or unitary character ascribed to this concrete case is a constructed wholeness. There are no concrete limits to any object or act. The limits imposed reflect the perspective and theoretical interest of the observer. The limits defining an individual may be dissolved when one is observing from the perspective of the group. In turn, the limits defining the group may be dissolved when one is conceptualizing in terms of social order. All units are thus constructs delineated for pragmatic purposes within the limits of empirical occurrence. Whatever unit has been abstracted out may be examined and described in its uniqueness. This is what the historian and ethnographer do, and the descriptive work that they produce constitutes important data to the social scientist interested in generalizing.

Whatever unit has been abstracted out is temporally and spatially bound. It has a particular historical development and is a unique configuration. This unit may be described as a case by an indefinite number of facts. These facts may be obtained from many diverse sources, depending upon what the case is. They may be obtained from documents, life histories, from the individual, from informants in a group, from participant-observation—from all the avenues open to the historian and ethnographer. The imputation of these facts to the case merely serves to describe; they do not have explanatory value in the comparative sense.

It is here that the social scientist with his procedure of constructive typology can make his special contribution. The sociologist, for instance, may be interested in the repetitive characteristics and uniform relations involved in revolutions. He desires theoretically to predict revolutions by use of the "if and when" proviso. This involves statements of uniformity and regularity with respect to revolutions. Such statements are based upon answering questions with regard to typical elements and sequences occurrent in revolutions in general. The ability of the sociologist to make such statements and answer such questions is based upon his ability to construct types on the basis of intensive examination of specific revolutions as empirical cases.

On the basis of his familiarity with empirical uniformities appearing in a thoroughly described case or several cases pragmatically classified as being similar, the constructive typologist erects a model revolution which in effect is a type. Initially this type will be dated and localized as an historic individual; it closely resembles the empirical case or type. The collection of such dated and localized types is representative of the first step toward generalization. Types of revolution that are relatively free from time and space markings can only be developed by accumulating these dated and localized types and modifying them to make them applicable to more and more empirical cases on a comparative basis. This means that the type becomes increasingly generalized and can consequently explain an increasingly wider range of cases of revolution.

The generalizing construct emerges out of the particularities of history, but applies in many diverse situations. Its quality of abstract generality gives it the capacity to serve as a basis of measurement and comparison of various empirical structures and courses of action. Its hypothetical typicality enables it to function as a tool of analysis in an indefinite plurality of individual cases, and enhances understanding of an indefinite number of concrete situations. It is the generalizing constructs of this sort that are of immediate scientific relevance in the predictive context.

In Sum. In the preceding analysis, emphasis has been placed upon the point that all types are constructed and that there are recognizable dimensions of the basis of construction. It should be made quite clear that no attempt has been made here to create a logical classification of types. The endeavor here is confined to pointing out the features of substantive typing that have been empirically persistent. No assertion is made, nor should it be implied, that the six polar variables listed above exhaust all the elements that might go into a formal classification. The variables dealt with here have been arrived at on the basis of an extensive review of the great bulk of modern sociological literature cast in the typological form. All the variables are found to be analytically applicable to all substantive types; hence, any formal system of classification of the construction of types would have to provide categories that would account for the phenomena dealt with here under our essentially empirical rubrics. In brief, we have constructed a typology of types. The primary object has been to indicate the attribute sphere within which types are developed and the bases on which they vary in terms of their construction. The principal assumption is that the function of a type or typology is dependent upon its structure. The structure of any particular type or typology is made visible by locating it in the attribute sphere of the general process of typification. Our typology of types is presented as a rough cognitive map of that attribute sphere and, therefore, is designed to differentiate between primary modes of type construction.

However crude or limited this particular typology may be demonstrated to be in the future, it is clear that construction in typological procedure varies with respect to at least six different dimensions. Consequently, types can vary greatly in terms of their structure, depending upon where they fall on the series of continua considered here to be the major dimensions. It is suggested that the user of types in social analysis and research could attain a greater understanding and, hence, control of those types by taking cognizance of these dimensions. This understanding and control, in all likelihood, would enable him to use types with greater precision, and would caution him to require of them only the function they can legitimately perform on the basis of their structural attributes.

SELECTED REFERENCES

Becker, Howard, *Through Values to Social Interpretation,* Durham, Duke University Press, 1950.

Bendix, Reinhard, "Max Weber's Interpretation of Conduct and History," *American Journal of Sociology,* vol. 51 (May, 1946), pp. 518–526.

Freeman, Linton, and Robert Winch, "Societal Complexity: An Empirical Test of a Typology of Societies," *American Journal of Sociology,* vol. 62 (March, 1957), pp. 461–466.

Hall, Richard, "The Concept of Bureaucracy: An Empirical Assessment," *American Journal of Sociology,* vol. 69 (July, 1963), pp. 32–40.

Lerner, Daniel, *The Passing of the Traditional Society,* New York, Free Press, 1958.

Loomis, C. P., "The Nature of Rural Social Systems: A Typological Analysis," *Rural Sociology,* vol. 15 (June, 1950), pp. 156–174.

Parsons, Talcott, *The Social System,* New York, Free Press, 1951.

Selznick, Philip, "Institutional Vulnerability in Mass Society," *American Journal of Sociology,* vol. 56 (January, 1951), pp. 320–331.

Stinchcombe, Arthur, "Bureaucratic and Craft Administration of Production: A Comparative Study," *Administrative Science Quarterly,* vol. 4 (September, 1959), pp. 168–187.

Weber, Max, *Theory of Social and Economic Organization.* Translated by A. M. Henderson, and Talcott Parsons and edited by Talcott Parsons, New York, Free Press, 1947.

II

John P. Dean
Robert L. Eichhorn
Lois R. Dean

THE SURVEY

Discussions about the survey method are frequently heated. Some social scientists argue that data gathered by a survey are of little or no value. Others maintain that the survey is just about the only way a social scientist can collect significant and reliable social data. Probably few social scientists would agree on just what the survey is and what it can do. Different conceptions of the method probably account for the vehemence with which it is either attacked or defended. The purpose of this chapter is to discuss both the conditions under which the social survey is an effective tool for the social scientist and the conditions that seriously impair its usefulness. We need to clarify what it can do adequately as well as what it should not be expected to do.

We will be concerned primarily with the use of the questionnaire in *face-to-face interviews* with *individuals drawn from a sample*. Questionnaires can also be administered by mail, telephone, and in supervised groups. Institutions and communities can be sampled as well as individuals. Subjects of an experiment, chosen on a non-random basis, can be asked to respond to questionnaire items. Many of the considerations discussed here would also apply to these other uses of questionnaires.

1. BACKGROUND OF THE CONTEMPORARY SURVEY

Some of the confusion about the survey method results from its being identified with a particular type of survey where limited use was made of it for census taking, market research, public opinion polling, or attitude measurement.

We are indebted to the discussions of the Cornell Faculty Committee on Structured Research Methods for many ideas presented in this chapter. The committee's members were Edward A. Suchman, Edward O. Moe, Gordon F. Streib, John Summerskill, John P. Dean, and Robert L. Eichhorn.

The Early Census Surveys

'These were surveys carried on during the late nineteenth and early twentieth centuries which were mainly designed to collect facts. The surveyors usually had their eye on some immediate social problem in a community, and they gathered facts that dramatized its pressing nature. They frequently turned over the census-type data they collected to public officials, hoping to influence governmental policy. Surveys gathered facts about housing conditions, kinds of employment, health, income and expenditures, the occurrence of crime, and so forth. Follow-up surveys sometimes tried to evaluate changes that had occurred.

The broad scope of these studies led many people to believe that a survey is primarily an instrument for getting an over-view of some social situation. Few of these early surveyors set out to test any explicit hypotheses or to relate their findings to any body of theory. Hypotheses were sometimes suggested in the kinds of data that were gathered or in the interpretation they made of the data, e.g., that poverty was a major cause of crime.

The first surveyors performed several services for present day social science. They stressed the need for going to the field and systematically collecting data rather than depending upon impressionistic or armchair speculations. More important, and frequently forgotten by those who think of the survey as solely a means of collecting attitude data about some issue, the early surveyors concentrated on factual data about the social environment of the respondents: they asked, "What do you eat?" "Are you working?" "How do you spend your wages?" "Do you have a bathtub or toilet in your house?"

These early surveys have had another effect—they led many social scientists to identify the method solely with the collection of facts about social problems. Social theorists sometimes disdain the survey because they equate it with a "social problems" emphasis; on the other hand, social reformers often feel that a survey is just a way of avoiding constructive action by studying the problem instead of doing something about it.

2. USES OF THE SURVEY

Use of the Survey in Market Research

Market researchers have used the survey in still another fashion. The manufacturer has an economic interest in understanding what the buyer's reaction is to his product. In attempting to answer this kind of question, market research people have made several contributions to the development of better survey techniques. They have perfected better instruments for getting at the "why" of respondents' reactions, feelings, and beliefs;

they have developed more standardized and systematic interviewing procedures; they have devised tactics for overcoming apathy and resistance,
thereby assuring more complete returns. Unlike many social scientists, the
market research surveyors have a means for evaluating their findings.
They can often test whether changes in the product or in the merchandiz-
ing techniques based on the findings actually are reflected in consumer
purchases.

Until recently the market research surveyors have had little interest
in theory or in testing general social science hypotheses. They have been
primarily interested in predicting the success or failure of a product in
the marketplace. Therefore, those social scientists who think of the survey
in this sense understandably feel that it is adequate only for studying
superficial problems.

Public Opinion Polling

The pollsters want to know how many people support the Republican candidate in the forthcoming election or favor agricultural price
supports, and how many are opposed. Since they want to generalize from
their sample to all of the voters in the United States or all the farmers in
the Wheat Belt, they need a representative cross-section of these people.
As a result, they have contributed much to field sampling procedures.
They have attacked the problem of how to make a sample most representative with the least cost and effort.

Since the public opinion surveyors are primarily concerned with
people's opinions and attitudes, some social scientists believe that the
survey is appropriate primarily for this purpose. For getting at sociological variables other than attitudes, they lean toward some other method.

Psychological Testing

Side by side with these developments, the psychologists were improving the testing instruments that they use for measuring intelligence, apti-
tudes, manual dexterity, and various kinds of attitudes. They gave more
attention to questions of reliability and validity than the surveyors and
were concerned about the relationship between their conceptual variables
and the question indices that stood for them. The psychometrists devised
new ways for defining variables (scaling, factor analysis, etc.) and stimulated interest in a mathematics for the analysis of data. All of these are
problems that concern today's survey researchers.

Today's Field Survey as a Research Instrument

While the survey can be used profitably for each of these special
types of investigation (census-type fact gathering, market research, opinion polling, and psychological testing), the social scientist who thinks the

survey method must be confined to these objectives underestimates the survey as a tool for social research. By incorporating and improving upon the achievements of these forerunners of the survey in sampling, questionnaire construction, interviewing, reliability and validity checks, and quantitative analysis, the survey emerges today as one of the more effective instruments the social scientist has for discovering and testing meaningful relationships among the variables of social science.

Those characteristics that make the survey an important research instrument also limit it and leave it open to criticism. Perhaps its major advantage is that it gives to social scientists *a quantitative method for establishing relationships and for generalizing about known populations.* The survey is able to do this because of its standardized or uniform data-collection procedures. What is the nature of this standardization? A systematically selected sample of individuals is exposed to a fixed set of questions; then their reactions to those questions are systematically classified so that quantitative comparisons can be made. The survey analyst can then establish whether a larger proportion of the clergy or of the legal profession favors participation in the civil rights marches; whether a higher proportion of respondents who said they had happy childhoods or of those who said they had an unhappy childhood agrees that, "Communists are taking over the country."

This standardization also creates one of the survey method's greatest weaknesses: *it exposes each respondent to identical questions and classifies his responses into a few simple types regardless of the distinctive qualities of each response.* Many things determine how a given respondent answers a given question asked by a given interviewer. Any particular respondent's answer is determined by such things as:

1. What he interprets the purpose of the question to be
2. What particular meanings he attaches to the words in the questions and in the response categories
3. How willing he is to say what he really thinks to an outsider
4. What he thinks he *should* say
5. How he thinks his family and friends might feel about his answers
6. How much he feels the interviewer is interfering with his work or his leisure
7. How much he thinks the questions are an invasion of his private world
8. How much guilt and anxiety he has about the subjects being discussed
9. What kind of mood he is in
10. How much he fears his answers may be revealed to people he knows
11. How much he wants to put himself in the best light to the interviewer
12. How much he lacks or has formulated information on, attitudes about, or feelings toward the subject being discussed
13. How willing he is to have his opinion written down
14. How objectionable he finds it to be pigeonholed by having to choose among a few limited categories.

The survey assumes that there is enough common understanding of the words in the questions and of the problems that are being inquired about for the response categories to apply realistically to a substantial number of respondents, *but not to all of them.* The survey analyst compensates for the limits this assumption imposes in two ways. First, he tries to construct meaningful questions and response categories and to understand the context in which they are answered. Secondly, he analyzes the data quantitatively by comparing groups or categories so that the misclassification of some respondents will not affect the major relationships he aims to establish. Quantitative comparisons are implicit in the logic of the survey method.

The survey used on a single occasion is at best an approximation of the controlled experiment.[1] The classical experimental model calls for a control group and an experimental group. After these groups have been equated on the crucial control variables by some measurement, the experimental group is exposed to the test variable or stimulus. Then both groups are remeasured on the effect variable and if all other possible causes of the effect have been controlled, the difference between the experimental and control group is assumed to be the result of the stimulus.

For example, pairs of Republican party members matched on socioeconomic status, age, education, religion, and birthplace of father are assigned at random—one to the experimental group and one to the control group. Both groups are interviewed in December on their political leanings and show no differences; then during the winter the experimental group is exposed to a barrage of Democratic propaganda. In May both experimental and control groups are reinterviewed on their political leanings. If no other influences can be discerned that might have influenced the experimental group more than the control group, the excess of pro-Democratic sentiment in the experimental group over the control group is assumed to be the effect of the propaganda (Figure 11.1).

Experiments of this sort are not possible for many problems where the survey can be used. Often there are multiple causes that make it impossible to isolate one variable as *the* experimental stimulus. At other times the respondents cannot arbitrarily be assigned to experimental and control groups. For example, suppose you are interested in studying why people vote for a particular Republican or Democratic candidate. There are many factors associated with a person's vote: his economic class, his family background, his current associates, his exposure to party propaganda, and so forth. We cannot arbitrarily take one group of subjects and expose them only to Republican friends, and another group and expose them only to Democratic friends in order to test the relative effects of

[1] We refer here to the survey used in conjunction with an *after-only* design, the one most frequently employed in field studies. Questionnaires can also be used to collect data within *before-after* or panel designs and within the classical experimental framework. The panel design will be considered momentarily, while references at the end of the chapter will lead the reader to discussions of the special problems of even more complex designs.

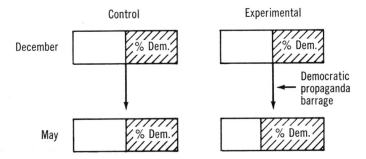

Figure 11.1. Classical experimental model.

friendships on voting behavior. But after we have surveyed a sample of voters, we can divide them into those who have predominately Republican friends and those with predominately Democratic friends. We can also divide them into those who have been exposed to Democratic propaganda and those who have not. Unfortunately *these will not be matched groups* as in the experimental model. In fact, it is highly probable that those exposed to Democratic propaganda will *also* be those who have more Democratic friends, have fathers who are Democratic, and so forth. So the survey tries to study specific effects of these variables by ex post facto analysis.

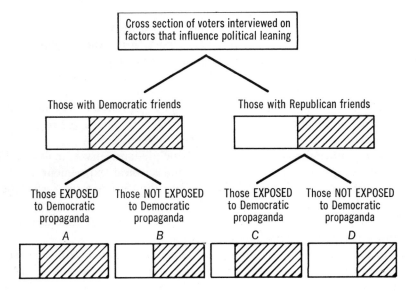

Figure 11.2. Model of survey analysis.

By comparing *A* and *B* (or *C* and *D*) we can see the difference exposure to Democratic propaganda makes while holding constant or controlling the political complexion of the respondents' friendship group. Of course, some of the other factors that are not held constant might account for the relationships established. Furthermore, by comparing *A* and *C* (or *B* and *D*) we can see the effect of friendship patterns on political leanings while controlling exposure to Democratic propaganda. And since it would be difficult to set up an experiment that systematically varied respondents' friendship groups, this is an advantage that even the survey administered on one occasion has over experiments: it can study the more realistic situations which cannot be brought into the laboratory.

The same group of respondents can be interviewed on more than one occasion. This is the "panel study," an approach that is clearly superior to a cross-sectional survey or even a series of cross-sectional surveys for studying change. While repeated surveys of comparable but not identical samples yield estimates of net changes in attitudes or behaviors that might occur, the panel adds to this the number and direction of individual shifts. Those who have remained consistently Democratic, for instance, can be compared to those who have switched (Republican to Democratic or Democratic to Republican) as well as to loyal Republicans with respect to influences brought to bear upon them between the first and second visits of the interviewer. The panel study somewhat frees the survey researcher from his dependence upon the respondents' ability to recall the past. By adding a control group that has been isolated from the influences one wishes to measure in the panel, the classical experimental design is even more closely approximated.

But the panel study has problems of its own. Repeated calls upon the same respondents can be a source of change itself; the respondent becomes sensitive to the interviewer's interests and prepares for his return. Furthermore, case loss is inevitable and one is never certain that this has occurred on a random basis. Thereafter *real* changes in the panel cannot be distinguished from sample bias. The advantages of the panel study must be weighed against its disadvantages by the survey researcher, and a decision made in light of the study's objectives.

Using either the cross-sectional or panel designs, survey analysis falls somewhere between the strict rigor of the classical experiment that is often hard to adapt to natural settings and the unstructured techniques (such as participant observation and interviewing without a questionnaire), that are adaptable to field conditions but do not generally yield quantitative comparisons among variables.

In summary, then, the survey as a research instrument aims to arrive at generalizations by making quantitative comparisons of data gathered by uniform question-answer procedures. Because of its stress on quantitative comparisons, the survey method is clearly inappropriate for studying problems on which quantification can throw little light. The survey is of little use for studying a unique historical event. Since survey data are collected from living individuals, the past must be reconstructed from the living memories of those persons most closely associated with the events. While a cross-section study throws some light on the event, and the panel study even more, the best reconstruction of an actual happening usually has to be made by also checking historical documents and the testimony of the most reliable witnesses.

Similarly, the survey is not generally useful for studying the on-going processes and structure of an institution such as a social club or union. A survey of the rank and file of a union may throw light on how the members perceive and feel about the leaders, but it won't yield information on how the leaders perceive and feel about the rank and file, or how they make their decisions about union policies and practices. Daily observation of the interaction among union leaders would be more productive.

Finally, since the survey method compares group or category differences and admits a margin of error in classifying individuals, it is not usually reliable as a means for understanding a particular individual in the sample. An individual questionnaire does give a kind of overview of how a person verbally reports his attitudes, opinions, and perceptions of other persons' and his own past. But it cannot substitute for the detailed history that analyzes the developing stages of a person's life in terms of the rich interpersonal experiences. The survey is just not suited to the detailed interweaving of qualitative, causal variables in analyzing social process.

The survey method involves a problem of theoretical importance explicitly stated hypotheses, and operational definitions of the major variables in the hypotheses. It operates through the conversion of these variables into a questionnaire for gathering data to estimate or measure the variables; the systematic exposure of a group of individuals to those questions and the systematic classification of their responses; the sorting and counting of different response patterns to establish quantitative relationships among variables and, thus, testing the initial hypotheses or suggesting new ones. The appropriateness of the survey for research purposes is not dependent upon the special uses made of it in the past, but upon the suitability of the method in the light of its underlying assumptions or logic for answering a particular research question. The method should be adopted or rejected on these terms.

3. THE SURVEY AS A PROBLEM IN COMMUNICATION

The crux of a successful survey is the communication process that takes place in the interview. In the question and answer exchange the information the researcher is interested in leaves the field and becomes data of the social scientist. There are two components of this process:

the interviewer's modes of interaction with the respondent as he solicits cooperation and handles the questionnaire during the interview, and the questions and response categories that the social scientist has incorporated in the questionnaire.

Good communication between the respondent and the interviewer depends upon the respondent's accepting the role and behavior of the interviewer as appropriate. One of the hardest problems for interviewers is conveying an understanding of social research. Respondents unfamiliar with social research often cripple communication by ascribing to the interviewers some role or set of motives with which they are familiar. For example, interviewers are sometimes thought to be tax collectors, salesmen, FBI agents, public opinion pollsters, IQ testers, university snoops, or foreign spies.

Good communication also depends on the respondent's feeling that interviewing itself is appropriate. In some cultures, direct questioning by strangers about personal matters could not be done. Even in societies such as our own, where this is acceptable, respondents sometimes feel that "outsiders" have no right to "barge right in and take up a lot of time asking questions." Such an attitude impairs good communication.

Finally, the survey method usually throws the interviewer and the respondent into an immediate face-to-face relationship. Good data, therefore, depend upon the interviewers being able to establish and maintain some level of rapport while meeting the demands imposed by the questionnaire.

The other aspect of the communication process involves the respondent's reaction to the questionnaire. For his responses to questions to be meaningful, he must understand the symbols of communication employed in the construction of the questions; the words must convey what the researcher wants them to. Therefore, in writing questions, the surveyor must not only be familiar with the language and culture of the different types of respondents in his sample, but he must also know something of their language habits, idioms of expression, and subtleties of word meaning. In the United States we can assume a rather wide universe of shared language and experiences to begin with. But if surveys are undertaken in other societies, other cultures, or even among sub-groups of our own society (such as ethnic groups, children, old people, or illiterates), the research worker must see the questions as these groups see them.

The survey method assumes that the respondent has information or experience that bears on the problem being studied. The respondent must also be able to communicate the information asked for or convey his reactions to experiences inquired about. In the survey this must be done verbally and thus requires a certain level of articulation about the research area. Finally, the respondent must be willing to communicate.

In a successful survey both components of the interview must operate smoothly. The communication via question-answer interaction must be as systematic and meaningful as possible. The interviewer must handle the fixed-question stimuli and response categories so as to bring about a uniform and unbiased collection of data. But at the same time, he must handle the interpersonal situation in terms of whatever peculiar social or human demands it poses. How reliable and how valid the data are depends on how skillfully the interviewers handle hundreds of these double-edged communication situations.

If the problems of communication in a given survey situation are insurmountable, then it does not make sense to try to get quantitative data by means of a survey. Many anthropologists feel that where wide differences in culture are present, surveys are useless. Yet successful surveys have been conducted among such groups as the Indians in the mountains in Peru. Many of the limitations of the survey can be offset by proper field procedures that minimize the biases of poor communication and maximize the validity and reliability of the data. The major field procedures that minimize bias are these: (1) careful construction and pre-testing of the questionnaire, (2) proper use of the questionnaire, (3) training interviewers how to contact respondents, (4) selection of appropriate interviewers, and (5) thoughtful and flexible administration of the survey in the field.

4. THE SURVEY PROCEDURE

A. Reducing Bias by Careful Construction and Pretesting of the Questionnaire

A number of potential obstacles to communication between respondent and interviewer may arise out of the survey instrument itself. Serious bias in responses can result. There are at least five such obstacles that survey researchers need to recognize and try to minimize in advance of going into the field with a finished questionnaire. These five, along with corrective precautions survey administrators should take, are listed below. Although the list does not pretend to be complete, it does include the sources of bias that are serious and consistently encountered in survey research.

1. *Irrelevance of the research problem to respondents.* This obstacle to communication is not, of course, exclusively a feature of survey research. It is basic to all social research and becomes particularly acute in the case of research that crosses cultural lines. Relevance or irrelevance of a research problem to respondents has two aspects.

The first involves relevance of the *central* problem of the research to a majority of respondents; the second, relevance of a particular sub-problem to an individual respondent. Obviously, the survey researcher solves the first problem by selecting his sample so that a majority of the population finds the main focus of the research relevant and meaningful. For example, if the research focuses on social and psychological problems of aging, with emphasis on retirement from employment, the sample should include only respondents over 60 years of age. Following the same example for the second problem, an interviewer would be embarrassed to find himself asking an elderly woman who has been a housewife through all her adult life, how she feels about retiring from her job. The point seems simple, but it can present real difficulties in questionnaire construction. The mechanics of the questionnaire should make it possible for an interviewer to skip irrelevant items without interrupting the smooth flow of the question and answer exchange. Very often, the questionnaire that flows most easily and naturally in the interview situation is the questionnaire most intricately constructed.

Sometimes, inapplicable items cannot be eliminated from the questionnaire by the mechanics of its construction. For example, the research may concern the effect of teen-age peer group friendships on adult friendship formation. An interviewer suddenly encounters a respondent who spent his adolescence with missionary parents in Western China. Since he had no opportunities for peer group friendships where he presently resides, the items concerning this problem simply do not apply to this respondent. But since a questionnaire clearly cannot make mechanical provision in advance for such unique respondents, the interviewer can do nothing but note that the items did not apply and explain why.

2. *Irrelevance or insufficiency of questionnaire items to the variable being investigated.* Construction of a survey instrument should begin with unstructured interviewing around the major variables the questionnaire is intended to measure. Before he can frame appropriate survey questions, a researcher has to know how people like those he will eventually sample think and talk about the problems he wants to investigate quantitatively. For example, he may be studying membership activity in a local union. He cannot assume that what represents high activity to him will also represent high activity to his potential respondents. Regularity of attendance at union meetings, for instance, might be an insufficient index of union activity for construction workers whose jobs frequently take them miles away from the town where meetings are held. In other words, if a researcher wants questionnaire items that will measure his variable realistically, he must know what constitutes this particular reality for the kind of people ultimately surveyed.

3. *Ambiguous or inappropriate item wording.* While the researcher is conducting an unstructured interview to determine what kinds of items are most relevant to his variable, he will also get some idea of how the items should be worded. To insure maximum communication a survey

question should mean, as nearly as possible, the same thing to the respondent as it means to the researcher, and be phrased in language that is familiar and natural to both the interviewer and the respondent.

For example, one survey, in an effort to measure respondents' perceptions of their own social class, asked, "Which of the following groups do you think your family belongs in—upper class, middle class, working class, lower class?" It soon became apparent that some people were taking the phrase "belongs in" to mean "deserves to be in" or "actually *should* be in" rather than "*is* in." The question was reworded to read, "If you were asked to put yourself (your family) in one of these four groups, would you say you are in—the upper class, middle class, working class, lower class?"

The same question could have read, "To which of the following social classes would you assign yourself (your family)?" The *meaning* here is more precise (in terms of the variable it is intended to measure), than is either of the other two wordings. But its disadvantages are glaringly apparent. It is pompous and stilted, and impossible to ask conversationally. And it states a concept, "social class," by no means universally familiar.

The best way to correct for ambiguous and inappropriate wording is to try out a number of alternative wordings informally with a few people similar to those who will eventually be interviewed, until the item wording is as nearly perfect as possible for the people and purpose it is meant to serve.

4. *Inadequate categories for responses.* A good questionnaire item must not only ask a question well, it must also provide response categories that permit respondents to answer it in a way that is meaningful to them. If the variables can be measured in terms of more or less, categories can be set up without much effort. Standard forms are "Often—Sometimes—Hardly Ever," "More—Same—Less," "Very (happy)—Fairly (happy)—Not so (happy)." But there are other questions that have no clear dimensionality. Consider, for instance, "Who is living in the household with you at the present time?" For theoretical reasons the researcher may decide that he is only interested in distinguishing those who live alone from those who live with their spouse or children and those who live with other persons. If so, he can arrive at categories in advance and ask the interviewers to check the proper place. If he is not sure of the categories he wants to use, he must phrase the question so that the interviewer lists everyone the respondent is living with. Responses are then classified at the coding or analysis stage. This is cumbersome since there are many combinations of people a respondent might be living with. It saves time if the categories can be worked out in advance by asking open-ended questions in a trial run, then classifying the spontaneous responses.

5. *Inappropriate item sequence; over-lengthiness; insensitivity to the emotional impact on the respondent of an item or series of items.* All of

these are sources of bias that can be minimized by careful pretesting. Some people apparently believe that the pretest is just a brief trial run that follows the construction of a questionnaire assumed to be ready for the field. A good pretest is a careful examination of the communication process that is going on in the interviewing situation. In one survey with only 350 respondents in the sample, there were 5 successive pretests with 20 respondents in each trial. While this almost doubled the cost of the survey, the questionnaire that was finally used was a well-constructed, sensitive instrument providing high order correlations in the analysis stage.

B. Reducing Bias by the Proper Use of the Questionnaire

No matter how good a questionnaire instrument the survey staff constructs, its effectiveness will be impaired by improper use. The major sources for bias in the interviewing situation are (1) that the interviewer will influence the respondent in giving his answer, or (2) that he will misrepresent the respondent's answer in the way he classifies it. These are more serious problems for "stimulus" questions than for "information" questions.

Information questions are designed to establish some fact about the respondent. For instance, the questionnaire might ask for the respondent's occupation. Probe questions may be necessary before the respondent answers the question satisfactorily. For example, a typical interview might proceed as follows:

Interviewer: What is your occupation?
Respondent: I'm in business.
Interviewer: What kind of business are you in?
Respondent: The machine tool business.
Interviewer: What sort of job do you have in the machine tool business?
Respondent: I'm foreman at Anderson Tool and Die Works.

The interviewer may find this adequate to classify the respondent and so move to the next question. It is not necessary that information questions and probes be asked exactly the same way to every respondent. If the study director is sure that the interviewers understand the purpose of the question, they can be shown how to probe for the required information. This probing may vary a little from one situation to the next. To make sure that uniform data are collected, a careful survey will include the specifications for given questions in the body of the questionnaire at the appropriate point. For instance, the instruction beside the occupation question might read, "Get job description in sufficient detail to tell how skilled or unskilled and how much responsibility job entails."

Instructions for handling the mechanics of the questionnaire also should appear in the questionnaire where they apply. Instruction sheets handed to interviewers separate from the questionnaire are often forgotten. Even with instructions built in, the procedure to be followed in the administration of the questionnaire can be quite complex and interviewers need practice in following these instructions. As an example, this section is reproduced from one questionnaire.

> Now, I would like to ask you some
> questions about your family.

23. Who are the people who live on the farm with you?

Name & Relation to Head	Sex	Age

24. (*if wife not mentioned*) Have you ever been married?
    _____ Married and living with wife
    _____ Widowed
    _____ Divorced
    _____ Separated
    _____ Never Married (*skip to question 27*)
25. How many living children do you have?
    _____ None (*skip to question 27*)
    _____ Children (*write number in blank*)
26. How many children do you see as often as once a week?
    _____ None
    _____ Children (*write number in blank*)
27. How many (other) close relatives do you have who live around this neighborhood?
    _____ None (*skip to question 29*)
    _____ Close relatives (*write number in blank*)
28. How often do you get a chance to see them? Would you say,
    _____ Almost every day
    _____ Several times a week
    _____ Less than once a week
29. Now about your friends. About how many really *close* friends do you have around this neighborhood that you sometimes talk over confidential matters with?
    _____ None
    _____ Friends (*write number in blank*)

Indentation and the use of *screening* questions can also guide the interviewer as this series of questions shows.

52. Have you ever had any other serious illness?
——— Yes. What was it? _____

_____

Did it cause any permanent change in your life?
——— Yes. What do you have in mind? _____

——— No.
——— No.

Note that the interviewer is poised to ask the next question, Number 53, if the respondent reports no other serious illnesses.

Before undertaking their regular assignments interviewers should run through a few practice interviews. This serves as a check on their knowledge of the mechanics of the questionnaires, gives them a chance to become familiar with the question wording, and creates an opportunity for them to practice handling the paper and pencil work of the questionnaire at the same time that they are handling the personal relationship with the respondent. Interviewers can be asked first to try out the questionnaire with someone in their own family, then with an acquaintance, and finally with a complete stranger. Interviewers who are having difficulty with interviewing can be given further training or discouraged from continuing. If the interviewing situation is too uncomfortable for them, they will usually decide to drop out of their own accord at this point.

Stimulus questions are designed to "take a reading," i.e., to get the respondent's reaction to a question as little influenced by the interviewer as possible. For instance, the questionnaire might ask:

75. How much unhappiness has there been in your life? Would you say,
——— Almost none
——— Some but not very much
——— A good deal

Stimulus questions present a real hazard of interviewer bias. Despite the best training, interviewers are likely to influence the respondent's answers by the way they ask the questions or by unconsciously revealing their approval or disapproval of the respondent's answer. If the responses to stimulus questions are to avoid being biased, interviewers must adhere to the *exact wording* of the question, use similar inflections, and persistently reoffer the response categories until the respondent makes a choice. Improperly trained interviewers often try to classify the respondent's freely-given answer into one of the categories on the questionnaire rather than insist that the respondent classify himself. An example will help to show how an inexperienced and an experienced interviewer might differ in handling stimulus questions.

Interviewer: Here are some statements that people have different opinions about. I wonder if you would tell me whether you agree or disagree with them. The first one is, "This country would be better off if there weren't so many foreigners coming in." Do you agree or disagree?

Respondent: Well, there certainly are a lot of foreigners coming in. The way the Italians are flocking into this neighborhood is a disgrace. I think it is just terrible. Don't you?

The inexperienced interviewer might nod feebly and check, "Agree." But the experienced interviewer would continue as follows:

Interviewer: Mrs. Jones, we would just like to know how *you* feel about some of these statements: Let me read the first one again. "This country would be better off if there weren't so many foreigners coming in." Now, do you agree or disagree to that?

Respondent: I certainly think that is true.
Interviewer: Then, would you say you agree or disagree?
Respondent: I guess I agree.

So the interviewer checks the category, "Agree," and goes on to the next question. After bringing the respondent back to the "Agree-Disagree" categories a few times, most respondents realize that they are to make a choice. The interviewer's job is to ease them into the swing of making these choices without annoying them or influencing the answers.

In order to avoid the biases the stimulus questions invite, interviewers need to be drilled in the uniform handling of them. To do this, the trainer should impress such things as the following upon them:

1. Ask all the stimulus questions exactly as worded.
2. Don't attempt to explain stimulus questions. Repeat the exact wording of the question slowly and distinctly, emphasizing the key words. Perhaps lead in with: Just let me repeat the question as it's worded here (then repeat); or, Well, generally speaking, what would you say? (repeat question). If the respondent still can't answer, record "don't know" as his answer. One answer to a query on what a question means is, Well, just as it seems to you, followed by How would you answer that?
3. Don't elaborate the wordings. If you ad lib you may distort the question.
4. Try to overcome preliminary "don't knows" and vague replies by reoffering the categories with some lead-in such as Well, on the whole . . . (repeat question); or, Well, in general . . . (repeat question). Do not accept a "don't know" or "can't decide" unless you are convinced that the respondent is not just sparring for time while he thinks it over. If the respondent does not want to commit himself, you can reassure him again that his views are as important as anyone else's, that there are no right or wrong answers, that what he says is confidential or that no names are taken, depending on the source of his hesitancy.
5. Never suggest an answer to a question. The respondent's replies are supposed to reflect his own reactions, uninfluenced during the course of the interview by the interviewer or any other outside source.

6. Don't give your own opinions, even if you are asked for them.

    If the respondent seeks your approval by asking, Don't you agree?, say, Well, I can understand how you feel about that . . . Then go on to the next question.

    If the respondent is bewildered and asks, I don't know, what do you think?, say, Well, that *is* a hard question. But generally speaking, what would you say?

    If the respondent seriously asks your opinion and demands, I've told you how *I* feel about that, now you tell me your opinion., say, As an interviewer, I'm not supposed to give my opinions. We're just the pencil pushers, you see.

7. Try to keep the respondent on the track. Try to avoid irrelevant chatter without abruptly cutting him off.

Some respondents resent being pushed into a choice among fixed categories instead of being allowed to express their opinions freely. Handling this problem successfully is the mark of a good interviewer. He asks a question, offers the categories, accepts the spontaneous response in stride, reoffers the categories, the respondent makes his choice, and he goes to the next question. By skillfully using the little leeway he has, an interviewer can relate himself to the respondent in a genuine and friendly way and at the same time standardize the data-collecting process.

C. *Reducing Bias by Training Interviewers How to Contact Respondents*

No matter how good a questionnaire you have, or how well trained the interviewers are in its proper use, if they are (1) unable to contact the proper respondents, or (2) unable to win their cooperation, major biases will exist in the data as it emerges from the field.

1. Interviewers' success in making initial contacts with respondents depends, of course, on how conscientiously the interviewers carry out the sampling procedures. In designing his sample, the survey researcher can range from the expensive and hard-to-carry-out area probability sample to the inexpensive but liable-to-bias quota sample.[2] Area probability samples are usually drawn by designating a primary sampling unit such as the city block or a segment of several blocks grouped together. A certain number of these are selected randomly, and interviewers are sent to enumerate all the dwelling units in each unit. Every nth house is then selected and the interviewer, when he calls, enumerates all members of the household above a certain age, for instance, 20. Then by a random procedure, one member of the household is chosen; he becomes the respondent.

In quota samples the interviewer is given specifications that the respondents he interviews must fit. For example, part of his assignment

[2] The strengths and weaknesses of various strategies for drawing a sample are discussed in Mildred Parten in *Surveys, Polls and Samples*, cited in the bibliography.

might be to interview four males of the lowest socio-economic level between 20 and 35 years of age. Where and how he locates these respondents is up to him. He may go down to the poorer sections of town and ring doorbells; he may stop persons on the street; or he may find them in the park sunning themselves. The invitations to bias here, of course, are enormous. The more leeway the survey gives the interviewers, the more carefully the interviewers must be trained to seek out a representative range of respondents and not just interview the most available.

Many surveys compromise between these two methods in drawing samples, thus hoping to keep down costs while also avoiding the main dangers of sample bias. For example, the survey could select primary sampling units randomly, assign the number of interviews to be done in each in proportion to the number of dwelling units, then leave it to the interviewer to select the actual respondents within the segment in such a way as to fill certain quota specifications he is given.

In any case, whether the sample is probability or quota, interviewers need careful instructions and recording forms for reporting the actual operations they did. Unless these instructions and forms have been thoughtfully worked out, errors of misunderstanding or sloppy adherence to instructions will be hard to catch and may create major cumulative biases.

2. A great deal can be done to train interviewers to avoid mistakes that result in refusals or break-offs. Most people are cooperative and friendly and welcome the opportunity to express their opinions. If they are approached in the right way, they seldom refuse. Of course, there is also a small number who appear hesitant when first approached by interviewers, and an even smaller number who appear downright uncooperative, hostile, or suspicious. But since the aim of the survey is to interview the hesitant and hostile as well as the cooperative, the interviewers must be trained to avoid mistakes that might lose the cooperative, and to be as resourceful as possible in finding a way of interviewing the hesitant. This training is important: it allays the natural anxieties of new interviewers as to whether they can get their foot in the door; it gives them some idea of the range of field situations they will be up against and thus cuts down the likelihood of panic when actually faced with a difficult situation; it teaches the interviewers a few of the techniques experienced interviewers have worked out; and it shows the genuine appreciation of the survey director for what they are up against.

To keep down refusals, the interviewer trainer should make special effort to impress on the interviewers certain features of the problem of winning cooperation on the doorstep. The trainer's rules of thumb might run as follows:

The interviewer should explain who he is, in a way that is understandable and non-threatening. He might say, for example,

Good morning, Mrs. Jones. I'm Mr. Robinson. I'm with the Cornell University Research Group that's making a study of this community. I wonder if I could talk to you for a few minutes.

The interviewer should make any explanation of the research as brief as possible. He cannot really explain the purpose of the research in the few minutes he has on the respondent's doorstep. The more thorough or elaborate the explanation becomes, the more confusing it will be to the respondent and the less likely he will be to cooperate. People do not like to get involved in things they fail to understand; they are apt to feel they might be taken in. In response to a query on what the study is all about, the interviewer might say simply,

You have been selected as one of our cross-section of people here in town. We'd just like to have your opinions about some things that concern the whole community.

If the respondent does not offer to cooperate immediately, he may be just stalling for time to learn more about what he is getting into before making up his mind. In this case the interviewer must decide *why* he is hesitant. The respondent may fear the interviewer is selling something, that the interview will take too much time, or that it will be too complicated for him to handle. The interviewer should handle the situation in accordance with his diagnosis of the difficulty. He might say,

I'm not selling anything. We'd just like your opinions on a few things.
I'll just take a few minutes of your time. I'm sure you'll find it interesting.
There aren't any right or wrong answers. We just want your opinions.
I really need your help. I'm supposed to get the opinions of all the people they assigned me. I need your answers to complete my assignment.
All your answers will be confidential. They won't be shown to anyone—just punched on a card like this. (Displays punch card)

If the respondent is busy at the moment, the interviewer can suggest that he ask the questions while the respondent continues what he was doing. Many respondents like to have company while they're washing the dishes or darning socks. Successful interviews have been conducted while respondents prepared lunch, ironed the wash, bathed the baby, washed the car, picked strawberries, and hoed the garden. Sometimes the respondent is genuinely busy at something awkward to interrupt, such as playing bridge with friends or leaving for a dental appointment. If the interviewer has caught the respondent at an inopportune time, or at a time when he seems irritated at being interrupted and may refuse, then the interviewer should try to arrange a convenient time to call back. He can offer a tentative time for the return call, such as,

I'd like to come back when you're not busy. How about 3:30 this afternoon? Or would tomorrow morning be better?

The tentative call back should be posed in terms of *when* is the best time to call back, not *whether* the interviewer should return.

Interviewers should be trained not to argue with respondents, but to agree with them, including objections to surveys or the hundreds of interruptions they put up with. Even if respondents break appointments, the interviewer should not appear critical or take the respondent to task. Interviewers should learn that these are commonplaces of interviewing that they must learn to take in stride. If they have been stood up, they should just try for another appointment at the most convenient time.

If the interviewers are carefully trained on these points, given practice at role-playing with each other and the staff in handling the various door-step obstacles, and then given actual practice in the field, they should be able to keep refusals down to a small percentage.

D. Reducing Bias by the Selection of Appropriate Interviewers

Of great importance in minimizing survey bias is the selection of appropriate interviewers. An example will help to make this clear. The staff of the Cornell Studies in Intergroup Relations decided to undertake a race-relations survey in Savannah, Georgia.[3] Knowing the explosiveness of the racial issue in the deep South, the staff had some doubts about whether they could carry on the survey at all. If they could, they were naturally concerned about the biases created by Northerners undertaking a survey in a section of the country and sub-culture with which they were only remotely familiar. If the survey director had brought with him a staff of trained interviewers from the university, the survey would undoubtedly have sustained many biases. The interviewer would have been perceived as an outsider as soon as he opened his mouth on the doorstep. If he convinced the respondent that "Even a Yankee has some legitimate reason for poking his nose into a Savannah family's business," the interview would probably be ended as soon as it became clear that most of the questions were on race-relations. Even if he succeeded in getting the respondent to complete the interview, the respondent would probably not give his spontaneous reactions to the questions, but in many instances would modify his responses to allow for what he would assume to be the interviewer's position on race-relations. And if the interviewer undertook to interview Negroes, the biases would be further enlarged. White Northern interviewers are just not appropriate interviewers for a white and Negro cross-section in the South when the subject is race-relations. No amount of training or experience would have made them so. Inappropriate interviewers are likely to get an excessive number of refusals and break-offs. The impairment of communication will bias the answers of

[3] The results of the various surveys conducted are summarized by Robin M. Williams, Jr. in *Strangers Next Door*, Englewood Cliffs, N.J., Prentice-Hall, 1964.

respondents interviewed. And because the interviewer is likely to experience a growing discomfort at his inadequacy in the situation, the survey may have an excessive number of drop-outs among the interviewers making the completion of the survey a further headache.

What are the characteristics of interviewers that keep interviewer bias to a minimum? They should have an *appropriate role and status* to be interviewing people in different walks of life in the area where they are assigned. It is desirable to assign the more fashionably-dressed interviewers to the better residential areas, interviewers with working class background to the factory sections, and so on. For this reason, an interviewing staff should have different types of persons. In the Savannah survey mentioned above, local Savannah interviewers from several different social classes were recruited and trained. White interviewers were assigned to white respondents, Negro interviewers to Negro respondents. Interviewers should be *naturally personable and friendly* people, free of peculiarities of mannerism, appearance, and personality that would alienate respondents. The survey can scarcely expect to train interviewers in the basic social graces or to modify their personalities during training. Since these are highly important qualities for winning the cooperation of the respondent and in establishing a friendly feeling during the interview, a survey that goes into the field with a peculiar set of interviewers is heading for bias. There is no real substitute for the genuine friendliness of a good interviewer. Interviewers should be *reasonably intelligent,* at least intelligent enough to follow the rather detailed mechanics of the questionnaire, the complexities of the sampling procedure and the administrative details of time sheets, reports, etc. One index of ability to handle this kind of paper work is educational achievement. A high-school education is just about the lowest limit for interviewers on a survey that is going to minimize paper work errors. Interviewers should have *conscientious work habits and the perseverance to carry out a job* under their own steam. Interviewers may at first perceive the chance to participate in a scientific survey, to interview many types of interesting people, and to earn some money in the process as an exciting experience they are eager to take on. But the novelty wears off fast; after a dozen interviews or so, many interviewers begin to see interviewing as the gruelling job it really is. If they are going to complete the survey accurately and without bias, the final interviews will need to be done as conscientiously as the first. To do this, interviewers need a stiff endowment of what we call "stick-to-it-iveness."

How can a surveyor recruit interviewers who meet these rather stiff requirements? Largely by recruiting friendly, interested laymen who would like the experience of working on the study, who are not dependent on the income for their livelihood, but who would like some spare money. Where can such people be found in the community? Our experience has been that it is difficult to choose good interviewers by personally interviewing them for the job; the characteristics of a good interviewer, such as conscientious work habits, ability to handle paper work, even qualities of friendliness and curiosity are extremely hard to judge in a brief face-to-face interview. It is wise to depend on persons who have known the interviewer candidate over a long period of time. If the study director can locate a few strategic persons in a position to know people who would make good interviewers and convey to them in some detail the kind of interviewers sought, there is a good chance that the persons recommended will prove suitable. The superintendent of schools may know some substitute or retired teachers who are qualified. The president of the League of Women Voters or the American Association of University Women may have some leads. An official of the local junior college may know some faculty wives who would be interested. Occasionally clergymen have contacts with persons in their parish who would make good interviewers. By letting persons of judgment and standing in the community pick the survey staff, the director probably will come up with a group more varied in background, yet reliable, than if he tries to hand-pick his own staff. Only this kind of staff can keep bias at a minimum.

E. Reducing Bias by the Thoughtful and Flexible Administration of the Survey in the Field

A number of biases can still arise *after* a polished questionnaire, in the hands of a trained interviewer, is actually being used in the field. Such bias results most commonly from:

1. *Cumulative interviewer errors.* Regardless of the training sessions, some interviewers will ask respondents the wrong questions or record the answers improperly. Sometimes these are the result of the interviewer not understanding the instructions; sometimes they reflect a shortcoming in the questionnaire that was not noticed in the pretest. Unless these errors are caught by the supervisor, the errors become cumulative and render some questions useless for the analysis of the data.

2. *Careless work by interviewers because of low motivation.* It is difficult to sustain the morale of interviewers and to convince them of the necessity of paying attention to the details of questionnaire administration without giving them an over-view of the total project so that they can see where they fit in. A training program might well begin with a description of the history of the research project, its scientific importance and some of the findings that have come out of a previous phase of the study. It is important for the interviewer to feel that the survey directors know what they are doing and that the interviewing they are asked to do can be handled by them. It helps to answer questions about different aspects of the research. In explaining the overall project, the director

might stress at first the theoretical importance of the research problem, then discuss the methods being used to study it. This finally brings the discussion to the point where the interviewers fit in. It is certainly no overstatement if the director winds up by telling the interviewers that everything depends upon how well they do their job; that through them the research data leaves the respondent and is transmitted to the social scientist, and that if the study is to be of any value they must learn to handle successfully the delicate communication process which is the crux of good interviewing.

While the survey is in the field, the director should give continuous attention to the morale of his staff. Extended interviewing is hard work. By listening to the interviewers' experiences, swapping yarns with them, and keeping them informed about the project, the director can do much to keep motivation high. It is good procedure to have the interviewers report into the office every two or three days, and to set aside one period every week when all of the interviewers meet together. This helps dispel the interviewer's feeling that he is the only person in the world who has met so many cranky respondents.

3. *Incomplete interviewer assignments and the "clean up" problem.* A field director usually expects a certain amount of incompleted work. He knows that some interviewers will not want to finish their assignments. This can be a blessing in disguise. Good interviewers like to interview, but some people who initially think they will like the job discover that they can't ask personal questions or meet people easily. Allowing them to drop out can preclude the collection of poor data. The good interviewers usually finish their work more quickly and are ready to take on the interviewing left by the less motivated interviewers.

The clean-up job may take nearly as much time as the main body of the survey because in this phase interviewers must contact the first refusals and the difficult-to-reach respondents. Respondents initially listed as "not-at-home" are best reached by sending the interviewers out at different times of the day and on different days of the week. Also, inquiries can be made of neighbors of the family about the best time to contact the respondent. Notes on this kind of information should be recorded to assist in the clean-up.

4. *Avoidable refusals by respondents.* Preparation for maximum cooperation is an administrative task that begins long before the interviewer knocks on the respondent's door. How much care is given to community relations and publicity, of course, depends in part on the magnitude of the survey and how controversial it is. But because of the danger that mistaken impressions, rumors, or adverse publicity may mobilize opposition or resistance to the survey in one or more strata of the community, it is generally wise to clear the survey with appropriate centers of authority and information. These will generally include the

mayor (unless it is a great metropolis), the police, the Chamber of Commerce, and one or more of the newspapers. An occasional respondent (perhaps mishandled by an interviewer) may object loudly to the survey or to some of the questions he was asked; it helps if he can be told that the police and the Chamber of Commerce know about the survey, have cleared it, and that he is free to call and check for himself. Newspaper publicity is often helpful in spreading the word that interviewers are making the rounds. Copies of a favorable newspaper story can be clipped from the paper and given to each of the interviewers; showing hesitant respondents the story from their own newspaper may help win their cooperation.

Refusals can also be kept down by carefully diagnosing the reasons why each respondent failed to cooperate and reassigning a more appropriate interviewer. A dapperly dressed young man may agree to be interviewed by a pretty girl, but not by the middle-aged man who first contacted him. A certain housewife may be interviewed by a "club woman" but not by a retired school teacher. Such reassignments are important in breaking down the resistance of respondents who initially refused.

Competent survey administration requires thoughtful planning, unflagging patience, and skillful handling of interpersonal relations. The value of a study can be seriously impaired by inadequate attention to the administrative problems.

5. THE ANALYSIS AND INTERPRETATION OF SURVEY DATA

There are many misunderstandings about the nature of survey analysis and interpretations. Many of these revolve around the contention that a table doesn't prove anything; that you can't attribute causation to a correlation shown in a table; that you still have to give an interpretation that goes beyond the data that is not quantitatively established. The survey analyst does not expect his tables to prove anything. He hopes merely to establish as firmly as possible the kinds of relationships that hold among variables that he has hypothesized and the conditions under which they hold. He is especially fortunate if the relationships he establishes run counter to prevailing scientific or common sense explanations. Out of disproof come new hypotheses and new theories.

For the most part the survey analyst does not expect the relationships he establishes to be high order correlations. He accepts multiple causation as a basis tenet: every effect has numerous causes modified by numerous intervening variables. He is more surprised when his correlations are high than when they are moderate or low. The most he hopes for is a more plausible demonstration of the way his key variables hold together.

For one thing, he knows the fallibility of the questionnaire as a measuring instrument and the biases of field survey procedures. Few

analysts are interested in the percentage of people who agree or who disagree with any one item in the questionnaire. These frequency distributions fluctuate with minor changes in question wording or question
sequence. Instead the analyst is interested in the relationship among the
variables his questions index. Let us suppose, for instance, that people
report that they go to church more frequently than we know to be the
case. Some people who never go to church respond that they go occasionally; some who attend occasionally say that they are in church most
Sundays; and some who go to church most Sundays answer that they go
to church every Sunday. As long as the people who say they go to church
every Sunday or most Sundays do, in fact, attend church more often than
those answering that they attended occasionally or not at all, correlations
between church attendance, *measured by this question,* and other variables related to church attendance will hold up. Most survey questions
probably misclassify a few respondents, some misclassify many. Surveys
often come up with a "male housewife" or a prize fighter who belongs
to the Ladies Aid. Because the survey analyst compares groups or categories arrayed along some variable, misclassification of a few individual
cases can be overlooked.

But even so, the survey analyst tries not to rest his case upon the use
of a single item index of a variable. In indexing a variable such as marital
happiness, the survey analyst may have several kinds of questions designed to tap the variable—the respondent may be asked to classify himself; the respondent may have been asked about symptoms assumed to
index marital happiness (e.g., "How often do you have misunderstandings
over the spending of money?" "How often do you disagree about dis-
ciplining children?" and "How many of your good friends are also your
husband's friends?"); or the interviewer may have been asked to give his
judgment of the respondent's marital happiness. Inclusion of all of these
kinds of questions in the questionnaire provides the analyst with several
different ways of estimating the major variables of the research.

Because of the unreliability of individual items the survey analyst
often tries to combine items into scales or scores (discussed in Chapter
8). The selection of items used to index the variables involves the whole
problem of establishing the reliability and validity of the indices, and the
usual tests for establishing reliability and validity apply here. Items can
be selected on the basis of their *manifest content;* objective, informa-
tional items especially can be evaluated on this basis. Items designed to
tap some less objective conceptual variable, however, generally require
evaluation by other methods. Items can be selected by testing to see if
they fit a scale model such as a Guttman scale or a latent attribute scale.
Factor analysis is sometimes used as a screening device prior to scaling.
Items can be evaluated in part by the kinds of meaningful relationships
they reveal when cross-tabulated with other variables. As our table running progresses, we learn how different items work. Finally, some items

we may be able to validate by an "outside check," such as whether or not the respondent voted or whether he was actually observed attending the union meetings he said he attended. The use of judges, expert informants, and one's own knowledge are also proposed as methods for validating the items, but while these are important for *choosing* the items there is some question as to whether they are methods for validating the choices.

There are numerous procedures for the analysis of survey data. The peculiarities of the problems being studied, the statistics to be employed, the equipment available for handling mass data, the personality of the analyst, and the ultimate use of the findings all influence the analysis procedure. Some analysts operate more empirically by running most of the items or indices against other items that might conceivably be related and then attempting to think of *ad hoc* explanations for the relationship they discover. At the other extreme we have analysts who more rigorously state the hypotheses they will test, specify the items that will index the variables, and test primarily those relationships hypothesized. A position between these would be both exploratory and reasonably rigorous by looking for recurring patterns of relationship among variables that are measured and indexed in several different ways. This analysis procedure need not be complex. When the hypotheses have been well formulated, the concepts clearly defined, and the study design thought out in advance, the analysis of the data should flow naturally from the overall design and be relatively straightforward. More complicated procedures, involved statistical manipulation, and abtruse indices are in some ways an admission of failure at earlier stages of research planning. Analysis should become involved only when things go wrong (poor indices are discovered, etc.) or when special problems not previously anticipated demand corrective or secondary analysis.

The survey researcher cannot, of course, provide for all of the eventualities of analysis, but neither should he avoid careful planning in the earlier stages of the survey, feeling that he can compensate for his negligence by complex analysis. Complicated analyses often show more glaring weaknesses than a simple analysis of a survey that was undertaken with a well thought-out design. With good planning and execution, a fairly straightforward analysis procedure, such as the following, should suffice:

The analyst should probably review the major hypotheses underlying the study and decide upon the major effect variables he wants to explain.

The analyst can then choose the indices he will use to estimate the major variables. This usually begins with an analysis of the content of the questionnaire with the major concepts in mind and the construction of scales and scores to represent them.

Having selected the indices of the major variables, the analyst might first sort on the effect variable and count on the background characteristics to see how the effect distributes in the population.

Then the analyst might sort on the effect variable and count on possible causal variables to establish the basic relationships. (Sorting first on the effect variable and then counting on the causal variables is a mechanical convenience permitting one to retain the original sorts while counting on a number of causal variables.)

The major or basic relationships the analyst establishes here become the central focus of the study. The tasks from here on are mainly designed to break down these relationships by showing that they are spurious or modifying them to provide more insight into the conditions under which they hold.

The analyst might next inspect the basic relationships to see if perhaps some of the background characteristics or other variables might be causing a spurious relationship (one that will be wiped out if a test variable is held constant). If this might occur, he introduces the test variables by sorting on both cause and effect and counting on the test variables.

Then the analyst will probably design further runs to clarify, interpret, or modify the basic relationships he has established among the variables. This involves the introduction of interpretive, modifying, and conditional variables. This also requires sorting jointly on both cause and effect variables and then counting on the interpretive variables.

Finally, the analyst runs any special tables he can design that might have further testing relevance for the interpretations that are emerging from the test variable analysis. These tables, if the findings are predicted by the interpretations, are important evidence.

This procedure for analysis adequately handles a limited number of variables at any one time and uses the language of an earlier technology. With high-speed computers replacing the counter-sorter the survey analyst might now consider "multiple correlation" or even "canonical correlation." [4] The first simultaneously relates many causes to a single effect, while the latter relates many causes to many effects. Yet the logic of survey analysis remains unchanged in its essentials: the analyst seeks causes (independent variables) whose relations to effects (dependent variables) persist after background and test variables have been introduced.

In interpreting survey data, the analyst seeks to tie together theoretically the numerous relationships he has found in the data. He hopes in doing this to relate the findings of his study to the findings of other studies and to the general body of theory in the field. No one has yet provided a model of procedural steps for arriving at reliable and valid interpretation. The survey analyst left to his own resources at this point often suggests interpretations that, in going far beyond his data, contradict the limited scientific assumptions of the survey method. At this point the social scientist has risen above the techniques of the survey method into the more abstruse methodologies of the armchair.

---

[4] Sociologists have rejected some of the more sophisticated techniques for establishing relationships among variables because of the failure of their data to meet the assumptions upon which the techniques are based. However, recent innovations help circumvent some of the earlier restrictions. See, for example, Harold L. Wilensky's use of "dummy" variables for analysis in "Mass Society and Mass Culture," *American Sociological Review,* vol. 29 (April, 1964).

6. SUMMARY

The essence of the survey is the uniform collection of data by means of a questionnaire, and the use of these data for establishing quantitative relationships that enable the social scientist to generalize to a known population. Because of the systematic way that the survey collects its data, it runs into many problems of communication—the standard form of the questionnaire is not always suitable for the wide variety of field situations about which the research worker is trying to gather information. The question may mean different things to different respondents; the context in which the question is answered may not be understood; the categories for classifying the respondent's answer are rather gross and overlook the subtleties of meaning the respondent may wish to convey; and so on. Much of the effort of a successful survey researcher goes into maximizing the validity and reliability of the communication between questionnaire and respondent by careful construction of the instrument and careful use of it during the questioning. Survey data can be seriously biased because the survey researcher fails to recruit his interviewers with great care, to train them effectively, and to supervise diligently their operation in the field. But even though the data-gathering process has been skillfully carried out, the survey analyst knows that individual questions occasionally fail to work and individual respondents are occasionally misclassified. But survey analysis can sustain these errors because its data are quantitative, and only classes, groups, or categories of individuals are compared. A modest amount of error at each stage of the investigation will not ordinarily alter the generalizable findings.

SELECTED REFERENCES

Ackoff, R. L., *The Design of Social Research,* Chicago, The University of Chicago Press, 1953.

Back, K. W., and J. M. Stycos, *The Survey Under Unusual Conditions: The Jamaica Human Fertility Investigation,* Ithaca, New York, The Society for Applied Anthropology, Monograph No. 1, 1959.

Backstrom, C. H., and G. D. Hursh, *Survey Research,* Evanston, Illinois, Northwestern University Press, 1963.

Cicourel, A. V., *Method and Measurement in Sociology,* New York, Free Press, 1964, chap. 4.

Coleman, J. S., "Relational Analysis: The Study of Social Organizations with Survey Methods," *Human Organization* (Winter, 1958–1959), pp. 28–36.

Deming, W. G., "On Errors in Surveys," *American Sociological Review* (August, 1944), pp. 359–369.

Edwards, A. L., *Techniques of Attitude Scale Construction,* New York: Appleton-Century-Crofts, 1957.

Festinger, L., and D. Katz, *Research Methods in the Behavioral Sciences,* New York, Holt, Rinehart and Winston, chaps. 1, 5, and 11.

Goode, W. J., and P. K. Hatt, *Methods in Social Research,* New York, McGraw-Hill, 1952, chaps. 11, 12, and 13.

Hyman, H., "Interviewing as a Scientific Procedure," in D. Lerner and H. D. Lasswell, *The Policy Sciences,* Stanford, Stanford University Press, 1951, pp. 203–216.

Hyman, H., *Survey Design and Analysis,* New York, Free Press, 1955.

Hyman, H., with W. J. Cobb, J. J. Feldman, C. W. Hart, and C. H. Stembler, *Interviewing in Social Research,* Chicago, The University of Chicago Press, 1954.

Jahoda, M., M. Deutsch, and S. W. Cook, *Research Methods in Social Relations,* New York, Holt, Rinehart and Winston, 1951, chaps. 6, 12, and 18.

Kendall, P., *Conflict and Mood: Factors Affecting Stability of Response,* New York, Free Press, 1954.

Kendall, P. L., and P. F. Lazarsfeld, "Problems of Survey Analysis," in R. K. Merton and P. F. Lazarsfeld, *Continuities in Social Research,* New York, Free Press, 1950.

Kish, L., *Survey Sampling,* New York, Wiley, 1965.

Lazarsfeld, P. F., "The Controversy Over Detailed Interviews: An Offer for Negotiation," *Public Opinion Quarterly* (Spring, 1944), pp. 38–60.

Maccoby, E., and R. Holt, "How Surveys Are Made," *The Journal of Social Issues* (May, 1946), pp. 45–57.

Maccoby, E. E., and N. Maccoby, "The Interview: A Tool of Social Science," in G. Lindzey, *Handbook of Social Psychology* (Cambridge, Mass., Addison-Wesley, 1954).

McNemar, Q., "Opinion-Attitude Methodology," *Psychological Bulletin* (July, 1946), pp. 289–374.

Miller, D. C., *Handbook of Research Design and Social Measurement,* New York, McKay, 1964, part 3.

Interviewing for NORC, Denver, National Opinion Research Center, 1947.

Parten, M., *Surveys, Polls and Samples,* New York, Harper & Row, 1949.

Payne, S. L., *The Art of Asking Questions,* Princeton, Princeton University Press, 1951.

Riley, M., *Sociological Research,* New York, Harcourt, Brace & World, 1963, units 4, 6, 8, and 9.

Rosenberg, M., and W. Thielens, with P. F. Lazarsfeld, "The Panel Study," in M. Jahoda, *et al., Research Methods in Social Relations,* New York, Holt, Rinehart and Winston, 1951, pp. 587–609.

Selltiz, C., M. Jahoda, M. Deutsch, and S. W. Cook, *Research Methods in Social Relations,* New York, Holt, Rinehart and Winston, 1959, Appendices B and C.

Sheatsley, P. B., "The Art of Interviewing and a Guide to Interviewer Selection and Training," in M. Jahoda, *et al., Research Methods in Social Relations,* New York, Holt, Rinehart and Winston, 1951, pp. 463–492.

Stephan, F. J., and P. J. McCarthy, *Sampling Opinions,* New York, Wiley, 1958.

Stouffer, S. A., "Some Observations on Study Design," *American Journal of Sociology* (January, 1950), pp. 355–361.

Wilensky, H. L., "Mass Society and Mass Culture," *American Sociological Review* (April, 1964), pp. 173–197.

Williams, R. M., *Strangers Next Door: Ethnic Relations in American Communities,* Englewood Cliffs, New Jersey, Prentice-Hall, 1964.

Zeisel, H., *Say It With Figures,* New York, Harper & Row, 1957.

12

John P. Dean
Robert L. Eichhorn
Lois R. Dean

OBSERVATION AND INTERVIEWING

Many sociologists feel that a newspaper reporter is greatly removed from a social scientist. Yet much of the data of social science today are gathered by interviewing and observation techniques that resemble those of a skilled newspaper man covering, for instance, a rent strike or a political convention. It makes little sense for us to belittle these less rigorous methods by claiming them unscientific. We will do better to study them and the techniques they involve so that we can make better use of them in producing valid, scientific information.

As scientists we naturally want to be as rigorous as possible. Whenever a crucial experiment or a survey will provide data of testing relevance for our theories, we will want to use them. But there are many areas of social science where this cannot be done. Sometimes quantitative data are difficult, almost impossible, to obtain; sometimes the relationships we want to examine are not explicit; often the problem is in the exploratory stages of research; or perhaps we want to obtain elaborate qualitative data on an individual case history. For these or other reasons the more structured methods are often not in order. Among the most frequent uses of observation and interviewing are the following: testing of hypotheses where structured methods cannot be employed; reconstruction of an event or series of events; case histories of an individual, an organization, or even a community; and pilot inquiries into new problem areas where the purpose is the production of hypotheses rather than the verification of them.

One hesitates to characterize unstructured field inquiry as a *single*

This chapter will deal primarily with *unstructured* observation and interviewing in a *field setting*. Observation and interviewing need not be unstructured or limited to the field. Both methods, employing highly refined categories for recording events and comments, are used in the laboratory. And unstructured observation and interviewing are used for research purposes in the privacy of the psychiatrist's office.

method. Research workers make use of observation and interviewing, as we have seen, in different ways depending on the specific purposes at hand. The hallmark of the survey method is standardized data gathering. *A major characteristic of observation and interviewing in the field is its non-standardization.* In fact, it aims to make a virtue of non-standardization by frequently redirecting the inquiry on the basis of data coming in from the field to ever more fruitful areas of investigation. Changes in the research direction are made in order to chase down more critical data for the emerging hypotheses. Informants are not treated uniformly but are interviewed about the things they can illuminate most. Each field situation is exploited to yield the most helpful data without unduly worrying about their comparability for statistical purposes. The aim is usually a flexible and skillful guiding of field work to make the most of the individual peculiarities of the situation in which you find yourself.

A second characteristic of observation and interviewing is that it makes effective use of the relationships the researcher establishes with informants in the field for eliciting data. He aims to establish himself as a friend who can be trusted: he often wants to ask questions that touch confidential and personal subjects; he often wants to participate in informal situations where informants are relaxed and spontaneous; he may want to be admitted to conferences or meetings that are off the record. To do these things he must have the confidence of persons around him. For some kinds of inquiries this trusted relationship is more important than for others. Studying an underworld gang would be almost impossible without a confidential relationship; it would be less necessary for studying a community chest campaign.

1. LIMITATIONS AND ADVANTAGES OF UNSTRUCTURED METHODS

The major limitations of observation and interviewing in the field are directly related to the characteristics noted above. *Because of the non-standardized way the data are collected, they are not generally useful for statistical treatment.* This means that quantitative relationships usually cannot be established and the researcher has to depend on a more impressionistic interpretation of the data for arriving at generalizations. In the long run, social science will have to rest on rigorously established generalizations, and methods that yield quantifiable data are probably best suited for establishing them. Field inquiries, using unstructured methods, will often suggest hypotheses to be tested, but seldom provide the data for testing them.[1]

[1] The validity of one's conclusions is a relative thing, and unstructured observation and interviewing are sometimes the only means for data collection suitable for testing hypotheses. Yet, the refinements of the experiment still serve as the model toward which we strive.

Because of the obvious difficulties of generalizing from field notes collected under disparate conditions, observation and interviewing frequently end with masses of undigested data, the meaning of which are not clear. Because of the elaborate detail that can be apprehended by a good field worker, each situation or person is likely to be perceived as unique as indeed they actually are. This very uniqueness inhibits attempts to define variables and to specify relations among them. If a researcher becomes genuinely familiar with a local political party committeeman, for example, he can judge to his own satisfaction from the various activities of the committeeman how motivated, active, and energetic the party worker is in promoting the interests of the organization. He can see the ways that one committeeman differs from another in his activities. He may never actually force himself to formulate what he means by "very active," "fairly active," and "not active." He may find himself reluctant to classify committeemen into types in accordance with certain common patterns that apply to their activities, and to relate these types to race or class origins. This lack of formulation is not an inherent shortcoming of the method, but it is a frequent concomitant. The more structured methods require an operational definition of variables and a statement of relations among them. Unstructured observation and interviewing do not necessarily do this.

A second major limitation flows from the researcher's use of the relationships he establishes in the field, that is, *the likelihood of bias.* Since the direction the investigation takes frequently changes on the basis of the emerging data, there is great danger that the research worker will guide the inquiry in accord with wrong impressions he has gotten from the first informants contacted. Or his own personal characteristics or personality needs may attract him into stronger relationships with certain kinds of informants than with others, and thus prepare the way for his receiving an undue amount of information from persons who are biased toward one point of view. Perhaps, too, the first hunches or hypotheses that emerge attract the field worker to instances that confirm these notions and blind him to data that point the other way. It is difficult for the researcher to tell how representative a picture he is getting. Some biases are almost certain to be present when the field situations the researcher can participate in, or the relationships he can establish, are limited by his role and status. A man may be able to join a precinct captain he wants to know for a drink in a tavern, but not interview the politician's wife at home during the day. A woman researcher might find the circumstances reversed. The great flexibility of unstructured observation and interviewing, besides being a major advantage, is also a clear invitation to bias that must be guarded against.

In compensation, unstructured observation and interviewing have a number of advantages over the survey. The field worker is not as bound by prejudgment: *he can reformulate the problem as he goes along.* The Erie County Voting Study, a panel survey undertaken in 1940, based much of its data gathering upon the hypothesis that the mass media strongly influenced how people made up their minds about candidates.[2] It paid only scant attention to interpersonal influences. When the analysis began to suggest that personal contacts were extremely important, the data for establishing this fact were quite scanty.

Because of his closer contact with the field situation, *the researcher is better able to avoid misleading or meaningless questions.* Respondents in one cross-sectional sample of a middle-sized city were asked if they belonged to the AFL or the CIO. The largest union in town was an independent union formerly affiliated with the AFL. As a consequence, many union members said, "AFL," while many more fell into the "other" category, having rejected both the AFL and the CIO as appropriate to their situation.

The impressions of a field worker are often more reliable for classifying respondents than a rigid index drawing upon one or two questions in a questionnaire. The field worker can classify party members as "more active" or "less active" on the basis of considerable information about them. A survey, using the number of hours spent working for the party on election day, might lump together the tireless worker who hauled voters all day long in his car and the idler who stayed around party headquarters.

Unstructured observation and interviewing usually uses the highest paid talent in direct contact with the data in the field. The survey director is typically several steps removed from the data-gathering process. This remoteness frequently impairs the researcher's understanding of the difficulties of communication that his questions evoke when asked by a semi-skilled interviewer.

Using unstructured methods, *the researcher can ease himself into the field at an appropriate pace* and thereby avoid rebuff by blundering into delicate situations or subject matter. The survey researcher may find to his surprise that some aspects of his questionnaire are explosive in certain localities.

The field worker can constantly modify his categories, making them more suitable for the analysis of the problem he is studying. The survey researcher is often stuck with the categories or variables he originally used in conceiving the problem.

Imputing motives is always hazardous in social science, even though often essential. *The field worker can generally impute motives more validly* by contrasting stated ideals with actual behavior, supplemented by the informant's reactions to "feed-back." Here, the researcher describes

2 P. F. Lazarsfeld *et al., The People's Choice,* New York, Columbia University Press, 1948.

the informant's motives as they appear to him for corroboration or modification.

The field worker can select later informants in such a way as to throw additional light on emerging hypotheses. Suppose several young party workers insist that the older leaders are afraid the younger men will take away their party posts. The researcher can then approach some of the older party leaders who are in close contact with energetic, younger workers to find out what their reactions are. The survey researcher is likely to find such a diversion limited by his sample and questionnaire. This problem of redirection may be solved by *repeated* surveys, if time and budget permit.

The field worker can generally get at depth material more satisfactorily than the survey researcher. He can postpone immediate data gathering to cultivate the relationship and draw out depth material only when the informant is ready for it. In one instance, preparatory to designing a questionnaire on the problems of elderly persons, a field worker using unstructured interviewing found half of his informants moved to tears at some time in the interview. When the questionnaire was used by trained interviewers, weeping was rare.

The field worker absorbs a lot of information that at the time seems irrelevant. *Later, when his perspective on the situation has changed, this information may turn out to be extremely valuable.* The survey researcher limits himself to what he considers important at the offset even though he has some serious misconceptions about the problem.

It is much easier for the field worker to make use of selected informants' skills and insights by giving these informants free rein to describe the situation as they see it. The field worker frequently wants his informants to talk about what they want to talk about; the survey researcher has to get them to talk about what he wants.

The field worker can usually move more easily back and forth from data gathering in the field to analysis at his desk. He has less of an investment to junk, if he started out on the wrong track, than the survey researcher does.

Difficult-to-quantify variables are probably less distorted by unstructured observation and interviewing than by an abortive effort to operationalize them for quantification by a survey. There is no magic in numbers; improperly used they confuse rather than clarify.

The field worker has a big advantage over the survey researcher in delicate situations where covert research is essential, that is, where he wants to make observations while ostensibly just participating. For example, if the researcher wanted to establish the existence of police protection for underworld operations, he might try to place a bet with the bookies in a poolroom while an officer was present: he would have trouble in direct questioning.

Finally, there is the ever-present dollar sign. Because the survey involves expenses such as recruiting and training interviewers, administering and supervising the field work, coding and punching the questionnaires, and running the hundreds of tables for analysis, *surveys are generally more expensive than field observation and interviewing.*

2. THE ADVANTAGES OF INTERVIEWING AND OBSERVATION COMPARED

The relative weight the researcher gives to observation as against interviewing depends upon the problem. Interviewing and observation have their respective advantages and limitations. By and large, interviewing serves best to get at information, impressions, and feelings that can be verbally reported. Of course, we must always beware of *distortion in reporting,* but frequently distortions or selective perceptions are precisely what we want to get at. When distortion occurs, it is usually for one of the following reasons:

The informant unconsciously modifies his attitudes or feelings in reporting them in order to make them more socially acceptable.

The informant unconsciously modifies his report because of some emotional need to shape the situation to fit his conceptions. Awareness of the true facts might cause anxiety the informant unconsciously protects himself against.

The informant reports as accurately as he can, but because he has selectively perceived the situation, the data reported give a biased impression of what occurred.

The informant just forgets the details of what happened or reports what he *supposed* happened. Data below the informant's memory threshold cannot be reported.

A skillful interviewer can often tell when distortion is occurring: perhaps the facts reported support, equally well, an interpretation other than the informant's; perhaps the biases are so clear that the interviewer can spot ways the informant is modifying the report; perhaps the interviewer has data from other sources that reveal to him the nature of the distortion. The fact that an informant's report is distorted does not invalidate it as data. It is still useful in revealing how the situation *looks* to the respondent and facts that may have escaped other observers who perceived the situation differently.

We must remember that an informant, familiar with the problem being studied, may be in a much more advantageous position to analyze and interpret on-going events than the researcher. He is likely to know the local jargon or technical terms that are necessary to understand the events; he may understand the people involved well enough to know the meaning of their reactions; he may be a better observer than the researcher.

Even when observation might be superior, interviewing will have to be substituted where the data are unavailable for observation. Examples include past events, privacy situations where an observer would not be tolerated, and situations where outsiders would so alter behavior as to give a misleading impression.

Interviewing has one major advantage over participant observation. The researcher can ask about events that might not naturally occur during the time he is with those he wishes to observe. Of course, the field worker is often free to do some interviewing along with his observation but, if several other people are present, this may be difficult. And if the researcher wants to reconstruct past events or explore relationships within a group, it may be much more satisfactory to pick off participants one at a time. In privacy he can get the informants' impressions and reactions about a situation, uninfluenced by the presence of others.

Where informants are relatively uninhibited and not inclined to slant their comments to protect themselves or others, interviewing is a quick and efficient means for collecting data. These data need not be trivial or public, but may be laden with emotion exposing the innermost recesses of the informant's existence. Key data are likely to be at the forefront of consciousness of a despondent informant, for instance, and easily within reach of the skillful interviewer.

But there are settings in which interviewing has serious limitations for data collection. Sometimes behavior reveals more than words. For example, behavior is often more revealing than verbalizations about behavior when we are dealing with matters of personal influence, aggression, and interpersonal manipulation. To distinguish between spontaneous behavior and conventional behavior often requires on-the-spot observation. Situations where conventional patterns of behavior are the apparatus for conveying hostile intent are hard to pick up by interviewing. A mother may employ the culturally approved act of keeping her child clean as a thinly veiled punitive device. Watch, for example, the way a rejecting mother scrubs her youngster's face and imposes physical restraints and taboos upon him.

An observer, then, seems to have the advantage over an interviewer in getting at the following:

Expressed affect evoked by interpersonal situations. The observer can make use of tones, gestures, facial expressions, body tensions, and mannerisms that the interviewer cannot reconstruct.

Unexpressed affect. Situations in which unresponsiveness or avoidance are important are best viewed. Observation is often necessary when what *doesn't happen* is critical.

Sociometric relationships that involve proximity, physical arrangements, changes of place or speed, objects manipulated, or impressions of the whole.

Social interaction that involves several people. Interpersonal influence, inappropriate over-reaction or under-reaction, manipulative behavior, ingratiating or defensive behavior are better apprehended by a good observer at the scene of action.

On the negative side, observation is often hampered by the time that it requires. An inordinate amount of observation time may be necessary to be present when the crucial events occur. Sometimes, too, the events to be observed are scheduled at times and in places that eliminate the researcher. And unless the researcher interviews, he must infer what the participants' perceptions and interpretations of the situation are. Most of what transpires in a group depends upon role taking, empathizing, perceptions of others' perceptions, and hidden motives—these may be difficult to infer without interviewing the members of the group. Clearly, in many instances, some combination of observation *and* interviewing is called for.

3. ESTABLISHING FIELD RELATIONS

Because the relationship between the research worker and the persons in the field is the key to effective observation and interviewing, much depends on the initial field contacts. They often determine whether the door to research will be open or shut. Although each field setting has its own peculiar characteristics to be taken into account, a few rough principles guiding entry into the field are worth noting.

1. *Generally field contacts should move from persons in the highest status and authority positions down to the actual participants in the field situation one wants to study.* Where there are two lines of authority (in a plant with both union and management organizations present or in a local political campaign with two contending parties, for example), early contacts with leaders of both groups may be essential to prevent either from identifying the researcher as a partisan. Top leaders are often in the best position to have the vision and perspective to understand what the research is trying to accomplish. Once they have offered cooperation, persons farther down the hierarchy will generally go along with the research if they are properly approached.

2. *The field worker needs to have a plausible explanation of the research, that makes sense to the people whose cooperation he seeks.* While this sounds obvious, it is not an easy thing to provide. If informants get the impression that they are going to be carefully scrutinized in all they do and perhaps compared to others, resistance may develop. Compare the following explanations.

We want to study what makes for good and bad union leadership.	We want to learn how a union carries on its day-to-day work.
We want to learn what the roots of effective political organizations are—how much patronage, hired help, volunteer help, figure in local party campaigns.	We want to understand how a local political party goes about a campaign.
We are interested in racial tension, discrimination, and prejudice and how they are related to each other in a community.	We are interested in the different groups that make up a city like this—the Jewish community, the Negro community, the foreign-extraction groups—how they are organized and participate in the total life of the community.

This principle underlies the better examples above: *the researcher should indicate interest in understanding the legitimate activities of a person or group, rather than evaluating them.* Field workers who do not give careful thought to the explanation of their research in advance, even to the selection of specific phrases they will use, often find themselves turned down.

3. *The field worker should try to represent himself, his sponsors, and his study, as honestly as possible.* Bluffing, pretending naiveté, misrepresenting oneself or one's sponsors, or pretending that the study is more or less important than is the case are all dangerous tactics. Subsequent events or other sources of information may bring to light the real situation and seriously damage field relations. Further research may become impossible.

4. As the first research step *the field worker should have in mind some rather routine fact-gathering that makes sense to those in the field.* This will provide him with an acceptable reason for contacting people where he wants to work. Gathering these facts will give others an opportunity to become accustomed to his presence and will generate contacts for further inquiry. Acceptance of the field worker depends more upon the kind of person he is than the perceived value of his research. Informants want to be reassured that the researcher is a "good guy" and can be trusted with what he uncovers. They are not usually interested in the complete rationale for the study. The researcher should not, of course, appear to be reticent in talking about his study; a willingness to tell people more about the study than they want to know allays fears and suspicions.

The field worker's aim is to participate *naturally* within the group he is studying (he would probably retain his identity as a researcher, although this would not be the case if his mission was covert). He hopes this will give him greater understanding of its members and of their social circumstances. At first the presence of an outsider may seriously inhibit behavior. But as he becomes fully accepted, others will behave quite spontaneously in his presence. Acceptance depends in part on the field worker having an appropriate role in the eyes of the informants. But even though he may appear novel, a pleasant, sincere researcher can become accepted.

5. Acceptance depends upon time spent in the field, a legitimate role in the eyes of the informants, and the expression of a genuine interest in the people being studied. Therefore, *the researcher should sacrifice initial data in order to speed acceptance.* He should not be overly eager to collect crucial data; instead, he should let circumstances carry him along. He should not give the impression that his only reason for being there is to collect data, but that he genuinely enjoys the informants' company and is interested in the activities of the group. He should avoid constant probing with questions—he is better advised to inject his comments or questions when the conversation naturally turns to his area of concern. Once he is accepted, he will have time to ask more direct questions, and while he waits he can win the informants' confidence, identify those having the most insight, and judge which questions will be threatening.

In general, field work progresses from passive observation, to participation in group activities, to interviewing and, finally, to experimental intervention. Trying to move too quickly from one phase to the next can destroy good working relations and delay data collection.

4. FRUITFUL SITUATIONS FOR FIELD WORK

How does the research worker find fruitful situations in which to interview and observe? Entry into some situations, of course, can be arranged by negotiation with key leaders. If the researcher wanted to study a union, he might be able to arrange with its officers to be present at union meetings. He could start by simply watching what went on at meetings. But to make the most of this opportunity, he would try to develop informal contacts outside the meetings. It would be a good idea for him to get to meetings ahead of time and remain afterwards chatting with members still in the union hall.

Observation is especially likely to be productive in informal settings. These may be places the research worker can enter without fanfare such as a tavern or a restaurant "where the boys hang out." But sometimes he will need an invitation in order to be there, i.e., if they meet in a private club house of some sort. In either case it is better for the field worker to get himself taken along than to barge in on his own. If he knows a person who usually stops at an informal meeting place, the field worker may be able to chat with him at a time when he is likely to be on his way there. For instance, if the union members generally go somewhere after the meeting for a glass of beer, the field worker might even suggest to one of the men that they have a glass of beer together. Just how these things can be arranged naturally varies from one situation to another. But in most cases a little careful thought will suggest the most appropriate way for the informal participation to be initiated.

After the field worker is accepted by the group, various research opportunities will present themselves. The researcher may be able to bring up certain subjects himself so that he can get the reactions of different individuals and perhaps get a discussion going. Even touchy subjects can be brought up if properly introduced. The researcher might say, "I've heard it said that . . . (such and such) . . . I've been wondering if there's any truth in it."

Sometimes in field situations the researcher can do some on-the-spot group interviewing. He might say to those assembled something like this, "One thing that I am especially puzzled about that maybe you fellows can clear up for me is this . . . ," and then ask about an important subject.

Occasionally the field worker has opportunities to bring together people who are important to the research in order to study their reactions to each other and to a topic with which he confronts them. One possibility along these lines is the formation of an advisory committee to the research project that will bring in strategically situated people.

Often the field worker can establish personal relations that he can develop socially outside the informal congregating spots. If he gets to know informants well enough to invite them out to lunch or to his home, he will have unusual opportunities to ask about the things he wants to know. And he may find himself invited to the informant's home. It is especially helpful to see an informant in his own social context. Intense affective reactions usually arise from charged interpersonal relations. Often, therefore, motives can be imputed more validly through observation of the informant interacting with those close to him. A person, placed in his family or among his friends, is in a good diagnostic setting: one might almost say it is a type of projective test.

5. FRUITFUL INFORMANTS FOR INTENSIVE INTERVIEWING

The experienced field worker is well aware of the unevenness of interviews in providing new insights, hypotheses, and interpretations. One informant will provide rich and provocative data, while another will yield almost nothing. If the interviewer can find the more fruitful informants, he can save himself much time. Naturally, no rigid rules can be laid down; luck will always play a part.

There are several kinds of informants who are generally more helpful than the person selected by chance. These include:

1. *Informants who are especially sensitive to the area of concern.*

The *outsider,* who sees things from the vantage point of another culture, social class, community, etc.

The *rookie,* who is surprised by what goes on and notes the taken-for-granted things that the acclimated miss. And, as yet, he may have no stake in the system to protect.

The *nouveau statused,* who is in transition from one position to another where the tensions of new experience are vivid.

The naturally *reflective and objective person* in the field. He can sometimes be pointed out by others of his kind.

2. *The more-willing-to-reveal informants.* Because of their background or status, some informants are just more willing to talk than others.

The *naive informant,* who knows not whereof he speaks. He may be either naive as to what the field worker represents or naive about his own group.

The *frustrated person,* who may be a rebel or malcontent, especially the one who is consciously aware of his blocked drives and impulses.

The *"outs,"* who have lost power but are "in-the-know." Some of the "ins" may be eager to reveal negative facts about their colleagues.

The *habitué* or *"old hand,"* or *"fixture,"* who no longer has a stake in the venture or is so secure that he is not jeopardized by exposing what others say or do.

The *needy person,* who fastens onto the interviewer because he craves attention and support. As long as the interviewer satisfied this need, he will talk.

The *subordinate,* who must adapt to superiors. He generally develops insights to cushion the impact of authority, and he may be hostile and willing to "blow his top."

3. *Critical cases.* A case is critical when the variables one is not studying are held constant so that the causal influence of the others are more easily discerned. Thus, critical cases are selected where one or more of the important variables are equated. Youth recently moved from states that have segregated schools to a state that has integrated schools potentially would be good sources for information. But cities that are desegregating their schools would yield critical cases since the home and community environment of the school children would be held constant. Often the best informants for sociological studies are those with similar psychological and social characteristics placed in *different* sociological environments.

Where sample surveys have been made, one can use data already collected to isolate critical cases. Follow-up interviews with these critical cases will yield data of great testing relevance and permit "before-and-after" comparisons that may be especially helpful.

4. *Trained persons in the field.* In many field situations there will be persons with special training in social work, clinical psychology, or psychiatry who, by virtue of their present job, are closely in touch with

those the researcher wishes to study. The researcher can sometimes profit enormously from their experience and familiarity with the field setting.

Selection of the best informants results in an unrepresentative sample, subject to bias. Therefore, the field worker should be cautious in his interpretations of the information he collects and corroborate it with data from systematically selected cases where this is feasible.

6. WHAT CHARACTERIZES GOOD INTERVIEWING AND OBSERVATION?

Actually, little is known about the specific techniques for good interviewing and observation in the field. Each research worker adopts whatever devices seem natural to him, perhaps modifies them under supervision or through experience when gross mistakes have been made, and finally comes up with a set of custom-made techniques that are his own. In every sense, good interviewing and observation remain an art.

The interviewer faces a dilemma. The research value of the interview depends on the amount and quality of the data the interviewer can elicit. Good data usually require intensive and detailed questioning. But intensive and detailed questioning is more feasible after a firm and friendly relationship has been established. In establishing such relationships the interviewer is generally warm and responsive, accepting spontaneous comments and permitting the informant to lead the conversation where he will. Thus, the interviewer must decide how much he should guide the interview to probe for specific data as against giving the informant free rein to cultivate the relationship. A skillful interviewer balances these alternatives by being an *insightful, sympathetic,* and *curious listener.* He tries to be natural and friendly throughout the interview. He frequently indicates by nodding or saying, "of course," or, "I understand," that he *accepts the informant's feelings.* A good interview resembles a conversation between friends more than a cross-examination. A good interviewer frequently seems to be just an interested listener encouraging the informant to talk. But it is not enough to be an attentive listener who nods incessantly. The interviewer must indicate by his responsiveness that he follows the feeling tone expressed by the informant and understands why he feels that way. Comments or questions that indicate that he grasps the significant features of the situation *as they appear to the informant* usually encourage him to amplify and reveal feelings, thoughts, and facts that he might at first hesitate to expose to a relative stranger.

Furthermore, *insightful listening* enables the interviewer to analyze and interpret what is being said—to piece together the little clues that reveal what is meant or *implied* by the informant. Inexperienced interviewers are often taken in by glib and articulate informants, their explanations often represent justifications or rationalizations customarily used to convince others and themselves that they are measuring up to expected standards of performance or morality. This does not mean that the interviewer should cut off or lay bare these pronouncements, even though he suspects them to be false. Where the informant's ego is involved and exposure would threaten or antagonize him, it is usually best to wait out the exposition, allowing the respondent to establish his integrity and recite his accomplishments—then he will feel more inclined to reveal some of his shortcomings, pet peeves, and irritations to a sympathetic listener.

The skillful interviewer is careful not to push the informant but to fall into step with his pace. He tries never to give the informant the feeling that he is pressuring or pumping him. The word "probe" is, perhaps, unfortunate, it gives the impression that a good interviewer is always cutting in deeper with his sharp interviewing techniques. Actually, good interviewing is not analogous to a dissection. Good interviewing is much more akin to feeding pigeons in the town square. First you throw a few grains near the birds to see if they won't move a little closer; gradually you establish confidence until hesitantly and tentatively they sidle up to take from your hand. Any false move or slip on your part and they retreat, and you have to begin anew. The rapport that exists between the interviewer and the informant is very much like this. A sensitive interviewer can feel its approach and recession. Only genuine warmth and reassurance can establish rapport.

Even though the interviewer succeeds in establishing a good relationship with the informant, the interview can still be a waste of time unless it contains data of relevance to the research problem. An interviewer must learn to distinguish between "generalities" and "data." Generalities are loose summary statements that convey a judgment, inferred by the informant on the basis of his selective perception of some situation or event. Data or facts are verifiable statements that require little generalization or inference. Here are a few examples:

Generalities	*Data*
The organization does not admit Negroes.	Mr. Choate, a Negro, applied and was refused.
Committeemen are not as interested in the party as they used to be.	Only 15 or 20 of the committeemen showed up at the political rally we held last fall.
Older workers are easily demoralized in trying to get jobs.	Of 100 older workers that come to the employment service, I would guess that 25 have jobs within a week. Most of the other 75 won't get placed for maybe 3 or 4 months or even longer. After a month most of them stop coming in.

Generalities may be important leads to good data. The generalities of an insightful and well-versed informant may represent excellent inferences from the data, but they are not the data themselves. Generalities are usually built up by piecing together the *circumstantial evidence surrounding discrete events selectively perceived.* It is the job of the interviewer to cut through the informant's perceptions to whatever circumstantial evidence there is that can provide the interviewer with data for making his own inferences and for verifying the validity of the generalities. A perceptive and strategically located informant may provide better inferences than the interviewer can arrive at from any available data. But without data that agree with the inferences, the generalities of neither interviewer nor informant are useful. To avoid this most recurrent of interviewing errors, the interviewer should always keep this in mind, and scrupulously try to differentiate generalities from data.

A brief analysis of a generality may make this clear. It is asserted that "the organization does not admit Negroes." Who or what is meant by "the organization"? Sociologically, the organization is a reification of the roles and operating practices of the people joined in an enterprise. Seen in this light, we want to know what steps must be taken by an individual to be admitted. Who passes on whom under what conditions? Then, what is meant by "does not admit?" Possibly, if a Negro were to try to comply with the admission procedures, he would be refused. But this is really a prediction of future action in the case of an unknown applicant. What is meant by "Negroes?" Does it mean Negroes of all economic classes, educational levels, and backgrounds? Experience has shown that often one Negro will be accepted, while another Negro is rejected.

If an informant replies to a question about discrimination with a generality that "the organization does not admit Negroes," the interviewer should not be content. He should seek out the data. He might say, "Have any Negroes ever applied for admission to the organization?" If he is told that they have applied, he goes on to get details, especially those that reveal who passed on the application and under what conditions, and those that would tell him whether white men with the same social, economic, and psychological characteristics have been admitted.

To enrich the data that bear on his research problem, the interviewer quickly analyzes a generality and phrases conversational questions to reduce them to concrete events. When he can do this spontaneously and effortlessly and at the same time maintain and improve his relationship with the informant, he can be called a skilled interviewer.

7. *GUIDING THE COURSE OF AN INTERVIEW*

To avoid offensive probing for specific data and permissiveness that allows the informant to ramble requires skillful guidance of the course of the conversation. Although rules of thumb are always hazardous, here are a few that some interviewers find worthwhile.

1. *An interviewer generally should open an interview by asking factual, non-threatening questions.* Suppose, for example, an interviewer wants to know whether an organization discriminates against Negroes, and is starting to interview an officer of the organization. His questions might progress as follows:

> I really know very little about your organization, so perhaps we'd better start from scratch. When did your organization first get going?
>
> Stay with the informant until he has traced a rough history of the organization, then inject, I see. About how many members do you have today?
>
> What does one have to do to become a member?
>
> Are people ever turned down? If he answers affirmatively, ask, Why is that? If he denies that they have been turned down or only when they were "not qualified," comment, Then I suppose you have all types of people in your group.
>
> Do you get people of different foreign extractions, like the Polish or Hungarian?
>
> What about Jews?
>
> Any Negroes? If there are no Negroes, ask, Has anyone ever proposed a Negro member?
>
> What happened?
>
> Was there any discussion about the fact that he was Negro?
>
> How did you feel about it? And so the interview progresses.

There is usually background information that an interviewer needs to collect. He is wise to spend the first five or ten minutes on these questions before he moves into more sensitive areas. They offer a chance for him to show genuine interest in things the informant likes to talk about and to put the informant at ease.

2. *The interviewer should locate the major data by unstructured "lead" questions.* The initial factual questions may lead the interviewer to key data he wants to ask about in greater detail, but often areas of interest are not touched upon. In trying to locate the significant data in these areas, it is usually wise to let the informant mention them in response to unstructured lead questions such as these.

> What impressed you about your experiences as a nurse?
>
> How did you feel about the meeting?
>
> What stands out in your mind about the various contacts you have had with Negroes?

After leads of this sort, follow-up questions on concrete examples that come to the informant's mind will provide specific data about experiences that are especially meaningful to him.

Of course, if the informant's concerns are too tangential to the research problem, the lead questions must be sharpened. Compare the following questions to those suggested above.

How did you get along with doctors when you were a nurse?

Did you feel the meeting came out satisfactorily?

What would you say is the first really *significant* contact you ever had with a Negro?

Since the interviewer can always sharpen the focus of his questions to bring into perspective what he wants, he can afford to *ask unstructured questions first.*

3. *The interviewer should make use of occasional guide questions.* A "guide" question is a pre-formulated and pre-worded question. In unstructured interviewing it is often helpful to have a few guide questions in mind before each interview. Well-prepared guide questions serve the following functions:

They provide the interviewer with something important to ask when sudden pauses occur such as when a sub-topic being discussed is exhausted.

They protect the interviewer against awkward or misleading wording which might occur if he suddenly finds himself grasping for appropriate words.

They provide a carefully planned way for introducing a delicate or touchy subject.

If used in several interviews, they provide a standardized stimulus; the different ways various informants respond to the same question is likely to be revealing.

They help to guarantee that an interview will cover all of the important sub-topics.

4. *The interviewer should make an effort to pick up leads.* In his spontaneous rambling, an informant will drop hints or clues that are interesting, but not really illuminating without further exploration. An interviewer is reluctant to keep interrupting once he has the informant talking freely, but if the item seems important, the interviewer should make mental note of it and at the first opportunity return to it. The manner in which this is done is important—he should not appear to be prying but simply interested in clearing up some little point he did not quite grasp. Compare the following:

Bad	*Good*
Why did you say that Mr. Kress was "obstructing" the meeting? (The informant may feel you are accusing him of saying something unkind.)	You say that Mr. Kress was "obstructing the meetings. In what way?
Do you think the Jewish community should fight anti-semitism? (The informant will give his opinion rather than data about the community.)	How do you think the Jewish community feels about fighting anti-semitism?

If the informant starts to wander from a subject you want to pursue, pick up at the point where he started to go astray. But, remember, you are after data.

Bad	*Good*
You said good committeemen are hard to find. Why is that?	You were saying that good committeemen are hard to find. How do you go about finding someone when there is a vacancy?

5. *The interviewer should cut through generalities with well-formulated probes.* Many interviewers use a few standard probes that have been shown to be especially helpful in cutting through generalities. Consider these examples:

Informant: His behavior was ridiculous.
Interviewer: How do you mean—ridiculous?
Informant: Of course, there are pressure groups on the inside.
Interviewer: What sort of "pressure groups?"
Informant: They seem to object to having Negroes around.
Interviewer: How does that come to your attention?
Informant: Politics come up once in awhile.
Interviewer: In what connection?

If these standard probes are thoroughly ingrained, they will spontaneously, almost involuntarily, come to the fore when appropriate.

It is often helpful to have the informant concentrate upon a concrete example that he knows well or to describe the most recent or most significant instance in his experience. The interviewer can usually get the informant onto concrete events by some probe such as these:

I wonder if you could give me an illustration of something like that?

How recently has something like that occurred? Could you tell me about that?

When an informant has set forth a generality, the interviewer should try to find out what caught his attention that made him form this judgment. He should not accept his judgment naively, but instead should look at the situation through the informant's eyes. He should ask the questions that illuminate what the informant selected to see, hear, and notice.

6. *The interviewer should stick with the fruitful areas once they open up.* If good data are pouring forth about some topic of interest, the interviewer should stick with it. It is usually better to forego exploring other facets of the problem in order to enrich the data on the subject under discussion: the interviewer can usually return another day to ask about other things. But if he cuts off the flow of data to ask about something else, he may never again have another chance to get it.

Perhaps the most common fault of inexperienced interviewers is their failure to stay with a topic until the good data are teased out. The novice sometimes feels that once he asks a question about something, and an answer is given, he should move on to the next subject. However, the lead question is just the beginning. Patient questioning may be required before something of consequence is uncovered: much useless verbiage is the by-product. When the interviewer hits upon a topic of concern to the informant, he should amplify the data to get it in fuller perspective. He might inquire about the actions or feelings or views of other persons who were involved in the situation. Of course, there are no formulae to be offered interviewers for reaching crucial data. But it helps to know in advance or to be attentive to the informant's special areas of interest, experience, and competence. Here the data will probably be more useful and the informant's insights of greater value. The interviewer may want to steer the conversation into these areas.

7. *The interviewer should reflect on the meaning of emerging data and ask questions that clarify or amplify their meaning.* Only the interviewer, who clearly understands the object of his research, is in a position to judge the significance of the data that are emerging and frame appropriate questions to illuminate their meaning. Too often interviewers think their job is to get the data flowing, and then passively absorb it. Interviewing requires intelligent analysis of what is being said during the interview. As the story unfolds, the interviewer should think about the implications of the data and stand ready to explore the sidelines that the informant takes for granted. New and important data are often implied by what the informant has already said. For example, a woman who has been ill may explain that the doctor has forbidden her to do any housework until she regains her full strength. This implies that the housework either goes undone or is done by her children and husband or by a paid housekeeper. Any of these could have serious repercussions for family adjustment and might be inquired about.

In interviewing about subjects that require specialized knowledge, the interviewer needs considerable preparation in advance. Otherwise, he will find himself either interrupting the informant to clear up technicalities that are important for understanding what is being said or stringing along without understanding in hope that it will become clearer to him later. Both are unsatisfactory, of course. Perhaps the lesser evil is to plead ignorance at the first sign of getting lost and ask for help in clearing up the details that are confusing. Then it may be possible to follow the rest with only minor difficulty.

8. *The interviewer should be especially alert to follow up in those areas where the informant shows emotional involvement.* Significant data are likely to emerge where the informant feels strongly. It is here that the research problem has the most meaning for him, and his tears or anger are of great help in enabling the research worker to see the problem through the informant's eyes. Because of this the researcher should frequently *inquire after feelings* and then *pursue the feeling tone* if there are signs of affect. He might ask questions such as these:

How do you feel about what happened?
What made you feel that way?

How did you react to that? Did you feel strongly about it?

He should try to re-create the feeling tone of situations long since past. A question like this might serve his purpose. Now that you think back, how did it feel to be refused just because you were a Negro?

With insight and interpretation the interviewer can often bring forth depth material by some question such as, You seem to feel that . . .

He should listen not only to what the informant says, but also to *how* he says it. And he should watch especially for unexpected affects. There is often something significant going on when the emotions shown by the informant are out of line with those that seem appropriate. The emotions may seem unduly extravagant or subdued. Unexpected affect is often indicated by such things as changing one's words, flushing, stammering, tremulous voice, ambivalent reactions, embarrassed silences, protesting, or over-concern with some idea. The skilled interviewer watches for any emotional blocking or noticeable checking of spontaneous responses on the part of the informant. He may be able to detect subtle meanings in associations of words or ideas, inconsistencies, questions to the interviewer, obvious gaps or oversights in reporting, sudden transitions, or the assumptions and practices that are taken for granted by the informant. The interviewer should have the perspicacity to *wait out the pregnant silences.* When in doubt as to what to say or what to ask, many interviewers just *pause.* If he is not sure what to say, the interviewer may say the wrong thing or, by speaking, still some comment the informant was about to make. "Dead air" presents a powerful incentive for the informant to speak and will often elicit data he had not intended to reveal.

The field worker has to break through the traditional taboos operating in any society which prove especially misleading to strangers. Social interaction often takes place on two levels: the socially expected and what really goes on. A guest leaving a party says he had a lovely time even though he was bored stiff. A person who stepped on your toe asks if it hurt, and you reply that it did not as you limp away. A host and hostess bring out the specials and act as if this was the way they lived everyday. One of the greatest skills in interviewing is calling the bluff of the informant, thus letting him know that *you* know that this is a sham. But this must be done in such a way that it does not antagonize the informant and give him the feeling that you doubt his word. When done successfully, the informant seems relieved, making it unnecessary for him to maintain pretenses and be on guard. Thereafter, he can talk more freely.

9. *The interviewer should redirect the interview to more productive areas when useful data are no longer emerging.* Sometimes an interviewer will have exhausted a topic and want to move along to a new area for exploration, but the informant keeps rambling on. He should, of course, *try not to interrupt.* If he watches for an opening, he can usually jump

in with something that will enable him to guide the interview in a different direction. These could be tried, for example.

> That's very interesting. It puts me in mind of one thing I want to be sure to ask you about . . . .
> Yes, I understand how (difficult) it must have been, but what puzzles me is . . . .

If it does become necessary to redirect the interview, the interviewer should take the informant's feelings into account.

> I can see that you feel quite strongly on that and I want to ask you more about it, but while I think of it I want to get your impressions on one thing we haven't talked about yet . . . .

Sometimes the interviewer can effect a transition by relating some aspect of the topic being discussed to one he wants to take up next.

> You just mentioned . . . (how difficult it was to get committeemen interested in politics). What about . . . (the actual work the party does in getting out the vote)?

Note that there is little relation between the two topics. It is not necessary that they be logically related as long as the progression seems natural to the informant.

> If the interviewer must interrupt, he should carry the informant along with him by using something like the shortage of time to explain his somewhat rude behavior.

> Your ideas on that are very interesting. But since I don't want to take too much of your time, would you mind if I asked you about another incident you can help clear up for me?

If there are certain specified areas that must be covered, the interviewer should have a check list of those thoroughly committed to memory. Then he can watch for easy transitions from one to another. But in addition it is helpful to have lead questions prepared for each area in case there is no easy and natural transition, and the interviewer has to use one of the foregoing devices for redirecting the interview.

10. *The interviewer should be alert to touchy subjects and not inadvertently blunder in.* If the informant seems reluctant to talk about a touchy subject that has come up, the interviewer should not move in too fast. Maybe he can skirt the edges of the subject, waiting for the informant to leave an opening. He can certainly watch for opportunities to put a mild question that will permit the informant to reveal what he is holding back. Where he suspects votes are being bought, for instance, he might ask this:

> How do you get out such a large vote in the 4th Ward? Do you make any special efforts? Make any special appeals or anything?

Things held back often seem to gain pressure within the informant. Coming close to the subject that is being avoided, especially if the interviewer indicates that he is familiar with this sort of thing, often melts resistance and calls forth a frank revelation.

Well, it's really like this. And this is off the record. Both parties spend a good deal of money on the Negro vote in the 4th Ward.

A statement that is somewhat inaccurate will often call forth a correction from the informant that opens up a sensitive area.

Interviewer: I suppose you have to use a lot of cars to get out the Negro vote.

Informant: Not any more than in the other ward . . . (The respondent pauses and the interviewer should pause too!) Of course, we usually have to give the committeemen up there something to spend on "helpers."

The words, "I suppose . . . ," are good for beginning these statements: they permit the interviewer to retreat if he has gone too far.

11. *The interviewer should try to turn back informants' direct questions.* The informant sometimes asks the interviewer a direct question, creating an awkward situation for the inexperienced. For the most part, an interviewer should not express opinions that would influence the informant's subsequent comments, yet he cannot be put in the position of refusing to answer a question or seeming to withhold information. Frequently, the best thing to do is *apparently* to answer, but actually evade giving his own opinions. Suppose an informant says, Well, I don't know. What do you think? One could answer this way:

Well, it *is* hard to form an opinion on that, isn't it? Do you ever get the feeling that . . .

This is much better than the following:

We interviewers are not supposed to express our opinions, so I really can't tell you.

Suppose an interviewer who favors legislative reapportionment is questioning an informant who says this:

I'm strongly opposed to reapportionment. It gives the big city bosses too much power. I'll fight every move to get it in. Don't you feel that way about it?

If the interviewer agrees, he may be embarrassed later when his views are made known—it is very poor strategy to misrepresent one's own beliefs. This is especially dangerous if the interviewer is talking to people on both sides of a question; they may compare notes and find that the interviewer was giving each faction the impression that he agreed with it. Perhaps the best response to such a question is something like this:

I think you make some very telling points. What about . . .

Then he can quickly move to the next question. Turning back direct questions is an important interviewing skill.

12. *The interviewer should end the interview before the informant becomes tired.* To maintain friendly relations with the informant so that he can return again, the interviewer should stop well short of the exasperation point. When to stop is a matter for the judgment and sensitivity of the interviewer. In part it depends on objective circumstances (how busy the informant seems to be, arrival of others, and other things to be attended to). In part it depends upon how much the informant is enjoying the interview. In most instances it is risky to extend a regular interview beyond 45 minutes. If one can return, the interviewer should end the interview after this period of time and come back in a few days for, "a few other details."

Of course, if the informant seems eager to go on, interviews can last longer. But the interviewer should remember that, even though the informant seems willing at the time, he may later begrudge the time spent for he may be more exhausted than he realizes or he may be too polite to indicate that he has other things to do.

13. *Whether an interviewer should take notes depends on the situation.* There are some situations where taking notes would impair relations with the informant. If the field worker is observing more than interviewing, it could be inappropriate for him to take out a pad and pencil and start jotting down notes. But it is often quite possible to structure an interview so that note taking does not seem amiss. If the conversation is clearly understood to be an interview or if the field worker is known to be a researcher, then the informant may actually *expect* the interviewer to take notes. And if the interview begins with factual nonthreatening questions, most informants will have little cause for objection. If a friendly and informal atmosphere develops in the course of the interview, the informant will hardly notice that the interviewer is continuing to take notes even though the discussion has moved to more delicate subjects. If the field worker is an observer at a meeting and it is understood by the leaders that he is gathering data, he can usually take notes. Note-taking is most difficult in situations where the field worker wants to be accepted as a participant. But even here, if the field worker waits until some noncontroversial information comes out (such as the name of a person he should see or date or address he needs to remember), he might then pull out his pad and announce, "Say, I'd better make a note of that or I'll forget it." Following this, he might be able to keep the pad handy and gradually increase his note-taking.

Actually, note-taking is more likely to interfere with the interviewer than the informant. He needs all his wits about him to guide the interview, ask penetrating questions that will draw out significant data, and maintain a friendly relationship with the informant. Note-taking distracts his attention and frequently results in a less productive interview. In most field work, note-taking should probably be limited to those situations where it is absolutely essential to get accurate factual information about something. The field worker's feelings, hunches, and perceptions can be put down after the interview. Since they represent an analysis of the interview data, they will probably be based upon material from different parts of the interview anyway.

8. RECORDING THE DATA

While in the field, the interviewer or observer must somehow manage to organize the mass of data that comes to his attention. While guiding the inquiry so as to elicit good data, he must sift and sort the raw data to separate the valuable from the inconsequential. He must note the key facts before they escape his memory, record leads for further investigation, reflect upon the data and derive refined hypotheses to guide further inquiry, and seek additional evidence in the field for testing these hypotheses.

Recording is the first step in the actual analysis of field data. The information collected might best be organized according to the way it will be used. The major purposes for recording field data include (1) training and monitoring field workers; (2) orienting other researchers to a particular field setting; (3) refreshing the researcher's memory; and (4) providing data, collected to fall into predetermined categories, for testing hypotheses.

1. *Training and monitoring field workers.* Recording is a good medium for informing a supervisor of what took place in the field. The supervisor can then constructively evaluate the interviewing or observation, point out places where different tactics might have been successful, and detect voids in the data. This purpose is served best by a detailed transcription of the interview. Where possible, key words or phrases can be jotted down during the interview and amplified *immediately* afterwards before the significant details are lost. Editing penciled interview notes in ink helps to preserve the notes later. When these amplified notes are typed, opening and parting statements should be added as nearly as they can be recalled. Descriptive phrases that give the tone or affect of the interview, or the scene viewed can also be inserted. Articles and other less essential words, omitted from the field notes, can be put in the final report. The main objection to such complete recording of field experiences is the enormous investment of time that it entails. Detailed recording probably consumes two or three times as much time as was actually spent in the field. This means that time in the field must be considerably reduced to allow for it. Any researcher would prefer to

have a full record to a scanty one. But a choice must often be made between 10 interviews per week recorded in great detail and 25 interviews with only the most pertinent data and interpretation set down. Depending upon the research problem, one is superior to the other.

2. *Orienting other researchers to a particular field setting.* A second purpose for recording is to inform one's fellow field workers about some person or event. These field reports suggest hunches and hypotheses to others and indicate new lines of investigation in their work. The reports contain the informant's perceptions. From the perceptions of many informants the researchers try to piece together the significant variables operating in the field situation.

Recording of this sort is generally most useful if it includes not only the opinions of the informant but also the impressions of the field worker, his evaluation of the informant's opinions, and any hypotheses the data suggest to him. It even includes diagnoses that rest on details fleetingly remembered or fuzzy in detail. Detailed reporting of the facts should enable the reader to diagnose for himself. But since the facts selected for reporting grew out of the field worker's understanding of what was happening, his impression is often more trustworthy than that of a reader with only partial data before him. If the field worker is attuned to the feelings of his informant, listens for what is *not* said, picks up the gestures, and notes how things are said or done, he may absorb from these a more valid impression that can be set down as a revealing word-picture. This challenging task combines psychiatric insight, scientific selectivity, and poetic succinctness.

The researcher should reflect on the field situation *before, during,* and *after* the interview or observation. He should also think about the data *at the time* he records it. He should anticipate the data that will be important prior to entry into the field, draw it out of his informants, ponder its meaning, and set down that worth saving. In field work, *a few relevant details are worth notebooks filled with run-of-the-mill data.* In some ways field inquiry resembles detective work. Several clues that do not fit will pique the researcher's curiosity and stimulate further reflection upon the meaning of the data, perhaps suggesting an hypothesis that ties together the loose ends. Or the researchers may be impelled to search for additional data that will eventually yield a new interpretation. Good field notes prompt further thought about what has been heard and seen.

3. *Refreshing the researcher's memory.* A third purpose of field recording is to provide refresher notes. Relevant information gathered from the field situations can often be noted in brief form. Each bit of information should be identified to indicate who said it and on what occasion. Time and place may also be important. Then the gist of an interview or observation can be reduced to a series of brief statements in this manner:

Leonard Green (Southside precinct committeeman, interviewed in his office by
    Weber) 9/21/66
The liquor dealers contribute to the campaign funds of both parties;
The supervisor in the 13th District feels he has to have at least three cars on
    hand election day to haul voters to the polls;
Some of the older Italian voters are the only ones who still expect to be paid for
    voting. Couldn't tell how prevalent this is.

The pertinent points gleaned from a large number of interviews can be
reviewed quickly when stored in this form.

4. *Providing data for testing hypotheses.* Unstructured observation
and interviewing are preferred methods for exploratory studies. Before
the researcher has formulated hypotheses there is little he can do other
than enter the field to look and to listen. But, in time, ideas begin to
crystallize, hypotheses take shape, and concepts seem clearly delineated.
Then the researcher is in a position to collect only those data of testing
relevance. He may do this among the informants he already knows, or
he may move into a new setting, prepared to be very selective in the data
he seeks.

With specific categories for data storage in mind, the field worker's
observations and interviews can more easily be quantified. For instance,
he might hypothesize that the academically deficient students sit at the
back of the classroom. To test this hypothesis he would note where the
members of the class sit, and then by a brief interview or from school
records he would discover the grades for each student. His methods
combine elements of the questionnaire, structured observation in the
laboratory, and content analysis. His questions are carefully selected and
perhaps worded ahead of time. He expects the answers to fall into predetermined categories or lend themselves to systematic analysis at a later
time. Yet, he still enjoys greater freedom than those who use the other
methods in the way he adapts himself to the field setting and to the
uniqueness of each informant.

If the field worker is prepared in advance with clearly stated hypotheses, well-defined concepts, and the data of testing relevance identified, he can be discriminating in what he records. Accounts of attendance
at meetings, seating arrangement, frequency of complaints about the
leadership, and other data that lend themselves to enumeration will
figure more prominently. Data may be recorded on maps, graphs, and
charts with less dependence upon lengthy descriptions of events and
conversations so characteristic of exploratory work.

Sometimes taped interviews or detailed field notes are subjected to
content analysis. Here the hypotheses were not clearly stated prior to
entry into the field and important data could not be distinguished from
the trivial. However, enough good data were recorded that categories
corresponding to the concepts in the emerging hypotheses can be spec-

ified and counts made to test the hypotheses ex post facto. This can be done crudely or with some degree of sophistication. Clearly, however, where the stage of research and the field situation permit, hypotheses should be stated before the data are collected.

By now, it is obvious that sound knowledge about the techniques for field interviewing and observation is quite limited. Yet many disciplines other than sociology depend upon these methods for gathering information: the social case worker, the doctor, the lawyer, the administrator, the criminal investigator, the journalist, just to mention a few. Research in future years can put these methods of inquiry on firmer footing. But until this happens, the field worker remains an artist and his conclusions are somewhat suspect.

9. ANALYZING INTERVIEWS AND OBSERVERS' REPORTS

The analysis of field interviews and observations cannot easily be separated from the data collection phase itself, since it occurs while the researcher is with the informant, after he has left him and in preparation for his next encounter. The freedom to evaluate data as it is being collected and to alter the course of the inquiry in light of new insights is the distinct advantage field interviewing and observation enjoys over the survey or the laboratory experiment. However, at some point the researcher must reflect upon his data, subjecting it to more or less rigorous analysis if he is to reach conclusions. This is so if his object is to formulate hypotheses or to test them.

The analysis of field notes may be casual (though thoughtful), or quite systematic, depending upon the purpose of the inquiry and the quality of data available. The participant observer, guarding his identity while attempting to formulate hypotheses, represents one extreme. While convincing his informants that he is one of them, he must make observations, ask questions, and reach conclusions. Note-taking will be done in his room at night. He returns to the field each day with new hunches to check, and in the end he is prepared to set forth plausible hypotheses for testing. In his case, reflection upon what he saw and heard constituted analysis of the data.

Next in order of rigor would come the anthropologist, for instance, who is recognized as an outsider. He is permitted to ask questions, attend ceremonies, and take notes. Very often he has formulated hypotheses before he enters the field or at least categories of information he wishes to collect and some notion about the ways societies function. Typically, he returns from the field with boxes of 5 × 8 cards, each preserving a piece of datum.

Finally, there is the field worker, who has reached the stage in his research where he enters the field with specific hypotheses to be tested and the data of testing relevance identified. He may return with tapes of interviews, minutes of meetings, or interaction counts taken in a coffee shop. But he knows where the data will fit and what he must do to analyze them.

In each of the preceding instances, some forms of content analysis are used to impose order upon the mass of data that field interviewing and observation produce. Content analysis involves the editing of field notes, developing categories for the classification of data, deciding upon the units to be tallied, counting and cross-tabulation, or in some other fashion establishing relations among variables.

Field notes are seldom in a form prepared for analysis. At least key points must be underlined or comments about a single individual or event, scattered through several interviews, must be starred or set-off in some way. One might want to consolidate all of the materials about a subject on a single card or sheet of paper. A system of cross-referencing would be the next step. Editing would reveal the inadequacies of the data, informants one failed to contact, or questions one forgot to ask. Unstructured interviewing and observation characteristically have sampling problems of both sorts.

Simultaneously, the researcher must consider the categories that are meaningful for grouping his data. If the belief in witches is important for testing some hypothesis an anthropologist entertains, all references to their presence, characteristics, potential powers, and recent behavior could be pulled out of the interviews and entered on cross-referenced cards. The categories for classifying data should be *unidimensional*, *mutually exclusive*, and *exhaustive* of the possibilities in a given field setting. Otherwise, unreliability will result from misclassification. Of course, the same data can be classified in more than one way. The anthropologist might be interested in what was said and the intensity with which it was said. A single comment would be entered in two categories, one for content and one for depth of feeling.

Sometimes an informant will devote a three or four hour interview to a single topic while another will mention it only in passing. Furthermore, the second informant's position in the community may be of greater consequence and, therefore, his brief remark could outweigh the lengthy discourse. The analyst must, therefore, decide upon the "units" that he will count. Will he enter a tally when a word is mentioned? A phrase? An idea? Or will he assess the entire interview? Finally, will he accord each informant's remarks equal weight? Ambiguity in either the definition of categories or units leads to unreliability in coding.

With the field notes prepared, the categories established, and units defined, the analyst begins to count. This may be done with more or less precision. The anthropologist might think to himself, "These people are preoccupied with witches," a rough estimation of frequency. While a field worker, who has systematically asked every informant how many times he had attended church in the last year, could quantify his data with greater precision.

With the dimensions measured, the analyst is ready to relate variables to each other. This may take the form of quantitative analysis, using punch cards, computers, and advanced statistics. Simpler tasks can be handled with McBee Keysort cards or, with patience, 5×8 cards on which the data are recorded. Such refined analysis defeats the purpose of unstructured interviewing and observation for studying some problems. If the object is to understand in depth the psychological world of an individual or the significance of rites of passage within the framework of the total society, this fragmenting approach would not suffice. Then. the analyst must still sort through his data, weigh its significance, fit the parts into the whole, and come to some conclusions. He works in the quiet of his study rather than in front of a computer.

Where theoretical development, methodological refinement, and the exigencies of the field of setting permit—explicitly stated hypotheses, carefully measured variables, and systematic analysis of the data are to be preferred.

10. SUMMARY

The essence of field observation and interviewing is the freedom it permits the researcher. He constantly aims to direct the data-gathering into more productive areas of inquiry. He does this largely by establishing sound relations with his informants and encouraging them to lead him by their greater involvement and familiarity with the field situation to the most significant data. He is especially interested in the perspective of his informants and often uses their views to reconstruct his own version of past events, organizational structures, informal leadership processes and other phenomena for which the approach is so well adapted. To do this he cuts through generalities and leads the informants to reveal the data that resulted in the particular views they hold. Guiding the interview to the significant data is the skill that distinguishes the good field worker from the poor. But unfortunately little is known about these skills, and they undoubtedly vary from situation to situation depending upon the nature of the informants and the problem investigated. But we know that the researcher should be a thoughtful and analytic listener or observer, who appraises the meaning of emerging data for his problem and uses the resulting insights to phrase questions that will further develop the implications of those data. This is an art.

SELECTED REFERENCES

Argyris, C., "Diagnosing Defense Against Outsiders," *Journal of Social Issues*, vol. 8 (1952), pp. 24–34.

Bain, R. K., "The Researchers Role," *Human Organization* (Spring, 1950), pp. 23–28.

Bales, R. F., *Interaction Process Analysis*, Cambridge, Mass., Addison-Wesley Press, 1950.

Becker, H. S., "Problems of Inference and Proof in Participant Observation," *American Sociological Review* (December, 1958), pp. 652–660.

Becker, H. S., and B. Geer, "Participant Observation and Interviewing: A Comparison," *Human Organization* (Fall, 1957), pp. 28–32.

Becker, H. S., and B. Geer, " 'Participant Observation and Interviewing': A Rejoinder," *Human Organization* (Summer, 1958), pp. 39–40.

Bennett, J. W., "The Study of Cultures: A Survey of Technique and Methodology in Field Work," *American Sociological Review* (December, 1948), pp. 672–689.

Berelson, B., *Content Analysis in Communication Research*, New York, Free Press, 1952.

Birdwhistell, R. L., "Body Motion Research and Interviewing," *Human Organization* (Spring, 1952), pp. 37–38.

Cicourel, A. V., *Method and Measurement in Sociology*, New York, Free Press, 1964, chap. 3.

Dollard, J., *Caste and Class in a Southern Town*, Garden City, N.Y., Doubleday, 1957, chaps. 1 and 2.

Festinger, L., and D. Katz, *Research Methods in the Behavioral Sciences*, New York, Holt, Rinehart and Winston, 1953, chaps. 2 and 3.

Festinger, L., H. W. Riecken, and S. Schacter, *When Prophecy Fails*, Minneapolis, University of Minnesota Press, 1956.

Garrett, Annette, *Interviewing: Its Principles and Methods*, New York, Family Welfare Association of America, 1942.

Gold, R. L., "Roles in Sociological Field Observations," *Social Forces* (March, 1958), pp. 217–223.

Goode, W. J., and P. K. Hatt, *Methods in Social Research*, New York, McGraw-Hill, 1952, chaps. 10 and 13.

Hyman, *et al.*, *Interviewing in Social Research*, Chicago, University of Chicago Press, 1954.

Jahoda, M., M. Deutsch, and S. W. Cook, *Research Methods in Social Relations*, New York, Holt, Rinehart and Winston, 1951, chaps. 5 and 6.

Junker, B. H., *Field Work: An Introduction to the Social Sciences*, Chicago, The University of Chicago Press, 1960.

Kahn, R. L., and C. F. Cannell, *The Dynamics of Interviewing*, New York, Wiley, 1962.

Kluckhohn, Florence, "The Participant Observer Technique in Small Communities," *American Journal of Sociology* (November, 1940), pp. 331–343.

Lazarsfeld, P. F., *et al.*, *The People's Choice*, New York, Columbia University Press, 1948.

Leighton, A. H., *The Governing of Men,* Princeton, Princeton University Press, 1946, pp. 373–394.

Madge, J., *The Tools of Social Science,* Garden City, N.Y., Doubleday, 1965, pp. 120–194.

Malinowski, B., *Argonauts of the Western Pacific,* New York, Dutton, 1932, pp. 2–25.

Merton, R. K., M. Fiske, and P. Kendall, *The Focused Interview: A Manual,* New York, Bureau of Applied Social Research, Columbia University, 1952.

Merton, R. K., and P. L. Kendall, "The Focused Interview," *American Journal of Sociology* (May, 1946), pp. 541–557.

Murdock, G. P., *et al., Outline of Cultural Materials,* New Haven, Human Relations Area Files, Inc., 1950.

Richardson, F. L. W., "Internal Mapping," *Human Organization* (Summer, 1950), pp. 31–32.

Riecken, H. W., "The Unidentified Interviewer," *American Journal of Sociology* (September, 1956), pp. 210–212.

Riesman, D., and M. Benney (eds.), "The Interview in Social Research," special issue of the *American Journal of Sociology* (September, 1956), pp. 137–217.

Rogers, C. R., "The Non-Directive Method as a Technique in Social Research," *American Journal of Sociology* (January, 1945), pp. 279–283.

Selltiz, C., M. Jahoda, M. Deutsch, and S. W. Cook, *Research Methods in Social Relations,* New York, Holt, Rinehart and Winston, 1959, chap. 6.

Strauss, G., "Direct Observation as a Source of Quasi-Sociometric Information," *Sociometry* (February–May, 1952), pp. 141–145.

Trow, M. A., "Comment on 'Participant Observation and Interviewing: A Comparison,'" *Human Organization* (Fall, 1957), pp. 33–35.

Whyte, W. F., "Observational Field-Work Methods," in M. Jahoda, *et al., Research Methods in Social Relations,* New York, Holt, Rinehart and Winston, 1951, pp. 493–513.

Whyte, W. F., *Street Corner Society: The Social Structure of an Italian Slum,* Chicago, The University of Chicago Press, 1955, Preface and Appendix.

Young, P. V., *Scientific Social Surveys and Research,* Englewood Cliffs, N.J., Prentice-Hall, 1956, chaps. 7 and 9.

Zander, A., "Systematic Observation of Small Face-to-Face Groups," in M. Jahoda *et al., Research Methods in Social Relations,* New York, Holt, Rinehart and Winston, 1951.

Zelditch, M., "Some Methodological Problems of Field Studies," *American Journal of Sociology* (March, 1962), pp. 566–576.

Part three

RESEARCH
ADMINISTRATION

13
Edward A. Suchman

THE PRINCIPLES OF RESEARCH
DESIGN AND ADMINISTRATION

1. INTRODUCTION

The design and execution of a research study is basically a problem in the *practical application* of the fundamental rules of scientific method to some specific research problem. However, the conduct of research involves far more, in actual practice, than an adherence to the general rules of scientific method. While it is essential to understand basic principles, the actual conduct of a research study raises specific problems which require specific answers. This chapter presents some of these problems, together with examples of how they were met in a realistic research situation.

Before presenting concrete materials, it might help to illustrate the problem by an analogy to a game or sport. The rules of a game, for example baseball or chess, are well known and clearly stated. It is expected that one will obey these rules. However, it is not the obedience of the rules alone, but how the game is played *within* the rules that determines whether one is a skilled professional or an unskilled amateur. To play a *good* game one must have not only a sound knowledge of the rules of the game, but also skill based on practice and aptitude, resourcefulness in capitalizing on opportunities, and ingenuity in inventing better ways of performing.

To a large extent, scientific research may be viewed as a problem-solving process. The design and administration of such research involves the making of decisions by the research worker at every step of the process. These decisions represent a working compromise between the rigorous demands of the scientific method and the realistic conditions of available resources and the exigencies of the research situation. Such compromises are usually evaluated as acceptable and appropriate in terms of the prevailing norms of the scientific community. In this sense, research is a social enterprise in which constraints are imposed not only by the requirements of the scientific method, but also by the normative structure of science.[1]

The Definition of Research Design

The challenge of research design is to translate the general scientific model into a practical research operation. As used in this chapter, *research design will refer to the entire process of planning and carrying out a research study.*[2] This is a crucial point—problems of design are not limited to any specific type of method or to any single stage of a study. To be sure, different methods lend themselves more readily to different kinds of research situations. It will not be possible in a chapter of this general nature, however, to cover systematically each of the major methods. Rather an attempt will be made to deal with these different methods and techniques by drawing on examples from a broad research project on intergroup relations which made use of many different methods and techniques.[3]

Problems of research planning will be shown to arise at each of the following stages in the execution of a research project: (1) the design of hypotheses; (2) the design of sample; (3) the design of instruments; (4) the design of administration; and (5) the design of analysis. The plan of this chapter is to take each of these steps in a research project and to examine them in terms of the problems of design that they create. Section 2 will

[1] A forthcoming book by Gideon Sjoberg and Roger Nett proposes an approach to social research methods as norms of behavior involving a socialization process of the scientist into the normative order of science.

[2] As described by Miller, "Designed research refers to the planned sequence of the entire process involved in conducting a research study." Using Ackoff as a guide, Miller lists the following ten essential steps: (1) Selection and definition of a sociological problem; (2) Description of the relationship of the problem to a theoretical framework; (3) Formulation of working hypotheses; (4) Design of the experiment of inquiry; (5) Sampling procedures; (6) Establishment of methods of gathering data; (7) Preparation of a working guide; (8) Analysis of results; (9) Interpretation of results; and (10) Publication or reporting of results. Delbert C. Miller, *Handbook of Research Design and Social Measurement*, New York, David McKay Co., 1964, p. vii. See also Russell L. Ackoff, *The Design of Social Research*, Chicago, University of Chicago Press, 1953.

[3] It might be worthwhile to look for a moment at this animal—the research project. There is little mention of research projects in textbooks of methodology. Forced into necessary categorization of methods, most textbooks treat techniques as if they existed by themselves and apply them to single studies also conceived of as separate entities. However, a great deal of research in the social sciences today is conducted in terms of broad projects encompassing many hypotheses and using many varied methods. A research project, characterized by long time execution and a relatively high financial budget, does create some of the most serious problems in research design today. It requires the combination and integration of many hypotheses and many separate study designs into a meaningful overall project structure. Too many projects end up as a series of loosely related studies. They are undertaken as projects in the first place because of the complex interwoven nature of the phenomena studied. If successful, they should end up as a synthesis of the separate analyses carried out in the different units of the project.

deal with design problems in the *planning* of research, while Section 3 will deal with problems in the *operation* of research. These problems will be illustrated, for the most part, by examples drawn from the Cornell Study of Intergroup Relations.[4] An attempt will be made in presenting these examples to give a realistic, clear picture of the many daily decisions and revisions made in the course of an actual research operation.

Some General Considerations

Before looking at specific design problems, let us state briefly some general considerations. First, it seems to us futile to argue whether or not a certain design is scientific. The design is *the plan of study* and, as such, is present in all studies, uncontrolled as well as controlled and subjective as well as objective. It is not a case of scientific or not scientific, but rather one of good, or less good, design. The degree of accuracy desired, the level of proof aimed at, the state of existing knowledge, etc., all combine to determine the amount of concern one can have with the degree of science in one's design.

Second, the proof of hypotheses is never definitive. The best one can hope to do is to make more or less plausible a series of alternative hypotheses. In most cases multiple explanations will be operative. Demonstrating one's own hypotheses does not rule out the alternative hypotheses and vice versa.

Third, there is no such thing as a single, correct design. Different workers will come up with different designs favoring their own methodological, theoretical, and personal predispositions. Hypotheses can be studied by different methods using different designs.

Fourth, all research design represents a compromise dictated by the many practical considerations that go into social research. None of us operate except on limited time, money, and personnel budgets. Further limitations concern the availability of data and the extent to which one can impose upon one's subjects. A research plan must be *practical*.

Fifth, a research design is not a highly specific blueprint to be followed without deviation, but rather a series of guide posts to keep one headed in the right direction. One must be prepared to discard (although not too quickly) hypotheses that do not work out and to develop new hypotheses on the basis of increased knowledge. Furthermore, any research design developed in the office will inevitably have to be changed in the face of field considerations. For example, a study of high school students involved a careful design which required identification of the students so that, (1) sociometric diagrams could be made between differ-

4 A comprehensive report of this research project including detailed methodological analysis is given in Robin M. Williams, with the collaboration of John P. Dean and Edward A. Suchman, *Strangers Next Door: Ethnic Relations in American Communities*, Englewood Cliffs, N.J., Prentice-Hall, 1963. Basic Books, Inc., Publishers, 1959.

ent ethnic groups; (2) the answers of the students could be compared to those of their parents; and (3) follow-up interviews could be made. However, in the course of field administration, a controversy between the local newspaper and the high school superintendent in which the newspaper attempted to use the survey against the superintendent, forced the deletion of all identification from the questionnaires.

2. DESIGN PROBLEMS IN THE PLANNING OF RESEARCH

Design problems begin with the formulation of one's hypotheses. To a large extent hypotheses are tentative predictions of expected relationships between variables developed from existing knowledge and theory. Thus all research planning must begin with an examination and evaluation of what is already known about one's problem.[5] The proof of one's hypotheses will consist of a more exact statement of the kind and size of relationship based upon data collected by systematic observation. It is this intimate connection between theory, hypotheses, and data that makes the initial "design of ideas" such an important one in the research process.[6]

This problem may be divided into two stages. First, there is the overall design of the study. Second, there is the translation of specific hypotheses into observable phenomena. In the first stage we are concerned with whether the method used will produce the kind of data needed to test the hypotheses. This stage involves such decisions as whether a statistical sampling survey, a qualitative unstructured observation, or controlled experimentation is needed. At this point one must decide on the nature of proof desired, taking into consideration the level of one's hypotheses, the size of one's budget, the amount of personnel and their skills, etc. For example, the study of intergroup relations was faced with two conflicting types of hypotheses concerning prejudice. One set of hypotheses viewed prejudice as stemming from an individual's "psychological needs," while the other set interpreted prejudice as the

[5] Merton offers a highly reasonable analysis of the way theory contributes to research and vice versa. It is fruitless to argue which is more significant or which comes first, theory and research are inseparable. Robert K. Merton, "The Bearing of Sociological Theory on Empirical Research," in *Social Theory and Social Structure*, rev. ed., New York, Free Press, 1957, pp. 95–99.

[6] All too often a research study will be divided into three tenuously connected parts. The first will deal with the hypotheses, the second will deal with the data, while the third offers a theoretical interpretation. The specific connections between the three are often hard to discern. This is also true for many research plans wherein the statement of the problem discusses the theory and hypotheses to be studied, while a separate section on method of study lists the techniques to be used. It is rare that the research proposal indicates how the proposed methodology will provide answers to the stated hypotheses. A most serious problem in hypothesis design, therefore, springs from the need for close integration between the statement of hypotheses, the method of study, and the plan of analysis.

result of, "acceptance of customary beliefs and practices." To investigate the psychological explanation, one's research design would involve depth level, possibly projective techniques aimed at individual cases. The alternative set of hypotheses could probably be demonstrated more adequately by a design aimed at the study of processes of group membership and communication.

To a large extent the controversy itself is a false one, attributable to the different methodological approaches used by two opposing groups of researchers. On the one hand, there are the "depth" psychologists who, using a clinical design on a sample of bigots, find prejudice resulting from personality defects, while on the other hand there are the "institutional" sociologists who, using field observation of discriminatory situations, find prejudice rooted in the thoughtless acceptance of current operating practices. Both approaches are valid, but require integration.[7]

In many cases the overall design of the study will spring directly from the nature of the hypotheses. For example, in studying the effect of participation in a common enterprise upon the reduction of prejudice, the general plan will determine whether one demonstrates the effectiveness of a total program or the effectiveness of a single variable. In planning a study of mixed Negro and white Boy Scout troops, it becomes important to decide whether one wishes to test effectiveness of an optimum combination of circumstances conducive to successful intergroup

[7] Another example illustrating the problem of overall design is provided by A. H. Leighton's study of social stress and mental disorder. Initially, the project was conceived as a study of the relative prevalence of mental disorder occurring within groups which differed according to the amount of social stress as observed by a team of anthropological and sociological observers. The analysis design was one of rank correlation between mental disorder and social stress for different groups. It became obvious, however, that such correlations could not serve as adequate proof for many of the hypotheses. (Many studies which make use of ecological research designs contain a basic weakness in inferring individual correlations on the basis of ecological correlations.) The design was subsequently changed to permit the determination of both ecological and individual correlations. The design consisted of the following four parts.

Social Stress	Mental Disorder
A. Anthropological observation of stress areas	C. Psychiatric clinical observation of mental disorder
B. Sociological survey of individual stress	D. Psychological screening test of mental disorder

This design permits the comparison of data obtained by four different methods. A comparison of A and B will show to what extent a climate of social stress is experienced as individual stress. A comparison of C and D will indicate to what extent standardized instruments of screening can diagnose cases of mental disorder in the same way as a trained psychiatric team. A comparison between A and C will offer the correlations desired initially. A comparison between B and D will afford the individual correlations necessary for studying individual mental disorder and individual social stress. Perhaps even more important in this design are the partial correlations which become available. For example, one can study the relationship between B and D for different social climates determined through A. Alexander Leighton, *My Name is Legion*, New York, Basic Books, Inc., 1959, and others in the Stirling County Series.

relations, or whether one is interested in some such single aspect as whether the first Negro to be introduced should be a person of outstanding abilities or of average abilities. Similarly, in the overall design one must decide whether the experiment is to be conducted in a natural or artificial situation. The inferences for action to be drawn from the experiment will be highly conditioned by the degree of naturalness retained in the experiment. If a scoutmaster tends to be prejudiced does one proceed with this handicap, or does one attempt to introduce a cooperative scoutmaster? [8]

The way in which the type of question asked will indicate the kind of data needed and, therefore, the best method to be used is illustrated by the study of a court case on discrimination in Elmira. First, an attempt to answer the question, "Did the court case affect the attitudes of the Negro community?" dictated the use of a cross-sectional survey which both directly asked about the effect of the court case and indirectly measured the respondent's attitudes to be compared with his attitudes before the court case. Second, the question, "What motivation leads a Negro to institute a court case?" resulted in a detailed case study of the Negro individuals concerned with bringing the case to trial. Third, an answer to the question, "Do Negroes behave differently as a result of the court case?" was sought through participant observer reports on the change in behavior of the Negro community. Fourth, a documentary

[8] In deciding upon the basic overall design of a study, one should keep in mind the essential logic of each of the main methods of social research. Each method represents some modification or approximation of the controlled experimental design. In the experimental design we have four cells representing before and after observations for an experimental and a control group. A good experiment will concentrate upon designing matched experimental and control groups, the isolation of a stimulus to be applied to the experimental group only, and the definition of some criterion of effect to be observed in both groups before and after the stimulus has been applied. The survey design attempts to reproduce this pattern by statistical controls which match pseudo-experimental and control groups and by correlation analysis which attempts to isolate stimulus and effect. A good survey design, therefore, will include information on necessary matching characteristics and a carefully thought out classification of stimulus and effect variables together with their most important preceding, intervening, and conditional variables. The panel design comes closer to the experimental design in that before and after observations are made of what may be thought of as the experimental group. From such a design it is possible to increase the plausibility of one's inference of which variable in a correlation analysis should be viewed as cause and which as effect. A trend study design uses a comparison between an experimental group before and a control group after. The problem in this design comes from the fact that there is no way of observing internal changes or of only a limited check on the matching of the experimental and control groups. Finally, there is the one cell design involving only the experimental group after exposure to the stimulus. This design is most common in the case study method or in uncontrolled observation. Here we observe the behavior of an individual or group and infer what this individual or group was like before the stimulus and how he differs from control groups not subjected to the stimulus. See S. A. Stouffer, "Some Observations on Study Design," *American Journal of Sociology* (January, 1950), pp. 356–359, and Hans L. Zetterberg, *On Theory and Verification in Sociology*, 3rd ed., Totowa, N.J., The Bedminster Press, 1963.

content analysis approach was used in relation to the question, "What kind of treatment did the media of communication give the court case?" Finally, a fifth approach, not used in the present study, would have been to set up experimental and control groups (the experimental group taking part in some form of group discussion concerning the court case), in order to study the effectiveness of such discussion. Depending upon which method is used, a different type of data is collected and a different kind of question answered.[9]

The Definition of Concepts

In the previous discussion the problem of research design has been limited to the determination of the overall framework. A more frequently discussed design problem concerns the translation of hypotheses into operational terms. For the most part, such discussions have been of a general nature either attacking or defending the process of operationalism. Little has been said about the actual problem of designing operational hypotheses.

Our position will be that hypotheses to be studied empirically must be stated in operational terms. This means on the one hand a definition of concepts in terms of observable phenomena, and on the other hand an analysis of the causal or interpretative sequences relating these phenomena.

Problems of design involving concept formation are basically problems in description and measurement involving such technical procedures as *scale analysis, index construction,* and *typological classification.* One must decide to begin with, whether the concept is to be viewed as uni-dimensional or multi-dimensional. If uni-dimensional, the design should incorporate some empirical test of common meaning such as scale analysis. If the concept is multi-dimensional, it becomes important to

[9] An important design problem which needs more methodological attention concerns the integration of different methods into a meaningful whole. One useful approach might be as follows. Observation supplies the impressionistic, organized, total picture necessary for the development of hypotheses and the interpretation of structured data. Surveys supply objective data concerning the range of variation (marginal distribution), comparisons between groups (individual differences), and the study of relationships (interpretative and conditional). The case study offers a connected sequence of variables to illustrate and explain how and why relationships exist. Finally, the experiment provides a control test of the effectiveness of specific variables.

The study could be designed to permit an interweaving between the various methods. For example, unstructured pilot inquiry would yield hunches and hypotheses. These hypotheses could be welded into a questionnaire instrument to be administered to a cross-section sample. Out of the cross-sectional statistical analysis would come correlation tables which would enable the selection of crucial follow-up case studies. These cases would be studied by detailed interviews and personal observation. The follow-up cases could also be "followed-out" into the community at large in a study of significant institutional environments. Finally, to come full circle, these institutional environments would be related to the initial pilot inquiry.

define the different dimensions involved and to provide for the study of their inter-relationship and the development of typologies. A great deal of so-called "secondary analysis" results from an inadequate, preliminary definition of one's concepts. Such secondary analysis is characterized by ex post facto rather than a priori operational definition.

The definition of prejudice provides an illustration of concept formation in the study of intergroup relations. It is essential in the study of prejudice to determine what dimension or dimensions one is concerned with. In the present study we were concerned with three concepts of prejudice—cognitive expression, affective feeling, and discriminatory behavior. We hypothesized three types of prejudice to fit these concepts—stereotyping, tension, and social distance, each of which we postulated as being uni-dimensional. Questions were formulated to provide for a Guttman scale analysis of each of these dimensions. Subsequent analysis showed that the only clear-cut single dimension was social distance, with a coefficient of reproducibility of .94. The stereotype scale was greatly affected by educational level, while the tension items broke down into two dimensions of "liking" and "competition." [10]

Concept formation for research purposes might usefully proceed in two steps. First, one would perform a logical analysis aimed at (a) discovering the various dimensions involved within the concept, (b) correlating these different dimensions so that all possible types can be discerned, and (c) reducing the number of types to be studied. After this logical exercise one may proceed to the second step of translating those types selected for study into operational categories and empirical indices. An example of this process is seen in the attempt to define the concept of the "exemption mechanism" in the study of intergroup relations. One of the major hypotheses concerned the ability of individuals to keep their prejudices intact even after favorable contact with a member of the minority group, by exempting this individual from the total group. In an attempt to define and study this concept a logical analysis indicated that exemption involved a relationship between the number of in-group and out-group members. Four types were derived in this way; they are,

---

[10] The problem of concept formation is basic to the process of research design. The main difficulties are first, to find adequate categories to cover the general concepts and second, to translate these categories into meaningful, observable indices. Perhaps one of the most important causes of difficulty comes from the attempt to include in the definition of the concept, correlated variables which are not themselves a part of the definition. For example, if one is asked to define a cow, one ordinarily would not attempt to squeeze into this definition the economics of the dairy industry. Similarly, many individuals might question the completeness of William Whyte's definition of group structure as the reciprocal relations between members occupying hierarchical positions in the group. Certainly this type of operational definition is a perfect one for research purposes. It contains within it a picture of the actual observations to be made. However, one feels that there is more to group structure than this definition implies, as there certainly is, but it is extremely important to recognize that these other things become correlates to be studied in relation to the definition rather than something to attempt to incorporate into the definition itself.

(1) where all of the in-group accept all of the out-group, (2) where certain members of the in-group accept most members of the out-group, (3) where certain members of the in-group accept certain members of the out-group, (4) where most members of the in-group accept most members of the out-group. Type 3 seemed to come closest to the concept of exemption. This limits the concept to those instances where only some out-group members are exempted by some in-group members. In Type 1 where all in-group accept all out-group persons, the notion of individual exemption does not seem to apply (these are the situations commonly described as non-discriminatory, such as riding in buses, etc.). Type 2 where some in-group members accept most out-group persons seems to be a form of "situational exemption" in which certain areas are defined as non-discriminatory. Type 4 where most in-group accept some out-group members is a form of exemption but seems to be limited to a kind of "honorific" acceptance, rather than real exemption.

From this logical analysis it was decided to concentrate the operational definition around the partial acceptance of only certain members of an out-group by certain members of an in-group. This operational definition was translated into categories of "feeling different" toward specific contacts, arrived at from the specific index question, "Would you say he (she) is typical of the (ethnic group) or different in some respects?" asked concerning individual contacts with ethnic group members by majority group members.

The usefulness of a logical analysis preceding the operational definition lies in the awareness it creates of the underlying dimensions. If the concept is defined as uni-dimensional by such an analysis, one knows that the problem of research design must center around some form of scale analysis which would permit one to differentiate the *degree* to which this concept is present in individuals or groups. If the concept appears to be multi-dimensional, the procedure of typological classification permits one to decide what relationships one must observe and correlate before the individuals or groups can be classified. Such a correlation between dimensions also serves to check on the completeness of one's typology—all cells in the table must be accounted for. Furthermore one can proceed on the basis of a complete table to reduce the total number of possible types in which one is interested.[11]

The Statement of Relationships

Most hypotheses involve the statement of relationships between concepts. The design problem becomes one of determining how one can best study such statements as, "the more *A*, the less *B*," or, "if *A*, then *B*,"

11 Paul F. Lazarsfeld, and Allen Barton, "Qualitative Measurement in the Social Sciences: Classification, Typologies, and Indices," in H. Lasswell, and D. Lerner (eds.), *The Policy Sciences*, Stanford, Stanford University Press, 1951.

followed by other statements introducing a third concept C such as, "if A, then B, under condition C," or, "if A, then B, due to C" or, "if A, then B by way of C." The problem for research design seems to be one of first stating the basic relationship one wishes to investigate in terms of an antecedent-consequent relationship between one's independent (causal) and dependent (effect) variable. The second step is then to introduce additional variables (intervening) into the hypothesized relationship which either test the validity of this relationship or elaborate upon the conditions affecting it. Basic to this model are the concepts of the multiplicity of causes and the interdependence of events in social analysis. Any single event has many preceding causes and multiple consequences. The segment one chooses to study out of this continuous chain of events determines which variables will be arranged in a sequence of preconditions— independent cause—intervening process—dependent effect—consequences. Such classifications are fairly arbitrary depending upon the definition of one's problem. It is extremely important in the design of one's research to trace carefully the sequence of relationships involved in the hypotheses. As we shall see later, the formulation of such a causal sequence and the identification of one's independent, dependent, and intervening variables serves also as the basis for the analysis design.

An example of this kind of design of hypotheses can be shown from the study of the relationship between intergroup contact and prejudice. The major hypothesis concerned the relationship between personal contact of minority and majority group members and prejudice toward each other. First, the two concepts of contact and prejudice were defined in observable terms. The formulation of hypotheses then proceeded by taking this basic relationship and logically determining the intervening variables—those variables which would help explain *how* it was that contact led to less prejudice. A listing of such variables included understanding (empathy and sympathy), familiarity or feeling at ease, cooperation based on common goals, etc. Similarly, a negative list of intervening variables was determined to explain how non-contact might lead to prejudice. Such variables were suspicion, ethnocentrism, isolation, etc. To complete the picture, intervening variables were hypothesized for deviate cases in which contact would result in prejudice or no-contact in tolerance. Such variables were competition, exploitation, insecurity, etc.

The design of the above hypotheses is that of A (the contact) leading to C (intervening variable) which in turn leads to B (prejudice). Observations would be required of all three variables, the cross-tabulation of which would show the disappearance of the correlation between A and B when C was held constant. The second type of interpretive variable included in the design would be where C preceded A. Such variables in a case of contact leading to tolerance would be the initial level of prejudice, previous experiences, personality, self-selection of contacts, etc. Finally, in deviate cases where contact might lead to prejudice such preceding variables as competition, forced association, etc., were to be studied. The above type of design would again find the correlation between A and B disappearing when C is held constant, but in this case C is interpreted as preceding A rather than intervening between A and B.

Finally, there are the conditional or modifying variables which have to be included in the design of hypotheses. These are the variables which do not destroy the correlation between A and B, but rather alter it depending upon the nature of C. Such variables would be the type of contact (relative status, closeness, situational pattern, etc.), types of prejudice (cognitive, discriminatory, tension), expectations, existing definitions, personality, and status and role or background characteristics. These conditional variables do not explain or interpret the relationship between contact and prejudice, but instead show the conditions under which this relationship becomes stronger or weaker.

A summary statement of what has happened to the initial contact-prejudice hypothesis might take the following form: "Certain preceding variables will tend to promote or limit contacts, which contacts in turn tend to produce certain intervening variables, which variables in turn tend to promote prejudice or tolerance. These relationships become modified (strengthened or weakened) by certain conditions of contact, types of prejudice, and kinds of individuals involved." A hypothetical statement involving the basic conceptual variables of contact and prejudice, but combining many variables of different kinds might read as follows: "Especially among women (modifying variable) social isolation (preceding variable) affords the opportunity for very limited contact with ethnic groups (independent variable), usually of an impersonal, inferior-superior, relative status nature (modifying variable) which tends to produce a stereotypic labeling of ethnic groups (intervening variable), especially if the individual has an authoritarian personality (modifying variable) which finds expression in prejudice toward the ethnic group (dependent variable) especially of the social distance, discriminatory type (modifying variable)." To be sure one cannot hope to include all of the above variables in a single demonstrative table, but some such statement must be built up, based upon the integration of disparate hypotheses.[12] This problem will be discussed further in the section on the analysis design.

[12] One of the main problems in the above type of hypothesis design concerns the need to place the variables A, B, and C in some sort of time sequence. Whether A leads to B or B to A, and whether C is to be considered preceding or intervening, all depend largely upon one's ability to arrange these in order of occurrence. This is of course the basic purpose of the controlled experimental design wherein one administers the stimulus in a known time sequence. The best research design for doing this outside of the experimental set-up involves the panel design. If one can determine whether or not A, B, and C are present and how they are related at one period of

3. DESIGN PROBLEMS IN THE OPERATION OF RESEARCH

The problems of design discussed in the previous section occur during the planning of a research study. It is customary to conceive of research design as limited to this stage of work. However, design problems continue to arise at each stage of the actual execution of a research project. The remainder of this chapter, therefore, will attempt to single out the more general types of design problems that are common to most studies. These will be treated in separate sections on (1) the sample design, (2) the instrument design, (3) the administrative design, and (4) the analysis design. A general characterization of the problems involved in each of these stages will be given together with brief illustrations.

The Sample Design

Of all design problems probably sampling design has received the greatest amount of attention. This is also an area in which the concept of efficiency of design based upon practical considerations is more likely to be used as a basis of evaluation rather than an all-or-none, good or bad criterion. As discussed previously, efficiency is a much more apt basis for evaluation than scientific.

Design problems in sampling may be divided into those which affect (1) the definition of the population, (2) the size of the sample, and (3) the representativeness of the sample. In regard to the definition of the population, one faces the important problem of deciding what group it is about which one wishes to generalize one's findings. For example, what does a cross-section of the population of Elmira stand for? A series of cross-community studies would help to determine more exactly the degree to which generalizations can be viewed as applying to human behavior rather than Elmiran behavior.

The definition of sampling variables requires a consideration of one's initial hypotheses. All too often a cross-section is selected when it would

time, and then study the same variables for the same group at a later period of time, then it is possible by means of a 16-fold table design to overcome many of the disturbing weaknesses of the usual static analysis. For example, the panel study design used in the Elmira intergroup study permits one to determine for each individual his contact and prejudice at two periods of time. By composing separate questions and analyses for each of the 16 possible types of contact and prejudice at two periods of time, it is possible to discern the manner in which the interpretive and conditional variables are to be analyzed. For example, an individual who had no contact and no prejudice when first interviewed, but who on the second interview has gained contact and continues to be unprejudiced, could be questioned in detail on whether or not the lack of prejudice was an important causal factor in the acquisition of the new contact. It is only by means of some such dynamic design that the interpretation of intervening variables can be removed from the plausible and argumentative realm. For a more complete discussion of this method of panel analysis, see Hans Zeisel, *Say it With Figures,* New York, Harper & Row, 1957.

be much more efficient to select some subgroup of the population. For example, in the study of contacts between minority and majority groups, it was found unnecessarily costly to include "old ladies on the shelf" who shed very little light on the problem of intergroup contact.[13] Defining the universe one wishes to sample requires both a knowledge of relevant population characteristics and some method of identifying these in the study population.

In regard to the size of the sample one must again keep clearly in mind, simultaneously, the purpose of the study and the number of variables to be analyzed. A descriptive study will require fewer cases than an analytic study of interrelationships. For the latter, there is the inevitable problem caused by the disappearance of one's cases in a breakdown analysis. It is difficult to see how this problem can be answered except through increasing the size of one's sample. One interesting type of sampling design that often has been overlooked in this respect is "double sampling." In double sampling one proceeds to study the variable which is expensive to observe by substituting a related but cheaply observable variable. For example, one can increase the size of one's sample by asking one family member about the behavior of other family members and friends. A check on the accuracy of these reports by a sub-sample of family members and friends affords some basis for adjustment of biased reporting. A new development which holds great promise is sequential analysis wherein current analyses of incoming material permits one to estimate sampling error without the full completion of the entire sample.

The third and perhaps most intricate sampling design problem arises in connection with the method used to secure a representative sample. The controversy of probability versus judgmental sampling has limited its arguments too often to national public opinion sampling. It is quite often more efficient to use a combination of both methods, especially when, as is most often the case, one is not so much concerned with distribution estimates as with the description of relationships. This problem of marginal versus breakdown analysis has been neglected in most discussions of sampling error. A particularly common problem occurs in relation to the representativeness of subgroups used in breakdown analysis. For example, how representative is a group of 30 young, uneducated women being compared with a group of 50 old, educated men? A related type of sample design problem which is often overlooked has to do with type I or type II errors. For example, how many conclusions are made

13 Sampling problems which do not deal with a population of individuals also call for different decisions. For example, the study of contact situations required the setting up of some form of inventory of the kinds and number of situations that existed in Elmira. We attempted to establish such a population base by having Negro members keep diaries indicating all situations occurring during the day in which white people were present. Time sampling in the observation of individual or group conduct is also a problem which needs careful formulation.

that a relationship is not significant when what one means to say is that the population difference is not large enough for a sample of this small size to determine, although of course a larger sample might very well show a significant relationship.

In summary, it would seem that many sampling design problems must be viewed more from the point of view of the hypotheses being studied and the level of demonstration desired, than from the current emphasis upon theoretical sample error although, of course, this is still important. To a large extent it is "like using a scalpel in a butcher shop." [14]

The Instrument Design

Regardless of the method used in the study, some form of reporting device is necessary. This may be highly structured (as in a check-list questionnaire), less structured (as in the open-ended interview), or simply a topical outline (as in a participant observer's report). Such reporting instruments are basically tools and, like the design of any tool, must be evaluated in terms of how well it does the job for which it has been constructed. Too many discussions on principles of question wording fail to realize that the validity of a question cannot be determined in the abstract.

The basic problem of instrument design, therefore, is to tailor it to the job—which requires, once again, a clear statement of initial hypotheses. The purpose of an instrument is to secure the data required by the hypotheses. These data may be evaluated in terms of reliability and validity. The concepts, reliability and validity, are greatly in need of more careful definition for social research. The design of a reliable instrument has traditionally centered around the construction of an instrument which produces the same measurement upon repeated use. Since repetition is an almost impossible criterion in social research (for even if one could repeat studies, one would never know whether the instruments were unreliable or whether the individuals had changed), it would seem that the problem could be stated better as one of internal consistency of operational indices. To check the reliability of a question or observation one would have to repeat the question or observation from another point of view which does not destroy the conceptual meaning of the datum. It is seen, therefore, that the reliability of an instrument relates directly to the problem of concept definition discussed previously, and concerns the interrelationship of different indices of this same concept. For example, the reliability of a question designed to measure prejudice can best be

[14] An excellent chart summarizing the characteristics and the main advantages and disadvantages of eight major types of sampling may be found in Russell L. Ackoff, *The Design of Social Research,* Chicago, University of Chicago Press, 1953, pp. 124–125.

determined by asking other questions also hypothesized as measuring prejudice and then studying the pattern of interrelationship between these questions.

Similarly, the problem of *valid* instrument design requires a unique solution in social research. *No estimate of validity can be given until a statement of purpose exists.* Any piece of data may be valid for one purpose and invalid for another, at one and the same time. Reliability, however, has only one possible measure independent of the purpose to which the instrument will be put. While an instrument may have many measures of validity it has only one reliability. Reliability is a necessary prerequisite to validity. Unless a measure is reliable, it cannot possibly be valid. Thus, if one can demonstrate the validity of one's instrument, one can presume that it is reliable.

To provide for a check on the validity of one's instrument in the design of the study, one must know the purpose for which the data are being collected. If, for example, one is attempting to define a concept such as prejudice, then the check on the validity of the observations made is the same as a check on the reliability of the items used in the definition. The use of the traditional criterion of comparing what a person says with what he does makes sense only when one's hypothesis involves the prediction of overt behavior from verbal responses. In many cases, even a low correlation between verbal and overt observations may be a valid measurement of the existing inconsistency between attitude and behavior. For example, we found many white storekeepers who said they would refuse to sell to Negroes. However, when we sent Negroes to these same stores they were generally waited upon. If our initial question was intended to predict actual behavior, it was indeed invalid. If, however, the initial question was asked to compare behavior in hypothetical situations with behavior in actual situations (its real purpose), then the question was certainly valid.

Apart from the above general statements, a great many problems exist in the design of recording schedules. The type of item or question to be used, the check list, multiple choice or free answer, the wording of the question (direct or indirect), the ordering of the items or questions, etc., all of these contain peculiar problems of design which cannot be treated in this brief chapter. Every study will create specific problems of question design. Many of these are answered on the basis of criteria of understandability, i.e., simple, clear-cut wording. Other problems are more difficult, such as the translation of questions into different wording for different subgroups. For example, in studying intergroup relations among majority group adults, Jewish and Negro adults, majority group youth, Jewish and Negro youth, it became extremely difficult to keep the same wording for all groups. There can be no doubt that direct comparisons of marginal distributions are impossible without identically worded questions. The decision was to leave questions identical where the hypothesis called for a direct comparison of marginal distributions and to change wording where we were more interested in the relation between different concepts. In summary, an instrument is basically a tool which must be evaluated in terms of its success in securing the information needed to demonstrate some hypothesis.

The Administrative Design

The administrative design of a research study concerns the execution of one's original study design. The principle goal is to stay as close as possible to the previously prepared model. Field or administrative conditions will invariably create the need to change the original design. The problem is how to compromise and improvise without destroying the ideal model.

Perhaps the first problem in field administration occurs in fulfilling the sampling requirements. The design of the administration will do much to determine how large a mortality one will have.[15] The use of call backs, telephone interviews, mail questionnaires, abbreviated questionnaire forms containing only the key questions, special inducements or rewards, etc., will often determine whether or not an interview is completed. Participant observation is particularly susceptible to sampling problems. For example, the observer in the Negro community in Elmira thought that he knew almost all the Negro families. However, a check on those he knew against a cross-section obtained in a survey showed the almost inevitable under-representation of uneducated respondents.

In regard to the administration of the schedule or instrument, the major design problems center around the interpersonal situation between investigator and subject. How is the field worker to define his role? How are the subject's behavior and responses affected by the presence of the investigator? This problem of definition of role is most apparent for a participant observer (it has been claimed by more than one anthropologist that there can be no such thing as a nonparticipant observer). In the case of one Negro observer, we found that after three years his role had almost completely shifted from that of a non-participant observer to one of a non-observing participant—a new role which proved very useful to us in subsequent action experiments.

An important principle to keep in mind in administrative design is the close, continued relationship between the field worker and the study

---

15 A major administrative decision is when to call a halt to attempts to reach all members of a selected sample. The more one is concerned with reproducing the marginal distribution of the total population as opposed to an emphasis upon the study of interrelationships, the more important it is to complete the sample. One helpful technique is to select a random sample of non-respondents for intensive follow-up and then to weight their responses in proportion to the size of the non-respondent group.

designer. The need to change design in the face of developing data is inevitable, and not always undesirable. Too many research designs, once in the field, are carried to completion despite an apparent need for redesign. One should benefit by the additional evidence accumulated in the course of field administration. Field conditions do not always act in a negative way. For example, in the study of intergroup relations among high school youth, a field administration problem arose requiring the singling out of Jewish, Negro, Catholic, and Protestant children. This addition, not contemplated in the original design, proved extremely valuable in subsequent analyses.

An interesting possibility in administrative design would involve the completion of a study in 2 or more stages. For example, if one wishes a total sample of 500 cases, one could select 2 random samples of 250 cases each. Upon completion of the first sample of 250, a preliminary tabulation and analysis could be made. This analysis would result in a new schedule to be administered to the second sample of 250 containing the following kinds of changes: (1) questions to be repeated without change in order to secure more cases; (2) questions to be repeated with change in wording because the analysis has cast some doubt upon the meaning of the first wording or because the distribution of responses is such as to prevent a breakdown analysis; (3) new questions to be asked in order to provide additional data; (4) new, follow-up questions to be asked of specific subgroups or individuals showing specific relationships between variables in an attempt to get at more detailed information. If necessary, the above procedure could then be repeated in 3 or 4 stages. This technique would help to eliminate the current overload of "pilot" inquiries, whose main asset lies in pointing out the problems that should have been studied.

The Analysis Design

Ideally, the design of analysis should be largely worked out in advance of the collection of data. If the design of hypotheses is any good, then the design of the analysis will follow from it almost automatically. In fact an hypothesis should be called operational only if the analysis to be made is explicit in the statement of the hypothesis.

For example, the analysis design for the study of the relationship between intergroup contact and prejudice would follow through the basic hypothesis design presented previously. First would come the test of one's operational definitions of the concepts involved. We hypothesized three separate dimensions of prejudice—social distance, stereotype, and tension. The analysis design therefore requires some form of scale analysis to test the dimensionality of each of these definitions of prejudice. The same would apply to the construction of an index of intergroup contact. What definition of contact would be most productive—availability of contact, actual contacts, or actual close friendship? Or should the contact index consist of some ratio between available contacts and actual contacts? [16]

In a similar way the basic interrelationships to be studied should have been specified in the design of hypotheses. For example, following the analysis of the relationship between the dependent variable (prejudice) and the independent variable (contact), one would proceed to study the interpretive variables, both preceding and intervening (understanding, familiarity, ethnocentrism, etc.), and the conditional variables (status and role attributes, personality, type of contact and prejudice). This much of the analysis design at least should be provided for in advance.[17]

[16] An example of a scale analysis which helped to clarify the meaning of an index is seen from the study of intergroup situations by means of hypothetical examples. In an attempt to find out how individuals react within specific situations, we formulated a series of questions which asked about their behavior in actual situations they had experienced, or if they had not experienced these situations, about their hypothetical behavior. Subsequent scale analysis showed quite decisively that the individuals were answering these hypothetical questions from an attitudinal rather than a situational point of view. Briefly, all of the hypothetical situations scaled together and were closely related to general scales of prejudice, whereas feelings expressed about actual situations did not scale together. This raises a very interesting design problem involving such techniques as socio-dramas, projective tests, etc. It would seem that wherever the subject is asked to construct an artificial situation, he will do so in general, stereotyped terms rather than with any real awareness of the specific situational components.

[17] The basic objective of a breakdown analysis is to study the effect of a series of test variables upon the main cause and effect relationship between the dependent and

(Where a = contact, b = prejudice, and c = test variable; + = presence, − = absence)

	Difference in $b+$ present	Possible Interpretation
	$a+ - a- = +$	The basic relationship-contact decreases prejudices.
1. $c+$	$a+ - a- = 0$	Explanatory variable.
$c-$	$a+ - a- = 0$	Total explanation. c precedes a and destroys relationship between a and b.
2. $c+$	$a+ - a- = +$	Independent variable.
$c-$	$a+ - a- = +$	Cumulative effect. c and a both remain related to b.
3. $c+$	$a+ - a- = -$	Improbable result, given initial positive
$c-$	$a+ - a- = -$	relationship.
4. $c+$	$a+ - a- = -$	Conditional variable.
$c-$	$a+ - a- = +$	Cancellatory effect. a has opposite effect depending upon $c+$ or $c-$.
5. $c+$	$a+ - a- = +$	Same as above.
$c-$	$a+ - a- = -$	Types 4 and 5 would have to show + effect outweighing −.
6. $c+$	$a+ - a- = 0$	Conditional variable.
$c-$	$a+ - a- = +$	Partial explanation. a is effective only if $c-$ present.
7. $c+$	$a+ - a- = +$	Same as above, but for $c+$.
$c-$	$a+ - a- = 0$	
8. $c+$	$a+ - a- = 0$	Improbable.
$c-$	$a+ - a- = -$	
9. $c+$	$a+ - a- = -$	Improbable.
$c-$	$a+ - a- = 0$	

However, it would be a great mistake to think of the analysis design as cut and dried, following the original design of hypotheses without deviation. The hypotheses serve as a point of departure, but ingenuity and imagination come into play as strongly as ever. The ideas one gets at this stage of research are no longer free floating, as in the hypothesis stage, but are closely limited to the data at hand. In the design of hypotheses one takes the total picture and cuts it up into a jigsaw pattern. In the design of analysis one attempts to fit the jigsaw pieces together but inevitably finds some pieces missing and other pieces added. The final picture established after the analysis should certainly resemble the hypothesized picture but undoubtedly will be changed in many respects.

The analysis stage, therefore, is a combination of the demonstration of previously formulated hypotheses and continued conceptualization leading to the development of new hypotheses. For many researchers who work better with tangible evidence, the analysis stage represents the highest moment of reflective thinking. The analysis design therefore should provide for the study of new hypotheses which become evident only in the face of the contradiction of one's original hypotheses. There is an obvious danger in the too-loose reformulation of one's hypotheses—but that is more a problem of personality than of method.

4. SUMMARY

What we have tried to show in this chapter is that problems in research design are practical problems that occur continuously from the beginning to the end of a research study. The research process is one of constant decision and revision—and each decision must be made with an eye toward its effect upon a balanced study design. While the basis for many decisions will rest upon fundamental rules of scientific method, the

---

independent variables. One begins with some relationship between two variables a and b, to be explained or modified by a third variable, c. What happens to the difference between $a+$ and $a-$ in the amount of $b+$ present, when observed separately for $c+$ and $c-$? Or to use the example of contact and prejudice, what happens to the difference between those people who have intergroup contacts and those who don't in the amount of prejudice present, when observed separately for individuals with authoritarian or non-authoritarian personalities? Does personality explain or modify this relationship? The preceding scheme lists the nine different possibilities and their interpretation.

From the listing of possibilities, we see that an explanatory variable wipes out the initial relationship. If this variable precedes a, or intervenes between a and b in a meaningful way, we say we have a "true" causal explanation. If no logical sequence can be discerned between a, b, and c, but rather c appears independently related to a and b, we say we have a "spurious" causal explanation.

If the initial relationship persists when controlled on variable c, then, we have a conditional effect. In this case both c and a may contribute to b independently, and therefore cumulatively, or dependently, either in a cancellatory way, or in a partial way. See Herbert Hyman, *Survey Design and Analysis*, New York, Free Press, 1955, and Paul F. Lazarsfeld, "Interpretation of Statistical Relations as a Research Operation," in Paul F. Lazarsfeld, and Morris Rosenberg (eds.), *The Language of Social Research*, New York, Free Press, 1955, pp. 115–125.

translation of these decisions into specific operational procedures requires skill and ingenuity.

The criteria of good research design are similar to the criteria of any good structural design. The architect of a research study, like the architect of a building, strives to satisfy the following general conditions:

1. basic soundness of construction (the rules of scientific method)
2. practicality of construction (availability of techniques and data)
3. suitability to purpose (validity of findings for the problem)
4. originality and inventiveness (the development of new techniques and new designs)
5. aesthetically pleasing (the "beauty" of a balanced design)
6. fitted to the construction budget (research without deficits or "free time" writing).

In short, *research design is science plus art.*

SELECTED REFERENCES

Ackoff, Russell L. *The Design of Social Research,* Chicago, University of Chicago Press, 1953.

Chapin, F. Stuart, *Experimental Designs in Sociological Research,* New York, Harper & Row, 1947.

Churchman, C. West, *Theory of Experimental Inference,* New York, Macmillan, 1948.

Hammond, P. (ed.) *Sociologists at Work,* New York, Basic Books, Inc., Publishers, 1964.

Hyman, Herbert, *Survey Design and Analysis,* New York, Free Press, 1955.

Kaplan, Abraham, *The Conduct of Inquiry,* San Francisco, Chandler Publishing Co., 1964.

Lazarsfeld, Paul F., and Morris, Rosenberg, *The Language of Social Research,* New York, Free Press, 1955.

Madge, John, *The Tools of Social Science,* Garden City, N.Y., Anchor Books, Doubleday, 1965.

Miller, Delbert C., *Handbook of Research Design and Social Measurement,* New York, McKay, 1964.

Stouffer, Samuel A., *et al., Measurement and Prediction,* Princeton, Princeton University Press, 1950.

Zetterberg, Hans L., *On Theory and Verification in Sociology,* 3rd ed., Totowa, N.J., The Bedminster Press, 1963.

14
Edward A. Suchman

PRINCIPLES AND PRACTICE OF EVALUATIVE RESEARCH

1. INTRODUCTION

An increasingly important aspect of social research deals with the evaluation of social action programs. As social scientists attempt to influence as well as understand the society they live in, they are forced to test the validity of many of their concepts and theories of social change. It is one thing to describe and analyze social phenomena; it is quite a different matter to deliberately influence the development and course of these phenomena.

Social scientists have long been concerned with the problem of induced social change. This interest has both an applied and basic scientific orientation. On the one hand, social scientists have been pressed to demonstrate the utility of their different disciplines for the solution of important social problems. On the other hand, the social scientists themselves have been challenged to test the validity of their knowledge under experimental field conditions.

The social experiment in the past has occupied a rather ambivalent position in social research.[1] As a controlled laboratory method for basic research, it has produced findings of limited significance, while as a research design for testing the effectiveness of applied social programs it has only rarely been able to satisfy the rigorous requirements of the experimental method. It would seem that some compromise between the too-limited focus of the laboratory experiment and the too-general approach of the field study will be required if social science is to develop a

The author wishes to acknowledge the contribution of George James and Jack Elinson to the development of the ideas presented in this chapter as part of a joint seminar supported by a grant from the Russell Sage Foundation. An extended treatment of the problems discussed in this chapter may be found in Edward A. Suchman, *Evaluative Research: Principles and Practice in Public Service and Social Action Programs*, New York, Russell Sage Foundation, in press.

[1] For historical accounts and current approaches, see Ernest Greenwood, *Experimental Sociology*, New York, King's Crown, 1945, and F. Stuart Chapin, *Experimental Designs in Sociological Research*, New York, Harper & Row, 1947.

methodology for the study of planned or deliberate social change, whether the objective be basic knowledge or applied action. This chapter examines the principles and techniques of evaluative research as one possible avenue for the development of a more productive experimental sociology, as well as for the more traditional use of evaluation to determine the success or failure of applied programs of social action.

2. DEFINITION OF EVALUATIVE RESEARCH

At the present time, the term "evaluation" is used to represent both an objective and a process. The objective is one of defining social worth or value and may apply to an object, a person, or an act. The process is one of measuring the degree to which the object, person, or act possesses the valued characteristic. These two aspects of evaluation—the definition of social value and the determination of its attainment—constitute the basic *conceptual* and *methodological* components of evaluative research.

Evaluation is defined by Riecken as, "the measurement of desirable and undesirable consequences of an action that has been taken in order to forward some goal that we value." [2] The conceptual emphasis of this definition is quite clearly upon the relation of some activity to a desired goal, while the methodological problem is one of measurement of the consequences of that activity. There must be some rationale (theory) for hypothesizing that certain forms of social action will produce particular effects and that these effects do indeed represent the desired social values. And there must be some technique (method) for measuring the effects produced in a reliable and valid way and for attributing these effects to the action taken. Thus, in evaluative research we find the two main ingredients of any research project, basic or applied: (1) an hypothesis linking some independent causal variable (social action) with a dependent effect variable (valued consequences), and (2) a method of procedure for measuring variations in the dependent variable and for determining the extent to which these variations are due to changes in the independent variable.

Hyman supplies us with a further prerequisite for evaluation viewed as social experimentation when he states that "evaluation refers to the procedures of fact-finding about the results of planned social action." [3] The independent variable or stimulus must be planned, i.e., deliberate and controlled. The action taken must be under the control of the social experimenter and introduced into the situation with the hypothesis that it will produce the desired change. Thus, Riecken concludes that any intentional social action can be the object of an evaluation study. Given

[2] Henry W. Riecken, *The Volunteer Work Camp: A Psychological Evaluation,* Reading, Mass.: Addison-Wesley, 1952, p. 4.

[3] Herbert H. Hyman, Terrance W. Hopkins, and Charles Wright, *Applications of Methods of Evaluation,* Berkeley, University of California Press, 1961, p. 3.

modern society's strong commitment to "planned social change" and "intentional social action," it is not difficult to understand the increasing demand for evaluative research.

3. EVALUATIVE VERSUS NON-EVALUATIVE RESEARCH

Since most discussions of research methodology deal with non-evaluative or pure research, it might be worthwhile to look at the differences between these two forms of research, especially insofar as such differences might affect the design and conduct of the evaluative research project. Our position is that the scientific method is the only logical basis for all research. Therefore, it follows that both evaluative and non-evaluative research must obey the same rules and utilize the same techniques. Evaluative research must, first and foremost, be *research*. How, then, does it differ from non-evaluative research and what, if any, are its special methodological problems?

In general, evaluative research is applied research the purpose of which is to measure the effects of some operating program. However, this does not have to be the case since evaluative research can also be used to test the validity of basic theoretical propositions about induced social change. Action research, for example, may have as its primary goal not the determination of whether a particular social action or service program is achieving its goals, but rather the test of hypotheses concerning how and why a change in some independent variable will or will not produce a change in the dependent variable.

To some extent we can make a distinction between program evaluation which examines the effectiveness of a total program as a single stimulus, and variable testing which concentrates on specific aspects of a program especially insofar as these can be generalized to principles of social action rather than to operational procedures. As Hovland points out, program evaluation has limited generalizability unless an attempt has been made to formulate the independent variables in terms of their conceptual as well as their operational referrants.[4] Even when the evaluation study is conducted for purely administrative reasons, it is our position that unless an attempt is made to conceptualize the program activities into broader principles of action, one will not be able to apply the findings to other programs or even to the same program at a later time or in a different place.

From this point of view, the distinction between applied and basic research in terms of generalizability of findings becomes relative rather than absolute. We may paraphrase Lewin by stating that there is nothing as practical as theoretical research or as impractical as purely applied research. The differences between evaluative and non-evaluative research are ones of varying accent rather than of a completely foreign language.

4 Carl T. Hovland, Arthur L. Lumsdaine, and Fred D. Sheffield, *Experiments in Mass Communication,* Princeton, Princeton University Press, 1949.

Non-evaluative research stresses understanding rather than application, but one of the most valid tests of understanding is experimental application, while application of evaluative research findings without an understanding of the underlying causal process can lead to unexpected, and often undesirable results.[5]

The specificity of evaluative research as compared to the greater abstractness of non-evaluative research raises some significant questions related to the meaning of data. In non-evaluative research, the concept is of primary importance, and the observable data are only a sample of operational indices of the concept with little inherent importance in themselves. In evaluative research, however, the operational indices are often the phenomena of direct concern with the concept or underlying action principle having only indirect relevance. To a large extent the specific program activities *are* the independent variables, not simply indices of these variables, while the dependent variable is directly represented by the specific, observable criteria of change. Thus, the "sin of operationalism" in non-evaluative research (whereby indices are treated as if they were the concepts) tends to become a "sin of conceptualization" in evaluative research (whereby the specific activities and criteria of effect which are necessary for planning and conducting operational programs tend to be lost in overly abstract generalizations). In this connection, note the contrasting criticisms of evaluative research as frequently being too general (i.e. not directly applicable to the specific time, place, and activities), while the criticism of non-evaluative research tends to be too specific (i.e. bound by the particular time, place, and instruments of the study). These criticisms, we feel, indicate the inherent and unavoidable overlap between the two types of research—neither can be completely abstract or concrete.[6]

4. THE LOGIC OF EVALUATIVE RESEARCH

The same model of causality that underlies non-evaluative social research also applies to evaluative research. We conceive of a chain of interrelated events which for research purposes has only an arbitrary beginning and ending joined by a similarly arbitrary number of inter-

[5] Hyman classifies research studies into three types: (1) the theoretical or experimental, (2) the evaluative or programmatic, and (3) the diagnostic. A similar distinction is made by Zetterberg who differentiates between diagnosis as leading to descriptive studies aimed at the development of taxonomies, and explanation which requires verificational studies to test hypotheses. Evaluation would involve action programs with the objective of measuring change. Herbert Hyman, *Survey Design and Analysis*, New York, Free Press, 1955, p. 312; Hans L. Zetterberg, *On Theory and Verification in Sociology*, Totowa, N.J.: The Bedminster Press, 1963, pp. 5–10.

[6] Lewis describes this interdependence as follows: "Knowledge, action and evaluation are essentially connected. The primary and pervasive significance of knowledge lies in its guidance of action. Knowing is for the sake of doing. And action, obviously, is rooted in evaluation." C. I. Lewis, "An Analysis of Knowledge and Valuation," *The Paul Carus Foundation Lectures* VII, La Salle, Ill., Open Court, 1946, p. 3.

vening steps. All social events have multiple causes and multiple effects and the antecedent-consequent segment chosen to be understood (non-evaluative) or to be changed (evaluative) is dependent upon the research worker's definition of his problem. Thus, no single factor is a necessary and sufficient cause of any other factor and social change can be brought about through many different channels. Consequently the relationships between any two independent and dependent' variables, or any program and its effects, must be stated in terms of probabilities and not certainties, and analyzed according to a model of interactional effects in which neither complete explanation nor complete program effectiveness is possible.[7]

In relation to evaluative research, we may diagram this model as follows:

Preconditions	Independent Variable	Intervening Variable	Dependent Variable	Consequences

The main evaluative hypothesis, as is true for all research, concerns the relationship of the independent to the dependent variable. The statement of this hypothesis takes the form of experimental intervention following the stimulus-response pattern. Instead of the non-evaluative statement, "the more A, the more B," evaluation proposes the hypothesis that "as A is changed, B will change." In terms of program evaluation, the hypothesis becomes "Activities A, B, C . . . N will produce effects X, Z, Y . . . N."[8] The program of social action becomes the independent variable to be manipulated while the desired effect becomes the dependent variable according to which change is to be measured. Thus, we see that a clear statement of a hypothesis is as necessary to evaluative as to non-evaluative research. We shall discuss in section 11 the problems of isolating and controlling the action programs as the stimulus or independent variable, and in sections 7 through 10 of defining and measuring the criteria of effect as the dependent variable since these two problems

[7] This model is well represented in the following set of readings, Paul F. Lazarsfeld and Morris Rosenberg (eds.), *The Language of Social Research*, New York, Free Press, 1955.

[8] This formulation has been suggested for public health evaluation as, "Activity A reduces the frequency of morbidity M." *Planning Evaluations in Mental Health Programs*, New York, Milbank Memorial Fund, 1958, p. 14.

consatute fundamental methodological considerations for evaluative research.

As in all research, the major empirical task is first to test for the existence of a significant relationship between the independent and dependent variables and, then, to analyze this relationship in terms of intervening or control variables which either (1) challenge the validity of the observed relationship as causal, (2) establish the conditions which indicate the process by which the independent cause leads to the dependent effect, or (3) modify the effects of the independent variable upon the dependent variable. Thus the first question to be asked in evaluative research is, Does the program being evaluated produce the effects that are desired? The further, more analytic questions become, How do we know it was the program that really produced the effects? What did the program do that resulted in the effects? and What conditions modify the effectiveness of the program? The similarity between these kinds of evaluative questions and Hyman's [9] and Lazarsfeld's [10] approach to intervening variable analysis in terms of explanation, interpretation, or elaboration is not simply coincidental. Evaluative research has a significant contribution to make to the understanding of how, why, and under what conditions social action is effective for inducing change.[11]

5. THE METHODOLOGY OF EVALUATIVE RESEARCH

Evaluative research has no special research designs or special methodology of its own for the collection and analysis of data. As we have stated previously, evaluative research is still research and as such must adhere to the rules of scientific method and utilize existing techniques.[12] While the objective or purpose of evaluative research may differ from non-evaluative research, the study design and the techniques for the collection and analysis of data are largely the same.

[9] Herbert H. Hyman, *Survey Design and Analysis*, New York, Free Press, 1955.

[10] Paul F. Lazarsfeld, "Interpretation of Statistical Relations as a Research Operation," in Paul F. Lazarsfeld and Morris Rosenberg (eds.), *op. cit.*, pp. 115–125.

[11] Note the similarity between the following statement as an evaluation of mass media campaigns and any analysis is non-evaluative research. "It has been found that there are a number of social and psychological factors that mediate between the message for the campaign and its effect upon the audience. For instance, prior opinions, interest, past behavior, mood, conflicting attitudes, pressures from family and other personal influences are some of the factors which can influence the impact of communication." C. R. Wright, "Evaluating Mass Media Campaigns," *International Social Science Bulletin*, vol. VII, no. 3, UNESCO (1955), pp. 429–430.

[12] Klineberg makes this point quite explicitly. "The term evaluation should as far as possible be restricted to a process which satisfies such scientific criteria—objective, systematic, comprehensive. As such, it should be distinguished from all forms of assessment which take the form of one man's judgment of the success or failure of a project, no matter how sensible and wise that judgment appears to be. . . ." Otto Klineberg, "The Problem of Evaluation," *International Social Science Bulletin*, vol. 7, no. 3 (1955), p. 347.

Evaluative research most closely follows the experimental model. This is natural since the independent variable or stimulus is supposedly under the control of the research worker and the major objective is not to discover correlations, but to achieve certain hypothesized effects through manipulation of the program stimulus. Since this is the basic research design for evaluation, we will devote the major portion of this chapter to a discussion of how some of the problems encountered in the application of this model to evaluative research might best be met.

However, we would like to point out briefly that evaluative research can and should make use of the two other major social research models— the survey and the case study.[13] The evaluative survey, like its non-evaluative counterpart, can only study the ex post facto relationships to be found between reported exposure to an action program and the presence or absence of the desired effects. Thus a cross-sectional survey may find that respondents who report taking part in a particular program show a significantly higher proportion of the intended effects of that program than respondents who report that they were not exposed. These findings are subject to a wide variety of methodological weaknesses particularly in regard to the self-selective nature of exposure. However, they are also amenable to the same attempts at approximating the experimental design through the use of multi-variate analysis techniques as is the non-evaluative survey. For example, a survey of the relationship between intergroup contact and prejudice may be viewed as an evaluation of the effectiveness of intergroup action programs in reducing prejudice.[14] In other words, the before and after type of evaluative design with control groups, if properly planned, can be carried out, in which case the design is no longer a survey, but instead an experiment.

The application of the social survey to evaluative research is greatly enhanced by the use of the longitudinal or panel design. This design affords a closer approximation to the before and after condition of experimental research by studying a population at two points in time and by using earlier measures of subjects as a form of self-control against subsequent changes both in terms of exposure and effects.[15] The hypothesis of the longitudinal or prospective survey is actually formulated as an evaluation of whether change in the independent variable will be related to change in the dependent variable, i.e., "a change in a will be followed by a change in b." Thus, the use of the panel technique for studying voting behavior in many ways represents an attempt to evaluate the effectiveness of a political campaign for changing the voting behavior

13 See Chapter 13, "Research Design and Administration," for a discussion of these models as they relate to the experimental design.

14 Robin M. Williams, *The Reduction of Intergroup Tensions*, New York, Social Science Research Council, 1948.

15 Donald Pelz and Frank M. Andrews, "Detecting Causal Priorities in Panel Study Data," *American Sociological Review*, vol. 28 (December, 1964), pp. 836–848.

of the public.[16] Panel studies of changing student values in college are also basically evaluative studies on the effects of exposure to a program of college education.[17]

The use of the case study method for evaluative purposes is widespread in clinical research. Diagnosis and guidance are founded upon the ability of the professional worker to evaluate cause and effect within the individual case and to prescribe a treatment program designed to change the undesirable condition of the individual. All of the so-called helping professions in health, education, and welfare carry out their professional activities on the implicit basis of case study evaluation. Most forms of testing, whether academic examinations of achievement or personality tests of emotional disturbance, are evaluative measures. It would be shortsighted to deny the utilization of the case study method for evaluative research.

However, as for non-evaluative research, the crucial methodological question hinges around the validity of this method not for understanding (or evaluating) the individual case, but for *generalizing* about the effectiveness of a particular therapeutic approach or program. Just as the single case cannot furnish proof of the existence of a cause and effect relationship, it cannot validly test the effectiveness of an action program in producing social change. The unanswered question will always remain, How do we know it was our program that produced the desired results? This is the key question underlying the use of the experimental method and we now turn to an analysis of that method as it applies to evaluative research.

6. EXPERIMENTAL DESIGNS FOR EVALUATIVE RESEARCH

The following flow chart by Greenberg and Mattison lays out the optimum conditions and the sequence to be followed in conducting an evaluative study according to the experimental model.[18]

This model represents the ideal evaluative research design and, no matter what adaptation is made, the basic logic must be traceable to this model. Campbell presents this logic as follows:

$$O_1 \quad X \quad O_2$$
$$O_3 \qquad O_4$$

X represents the exposure of a group to the program being evaluated, and O refers to the observations or measurements made of the desired

[16] Paul F. Lazarsfeld, Bernard Berelson, and Hazel Gaudet, *The People's Choice*, New York, Columbia University Press, 1948.

[17] Philip E. Jacob, *Changing Values in College: An Exploratory Study of the Impact of College Teaching*, New York, Harper & Row, 1957, and Allen H. Barton, *Studying the Effects of College Education*, New Haven, Conn., The Edward W. Hazen Foundation, 1959.

[18] Bernard G. Greenberg, and Berwyn Mattison, "The Whys and Wherefores of Program Evaluation," *Canadian Journal of Public Health*, vol. 46 (July, 1955), p. 298.

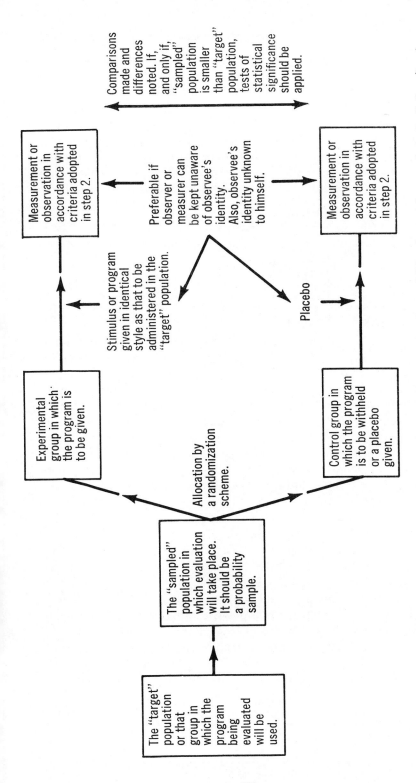

Source: This chart is reproduced from Bernard G. Greenberg and Berwyn F. Mattison, "The Whys and Wherefores of Program Evaluation," *Canadian Journal of Public Health*, vol. 46 (July, 1955), p. 298. With permission of the authors and the Canadian Public Health Association.

Figure 14.1. A flow chart to illustrate optimum principles and sequence to be followed in conducting a valid experimental design to evaluate a health program.

effects. X's and 0's in a given row refer to the same specific persons, while parallel rows represent equivalent or matched samples of persons. Temporal order is indicated by the left-to-right dimension.[19]

Quite simply, this design calls for the setting up of equivalent experimental and control groups, making a "before" measure to determine a base-line against which change can be measured, exposing the experimental group to the program or activity to be evaluated, and then making an "after" measure to see what changes have taken place. This design and the measurements to be made may also be diagrammed as follows:

	Before	After	
Experimental Group	X_1	X_2	$d = X_2 - X_1$
Control Group	X_1^1	X_2^1	$d^1 = X_2^1 = X_1^1$.

The test of effectiveness is given by the significance of the difference between d and d^1.[20]

This is the basic design of any evaluative research and, if the conditions of control are satisfied, its demonstration of effectiveness is infallible. However, only rarely can the requirements of the above design be fulfilled outside the laboratory. Deviations and compromises are essential if any evaluative research is to be done at all. As Greenwood points out, "Perfect control, while it is something to aim at, is almost never possible. The experimenter must therefore always aspire after the maximum control that circumstances will permit. As in everything else, gradations exist. There are good approximations to the ideal experiment and there are poor ones." [21] If it would help to avoid senseless debate over whether various adaptations are really experiments, we might better speak of these as "statistical comparisons with matched control groups" rather than experiments.[22]

We can only briefly summarize some of the major forms of adaptation as diagrammed by Campbell. The simplest, corresponding to the social survey discussed previously, is the "after-only" design $(X, 0)$. This is probably the most common, and weakest, form of evaluative research. After a group has been exposed to a program, a measurement is made to see whether they show the desired effect. There is no way to check the extent to which the effect was present before the program, or if the effect would have come about anyway without the program. There is always a strong possibility of a self-selective bias with those individuals who

[19] D. T. Campbell, "Factors Relevant to the Validity of Experiments in Social Settings," *Psychological Bulletin*, vol. 54, 1957, pp. 297–312.

[20] Samuel A. Stouffer, "Some Observations on Study Design," *American Journal of Sociology*, vol. 55 (January, 1950), pp. 355–361.

[21] Greenwood, *op. cit.*, p. 29.

[22] Hornell Hart, in a review of Chapin's "Experimental Designs in Sociological Research," *Social Forces* (October, 1948), pp. 96–98.

are most favorable or susceptible to begin with, being more likely to expose themselves to the program.

An improved design, still lacking a control group, would be the "one-group, pre-test, post-test" design $(0_1 \, X \, 0_2)$. This is similar to the panel study mentioned previously. The presence of a before measure permits the evaluator not only to measure the degree of change, but also to compare those who changed with those who did not. But five main sources of error are still possible: (1) extraneous events occurring at the same time as the program may be the real cause of the observed change, (2) the change may be due to what happens in time (natural improvement), and have little to do with the program, (3) the before measure itself may act as a stimulus for change, (4) changes in the after measure may reflect instrument unreliability, and (5) unreliability may produce statistical regression with values shifting toward the mean.

The introduction of a control group to the after-only design does provide a much closer approximation to the experimental method, provided there is reason to believe that both experimental and control groups were matched to begin with, i.e., $\left(\begin{smallmatrix} X0_1 \\ 0_2 \end{smallmatrix}\right)$. While this design does not permit an analysis of who changed (internal change), it does provide a fairly valid test of the effectiveness of the program in producing the desired change (marginal change).

Other designs suggested are variations of the above basic models and we need not to go into them here. Suffice it to say that, whichever design is used, the demonstration or proof of effectiveness must be related to the ideal experimental design with an awareness of the implications of the compromise design upon the evaluation study.

In the remainder of this chapter, we will examine each of the three basic requirements of experimental proof and discuss their importance for evaluative research. The three basic requirements are: (1) the definition and measurement of the effects desired (the criteria of the dependent variable), (2) the description and identification of program activities designed to produce the desired effects (the isolation and control of the independent variable), and (3) the selection of equivalent experimental and control groups (defining and sampling the target population). Most of the methodological problems of evaluative research fall into one of the above three categories.

7. THE DEFINITION OF PROGRAM OBJECTIVES AND CRITERIA OF EFFECT

Most research begins with the conceptual and operational definition of the dependent variable—evaluative research is no exception. The dependent variable indicates what it is that one wishes to explain or, in the case of evaluative research, to change. In the absence of any clear statement of what one is attempting to accomplish, it becomes impossible to develop criteria for evaluating success or failure. It is as if we were to conduct an experiment without defining what response or effect the stimulus was expected to have.[23] James recognizes this explicitly in his definition of evaluation as, "the measurement of success in reaching a stated objective." [24]

Perhaps, then, one of the most characteristic features of evaluative research is the presence of some valued goal or objective whose degree of attainment constitutes the main focus of the research problem. Evaluation does not exist in a vacuum. One must always ask, The evaluation of *what?* Every action, every program has some value for some purpose and inevitably will show some effects—therefore, it is meaningless to ask whether a program has any value without specifying what the value is for.[25] In reverse, if any activity has an objective then it is open to evaluative research. Thus, a research project may be evaluated in terms of the degree to which it successfully attains its own objectives, e.g., the test of some hypothesis, or a research technique in terms of its ability to produce reliable, valid, and relevant data bearing on an hypothesis, or a theory in relation to its value in organizing disparate hypotheses.[26]

The definition of what one hopes to accomplish with an action program, sufficiently detailed to permit translation into observable and measurable indices or criteria, is not a simple task. Most programs have multiple objectives consisting of a mixture of different dimensions of generality.[27] As described by one conference on evaluation, "there were

[23] Kendall states, "Obviously the evaluation of an experimental program presupposes fairly precise knowledge of the objectives of the program. Without such knowledge, it is manifestly impossible to say whether or not the program has been successful." Patricia Kendall, "Evaluating an Experimental Program in Medical Education," in Matthew B. Miles (ed.), *Innovation in Education,* New York, Teachers College, Columbia University, 1964, p. 344.

[24] George James, "Planning and Evaluation of Health Programs," in *Administration of Community Health Services,* Chicago, The International City Manager's Association, 1961, p. 124.

[25] As a parallel, the concept of evaluation is similar to that of validity in methodological research. Validity also implies some purpose and, to be meaningful, one must always specify validity for what. An insightful discussion of this problem in regard to validity may be found in Samuel Stouffer *et al., Measurement and Prediction,* Princeton, Princeton University Press, 1949.

[26] Methodological research is basically evaluative in nature, designed to measure the worthwhileness of some research technique or instrument. Reliability and validity are evaluative criteria.

[27] As described by Smith: "Most programmes will be found to have more than one objective. The first step in conducting an evaluation is thus to achieve consensus among those responsible for the programme as to the order of priority of these multiple objectives. As part of the same process, it is helpful to analyze the more general and far-reaching objectives into steps or sub-goals through which the programme seeks to achieve them. Often it may be found that achievement of specific sub-goals can be measured, while the less tangible ultimate goals (international understanding, for instance) remain inaccessible." Brewster M. Smith, "Evaluation of Exchange of Persons," *International Social Science Bulletin,* vol. 7, no. 3, UNESCO, 1955, p. 389.

long-range, short-range, broad, narrow, subsidiary, sub-objective, immediate, intermediate, and ultimate objectives." [28]

Objectives may be examined and classified according to a number of different schemes. Some of the pertinent questions to be answered are the following:

1. *What* is the content of the objective? Are we trying to change knowledge, attitudes, and/or behavior? Are we interested in affecting exposure, awareness, interest, and/or action? Answers to these questions determine what Hyman calls, "the regions within which the concepts are set." [29] Hovland and his colleagues, in evaluating the effectiveness of propaganda films, specify four different areas of interest: knowledge, beliefs, attitudes, and motivations. [30]

2. *Who* is the target of the program? Who is the program trying to change? Are we seeking to change individuals, groups, or whole communities? Are we attempting to reach the target group directly or indirectly through some related groups such as friends or relatives? Any program will have differential effects among various subgroups of the population and success or failure can best be measured according to whom one is attempting to reach.

3. *When* do we wish the change to take place? Are we seeking an immediate impact or do we wish to build toward some postponed effect? In general, we may distinguish between short-term, discrete programs of a single, one-shot nature and cyclical or repetitive programs that culminate toward some long-range goal. Some objectives require more time than others and the evaluation must keep in mind the length of time that the program has been in effect. The success of an evaluation study may disappear as the novelty and enthusiasm of a new program wear off, or there may be a sleeper effect which shows up at a later time. [31]

4. Are the objectives *unitary or multiple?* Is the program intended to produce one change or a series of continuous changes? The evaluator should include measurements of many possible effects. He must also pay careful attention to unanticipated or undesirable side-effects. Almost any social action will produce some boomerang effects.

5. *How much* effect is desired? Is the program aimed at wide-spread or concentrated results? Is any particular proportion of effectiveness necessary before the program can be considered a success? Are there any specified standards of performance that have to be met?

These five questions, among others, are highly relevant to the formulation of the objectives of an action or service program. While some of

28 *First National Conference on Evaluation in Public Health,* Ann Arbor, University of Michigan, School of Public Health, 1955, p. 21.

29 Hyman, *et al., op. cit.,* p. 9.

30 Carl Hovland, Arthur A. Lumsdaine, and Fred D. Sheffield, *op. cit.,* pp. 33–45.

31 Riecken states that, "All experience with action programs indicates that their real effects cannot be gauged without considering the long-run forces that may support, negate, or even reverse the immediate effects." Riecken, *op. cit.,* p. 22.

them may be unimportant for program operation, they are crucial in defining the criteria of effect and in designing the evaluation study. Such methodological problems as sampling, selection of controls, preparation of measuring instruments, method of field administration, and techniques of analysis are strongly affected by the kinds of answers provided to these questions.

8. TYPES AND CATEGORIES OF OBJECTIVES

Just as one may conceive of a causal sequence containing an unlimited number of antecedent-consequent relationships, one may visualize a social action program as composed of a potentially unlimited number of steps each with its own particular objective. Although these steps usually constitute a continuous series of events, for evaluation purposes they may be subdivided into a hierarchy of sub-goals each of which may be viewed as the result of the successful achievement of the preceding goal and, in turn, as a precondition to the next higher goal.

A useful distinction may be made between "objectives," "activities," and "steps" arranged in a descending order, with each of the lower steps denoting action taken to implement a higher step. According to this model, the objectives constitute an ordered series, each of which is dependent for its existence upon an objective at the next higher level, while each is in turn implemented by means of lower level objectives. This framework proposes a descending order of objectives ranging from the idealized objective as the ultimate goal down to the lowest level consisting of a subdivision of administrative tasks. Rosenstock and Getting point out that the division of labor in an organization is such that the *technique* or *methods* of work to be used at any level become the objectives of the immediately lower level. In turn, the objectives at any level provide the methods of attaining the immediately higher level. The functional relationship between any two contiguous levels, thus, is that of objective and the method for achieving that objective.[32]

This sequence may be broken down as follows: at the highest level are the ultimate objectives which constitute the basic rationale for the action program. These are then subdivided at the next lower level into a series of intermediate sub-objectives necessary for achieving the ultimate objectives. These sub-objectives, in turn, at the next lower level are divided into methods (programs, services) through which various sub-objectives may be attained. These programs or services may then be further subdivided into various immediate administrative objectives or

---

[32] Vlado A. Getting *et al.*, "Research in Evaluation in Public Health Practices," paper presented at the 92nd Annual Meeting of the American Public Health Association, New York, October 5, 1964.

actions deemed necessary to put the program into operation. Evaluation at each stage attempts to establish the validity of each method for accomplishing the objective of the next higher stage.

The idea of the interrelatedness of these various levels of evaluation is expressed by Herzog as one of movement "from the abstract to the concrete, from the whole to its parts, with the parts becoming ever more limited, and specific," characterized by a paraphrase of the old jingle:

> Big criteria have little criteria upon their
> backs to bite 'em.
> The small ones have still smaller, and so on
> *ad infinitum.*[33]

A difficult question concerns the extent to which immediate and intermediate goals can be divorced from ultimate goals as valid in themselves. MacMahon and his associates distinguish between intermediate goals as an "evaluation of technic" and limit "evaluation of accomplishment" to ultimate goals only. Surgery as a treatment for breast cancer provides an illustration. An evaluation of accomplishment would try to show whether surgical removal of the affected breast actually leads to a lengthening of life, while an evaluation of technique would be limited to the successful performance of the breast surgery itself. In an evaluation of technique, "cause and effect are not at issue." MacMahon maintains that an evaluation of technique in the absence of any evaluation of accomplishment becomes largely meaningless. "Unless it has been shown that the use of a certain technic is followed by beneficial results, what is the use of making sure that the technic is being followed?" [34]

An assumption of validity must be made whenever one moves down the scale from a higher order objective to a lower one. Hence, every lower level objective must contain all of the assumptions made for *all* of the objectives above it. Any program which is based upon a false set of major assumptions cannot be rescued by its lower level objectives, although quite sound evaluations might still be done for each of these individually as techniques or program components. There are only two ways to move up the scale of objectives in an evaluation: (1) by proving the intervening assumptions through research, i.e., changing an assumption to a fact, or (2) by assuming their validity without full research proof. When the former is achieved, success in meeting a lower level objective can be viewed as automatic progress toward a higher objective.

The scope or generalizability of findings will also be determined by

33 Elizabeth Herzog, *Some Guide Lines for Evaluative Research,* U.S. Department of Health, Education and Welfare, Children's Bureau, 1959, p. 17.

34 Brian MacMahon, Thomas F. Pugh, and George B. Hutchison, "Principles in the Evaluation of Community Health Programs," *American Journal of Public Health,* vol. 51 (July, 1961), p. 964.

the level of objective which one chooses to evaluate. The higher the level of objective, the more the number of activities that will be evaluated. Studies of high level objectives may be characterized as having higher evaluative power than those of lower level objectives. Such studies include more events and become generalizable to a greater variety of actions. For example, an immediate goal such as the readability of a pamphlet has little generalizability beyond the specific pamphlet and usually will have to be tested repeatedly for each separate piece of literature. However, the evaluation of information as an effective stimulus to a change in behavior, a higher level objective, has a greater degree of transferability to other programs. The degree of generalizability is, of course, related to the underlying assumptions at each level of evaluation with the assumptions themselves acquiring a greater degree of theoretical importance as one moves up the scale from practical to ideal objectives. In part, the greater significance of evaluative research at a higher level of objective also stems from the fact that the higher the evaluative power of a study, the larger the number of possibilities for its being proven ineffective. Effectiveness at the top of the scale generally subsumes effectiveness at lower levels.

9. CRITERIA OF SUCCESS

In addition to varying levels of objectives, evaluative research may be conducted according to different *categories* of effect. These categories provide different criteria of success or failure and help to define the type of measure to be used in judging an activity.

In general, we propose five types of criteria according to which the success or failure of a program may be evaluated; these are effort, performance, adequacy, efficiency, and process.[35] These criteria are interrelated with an evaluation of effort and performance necessarily preceding one of adequacy, efficiency, or process. Furthermore, in general, successful performance implies successful effort, although such performance may still be inadequate in terms of the total problem being attacked, or inefficient as compared to some alternative method.[36]

Effort. Evaluations of effort have as their criteria of success the quantity and quality of *activity* that takes place. This represents an assessment of input or energy expended regardless of outcome. It is intended to answer the questions, How much did you do? and How well did you

[35] Paul proposes a similar classification of three criteria—effort, effect, and process. Benjamin D. Paul, "Social Science in Public Health," *American Journal of Public Health*, vol. 46 (November, 1956), pp. 1390–1396.

[36] These categories were first presented by George James in "Evaluation and Planning of Health Programs," *Administration of Community Health Services*, International City Managers' Association, Chicago, 1961, pp. 126–218. They are revised and expanded in this presentation.

do it? Criteria for evaluating effort are based either on the capacity or resources available or the expenditure of effort itself. Effort evaluation assumes that the specific activity is a valid means of reaching higher goals. This is usually the simplest type of evaluation; it's easier to maintain administrative records than to measure results. Many of the so-called standards in public service areas represent assessments of available resources and activities.

Performance. Performance or effect criteria evaluate the *results* of effort rather than the effort itself. This measure of achievement requires a clear statement of one's objective in terms of outcome rather than input. How much is accomplished relative to the defined goal? Did the desired change occur? Were there any boomerang effects? In general, an evaluation of performance involves fewer assumptions than an evaluation of effort.

Adequacy of Performance. This criterion of success requires a measure of the degree to which effective performance is adequate to the total amount of need. For example, a program of intensive psychotherapy for a small group of mentally ill individuals may show highly effective results, but as a public health measure prove inadequate to meet the problem of mental illness in an entire community. Adequacy is obviously a relative measure depending upon how much of an impact one wishes to make upon the total problem.[37]

Efficiency. A program may show positive results but there may be better ways to attain the same results. A barometer may be used to measure the height of a building by tying it to a string and lowering it to the ground from the top of the building—but, is this the best way? Efficiency may be determined by the evaluation of alternative paths or methods in terms of costs (money, time, personnel, and public convenience). In a sense, it represents a ratio between effort and performance—outcome divided by input. Such comparative evaluations of competing approaches has both administrative and research utility.

Process. In the course of evaluating the success or failure of a program, much can be learned about how and why a program works or does not work. Some evaluators maintain that an analysis of the process whereby a program achieves the results it does is not an inherent part of evaluative research. For administrative purposes, an evaluation may

37 If a program has a high potency, but low exposure, total impact may not be great. This point was made by Bigman in evaluating the effectiveness of religious programs. "In the first place, the *number of persons* may be so small as to render the program relatively ineffective. Here we must distinguish between effectiveness and *impact.* By the latter term I mean the strength of the influence upon exposed individuals. A program or activity may have considerable impact, affecting markedly the thoughts and actions of those it touches; it will be necessarily judged ineffective if it is so designed that this impact is confined to a small fraction of the group it is intended to reach and influence." Stanley K. Bigman, "Evaluating the Effectiveness of Religious Programs," *Review of Religious Research,* vol. 2 (Winter, 1961), p. 113.

limit data collection and analysis to determining simply whether or not a program is successful without examining the why's and wherefore's of this success or failure. However, unless such an analysis is incorporated in the evaluative research design, it is difficult to determine the degree to which success was actually due to the program itself. Furthermore, different parts of the program will be successful to different degrees with different people, and an analysis of process can help to improve even a successful program.[38]

An analysis of process is particularly useful when a program is *not* working as expected. Locating the specific causes of failure may permit one to modify the program rather than discard it as a total failure. Interpretation of the reasons for success or failure can be made only from an analysis of process. This analysis may be made according to four main kinds of specification dealing with (1) the attributes of the program itself, (2) the population exposed to the program, (3) the situational context within which the program takes place, and (4) the different kinds of effects produced by the program. These elaborations of how, why, and among whom different aspects of a program are effective is similar to any analysis of intervening variables in non-evaluative research. These are the conditional variables which modify the relationship between the independent variable (the program) and the dependent variable (the effects).

10. RELIABILITY AND VALIDITY OF CRITERIA

Problems in determining the reliability and validity of criteria measurements are similar for evaluative and non-evaluative research. Both are concerned with the degree of consistency or dependability of a measure (reliability) and the "bias" or meaning of a measure (validity). Since reliability is usually determined by a comparison of measures repeated at two points in time, and since the basic objective of evaluative research is to measure change over time, it is easy to see that reliability constitutes a special problem for evaluative research. How does one tell whether an observed change is due to unreliability or to actual change? The most common way of meeting this problem is to determine reliability on the basis of simultaneous measures by different observers, or by subdividing the test or measure into equivalent parts (split-halves).

[38] Kendall makes this point quite clearly. "Even though one may feel some satisfaction in identifying the effects of an experimental program, thus being able to judge the extent of its success or failure, an evaluation study is more complete if one can at the same time specify what accounts for program effectiveness. One may be interested in this from a theoretical point of view, perhaps in order to classify the kinds of factors associated with attitude change. But the specification of effective factors also has practical implications. To strengthen an experimental educational program, or to duplicate it in another setting, it is essential to know just what features of the program account for its effectiveness, and with what type of student it is most likely to succeed." Kendall, *op. cit.*, pp. 356–357.

It is validity, however, which presents the most significant methodological problem for evaluative measurement. Herzog maintains that, "The problem of validity invades every aspect and every detail of the evaluative process, especially the selection, definition, and application of criteria." [39] She suggests three aspects of validity of special importance to evaluative research: "(1) Is the criterion selected a valid criterion of what is to be measured? (2) Is the indicator selected a valid reflector of the criterion? and (3) Are the various valid segments of the study combined in such a way as to preserve their individual validity and achieve validity of the whole?" [40]

Since validity itself is an evaluative criterion, it can only be determined in relation to some objective. Validity refers to the extent to which a criterion measures what it is supposed to measure: until one has a statement of purpose, one cannot determine validity. In evaluative research, the validity of any measure of effect, therefore, will refer largely to the ability of that measure to determine the degree to which the desired effect is present or absent. This may be broken down into two aspects: (1) How valid is the chosen criterion as a measure of the desired effect? (external validity) and (2) How valid are the particular measures made of the chosen criterion? (internal validity). Brogden and Taylor discern four sources of criterion invalidity in terms of "any variable, except errors of measurement and sampling error, providing a deviation of obtained criterion scores from a hypothetical 'true' criterion score." [41] These four sources are:

1. Criterion deficiency—omission of pertinent elements from the criterion.
2. Criterion contamination—introducing extraneous elements into the criterion.
3. Criterion scale-unit bias—inequality of scale units in the criterion.
4. Criterion distortion—improper weighting in combining criterion elements.

These sources of error are similar to those found in the construction of any measuring device in non-evaluative research. They are particularly significant for evaluative research because these criteria tend to represent the operational goals of the action or service program. Thus they have both operational and construct validity at one and the same time.

11. THE SPECIFICATION AND CONTROL OF PROGRAM CONTENT

Given a set of objectives, the next problem is to develop a program designed to meet these objectives. This program constitutes the stimulus or independent variable which is to be evaluated in terms of the criteria specified above. Too often in evaluative research one begins with an on-

[39] Herzog, *op. cit.*, p. 41.
[40] *Ibid.*, p. 44.
[41] H. I. Brogden, and E. K. Taylor, "The Theory and Classification of Criterion," *Educational and Psychological Measurement,* vol. 10 (Summer, 1950), pp. 159–186.

going, established program whose objectives have been lost or forgotten and the task is formulated in terms of evaluating the effects of the program, whatever they may be. A much more logical procedure would be to first determine what it is one wishes to achieve and then to develop and evaluate a program designed to achieve the desired objectives. For this reason, it is a well known fact among program evaluators that it is much more difficult to evaluate a firmly entrenched, traditional program or approach than a new, developmental program. The former are likely to have developed a rationale and support for their continuation that transcends their original purpose while the latter often need to seek the support of evaluative research to gain any acceptance at all.[42]

One of the major decisions to be made in planning an evaluation study is whether one is interested in evaluating a general concept or approach to social change or a program of specific operating practices. In the case of concept evaluation, the activities evaluated become only operational indices of the concept and one faces the problem of the construct validity of these activities. It may well be that the concept is basically sound, but that it has not been successfully translated into the proper activities. In the case of program evaluation, the activities are likely to have a justification of their own and therefore must stand or fall on their own. Concept evaluation is more likely to be aimed at ultimate objectives and to utilize criteria of achievement while program evaluation will, to a much greater extent, be directed toward immediate objectives and employ criteria of effort.

Whether one deals with concept or program evaluation, it is essential that the specific operations being evaluated be defined as clearly as possible. This is necessary for both research and administrative purposes. From the research point of view, the experimental model of evaluation requires that the stimulus or independent variable be as isolated and controlled as conditions permit. This is necessary if one is to be able to manipulate the administration of the program activities to the experimental group and to withhold them from the control group. Obviously, unless one knows specifically what the program activities are, one cannot manipulate or control them.

From an administrative point of view such knowledge is essential not only in order to put the program into effect but, even more important, to know how to duplicate or extend the program. This is particularly the case in regard to demonstration programs. Unless one knows what the demonstration program consists of, what is being demonstrated? If the demonstration program is to serve as a prototype for similar programs or approaches, then the evaluation must specify the essential ideas or com-

---

[42] We cannot in this chapter go into the many administrative considerations that lead to the support of or opposition to evaluative research or to the various uses and abuses made of evaluation studies. A forthcoming book by the author, *Evaluative Research: Principles and Practices in Public Service and Social Action Programs*, New York: Russell Sage Foundation, in press, will deal with some of these problems.

ponents of that program. If the program or activity is to be carried out under different circumstances, i.e., in a different location or with different populations than the study group, then conceptual equivalence is more significant than operational equivalence.

Given the inevitable social and cultural differences between communities and sub-groups of the population, it is probably more profitable to evaluate an approach than a specific set of operations. It is doubtful that the same activities will have the same meaning for different cultural groups or be responded to in the same way. However, the same conceptual approach could be carried out among different groups by translating it into the appropriate and acceptable activities for each group. To some extent, this problem has its parallel in non-evaluative research in regard to concept versus data equivalence especially for cross-cultural research.[43]

An essential aspect of any program is *how* it is organized and carried out as well as *what* it consists of. As Hyman and his colleagues point out, "Our conclusions are sounder and our understanding is greater if we can distinguish whether it is the formal program or the staff that is responsible for the outcome." [44] Evaluative studies of educational programs have shown that how a program is administered is as important as what the program encompasses.[45] For evaluative purposes, the way an activity is organized and conducted becomes an inherent aspect of the program itself. To some extent this variable is also subject to experimental evaluation in terms of alternative approaches and differing methods for conducting the same program.

12. THE SELECTION OF EXPERIMENTAL AND CONTROL GROUPS

The definition of the characteristics of the population universe from which one wishes to select groups for evaluation purposes and the procedures for selecting representative samples of these groups present similar problems for evaluative and non-evaluative research. In both cases, the crucial question is, What is the population about which I wish to generalize? In evaluative research, the target population is usually defined in terms of that group in the total population that one wishes to reach with the proposed social action program. Thus, the population universe is defined as comprising those individuals whom one wishes to change, or, in the case of service programs, those individuals who constitute the present or potential clients for the services being rendered.

Once having defined the target population, the crucial problem be-

[43] Edward A. Suchman, "The Comparative Method in Social Research," *Rural Sociology*, vol. 29 (June, 1964), pp. 123–137.

[44] Hyman, *et al., op. cit.*, p. 75.

[45] Philip E. Jacob, *Changing Values in College*, New York, Harper & Row, 1957.

comes one of exposing a representative sample of that population to one's program while keeping another representative sample from being exposed. In the laboratory, this problem is easily met by simple, random allocation of subjects to either the experimental or the control group. However, such random assignment is rarely possible in social action or service programs. Both administrative and ethical reasons prohibit one from dispensing services to one group (whether they wish them or not), and deliberately withholding these services from another group (whether they need them or not). As Blenkner points out, "No casework agency is so dedicated to science as to permit it to make a random sort of its applicants, offering to help one half, while merely following up the other half to see what happens to them." [46] Furthermore, there is the additional problem of the self-selection of people who seek help and the virtual impossibility of forcing people to accept help they do not want. Hyman and his colleagues maintain that, "The evaluator rarely has control over the flow of subjects into a program. Selection is governed either by the subject himself when he is favorably disposed to a program, or by the agency which recruits in terms of the wish to have particular subjects and programs joined." [47]

There can be no question that this sampling and random assignment problem is perhaps the most difficult one in evaluative research. Some would go so far as to maintain that this *sine qua non* of the experimental method precludes its use in evaluative research. To a large extent this is an unavoidable truth and evaluative research will always contain this type of sampling bias. Borgatta discusses why service agencies resist the use of randomly assigned control groups and challenges their argument that withholding treatment deprives clients of services to which they are entitled.[48] Certainly in medical research various treatments and drugs have been withheld until proven effective by rigorous experimental field trials.

While it is doubtful that social scientists ever will, or should, be accorded the same privileges for social experimentation, there are several design elements that can serve to lessen the penalty. The use of alternative social action or service programs given to a series of experimental groups allocated at random denies service to no one and, at the same time, it permits an evaluation of different approaches or programs. Similarly, since services cannot be given to everyone simultaneously, it may be possible to divide a waiting list of prospective subjects at random into those who receive treatment earlier or later. Finally, as in the case of all other non-evaluative social research techniques, approximations to the experimental model may be made either by matching exposed and non-

46 M. Blenkner, "Obstacles to Evaluative Research in Casework," *Social Casework*, vol. 31 (1950), p. 98.

47 Hyman, *et al., op. cit.,* p. 24.

48 Edgar F. Borgatta, "Research: Pure and Applied," *Group Psychotherapy*, vol. 8 (1955), pp. 263–277.

exposed individuals or groups according to personal or group characteristics, or by means of the statistical analysis of covariance. The rigorous use of these approximations has much to offer the field of evaluative research.

13. SUMMARY AND CONCLUSIONS

Evaluative research is an essential and expanding area of social research. As social scientists become increasingly involved in social action programs, not as agents of change but as research workers interested in studying the process of change, they will turn more and more to evaluative research models to study the consequences of planned social action. Such studies will be aimed as much at understanding the factors influencing social change as at measuring the administrative effectiveness of an operational program.

We stress the potential theoretical importance of evaluative research not only because such an emphasis is necessary if serious scholars are to enter the field, but also because it is our conviction that evaluative research aimed at testing principles of social action will have greater utility in the long run than evaluation limited to specific program operations. While the reciprocal relationship between theory and empirical research is widely accepted, this is not true for theory and evaluative research. And yet evaluative research can be a major source of empirical data bearing upon the process of social change. Williams recognizes this when he states, "It is not only that the attempts to apply the results of sociological research often force revision of our hypotheses and frames of reference; it is also true that the experience of practitioners, even when not utilizing research, can contribute very directly and importantly to our research orientation." [49]

[49] Robin M. Williams, "Application of Research to Practice in Intergroup Relations," *American Sociological Review*, vol. 18 (February, 1953), p. 80. As an illustration, note the following analysis from an evaluation of a mass X-ray survey. "The general theory, which has much evidence to support it, is that a spreading net of people mobilized through natural groups is at once more likely if pressed to reach lower in the social structure than could be done from the outside directly, and to reach them in the more acceptable form of verbal communication from friends and with the added weight of social pressure. All of this depends on there being a complete network of relationships, encompassing almost everyone and with unbroken links between the obvious leaders who can be approached by a small group of project workers and the vast hard-to-reach lower strata, and on the ability of the project people to awaken interest which can be communicated. The interest to be communicated need not be directly related to the project, that is, in this case it need not be health in general or tuberculosis in particular, but that common interest which defined community. The assumption of community, the assumption of direct health interest, and the assumption that the people are homogeneous, are all dangerous if untrue and will be explored in the report." Gerald Gurin and Charles A. Metzner, *Target TB Bronx: An Evaluation of a Mass Tuberculosis X-Ray Survey Conducted by the New York City Department of Health*, Ann Arbor, University of Michigan, School of Public Health, Bureau of Public Health Economics, Research Series No. 7 (October, 1957), p. 6.

To some extent evaluative research may offer a bridge between pure and applied research. Evaluation may be viewed as a field test of the validity of cause-effect hypotheses in basic science whether these be in the field of biology (i.e., medicine) or sociology (i.e., social work). Action programs in any professional field should be based upon the best available scientific knowledge and theory of that field. As such, evaluations of the success or failure of these programs are intimately tied into the proof or disproof of such knowledge. Since such a knowledge base is the foundation of any action program, the evaluative research worker who approaches his task in the spirit of testing some theoretical proposition rather than a set of administrative practices will, in the long run, make the most significant contribution to program development.[50]

To make this contribution, however, evaluative research must accept the responsibility of adhering as closely as possible to the basic requirements of the scientific method. Progress in this direction will depend largely upon the extent to which the evaluator attempts to specify the objectives of an action program including their underlying assumptions, develops reliable and valid criteria specifically related to these objectives, and then sets up an experimental situation consisting of equivalent exposed and non-exposed groups to determine the extent to which these objectives and any negative side effects are achieved.

To conclude, we summarize the range of variation in evaluative research by defining evaluation as the determination (whether based on opinions, records, subjective or objective data, etc.) of the results (whether desirable or undesirable, transient or permanent, immediate or delayed, etc.) attained by some activity (whether an approach or an operational program, a drug or a therapy, an on-going or one-shot attack, etc.) designed to accomplish some valued goal or objective (whether ultimate, intermediate, or immediate, effort or performance, long or short range, etc.). This definition contains four key dimensions: (1) process—the determination; (2) criteria—the results; (3) stimulus—the activity; and (4) value—the objective. The scientific method with its accompanying research techniques then provides the most promising means for determining the relationship of the stimulus to the objective in terms of measurable criteria.[51]

SELECTED REFERENCES

Borgatta, Edgar F., "Research Problems in Evaluation of Health Service Demonstrations," *The Milbank Memorial Fund Quarterly,* vol. 44, part 2 (October, 1966), pp. 182–201.

[50] Alvin W. Gouldner, "Theoretical Requirements of the Applied Social Sciences," *American Sociological Review,* vol. 22 (February, 1957), pp. 92–102.
[51] Edward A. Suchman, "A Model for Research and Evaluation on Rehabilitation," in Marvin Sussman (ed.), *Sociology and Rehabilitation,* Vocational Rehabilitation Administration, 1966, pp. 52–70.

Evaluation in Mental Health, U.S. Department of Health, Education and Welfare, Public Health Service Publication No. 413, Washington, D.C.: Government Printing Office, 1955.

Greenberg, Bernard G., and Berwyn F. Mattison, "The Whys and Wherefores of Program Evaluation," *Canadian Journal of Public Health,* vol. 46 (July, 1955), pp. 293–299.

Gruenberg, Ernest, ed., "Evaluating the Effectiveness of Mental Health Services," *Milbank Memorial Fund Quarterly,* vol. 44, part 2 (January, 1966).

Herzog, Elizabeth, *Some Guide Lines for Evaluative Research,* Washington, D.C.: U.S. Department of Health, Education and Welfare, Children's Bureau, 1959.

Hyman, Herbert, *et al., Applications of Methods of Evaluation: A Study of the Encampment for Leadership,* Berkeley: University of California Press, 1961.

Meyer, Henry J., and Edgar F. Borgatta, "An Experiment in Mental Patient Rehabilitation," New York: Russell Sage Foundation, 1959.

Planning Evaluations of Mental Health Programs, New York: Milbank Memorial Fund, 1958.

Riecken, Henry W., *The Volunteer Work Camp: A Psychological Evaluation,* Reading, Mass.: Addison-Wesley, 1952.

Suchman, Edward A., *Evaluative Research: Principles and Practice in Public Service and Social Action Programs,* New York: Russell Sage Foundation, in press.

15
Roy G. Francis

ADMINISTRATION OF
SOCIAL SCIENCE RESEARCH

1. THE PROBLEM OF BIGNESS

In years past the scientist was largely a "loner"—an isolated figure. The public's image of someone puttering around in solitary research was usually correct. The professor emeritus now can recall with fond memory the "bit of string and chewing gum" approach to physical research; yet no newly hooded doctor would imagine entering a lab with equipment involving less than two hundred thousand dollars.

Social scientists, too, are changing. Hardly 25 years ago university presidents imagined that social scientists needed merely a pencil, a pad of paper, and a reasonable amount of quiet for their research. Professors seemed to cooperate in maintaining this image: for a paltry sum, hardly sufficient to pay for supplies of paper and mimeograph materials, the professor would use students as interviewers (as a part of a class project) and eke out some information on a captive (i.e., student) audience. Statistical manipulation remained naive and theory was speculative more than rigorous.

As social scientists grew in sophistication so did their research designs. As the public became increasingly aware of the value of social knowledge, the scope of research broadened. Today, there are few worthwhile studies done by a single investigator with minimal support. One reason for this, and why it will be increasingly unlikely for the researcher without foundation support to do much research, is the emergence of the use of computers in sociological research. The consequence is that our research designs can now be as sophisticated as our imagination will permit. This most likely will result in our gathering rather enormous amounts of complicated data—a most expensive sort of research.

The presence of complicated data implies a research staff. Hence, the modern researcher is more likely to be an administrator in addition to being a scientist. He will employ statisticians who are far more rigorously trained than himself. He will employ other specialists to assist in questionnaire construction. He will employ still others to help design the sample; to recruit and train interviewers; to supervise the gathering, coding, and analysis of data; and so on.

In addition to specifying strategies of research, the scientist will have to contend with the logistics of research. He will incorporate the manipulation of time and money in his design: which dollar in-put will result in the most efficient use of his research staff? If the scientist heads a research organization, he must consider the on-going overhead in the calculation of research expense. Normally, this will imply continuous research operations, so as to minimize the per-unit cost of maintaining an organization.

The implication of these points are numerous. For one thing, we need to distinguish between methodology as instructions to the scientist, and the instructions a scientist gives his employees. The scientist must, for example, understand the theory of interviewing; the interviewer must be given a set of specifications to enable him to meet all predictable contingencies on the job. But one ought to derive his philosophy of science from statements to the scientist, not to the employee.

2. THE RESEARCH ENTERPRISE AND THE PUBLIC

The social sciences are social, not only by virtue of their subject matter, but also in their research strategy. Sociologists sample people, whether as random things in a population of individuals or as members of some form of organization. They interview people; send questionnaires to people; ask people for permission to study a school, hospital, business unit or whatever.

Sometimes the administrator is in charge of a project, which has a fixed beginning and end in time. The project is normally involved in a single research activity in a finite social space. Some administrators have acted indifferently to the public's reaction to their research behavior: they are oblivious to any sense of public responsibility. It is as though bad public relations may affect someone else's research, but not their own. Attitudes of this kind are quite unfortunate; for even in research, it often turns out that it's a small world.

An example of this would be the following. In a research regarding anxiety, a sociologist secured the support of a school administrator. Through this, he had access both to students and their records. When parental concern was shown, the researcher acted as though the parents had no right to become involved. As soon as the data were obtained he left and neither aided the administrator in encountering the parents in the community nor shared his findings with school personnel. Subsequent requests to do research were refused, of course, even though different scientists were making the requests.

In sharp contrast to this was the sociologist who, in making contact with school administration for permission to do a study, sought assistance by the social studies teachers. He shared with them the major point of his study and secured their criticism of the research instruments. It turned out that he had used a vocabulary which, in parts, was inappropriate for the particular area in which he was studying. The social studies teachers generally enabled him to avoid entanglements which were not critical to his research. *After* the data had been collected, the sociologist then talked to the social studies classes about sociological research, using the study which had involved some of those students as his example. In pointing out the assistance he received from the social studies teachers, their status was elevated in the eyes of the students. Quite naturally, the teachers welcomed this experience and subsequent researchers were welcomed.

This brief account illustrates a skillful use of sociological variables. The manipulation of self and public esteem is consonant with general theory; so is the need to secure a vocabulary to which the subjects can properly respond. But, from the point of view of administration, the "further research" that always seems to be necessary was made feasible. Unless the sociologist maintains a social situation in which it is possible for his research to take place, no one else is likely to do it for him.

The administrator of a research institute *cannot* avoid the problem of social responsibility. The project is a temporary thing; its administrator's concern for good public relations need stem only from his concern for professional colleagues who will follow. Indeed, in a large, metropolitan area of two or three million people, a sample of 1,500 will be quite invisible. But the administrator of an institute faces a continuous public, and even if one bit of research may seem invisible, his total public contact is not. In order that his administration may succeed, the director of an institute must develop strong relations with the public of which he is a part.

In a democratic society, sociological research depends upon a willing public. It may be that is true in any situation: a totalitarian situation may require people to participate in a research enterprise, but that does not imply acquisition of trustworthy data. It can be fairly said that for an ongoing sociological research agency to succeed, it must have the support of its community area. Put another way, unless the public which is used in the research activities has faith in the research agency, it simply cannot succeed. The research director must, then, utilize sociological theory in placing his agency in its setting. He must be aware of the power structure of the community, the general pattern of values which must be taken into account if his venture is to succeed. This means that he must be politically alert—aware of sources and uses of power.

Social research is variously visible. Two factors seem to be more significant than others in determining the visibility of the research. One is the character of the subject matter and its likelihood of resulting in conversation. Topics that do not arouse emotions and senses of identity are less likely to be visible than those which do involve emotionally tinged subjects. This is not to say that strategies to minimize public response to emotionally toned topics do not exist. They do, indeed. But a topic of toilet training is likely to cause more comment than one of choice of color of egg shells. The second factor is the size of the community. In a small community, a small sample can be quite visible. This is especially true if the small community is a rural one not used to being visited by sociological interviewers. A large community, on the other hand, can tolerate a much larger sample and still appear relatively invisible. This is because in the small community, every member of the population is likely to know the other which is not true in a large urban area. It would be a relatively rare occurrence if three or four individuals in a sample of 1,000 in a metropolitan area knew each other.

However, poorly managed research in a large urban area can suddenly become quite visible. This is especially true if the subject matter and/or the manner of research offends someone on or near the center of power. Thus, a research project on parent-child relations in a "pocket of poverty" may not become visible even if resented by the parents, as their access to power is limited. But let the daughter of a member of a suburban school board happen to be in a sample and the roof may fall in.

One strategy which has proven to be quite effective in minimizing the consequences of dealing with emotionally toned topics is quite simple to use. It is, essentially, this: not only use the sex of the interviewer to advantage, but provide an opportunity for catharsis at the end of the session. Ask the subject if there were objectional parts to the study, and how they could be avoided. This device tends to make the interviewer be the target of any hostility, but tends also to weaken any necessity to vent that hostility in public. Hence, there is less danger of a contamination of the population by a display of anger which could stop the entire project.

The use of the sex of the interviewer requires a sophisticated sense of social psychology. Recall that the interview is a social situation and that people are interacting, if only by chance (the implication of random sampling). A general rule of good interviewing is, "never force the subject to lie." That is to say, avoid presenting any threat to ego that you cannot control. Thus, in studies of homosexuality, males interviewing males or females interviewing females is fraught with tensions. Males interviewing females, and the converse, appears to be less threatening. The good administrator selects his research team accordingly.

The research institute, unlike the individual project, can become a victim of accumulated visibility. The longer the agency exists, the more problems it will be studying, and the more likely it is to threaten at least some highly visible people. Moreover, since sociology has proved its worth, an increasing number of agencies seek to have research done. Typically, most of them are directed towards social problems and it happens that social problems are, or tend to be, ecologically restricted. The fact that there is a correlation between ecological area and manifest social problems implies a concentration of research activity in certain areas. It is possible for an area to become saturated. When repetitive work occurs, not only is there a mounting irritation of the public which is convinced that they had been interviewed about the same topic just a few weeks ago, but the subjects learn how to manipulate the interview situation. They can become "research-wise" and can feed the interviewer what the subject thinks is most pleasing.

Moreover, not all who present themselves as researchers are, in fact, researchers. The presentation of self as interviewer for a research project has become a gimmick for sales people, for perverts, and for those who may want to make a book on a neighborhood (in the sense of a systematic casing of an area). Some sales people work in two stages: first an apparent interview, and then a selective drive on those most likely to respond. In any event, the researcher, if he is to achieve the faith of the public and keep it, must assist the public in protecting itself against the charlatan.

Every effort must be made to let responsible public agencies know about research, at least where the nature of the research allows it. As much information as possible, without jeopardizing the purpose of the study, should be revealed. Agencies such as a better business bureau, a chamber of commerce, and others depending upon the problem (the Labor Temple, a council of churches, and the like), should be informed of the project, its schedule for interviewing, etc., so that the public can turn to a trustworthy place to have questions answered. If the research project or institute is connected with a college or university, some office should always be informed so that an unambiguous response can be made to anyone desiring information.

3. THE DOLLAR AS THE UNIT OF MEASUREMENT

A major difficulty of any administrator is to know the cost of his several operations. This is particularly true when he seeks to submit a budget to accompany a request for funds. Whatever his emotional commitment to securing knowledge may be, in respect to budgeting he must take a role which permits him to regard facts or information as things. In some sense, he must identify a unit of information and associate with that some estimation of cost.

If the interview constitutes the unit, his problem is relatively simple. He identifies a cost per interview and proceeds directly to identify the total cost of securing his information given a stated size of sample. This is made possible if he can identify a cost per interview. If he proceeds on the basis of paying his interviewers by the completed schedule, that is, on a piece-rate system, his problem is simple. However, if he has a system of partial payment for incomplete schedules, his problem is a bit difficult. In that case he must estimate, in some sense, the probability that a given schedule will be completed. Then the expected value would be to multiply the probability of each kind of schedule by its proper cost and add. Of course, he would have to determine then the likely number of incomplete schedules that will accompany his achieving the stipulated size of sample. The task gets more complicated as the degrees of completion associated with different amounts of payment increases.

At some point, however, the administrator will decide that the fundamental unit is not a completed interview, but some bit of information. He will need to know how many bits of information he can hope to secure and at what relative price. The price, in part, depends upon the probability of the bit being correctly reported. The probability depends on such matters as subject matter, length of the interview schedule or questionnaire, and position. On long schedules, those appearing towards the end tend to have the lower probabilities of completion.

Cost analysis is refined when one inserts the cost of sample error into the problem. Of course, this makes computation a bit awkward, but with modern computers that difficulty is readily solved. Moreover, since sampling error estimations flow from existing data, it is clear that precise cost analysis requires the administrator to have sufficient previous experience (or can use reports by others) which will enable him to "plug in" reasonable estimations of error in his formulas.

There are a number of treatments of cost problems, some of them relating to estimations of desired sample size. One may, for example, use the argument of Ackoff,[1] or the one found in Deming.[2] Deming introduces his initial argument on allocation of sample cost with the problem of multi-stage sampling. He observes that large population areas would entail considerable cost if one attempted to make a roster of all inhabitants from which to take a random sample. Usually no study can afford such an expenditure. The typical solution is to divide up the area into segments and select samples of these segments. Within the chosen segments, one chooses his units for inquiry in a two-stage design. Obviously, one could continue to segmentalize further. But it is also obvious that the estimation of variance must take into account the various stages involved in the sampling procedure.

Deming argues, if any area is so great as to require a salaried supervisor, the overhead cost to the study has changed. He points out, however,

[1] Russell L. Ackoff, *The Design of Social Research,* Chicago, University of Chicago Press, 1953, Appendix IV.
[2] William Edwards Deming, *Some Theory of Sampling,* New York, Wiley, 1950, p. 153.

that the formulas needed for the estimation of variance may, with some modification, be used to allocate costs. His formulas enable one to choose the best sample size for the smallest segment used; from this the minimum cost of the study can be determined. With m primary units to be used in the design, he observes:

> If this calculated minimum cost is larger than permissible it will be necessary to take a smaller value of m and to accept a greater variance in X, or else to abandon the survey, unless some other way can be found to reduce costs.[3]

Some of the other ways to reduce costs would be to reduce overhead by less spacious quarters, fewer units of secretarial help, or reduced pay for various segments of the study. The latter is often resisted by those in the agency, and it is difficult to recruit the kind of talent needed with low pay. Should the administrator of an institute, or a person considering a formal research proposal find himself technically unable to make the proper estimations, he should know enough to go to a skilled statistician for this information. Indeed, this is one reason why research staffs normally contain a statistician and why projects at least allow for statistical consultation beyond the ability of the research team itself.

In any event, the planner of research sometimes must face alternative research strategies. He knows that his research instrument cannot be increased in length without limit. He knows, at least intuitively, that the instrument must be kept within reasonable limits. If he is faced with a complex research design, he may need to know the relative cost of securing a set of data by one instrument as over against the other. It is not sufficient merely to compare relative costs. It may turn out that a test which generates a high degree of statistical precision does so at extremely high cost, so high that he cannot afford that test. This would make sense, particularly if this particular test were of secondary importance to the research effort. Clearly, if precision is costly, it should be related to the significance of the information for the research. To gather completely precise data which are irrelevant to the research enterprise is no bargain.

Thus, the good research designer weighs the relative contributions of the several aspects of his project. Within limits, to be discussed more fully in a moment, the administrative unit which can be manipulated is money. He may decide to use his money by increasing the size of sample or by increasing the length of his instrument. He may employ a larger number of interviewers over a shorter period of time under different conditions than others. In any event, by translating his several operations into the common unit of money, he can make a number of realistic comparisons. Since his funds are at least relatively finite, this basis for decisions ought not be taken lightly. Textbooks may be written as though the cost of the study is irrelevant to problems of design. The sound administrator knows better. The brilliant one makes his conversions of information and ac-

[3] *Ibid.*

curacy to monetary units and makes a decision in terms of implications to his budget as well as to his theory.

4. THE PROBLEM OF TIME

Scientific research is a process. As such, it takes time. Logic recognizes the truth values of "true" (acceptable) and "false" (not acceptable)—or, perhaps, rejectable and not rejectable. But the scientist as a man of action entertains a third: doubt. The research activity is designed to remove that doubt in one direction or another. Logical relations are instantaneous. The removal of doubt is not; it takes time.

The time utilized in sociological research involves social relations. These relations include the interviewer and the respondent. They also include the interviewer(s) (and the relations existing between them), the project director, and the rest of the staff. In turn, the relations between the interviewers can involve competition, jealousy, and other characteristics of human behavior.

But the time spent in research may well involve forces acting upon the data itself. In a longitudinal study that stretches over one or two generations the passage of historical change can indeed be problematic. In shorter time spans the significance of social change to the study may be inconsequential. Consider a study regarding attitudes towards civil rights demonstrations. Suppose that the study had begun its interviews before the Rev. Reeb was assaulted in Selma, Alabama. It is virtually certain that the character of the response would have changed dramatically as a result of that event. When the President's message to Congress was aired over all networks on TV and radio, the attitudes being studied again were likely to be undergoing change.

Anytime the research project is involved in a problem that is in any way topical, the universe itself is likely to be changing. The study design for dynamic universes is not well known; indeed, the problems in sampling have not really been solved at all. Our sampling strategies are essentially geared to static universes. At best we assume we are sampling a fixed system before an event and another fixed system after the event.

Clearly, if the dynamics of the situation are undergoing rapid modification, the time spent in gathering data can make a difference. There are many good justifications for reducing that time to a minimum. There are at least two ways in which it can apparently be done. One is to reduce the size of the instrument (shorten the number of bits of information) so as to enable the interviewer to complete a large number of interviews in a fixed period of time than he otherwise would. The other is to increase the staff of interviewers. We are presuming, of course, that we are operating out of maximum efficiency in both cases. That is, for example, to arrange the interviews which have been determined by a random process such that there is a minimal amount of time spent between each attempt at interviewing. Normally, this would enable one interviewer to work in a restricted geographic space. It may be that some danger exists if it turns out that some ecological unit integral in the research package is covered completely by a single interviewer. In such a case one would not be certain that it was the area rather than the interviewer which accounts for any observed difference. Aside from such considerations, the normal practice is to minimize the travel distance between each selected interview for the interviewing staff taken as a whole. Shortening the time period by increasing the staff is not as simple a solution as it may appear. First, it requires a potential staff to be available. Second, it increases the amount of time necessary to train the interviewing staff. Third, it increases the cost of administration.

Good research administration routinely involves a "follow-up" or a "check-up" on reported interviews. It is vital that each respondent be identified sufficiently to enable the administrator to re-interview him to establish the fact of an interview having taken place. One of the great weaknesses of an uncontrolled quota sample is that the interviewer may have faked his entries and no one could possibly determine it. Sound administration involves taking a random sample of each interviewer's returns and determining whether or not the interview took place.

The increased staff implies, of course, greater costs in this type of administration. Moreover, it is likely that the probability of obtaining false results is a linear function of size of staff. That is to say, the larger the staff the more likely one will encounter this. Suppose that as an administrator you determine that at least one interviewer did not complete all of the material he turned in to you. What do you do?

It will be necessary to determine how much contamination has occurred. One way to attempt that would be to call each of the respondents to find out to what extent he grossly cheated on his returns. Even if you are able to show that only one or two reported interviews never took place, you could not be sure that on those that did all items were honestly reported. Some of the respondents would probably accept an explanation of why they were being interviewed again; but some would not. The replacement of those who refuse to be interviewed a second time often presents a difficult problem.

Interviewers, like anyone else in a social organization, can get involved with each other. This is particularly true if one has a large staff. A small staff can be selected on high criteria, but a large staff of interviewers tends to consist of people of unequal training. Hence, one may have graduate students, college graduates, and some high school graduates on the same staff. One obvious problem is that of pay. Another is the boredom that bright people experience when a novel experience wears off.

Though the administration of a large staff involves careful logistical work and may breed headaches, it is often the sounder path to follow.

When time is of essence, a small staff is improper. The decision as to the immediacy of the time factor is a theoretical question more than a technical one. Hence, a cost analysis is not the sole criterion.

Time is involved in yet another way. Research takes more time to complete than is ordinarily imagined. It may take years between the date one was first inspired to do a bit of research to any published report. When some non-scientific agent or agency is sponsoring or otherwise involved in the research, there may be a sense of impatience at the time taken. Often attempts are made to hurry various aspects of the research program. This usually results in a wastage of time.

One consequence of this drain on time has been the emergence of the research report published under the auspices of the sponsoring agency. Sometimes this involves an item in a project budget to cover cost of publishing. While such procedure hastens the day when the research findings are disclosed, it comes at a price. Journal publication is "refereed." That means that people other than the author pass judgment on its worth. Critical evaluation is made available.

Of course, journals may be involved in a bit of scientific in-fighting. Editors are not above personal preferences. It is conceivable that an unpopular conclusion may find it difficult to get into an accepted journal, especially if the author is relatively unknown. However, the journal's use of referees is still the best filter the scientific community has developed. It screens out many poorly written articles of poorly conceived studies. There are those who feel that if the journal fails in any way it is in permitting the publication of unnecessary materials.

Book publishers, in addition to any concern over merit, are often concerned with sales. Of course, if a study is an especially good one, the prestige value may offset any lack of sales. Unfortunately, the judges for book publishers are often those who edit journals; or, at least, are subject to the same prejudices and forces. Prestige may adhere more to a name than to a work.

Yet the general practice of turning out quantities of unjudged writing simply to show results from a study is hardly consonant with scientific values. However, as long as we continue to give honor to scholars in terms of the number of projects, or their total gross budget, we will have a continued growth of non-refereed publications. The administrator who has hastened the publication of his institute's work may thereby satisfy his sponsors. But he may not necessarily have shortened the time needed to get those findings into the world of science.

5. DEFINING THE STAFF

Modern science is taking on many characteristics of bureaucracy. There is a high division of labor, and a number of staff people are required for an efficient research operation who have nothing directly to do with creative research. The first task of an agency creating a research institute is to imagine a structural division of labor.

Obviously, there will be a director. Yet what his duties shall be are not obvious. To a considerable extent, of course, it depends upon the character of the research enterprise. If it is a part of a college or university, the director will be responsible to a committee of some sort. If the enterprise is multidisciplinary, the committee will consist of faculty members from the variously interested departments. If the research organization is to be a part of some public agency, its board will be chosen to represent relevant aspects of the public. A big difference is this: in the university or college setting, the board or committee members will be knowledgeable. In the public setting that is probably not so.

The director will require secretarial help. Usually, one or two secretaries will be sufficient for the kind of unit most students will become identified with. The college organization has the advantage of having so many special skills from the faculty to draw on: content specialists, methodological experts, and the like, who are readily available. Yet even there a formal way of making them part of the enterprise is needed: departments need to have their teaching time taken care of, and a person who devotes some time to the research structure must be relieved of time from other duties.

In any case, the research unit will need some group to decide on the worthwhile character of the research. This will flow in two directions. If the agency is funded, a decision is needed as to where the available time and funds will be directed. If the agency is simply a "holding agency," serving mostly as a device to obtain and administer funds, the decision must be made: which sort of project will the agency sponsor or assist in getting funds?

While the academic enterprise has a knowledgeable board to assist in the decision-making, in both cases the personality of the incumbent will largely determine the fate of the undertaking. Sociological theory of leadership indicates the existence of two major types of leadership: one involves a creative person who initiates action; the other involves a person who mediates contention. Both types can be successful in a scientific operation, but both also can encounter difficulties when the structure is contrary or contradictory to one's style of administration. Hence, those planning an institute must have in mind the sort of person who can best function in a given structure—or be willing to modify the structure to accommodate the incumbent.

To a considerable degree, the kind of permanent staff one can plan for depends upon the funding of the operation. Some agencies fund only the director and his immediate secretarial help. Remaining staff personnel depend upon the projects developed and separately funded. Some agencies regularly budget for project planning, which includes at least some support for consulting personnel. A few agencies have successfully funded a core staff of research personnel along with central direction. It should be clear that the larger the funded staff, the greater the need for non-scientific personnel, i.e., bookkeepers, receptionists, file clerks, statistical clerks, and the rest necessary for continued operation.

A good sociological research agency has at least a part-time training officer whose task it is to create a list of trained interviewers. This will require recruiting potential workers and providing them with a basic training in general interviewing. Later, for specific projects, the selected individuals receive further training for the particular instruments to be used.

Experience has shown that interviewing can best be taught under live conditions. Thus, in the initial stage of creating a list of trained people, it is best to work with a real instrument. After initial screening in terms of obvious characteristics (diction,[4] ability to relate to others, some measure, however crude, of ability to learn and take directions), a general introductory session is held. At this session, obvious points are developed such as: interviewing is simply an instance of organized conversation.

The training officer must always be aware that the interviewer is simply to act for the scientist. He is needed only because the scientist cannot take the time to interview everyone. Hence, he is not to introduce any element into the situation which the scientist cannot control. For that reason he must, within limits, follow instructions; for that reason, the scientist must write out detailed specifications anticipating difficulties in the instrument and working out solutions. One reason for a pre-test of a schedule or questionnaire is to learn these typical difficulties. Thus, one may use the word "prejudice" in a question (Is there any evidence of prejudice against Negroes in the plant where you work?), and find that he must work out a definition of the term. I recall using the cited question to find that many answers of no were based on the fact that the Negroes had their own rest rooms and the like.

Before the interviewers are introduced to the need for specifications (or, as they are sometimes called, "specs"), they should be introduced to the fundamental instrument. A good introduction should involve the following: each person is given a copy of the instrument. Then "on stage," a fully trained person interviews another. This other can be a member of the staff for this purpose. While this interview is going on,

---

[4] Diction here simply means the ability to be understood by some meaningful population. Care must be taken not to introduce a class bias in recruiting interviewers. The personnel officer must understand that his sample is to accept the interviewer and for certain segments of a population manners of speaking, that others may find offensive, are quite appropriate. Some even go so far as to try to match the respondent and interviewer on ethnicity and other characteristics.

each trainee fills out the instrument he has been given. Then results are compared. Usually, the interviewer who conducted the presentation will simply read what he recorded and the trainees check their own.

Each trainee is then given two more copies, and the specifications are distributed. The person in charge of the research then reads the questions or items in order and points out the instructions contained in the specs. Trainees should be encouraged at this point to raise any question they may have. They should make notes on one copy of the instrument to have for constant review. After this session is completed, they pair up and interview each other. The purpose of this is simply to get as familiar with the instrument as possible. The overnight assignment is to study the specs and the instrument as much as time permits. During this study, they should write out any question they have or any comment that occurs to them.

There are a number of recurring problems in interviewing: some respondents attempt to reverse the roles and become the questioner; some are recalcitrant; others talkative. The next few sessions at interviewing are best conducted with trained respondents (usually members of the staff, though if the agency is connected to a college or university, graduate students make able subjects for this part of the study). These are trained to attempt to introduce various distortions into the situation. The trainees interview these subjects and the interview is on tape. Later, in individual sessions, the tape is replayed to the trainee with both the shrewd maneuvers and the mistakes pointed out. These sessions are continued as long as necessary: either to indicate general training or to justify termination of the training. Ordinarily two or three sessions are adequate.

If time is short the training period can be adjusted. One such adjustment is to have the trainees take turns publicly interviewing the same respondent who is coached to introduce distortions. Each trainee records everything that develops. At the point of some shrewd work by an interviewer, the trainer calls immediate attention to the principle involved. Similarly, attention is called when the interviewer has lost control or made some misinterpretation of the specifications. This method relies on role-taking as its principal training device. It is assumed that each trainee takes the role of the interviewer in the public display.

This method can be used to advantage if the researcher is still considering modifications to the instrument. A person with considerable experience can benefit enormously from observing the difficulties that emerge. It sometimes happens that the instrument is faulty in that it tends to create unavoidable traps for the interviewer. Thus, this group method can be utilized both in hurried training and in some aspects of the pre-test.

The training officer should, in maintaining the file of capable interviewers, try to keep abreast of their experience. Moreover, he should record ratings by project directors of their relative skills. If some particular kind of interviewing is either well done or poorly done by the interviewer, a note should be made of this. Thus, one person may be unable to handle projective instruments, yet be highly adequate for other types of data collection.

Modern science, and apparently sociology in particular, is often described as being poorly written. Passive construction is often used where an active style is not only more readable but more to the point. Polysyllabic writing, redundancies, and violations of syntax characterize many articles appearing in professional journals. With current emphasis on "data retrieval," and the increasing use of computers in locating data, less attention is paid to the style of writing. In those papers which are structurally mathematical in character, this involves no great loss. But insofar as a paper is involved in a theoretical argument, and to the degree that neither a statistical nor a mathematical language is used, the loss can be great. If the thrust of the paper is trivial, writing bad enough to prevent one from reading it may be a blessing.

The point is, a large research structure can well afford to have an editor on its staff. Ideally, this person would be sufficiently trained in the content of sociology to be able to determine whether the sentence makes substantive sense. Of course, the person should be well trained in English to aid both in the creation of readable sentences and in the development of agrument as a literary piece.

Another role of increasing importance in large-scale research is the librarian. It is possible that this role and that of the editor can be combined. The librarian would serve two functions: to aid in the location of relevant literature and relative research instruments. One major reason why sociological research is not accumulative is that its instruments are ordinarily constructed for a specific bit of research. A good research library will consist not merely of books and journals, but files of instruments catalogued by type of problem. It would be advisable for the agency to collect as many instruments as possible, and not merely those used in the agency itself. Unless the instrument is copyrighted, one can often generate an instrument, items of which having been pre-tested in the crucible of real research, by selecting those items of interest. One would normally attempt also a file of reprints based on these instruments, with as many comments by their creators and authors as possible.

It is conceivable that each operation in a research project could have a specialist whose role is limited to that future. Thus, a staff could have an expert on questionnaire construction. Specialization could go so far as to a person being a "Likert Scale Man" or a "Guttman Scale Specialist," though, clearly, this can be carried to absurd lengths. It is advisable, however, to have a number of trained "code clerks," and others who can prepare completed schedules and questionnaires for statistical processing.

Again, the agency connected to an academic situation has the advantage in providing majors with valuable experience. A list of experienced code clerks from the student body is an asset for any research institute. In addition to the facilitation of research, it can provide an avenue for training as well as an opportunity for a person to earn some money. Both of these can contribute to a student's maturation as a qualified social scientist.

Some relation, by contract or otherwise, with a data processing unit must be established. Some universities are developing computer centers for various scientific areas. Thus, the social sciences may have a center for their own use. This assures the individual researcher of having access to some trained person who is sympathetic to his particular needs. A common complaint of social scientists who must share facilities with physical scientists is that the programmers are not likely to be interested in the problems (they are considered trivial), of the social researcher. However, with more and more graduate students taking special training in statistical analysis and in computer programming, it is likely that soon good research *projects* as well as every research institute will have programmers as part of their staffs.

When a research agency is created such that several projects are in various stages of completion at any given time, the administrator has the task of assigning various special technical skills from any pool the agency has. Normally, there are few difficulties encountered. But each administrator has to be alert to the possibility that there may be times of competition between different project leaders for available personnel, and have policy established to be used when necessary.

Generally, this can be avoided by careful logistics planning. An able administrator is aware of the progress of each project in his organization. This is not accomplished by a bureaucratic form unless the agency is an enormous one. Rather, the director establishes by personal knowledge what is going on in each sector. He will try to have projects initiated in such a pattern as to minimize the likelihood of a jamming at any point. Nothing can harm morale more than to have subordinates be confused and not knowing from whom they take instructions and assignments. No administrator can afford to have this preempted from him by an ambitious staff member. Hence, lines of authority, not having to do with the creative aspects of science but merely its technical completion, must be established and understood. This problem is most likely to be crucial in an academic situation in which the technical people are students who depend variously on the professional staff for academic advancement. The junior faculty members, too, may need protection from a domineering full professor who feels his project takes priority over all the others. Clearly, the administrator can provide a most useful function in the control over special functions of a technical staff.

6. SOME SPECIAL PROBLEMS

Modern large-scale research administration in the social sciences has raised some problems unanticipated by sociologists in the past. Many of these problems are critical and must be solved if the agency is to succeed. The solution will generally require an ethical or moral stand as well as any program of action.

A. The Problem of Invasion of Privacy

Modern research techniques include such devices as personality tests. Moreover, the subject matter of many projects is often in the domain commonly thought of as private—as, for example, sex. Included in this can be attitudes about others, members of the family, office colleagues, and the like. From time to time researchers have been sued on the grounds of "invasion of privacy." This stems either from the use of deceit in securing subjects or from the argument that the subject did not realize he would be revealing intimate information.

That such material is scientifically relevant is not the point. The point is, our culture has long traditions of the sanctity of the individual. Instances of a genuine invasion of privacy have occurred. With increased knowledge of electrons we are creating an enormous army of mechanical snoops. We can eavesdrop "for the sake of science."

The sociologist who engages in these behaviors must develop some ethical grounds for doing so. The problem is not a simple one. One can hold that any inference about an individual in the research sample constitutes an invasion of privacy insofar as the individual was not told, and could not be told, that this area of his life was to be studied. Telling the subject what the research is about can introduce a contamination that destroys the entire project. Hence, most researchers routinely do use deceit, or at least silence, where knowledge exists. The sociologist must draw a line somewhere between what is admissible procedure and what is not: surreptitiously bugging a bedroom to learn the nature of intimate husband-wife interaction probably would not be tolerated in any court in the land.

For the routine case, i.e., the standard procedures everyone uses, a routine solution has occurred—the insurance policy offering some protection against such lawsuits. It should be recognized that, although the scientist has a moral problem on where to draw the line between accepted and rejected practices, some members of the public will engage in lawsuits either for publicity or for the likelihood, however small, of getting some money for nothing.

One solution which has been advanced for the problem of invasion of privacy takes a positive stand, rather than the passive stand of simply securing insurance. Normally, social scientists obtain their data in one of two ways, or both. One, we beg for our data. We use various pitches to make the subject feel obligated to contribute. Under the rubric of "establishing rapport," we really are trying to establish ways in which we, the beggar, can obtain what we want. I am using the concept of begging here in the same sense that fund raising for charitable activities is a form of collective begging.

The other way to obtain our data is to steal it—take it under one guise or another. We may want to measure intelligence, but are fearful that if we overtly ask permission to measure it we will get rejects. So we think of something which is either a synonym for intelligence (at least in terms of operations the subject is to perform) or something known to be highly correlated with a known measure of intelligence, and then administer this other thing. In this way we are "stealing" a person's intelligence score. The reader can think of a number of strategies we employ to get data without the subject's noticing—projective instruments and the like abound with obvious instances.

A third way of acquiring data has been proposed. This is to hire the subject to be an interviewee. Sometimes market research agencies have given token payments, but that is not what we are considering here. We are thinking of paying people for the time we take from them, and in some measure relating it to the time they can earn in some other activity. Professional people (lawyers and doctors, etc.), may be more responsive to our inquiries if we would pay them $10.00 or $15.00 per hour of interview time. Others may be obtainable for as little as $1.75 (or whatever the minimum wage might be). It is true that the cost of research would skyrocket; but since we beg our money from some presumably affluent foundation anyway, this ought not be the real problem.

There are potentially many positive results from this sort of thing. No longer would we have to pretend that a three-hour schedule can be done in twenty minutes. It is possible that we may be able to study families together (other than those in trouble) by paying a reasonable rate to each member of the family. Since, under this notion, the relation between the interviewee and the research project would be a contractual one, the danger of invasion of privacy should be minimal: it was the person's job to reveal personal intimacies about himself.

Of course, the administrator would be forced to make more critical decisions regarding the necessity for various bits of information. We alluded to this before. Under this scheme, the administrator would have to consider the cost of each item and whether or not it was worth it to the total project. Under a forced accounting system that this strategy implies, we may have the side effect of rendering research administration more rigorous. It is conceivable that the long run effect would be to lower total costs of research as the immediate pressure would be to reduce waste and be as efficient as possible. As long as we can beg, borrow, or steal our data, there seems to be little pressure for efficiency. As long as we refuse to consider such a quantitative measure as money as the basic unit for comparison, we can scarcely talk about efficiency in a meaningful way.

Objectors to the plan appeal to more than the possible increased cost. They assert that some sort of bias is introduced: what kind of person is it who will give data for money? The insinuation is that this is a sort of prostitution to which the response is that there must be some kind of person who will give his data without monetary reward. The insinuation there is of promiscuity. The counter insinuation is, I think, a fair one. There is no more reason to believe that free data are truer than bought data. At least there should be some studies done to compare the kind of results one obtains from the two different strategies. I must admit that the possibility of there being professional and amateur respondents is an intriguing one. It would be somewhat amusing if it turns out that this strategy does not lessen the likelihood of invasion of privacy suits. That was what it was proposed to do.

B. The Problem of Subpoenaed Data

Sometimes, directly or indirectly related to the research project, the scientist secures some data that are interesting to the police or investigating committee. Suppose a person is studying political radicalism and discovers that some members of his sample are members of the communist party. Suppose, further, that some investigative officer happens to ask him about such a person. Since most research promises anonimity to the subject, what is the responsibility of the researcher? If he refuses to divulge his information he may find himself facing another inquiry. This second inquiry may find himself the subject of concern, or the information may be related to, say, a congressional committee and the scientist has been subpoenaed to testify. The problem is: does academic freedom stand as a protection for the scientist if he, in this instance, refuses to divulge his information?

To illustrate, here is another situation. Suppose you are conducting research on the problem of traffic accidents and their causes. It would occur to you that there may be some relation between the kind of accident a person has and the type of traffic violation that may have occurred. There is a small relation between the number of accidents and the number of known violations, according to research literature. But you may wish to know if violations not of public record are related to accidents and, possibly, if certain kinds of violations but not others are. Accordingly, in your research, you systematically gather information regarding all accidents (reported or not) and "all" violations, arrests or not, the subject has had.

Suppose police officers learn of this. Suppose they have access to your sample list (this is not too important, except that if they have knowledge they may be able to claim "probable knowledge") since you took your sample from the roster of drivers' licenses. Suppose the police, or some agency of the state, tries to subpoena your data: what is your moral responsibility to your respondents? To the public? Some may feel there are no issues, at all: one merely turns over the data to the public officials. Yet this is hardly possible since one is not likely to be able to get data of this sort without promising anonimity. If a promise of this kind has been made, which obligation is the stronger?

Moreover, suppose that during the course of research, you conclude that you can identify behavioral characteristics from which you can properly create a typology of drivers. Suppose, further, that this typology includes highly dangerous drivers, dangerous both to themselves and to others. Now, what is the issue?

This is something like the recurring problem in the case of studying deviant behavior. Two dramatic illustrations come readily to mind. One can conceive of doing research in mental health and uncovering a truly dangerous individual. It is possible to imagine learning of a threat to another which you, as scientist, must judge to be real or fanciful—and, if real, what course of action? If a demonstrable threat to another, there probably is little choice: but suppose the threat only has a certain statistical probability which rests in a range of sampling error. Now, what is the basis for action? Another illustration involves studying criminal or gang behavior. To establish rapport, one must become accepted as a confidant. This means accepting some secrets without reporting to police or other public officials. One may learn of a variety of crimes having been committed or about to be committed. Again, the scientist is put in the position of having to make a moral decision.

The administrator, too, must face these prospects as he considers or judges various proposals of research. He must consider his research staff and their interests; the source of data (whatever or whoever they may be); and the community at large. The problems are vexing, and cannot be solved by an appeal to any technical equipment in research design. It is an ethical question that requires considerations of other than scientific values for a decision. To claim that science is so precious that all such problems are not real is not only to accept the arrogant deification of science but it also can endanger the scientific enterprise if, as a result, the public loses faith in those doing research.

C. The Problem of Off-Base Research

From time to time a sociological research team is involved in securing data in an area some miles removed from the home base of operations. It might be a project has a number of interviews to be conducted in a rural county. Often, under such situations, the team of interviewers is taken en bloc to the area where research is to be done. These people can scarcely fraternize with the local residents for two reasons: as strangers in a rural area, they may not be freely accepted; as members of a research team, they could contaminate the locality by conversing with those whom they intend to interview. Because of the highly visible character of research in small towns, the topic of conversation is almost certain to touch on various aspects of the research operation. It is hard enough to take into account community discussions of a research program without contributing to it by conversations with the public. Generally speaking (unless the research design specifically calls for a maximization of public discussion), most teams are removed from the local patterns of after work interaction.

For a variety of reasons, they are likely to be all staying in one or two locations, depending on the number of hotels and motels available in the area. In any case, the members of the staff are away from home and, hence, away from many of the controls over daily activity. In many ways, the research excursion is a lark, often regarded as having festive overtones. If the research team is bisexual, and if the plans call for any length of time in this situation, problems of managing sexual relations sometimes emerge.

While we are not proposing any particular device for the handling of the situation, we feel it important enough to mention. Aside from any moral issue which exists, the research itself can be endangered by any overt or public display of sexual conduct. Not only do walls have ears, but a certain amount of listening can be presumed. And, in small towns, there is considerable talk. If there is anything about the research activity that is at all threatening to any sizable segment of the local power structure, any hint of impropriety can be used to discredit the research.

Hence, the administrator of research in this kind of a situation is well advised to make plans regarding these possibilities. Efforts must be made to minimize opportunity for behavior that could weaken the success of the research venture. Even if his interviewers look upon the situation as a free one, the research director must take his task seriously. We presume that his commitment *is* to the successful acquisition of all the data required for his study.

7. SUMMARY

Large scale research requires an awareness of sociological theory for its own completion. A research agency of any magnitude implies a social structure which takes on many characteristics of a bureaucracy. There will be a division of labor and a line of authority. Policy must be established in a number of areas and some part of the agency must be made responsible for the creation and implementation of that policy.

The public must have faith in the institute doing research. Thus, the administrator and his staff are responsible for maintaining that situation which makes their existence possible. Scientific projects vary in their visibility, and this visibility has various effects on scientific inquiry.

The capable administrator learns how to equate various aspects of research design to the common denominator of money. With this quantitative base he is able to make use of statistical arguments to assist in certain decisions (as whether to increase the length of the research instrument or the size of sample). This problem is related to the problem of time. If events are rapidly occurring in such a way as to have an effect on the data gathered, an increase in interviewing staff may appear as a way to reduce the effect of immediate history. However, this brings certain added costs in recruiting, training, and administrating a larger staff.

A well-designed research agency has a clearly established table of organization. This conveys the division of labor necessary for proper management in the most efficient (least costly) way. In turn, decisions have to be made defining the permanent and the temporary staffs. If more than one project is underway at any time, care must be taken to allow uncontrolled use of various pools of technical assistance. Administration of a large scale research organization is rapidly becoming a full-time job, a new identity matrix in certain career lines.

Some special problems were discussed. These all had the characteristic of involving the administrator and/or his supporting board in moral and ethical judgments. These moral issues could not be ignored and there was no simple decision regarding the ethics of a situation. This resulted from the fact that the acquisition of data by social scientists involves the scientist in a commitment to his subjects which cannot be ignored.

In brief, this chapter oriented the student to the major tasks of the research administrator. Despite the difficulties of the problems, they must be met and are being met in every day operations. By making the student aware of the several difficulties, it is hoped that the coming generation of sociologists will be able to make sound decisions in the face of moral dilemmas.

INDEX

Symbols, 5, 14
   concepts and, 45 ff.
System, science tendency toward, 15

T-scales, 196
t-test, 171
Tabular presentation of data, 70 ff.
Tarski, A., 218, 229, 232
Taves, M., 205
Taylor, E. K., 345
Teggart, F. J., 13
Theories, 31-33, 40-42
Thielens, W., 272
Thought, rules of, 22-23
Time problem in research, 359 ff.
Timeless–time-bound types, 237-238
Toby, J., 212
Tönnies, F., 237, 238
Torgerson, W. S., 212
Travel in research, 370-371
Trow, M. A., 304
Tschuprow's *T*, 150 ff.
Two-way classification, 134 ff.
Types
   general-specific, 235
   generalizing-individualizing, 239 ff.
   ideal-extracted, 232-235
   scientific-historical, 235-237
   timeless–time-bound, 237-238
   universal-local, 238-239
Typology, constructive
   explication of procedure, 213 ff.
   structure and function, 230 ff.

Uniformities, empirical, delineation of, 222-224
Universal affirmative and negative, 24
Universal law, 53
Universal-local types, 238-239
Universe of content, 194

Validity, 321, 344-345
Value-conflicts, group, 176-177
Variables
   continuous, 46
   design to control, 164-166

Variables—*Continued*
   discrete, 46
   one-way classification of, 109-110, 128 ff.
   two-way classification of, 134 ff.
   types of, 46
Variance, 79
   analysis of, 107 ff., 125 ff.
   between-group, 130 ff.
   between-treatment, 130
   concept of, 126-128
   statistics and, 65-66
Variation, concomitant, 115, 119 ff., 139-140
Von Wiese, L., 234

Walker, H. M., 112
Walters, E., 32
Watkins, J. W. N., 218
Weber, Max, 19, 218, 229, 232, 233, 236, 239, 240, 243
Weiss, P., 34
Whyte, W., 304, 314
Wilensky, H. L., 270, 273
Williams, R. M., 263, 273, 309, 333, 349
Wilson, Logan, 221
Winch, R., 215, 243
Winer, B. J., 126
Woodger, J. H., 49
Wright, C., 328, 332
Write-up of conclusion, 19, 361

x-axis, 72
X-value, 75-76
$\overline{X}$-value, 107, 135

y-axis, 72
Yinger, J. M., 216
Young, P., 217, 304
Yule, G. U., 148-150, 153, 155

z-scores, 105-106
Zander, A., 304
Zeisel, H., 273, 318
Zelditch, M., 123, 304
Zetterberg, H. L., 49, 223, 312, 326, 330
Znaniecki, F., 221